Caribou

Common
shrew

Raccoon

WITHDRAWN

Snowshoe hare

Virginia opossum

Tiger

National Geographic

Book of
Mammals

*Prepared by the
Book Division*

*National
Geographic Society,
Washington, D.C.*

NATIONAL GEOGRAPHIC BOOK OF MAMMALS

Published by

The National Geographic Society
Reg Murphy, *President and Chief Executive Officer*
Gilbert M. Grosvenor, *Chairman of the Board*
Nina D. Hoffman, *Senior Vice President*
William R. Gray, *Vice President and Director,
    Book Division*

Staff for this edition

Barbara Lalicki, *Director of Children's Publishing*
Barbara Brownell, *Senior Editor, Project Manager*
Marianne Koszorus, *Senior Art Director, Project
    Manager*
Carolinda E. Hill, *Editor*
Elisabeth B. Booz, *Research Editor*
Jennifer Emmett, *Assistant Editor*
Mark A. Caraluzzi, *Marketing Manager*
Vincent P. Ryan, *Manufacturing Manager*
Lewis R. Bassford, *Production Project Manager*

The *National Geographic Book of Mammals* was compiled by
    National Geographic staff with input from scientific consultant
    Henry W. Setzer and educational consultants Glenn O. Blough
    and Judith Hobart. Darrell K. Sweet painted the color
    illustrations, and Ned Smith created the black-and-white art.

Prior to the 1998 reprint, scientific consultant Dr. Ronald M.
    Nowak, Editor of *Walker's Mammals of the World,* reviewed
    the book, and changes were made to ensure its accuracy in
    light of current information and study.

Printed and bound by R. R. Donnelley & Sons Company, Willard, Ohio. Color
separations by The Lanman Companies, Washington, D. C.; Progressive Color Corp.,
Rockville, Md.; Stevenson Photo Color Company, Cincinnati, Ohio. Case cover and dust
jacket printed by Inland Press, Menomonee Falls, Wisconsin.

Library of Congress ℗ Data

National Geographic book of mammals.
    Includes index.
    Summary: A picture encyclopedia presenting a general introduction to the world's
mammals and the vital statistics and behavior for each of the entries from aardvark to
zorilla.
    1. Mammals—Encyclopedias, Juvenile. [1. Mammals—Encyclopedias]   I. National
Geographic Society (U. S.). Special Publications Division.   II. Title: Book of
mammals.
QL706.2.N37   599'.003'21—DC19   80-7825
                                                            AC r90
1998 Reprint by Book Division
ISBN 0-7922-7141-6

*Watchful oribi in southeastern Africa quietly feeds among tall grasses.
If startled, this small antelope will bound swiftly away.*

*PRECEDING PAGES: Heads up! Here comes an elephant—largest of all
mammals. Behind it, a parade of adults and young crosses a grassy
plain in Africa. PAGE 1: Young mountain goat gallops headlong
down a rocky slope in Washington State. ENDPAPERS: Making tracks,
mammals big and small leave their footprints.*

*COVER: Bold and majestic, a Bengal tiger runs through splashing water
in this re-creation of natural tiger behavior. Tigers are the largest of the
cats. A computer-generated image of the National Geographic Society's
trademark Yellow Border has been added to this remarkable scene.*

Foreword

FOR ME—and I suspect for almost everyone—mammals appeal deeply to the imagination. One of my favorites is the elephant. It's hard to imagine that such a massive beast can manipulate its trunk to pick up a tiny peanut and yet be able to heft a thousand-pound log of teak with obvious ease! In Sri Lanka, Raja, a movie-star elephant, once swung me up with his trunk and carried me across a river. That night, Raja gently led a sacred procession through a jammed crowd of ten thousand people—without stepping on anyone's feet.

Many people—my daughter, Alexi, among them—are intrigued by cats of any size. Others favor dogs, and still others are enthralled by whales and other marine mammals. This interest is natural, for we too are mammals—tied to the other members of this realm by myriad, complex relationships.

For those of us privileged to observe animals in the wild and to interact with them, the allure of the world of mammals is even greater. While snorkeling with humpback whales off Hawaii, I was amazed by these gentle giants—among the largest mammals ever to inhabit Earth. I watched one huge humpback swim—carefully it seemed—over a diver in its path. The mere slap of a fluke could have instantly killed the diver. As the whales glided silently past, I marveled at their sensitivity toward other creatures.

In Africa, I have followed herds of wildebeests across the Serengeti Plain. How do these large, shaggy antelopes live, forage for food, escape predators? Why do they move along established migratory paths, when other kinds of antelopes do not? How many kinds of antelopes are there? And what are their differences and similarities?

These are the kinds of questions that the *National Geographic Book of Mammals* answers. Educators, librarians, and specialists in many fields of mammalogy have contributed their expertise. In-depth information about habitat, food, and behavior—presented in a form that the entire family can enjoy—makes this volume unique. It greatly expands the opportunities for parents to teach our children about the world of mammals.

Illustrated with nearly a thousand exciting photographs of animals in the wild, the *Book of Mammals* is much more than a collection of wildlife portraits and a compilation of vital statistics. It is an extraordinary work, compelling in its breadth of information, in its variety, and in the quality and the range of its photographs.

Never in all my years with the National Geographic Society have I been so enthusiastic about a project. Since the Geographic's founding more than a hundred years ago, Society members have ranked wild animals and animal behavior among their chief interests. I believe that the *National Geographic Book of Mammals* sets a standard of excellence in the field of wildlife study. It not only reveals the heritage of the wild, free past, but it also points the way to greater understanding and concern for a new generation of readers.

GILBERT M. GROSVENOR
Chairman of the Board of Trustees
National Geographic Society

Contents

Coats damp from fishing in a river in Alaska, a female brown bear and her cub pause on a gravel bar.

How To Use the
Book of Mammals

IN THE *Book of Mammals*, you will learn about the habits and behavior of mammals of the world. Each entry concentrates on a single kind of animal such as the aardvark or on a closely related group of mammals such as monkeys. To learn about mammals in general, read "What Is a Mammal?" beginning on page 10. This is an interesting, in-depth essay, divided into ten short sections, which explains why scientists classify certain animals as mammals. It compares some of the ways that mammals find food and shelter, raise their young, defend themselves, and communicate.

The pages of the *Book of Mammals* are numbered consecutively from page 1 to page 608. At the end of the book, following the last alphabetic entry (zorilla), there are some pages with additional information. On page 600, the various mammals that make up this book are grouped together by the scientific order to which each of them belongs. The chart on that page also includes more information on the features that distinguish one order from another. A glossary appears on page 595. It is a small dictionary that defines words in the book that may be unfamiliar to some readers. An index begins on page 601. It lists the common and scientific names of species of mammals discussed or pictured in the *Book of Mammals*.

On page 9 (opposite), a sample entry for the ibex appears. It is slightly different in appearance from the ibex entry on page 286. It has been changed to bring together in one place all the elements that might occur on several pages. The numbered paragraphs below match the numbered elements in the sample entry. These elements appear consistently throughout the *Book of Mammals*.

1 The *Book of Mammals* is organized alphabetically. Each alphabetical section begins with a large letter at the top of a left-hand page.

2 Each entry is headed by the common name of the mammal covered on that page. Some entries, like the one on the cheetah, cover only a single species. Others, like the one on the ibex, include several species. Still others, like the entry on the llama, cover several related mammals—llamas, alpacas, guanacos, and vicuñas.

3 With the heading of the entry, you will find a pronunciation guide for the name of the animal. For ease in pronunciation, these guides use common words and syllables. The syllable in capital letters should be accented. For simple names like "goat" or "bear" there is no pronunciation guide. Difficult words in the entries also are followed by pronunciation guides.

4 Every entry includes a range map. The colored areas on the maps show where the animal lives throughout the world. The maps do not include the ranges of pets or farm animals.

Each of the 19 orders, or groups, of mammals has a different color for its range maps. The range of every mammal in that order is shown in that color. For example, the ibex is an artiodactyl (art-ee-oh-DAK-tul), or even-toed hoofed mammal. Its range is shown in green. Similarly, the ranges of all the artiodactyls appear in the same shade of green. The colors used for the orders are shown on page 17.

5 Each entry in the book includes a fact box that gives information about all the species of the animal in the entry. The symbol of a tiger's footprint immediately after the name means that some species are threatened with extinction. "Height" or "Length of Head and Body" indicates the size of the animals. "Weight" tells how heavy they can be. "Habitat and

Range" describes the terrain the animals live in and the parts of the world they inhabit. "Food" lists what the animals eat. "Life Span" reveals how long the animals live. "Reproduction" tells how long a pregnancy lasts for the animals and how many young are born at one time. "Order" shows the scientific classification of the animals.

6 All sizes and distances in the *Book of Mammals* are given both in standard United States measurements and in metric measurements. All metric conversions are rounded off to whole numbers.

7 Every photograph has a caption that describes the picture. For clarity, captions often are keyed to photographs by triangles.

8 Identification lines give the common names of the animals that are shown in photographs and the average sizes of adult animals. This information is given only once. If the entry includes only one species, there is no identification line. See the fact box for this information.

9 Cross-references are given when the information about an animal appears under another name or with the entry for another animal. Check the index for other animals that interest you.

What Is a Mammal?

By Henry W. Setzer
Curator of Mammals, Emeritus, Smithsonian Institution

FROM DOGS AND CATS to elephants and kangaroos—the world of mammals is filled with incredible diversity. Graceful porpoises, which spend their lives in the water, are mammals. So are bats, which fly through the night air. Tall giraffes and tiny mice are mammals, as are chattering monkeys and powerful tigers. Human beings are mammals, too.

What characteristics do all these animals share? What sets them apart from the other creatures that belong to the animal kingdom?

Scientists break the animal kingdom into two divisions: vertebrates (VURT-uh-bruts), or animals with backbones, and invertebrates (in-vurt-uh-bruts), those without backbones. Mammals are vertebrates, but so are fishes, amphibians, reptiles, and birds. Of these animals, however, only birds and mammals are warm-blooded. That means their bodies stay at almost the same temperature even when temperatures around them vary widely.

But birds and mammals have different kinds of body coverings. Birds have feathers, and mammals have hair. Of all the animals in the world, only mammals have hair, though not all hair looks the same. Whales have only a few coarse hairs near their mouths. Thick, curly wool covers the bodies of domestic sheep. Many pigs have scattered, coarse bristles. Hedgehogs have spines, and porcupines have quills. Fine fur covers cats and foxes.

Other characteristics besides hair set mammals apart from all other animals. An important trait is that every female mammal feeds her young on milk from her body. The word mammal comes from the Latin word *mamma*, which means "breast."

Scientists think that mammals first appeared

Nose-deep in grass, a lion watches for prey. Scientists ▷ *group lions among the carnivores, or meat eaters.*

What Is a Mammal?

Prehensile-tailed porcupine, found in Central and ▷ South America, sniffs a branch as it climbs. This tree-dweller has quills mixed with its other hair.
▽ Hanging upside down, a three-toed sloth of South America moves slowly but easily through the trees.

△ Australian hopping mouse licks its delicate paws. When startled, this rodent bounds away on its hind legs.

more than 200 million years ago. They descended from a group of reptiles called therapsids (thuh-RAP-suds). Therapsids resembled mammals in the number of bones in their feet and in the way the jaw muscles were attached to their skulls. A few therapsids may have been warm-blooded, had hair, and fed their young on milk. Scientists do not know for sure. Descendants of reptiles that had these characteristics, among others, became the first mammals.

Today there are thousands of species, or kinds, of mammals. Scientists have put them into 19 groups called orders. Which order a mammal belongs to may depend on the arrangement of its bones or the kind of teeth it has. It may also depend on how the mammal bears its young.

Monotremes (MON-uh-treemz) share several characteristics with reptiles. They lay leathery-shelled eggs that hatch into young animals—instead of bearing live young. Like all mammals, however, monotreme young are nourished by their mothers' milk. Instead of sucking from a nipple, a young monotreme gets milk from pores on its mother's belly. The only members of the monotreme order are the echidnas and platypuses.

Marsupials (mar-SOO-pea-ulz) give birth to living young that are tiny and underdeveloped. At birth, most marsupials crawl into a pouch or a sac on the underside of their mothers' bodies. Inside, each attaches itself to a nipple. There it remains, drinking milk and growing stronger. When it is more fully developed, it begins to spend time out of the pouch.

Many different kinds of marsupials live in Australia. Koalas and kangaroos are probably the most familiar. In the Western Hemisphere, only opossums belong in this order of mammals.

Mammals in all the other orders give birth to living young that can survive outside their mothers' bodies as soon as they are born. The offspring get their nourishment by nursing.

Curling back her lips, a huge female black rhinoceros ▷ stands ready to defend her calf.

What Is a Mammal?

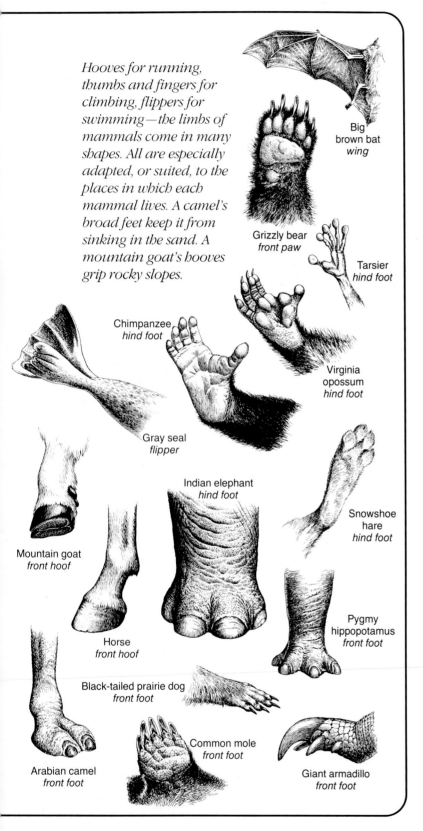

Hooves for running, thumbs and fingers for climbing, flippers for swimming—the limbs of mammals come in many shapes. All are especially adapted, or suited, to the places in which each mammal lives. A camel's broad feet keep it from sinking in the sand. A mountain goat's hooves grip rocky slopes.

Big brown bat
wing

Grizzly bear
front paw

Tarsier
hind foot

Chimpanzee
hind foot

Virginia opossum
hind foot

Gray seal
flipper

Indian elephant
hind foot

Snowshoe hare
hind foot

Mountain goat
front hoof

Horse
front hoof

Pygmy hippopotamus
front foot

Black-tailed prairie dog
front foot

Arabian camel
front foot

Common mole
front foot

Giant armadillo
front foot

Some orders include hundreds of species—chiropterans (kye-ROP-tuh-runs), or bats, for example. Others—like tubulidentates (too-byu-luh-DEN-tates), or aardvarks—include only one.

Sometimes it is easy to see why animals are grouped together. Carnivores (CAR-nuh-vorz) are basically meat eaters. Insectivores (in-SEK-tuh-vorz) eat mainly insects. Artiodactyls (art-ee-oh-DAK-tulz) are hoofed animals with an even number of toes on each foot. The illustration on page 17 lists all of the 19 orders of mammals and shows one representative of each order. A chart on page 600 tells what makes each

▽ *Bulky manatee swims in a river in Florida. These mammals spend all their lives in the water.*

Wings folded, a yellow-eared tent bat roosts on a ▷ branch in Panama. Of all mammals, only bats can fly.

order special. It lists all of the animal entries in this book by order.

Mammals live in almost every climate and terrain. Because their bodies stay about the same temperature in widely varying conditions, mammals do not rely on the sun to keep warm. They can move about after dark and in the cold, when cold-blooded animals seek shelter. The hair that covers most mammals serves as a blanket against the cold. When they get too warm, many mammals sweat or pant. This helps lower their body temperatures.

Armored with scales, a Cape pangolin (above, left) crosses a dry grassland in Africa. A brush-tailed possum (above, right) pauses in a tree fork in Australia. Like most marsupials, it has a pouch for its young.

Mammals are adapted, or suited, to their environments in many other ways. Polar bears and some seals have layers of fat that protect them in the icy climate of the polar regions. The streamlined bodies of whales and porpoises move easily through the ocean. Though they must come to the surface to breathe, these marine mammals spend all their lives in the water. Animals that live in deserts usually need little water. Kangaroo rats and fennecs get most of the moisture they need from their food. High on mountain slopes, the tiny pika survives by drying plants in summer to eat when food is difficult to find.

The feet, hooves, or paws of a mammal may give a clue to where the animal lives. Camels have broad, padded feet that keep them from sinking into sand. The padded hooves of mountain goats give them a good grip on steep, rocky slopes. An armadillo's thick front claws help the animal dig through sunbaked

Fine yellowish hair frames the dark face of a golden ▷ langur, a kind of monkey.

earth. A tarsier's padded fingertips help the tiny primate cling to tree trunks.

Sometimes animals become extinct, or die out, because they no longer fit into their environment. When the climate or the terrain changes sharply over decades or even centuries, the animals may not be able to adapt and to find the food and shelter they need. Millions of years ago, the hornless rhino probably died out when the trees it ate gradually disappeared and it could not digest other foods. Nowadays, many animals are becoming extinct because people have taken over their habitats, cutting down forests where they lived or turning wilderness into farmland.

People around the world have developed some special breeds of mammals. Domestic, or tame, animals—cows, horses, dogs, cats, goats, and sheep—all have been bred to provide things people want or need. Cows can be bred to produce increased amounts of milk or meat. Sheep can be bred for thicker coats. Cats and dogs can be bred simply for traits that please their owners.

On the following pages you can read more about how mammals in the wild survive in different environments. Though they all eat, move, find shelter, and care for young, mammals do these things in an amazing variety of ways.

Caribou trots through low shrubs. Like most male deer, caribou grow bony antlers every year.

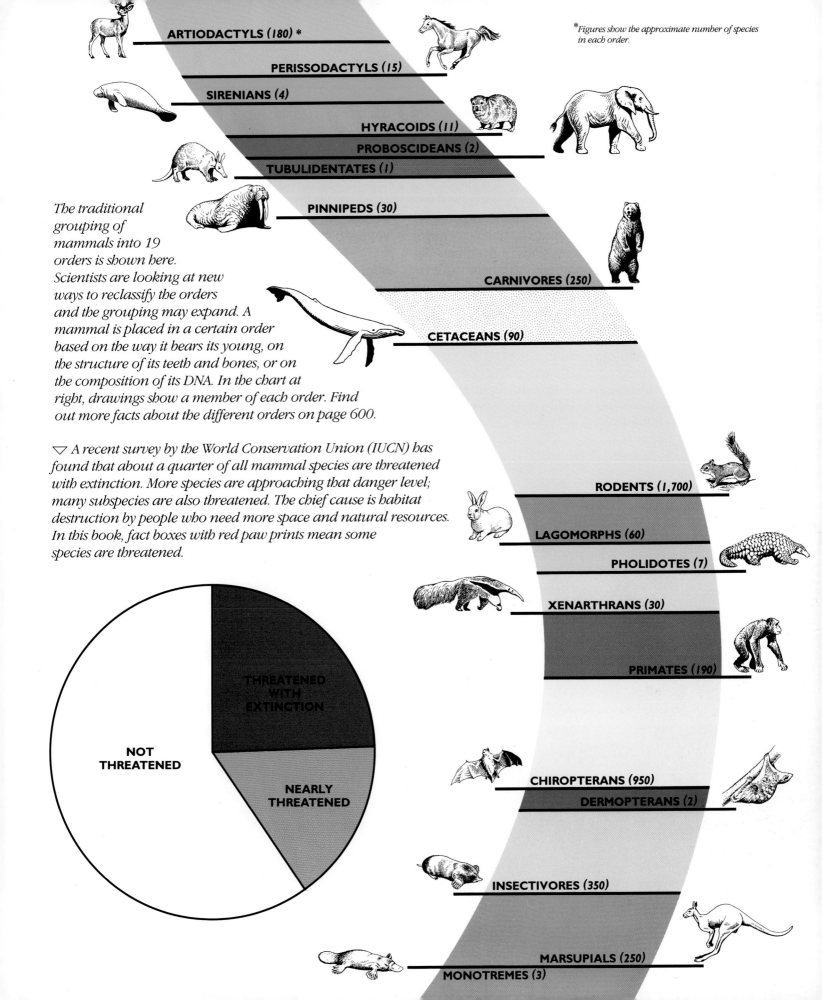

ARTIODACTYLS (180) *

PERISSODACTYLS (15)

SIRENIANS (4)

HYRACOIDS (11)

PROBOSCIDEANS (2)

TUBULIDENTATES (1)

PINNIPEDS (30)

CARNIVORES (250)

CETACEANS (90)

Figures show the approximate number of species in each order.

The traditional grouping of mammals into 19 orders is shown here. Scientists are looking at new ways to reclassify the orders and the grouping may expand. A mammal is placed in a certain order based on the way it bears its young, on the structure of its teeth and bones, or on the composition of its DNA. In the chart at right, drawings show a member of each order. Find out more facts about the different orders on page 600.

▽ A recent survey by the World Conservation Union (IUCN) has found that about a quarter of all mammal species are threatened with extinction. More species are approaching that danger level; many subspecies are also threatened. The chief cause is habitat destruction by people who need more space and natural resources. In this book, fact boxes with red paw prints mean some species are threatened.

RODENTS (1,700)

LAGOMORPHS (60)

PHOLIDOTES (7)

XENARTHRANS (30)

PRIMATES (190)

CHIROPTERANS (950)

DERMOPTERANS (2)

INSECTIVORES (350)

MARSUPIALS (250)

MONOTREMES (3)

NOT THREATENED

THREATENED WITH EXTINCTION

NEARLY THREATENED

Homes and Habitats

IN FREEZING POLAR REGIONS or in steamy tropics—wherever they live, mammals need places to take shelter from snow and ice, from sun and wind. They also need places to hide from enemies, to raise young, to store food, and to sleep.

Just as mammals come in many shapes and sizes, so do their homes. Beavers often build dome-shaped lodges of sticks, stones, and mud. Chimpanzees make leafy nests in the trees. Many kinds of mammals dig underground burrows. Some take over dens made by others. Warthogs and pangolins move into abandoned aardvark burrows.

Underground homes can range from a single hole in the ground to a complex network of tunnels. Prairie dogs build burrows that contain rooms for nurseries, for sleeping, and for toilets. They even have rooms called listening posts. There they can listen for enemies above ground. A ring of earth at the mouth of the burrow helps keep water out.

Mammals that are active at night need shelters in which to spend the daylight hours. The flying squirrel, for example, builds a nest in a hollow tree.

Jackrabbits and other hares live in open areas. They often use bushes for shelter. As the hot summer sun moves across the sky, the animals stay in the shade by moving around the bush. Mammals like these, with no fixed homes to hide in, often have young that are independent soon after birth.

Some mammals, such as caribou, live in a large herd that moves continually over a certain area, looking for food. Where food is hard to find, the home range can be very large.

Many mammals are now becoming extinct because their homes and ranges are being destroyed by people who compete with them for the same space.

On the next few pages, paintings show mammals of four climates and terrains. Though the animals shown in each illustration would not gather in the same place at the same time, they do inhabit the same general areas.

Polar bear wanders across the snow. These bears rarely seek shelter, except when they have young.

◁ *Black-tailed jackrabbit hides from enemies and from the Texas sun in a shady spot under a bush.*

Striped face and thick ▷ *claws sandy from digging, a young badger sits at the entrance to its burrow. It makes its home in a riverbank in Michigan.*

Northern flying squirrel peers from a hollow tree. Inside, a nest of shredded bark and small plants provides protection and warmth. Mammal homes range from simple shelters to complex ones.

ON THE DRY, OPEN GRASSLANDS of eastern Africa, large and small mammals—hunters and prey—gather at a water hole to drink and to eat. Most hoofed animals nibble bushes and grasses. Wild cats and wild dogs feed on meat. Others find insects or the remains of dead animals.

1. GIRAFFES
2. LIONS
3. ELEPHANTS
4. CHEETAH
5. IMPALA
6. LEOPARD
7. WILDEBEESTS
8. BURCHELL'S ZEBRAS
9. WATERBUCK
10. CAPE HUNTING DOGS
11. SPOTTED HYENAS
12. BABOONS
13. THOMSON'S GAZELLES
14. WARTHOGS
15. ROCK HYRAXES
16. DWARF MONGOOSES
17. BAT-EARED FOX

ALASKA'S COOL WATERS and stark, rocky coasts support many of the world's marine mammals. Whales and porpoises spend their entire lives in water. Seals, sea lions, and walruses go ashore to bear young.

1. HARBOR SEAL
2. SEA OTTER
3. NORTHERN SEA LION
4. PACIFIC WALRUS
5. NORTHERN FUR SEAL
6. HUMPBACK WHALE
7. RIBBON SEAL
8. HARBOR PORPOISE
9. ORCA
10. BAIRD'S BEAKED WHALE
11. DALL'S PORPOISE
12. BELUGA
13. GRAY WHALE
14. BLUE WHALE
15. BOWHEAD WHALE

IN THE DENSE FORESTS of South America, mammals live at different levels. Sloths and monkeys rarely come down from the treetops. A porcupine and an opossum clamber on lower branches. Such animals as agoutis and capybaras search for food among the tangled roots.

1. TWO-TOED SLOTH
2. SPIDER MONKEYS
3. UAKARI
4. KINKAJOU
5. EMPEROR TAMARIN
6. OPOSSUM
7. PREHENSILE-TAILED PORCUPINE
8. TAMANDUA
9. BROCKET DEER
10. JAGUAR
11. BRAZILIAN TAPIR
12. WHITE-LIPPED PECCARIES
13. CAPYBARAS
14. GIANT ARMADILLO
15. AGOUTIS

ALPS OF EUROPE provide varied habitats for hoofed and fur-bearing mammals. Red deer and a marten take shelter in the woods. A marmot, an ermine, and a hare live among boulders and bushes. Ibexes and chamois find footholds on rocky slopes.

1. CHAMOIS
2. ALPINE IBEXES
3. MOUFLON
4. ALPINE MARMOT
5. BLUE HARE
6. ERMINE
7. RIVER OTTER
8. BEECH MARTEN
9. RED DEER
10. WILD BOAR
11. LYNX
12. WOOD MOUSE

Finding Food

△ *Koala chews on eucalyptus leaves. These Australian animals feed in trees. Many kinds of mammals browse, or nibble on leaves and twigs.*

FOOD IS THE FUEL that keeps bodies working. But many different kinds of food—from berries and leaves to fish and meat—can provide the energy mammals need to survive.

Some mammals eat mainly plants and fruit. Others eat mostly meat. Still others, including humans, eat both plants and meat. Bears, for example, change their diet with the season. They may eat new shoots in the spring, fish in the summer, and nuts in the fall. At any time of the year, they may eat animals that they kill or find already dead.

To find food, most mammals probably rely on smell more than on their other senses. Squirrels sniff to find the nuts they have buried. Red foxes use their noses to detect the scent of nearby prey.

Other mammals use keen eyesight to spot prey. Cheetahs watch the grasslands of Africa for antelopes. When they see prey, they start to stalk, creeping closer and closer. Then they run it down. The serval, a kind of small cat, uses its ears to detect the rustling of small animals in the grass or underbrush. This hunter pounces on its prey.

Some bats use a very different system to find food. They hunt—and find their way—by echolocation (ek-oh-low-KAY-shun). These bats send out beeps or pulses of high-pitched sounds. The bats listen for the sounds that bounce back when the beeps hit an object. From the echoes, they know where the object is and if it is moving.

Toothed whales and porpoises also find food by echolocation. Other whales have comblike plates

With a long tongue, a Cape pangolin licks ants from the surface of an acacia log. These scaly mammals also feed on termites. A pangolin tears open a termite mound and reaches in with its worm-shaped tongue. The insects stick to the tongue and the pangolin swallows them.

called baleen (buh-LEAN) in their mouths; these plates serve as huge strainers. A whale opens its mouth as it swims through water rich with shrimplike animals. Then it closes its mouth and pushes the water out with its tongue. Caught in the baleen are thousands of the tiny animals that make up the whale's meal.

Anteaters and pangolins reach their food by using large claws to tear openings in ant or termite nests. The long-nosed animals put their snouts against the holes and push their long tongues in. Many insects stick to their tongues and are swallowed. Anteaters and pangolins have no teeth at all.

Mammals are the only creatures that have different kinds of teeth for different purposes. Meat eaters usually have sharp teeth with which to seize prey and rip flesh. Animals that eat plants often have shovel-shaped teeth that cut off mouthfuls of food. Both kinds of animals have strong back teeth for grinding plants or for shearing meat from bone.

Many hoofed animals, like cows and deer, swallow their food without chewing it thoroughly. After eating, an animal brings up a wad of partly digested food, called a cud. It chews the cud thoroughly, swallows it, and digests it.

△ *Cheetahs approach a herd of wildebeests on the plains of Africa. If the cheetahs can get close to a small or weak animal—perhaps a young wildebeest—they will begin to chase their prey down.*

▽ *As a fishing bat skims above water, its hind claws break the surface. Fishing bats use echolocation to find prey. They use their large claws to hook it.*

Getting From Place to Place

Leaping in unison, common dolphins speed through water off the coast of Mexico.

WALKING, HOPPING, crawling, swimming, or swinging, mammals travel from one place to another. Most mammals live on land and use all four limbs to move across the ground. Some, such as bears and raccoons, walk on the flat soles of their feet. Dogs and cats walk on their toes. Many fast-moving animals—horses, deer, and antelopes—run on hard toenails called hooves.

▽ *Over short distances, mammals travel at widely varying speeds. The sloth moves slowly through the trees at less than 1 mile (2 km) an hour. The armadillo ambles along more quickly. The cheetah, fastest land mammal, can reach speeds of 60-70 miles (97-113 km) an hour. The pronghorn comes close. A human sprinter can run a 220-yard, or 200-meter, race in less than 20 seconds—a rate of about 23 miles (37 km) an hour.*

1. Three-toed sloth: *less than 1 mile (2 km) an hour*

4. African elephant: *24 miles (39 km) an hour*

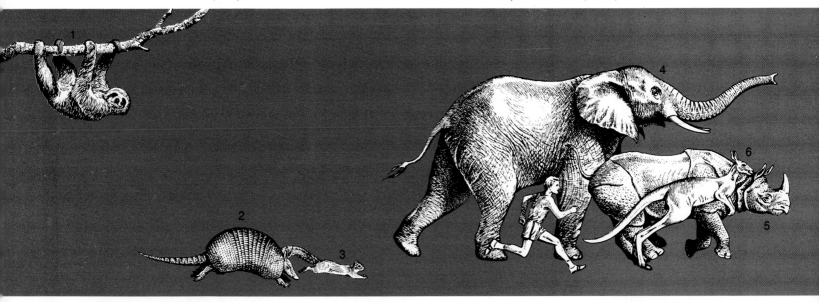

2. Nine-banded armadillo: *8 miles (13 km) an hour*

3. Gray squirrel: *12 miles (19 km) an hour*

5. Indian rhinoceros: *30 miles (48 km) an hour*

6. Red kangaroo: *30 miles (48 km) an hour*

What Is a Mammal?

Thick vine makes a natural jungle gym for a female ▷
orangutan and her young. Strong hands and long
arms equip these primates for life in the trees.

Other swift mammals have developed strong back legs. Big kangaroos and little jerboas use their powerful hind limbs to bound across open areas.

Moles and pocket gophers live underground. These animals have powerful shoulders, short arms, and long hard claws, which they use to burrow easily through the soil.

When faced with water, most land mammals can swim if they must. Some do so especially well. Beavers and otters have webbed feet that help them swim. Mammals that spend all their lives in the water, like whales and manatees, have large flattened tails. They propel themselves along by moving their tails up and down.

Animals that live in trees often move easily among the branches. The sharp claws of opossums and squirrels help them climb. Monkeys cling to trees with strong hands. Binturongs and silky anteaters use their tails to help hold on.

Flying squirrels and flying lemurs can glide through the air by spreading flaps of skin that connect their limbs. Of all the mammals, only the bats can actually fly.

7. Giraffe: *35 miles (56 km) an hour*   8. Mexican free-tailed bat: *40 miles (64 km) an hour*   12. Cheetah: *60-70 miles (97-113 km) an hour*

9. Thoroughbred horse:
   42 miles (68 km) an hour   10. Black-tailed jackrabbit:
   45 miles (72 km) an hour   11. Pronghorn:
   57 miles (92 km) an hour

Defense and Offense

RUNNING AWAY from danger is often the best defense for most mammals. However, not all animals are fast enough or alert enough to avoid predators (PRED-ut-erz)—the animals that hunt them. Sometimes mammals protect themselves by keeping perfectly still. As a predator passes by, it may not see or hear its prey.

Some mammals have coats that blend in with their surroundings. This kind of coloring is called camouflage (KAM-uh-flazh). It may save an animal

from attack. Camouflage also may allow a predator to hide from its prey. The predator can stalk undetected until it is close enough to attack.

Some mammals find protection in groups. As a defense against wolves, musk-oxen stand shoulder to shoulder and lower their heads. The attackers face a wall of thick, sharp horns. Prairie dogs guard their groups of burrows. If a prairie dog spots danger, it barks a warning to the others.

If they are caught or cornered, or if their young are in danger, most mammals will put up a fight. Zebras and horses kick. Anteaters slash with their claws. Even tiny mice bite.

Some mammals have special ways of defending themselves. A porcupine's quills can prevent attackers from harming it. A skunk sprays its enemies with a bad-smelling, stinging fluid. An opossum plays dead to discourage predators.

Teeth and claws, armor and quills all are used for

△ *Female hooded seal bares her teeth. Unlike many other seals, hooded seals fight to defend their pups.*

defense. Some of these features may be used in attacking other animals. Many mammals must be able to catch prey to get food.

Sometimes an animal's defensive features come in handy in several situations. In a tight spot, a walrus fights with its tusks. It also uses them in sparring with rivals and to nudge other walruses away from its area. Sometimes a walrus's tusks even serve as hooks. The animal plants them on the ice and hauls itself out of the water.

◁ *Wrestling match—more a game than a fight—erupts between two young male red kangaroos. The brief battle ended without injury to either.*

▽ *Spotted coat of a black-tailed fawn helps it hide among underbrush.*

▽ *Two sassabies stand alert on a termite mound. From this raised area on a grassland in Africa, these antelopes can spot an approaching enemy.*

Caring for Young

BECAUSE IT MUST FEED on her milk, a newborn mammal depends on its mother. Some young, however, need more attention than others.

Newborn marsupials are especially helpless. The kangaroo, the koala, the opossum, and the other members of this order all bear tiny, underdeveloped young. An offspring crawls into its mother's pouch soon after birth. There it remains attached to its mother's nipple. Only after several weeks is it large enough to move around—even in the pouch.

Mice, wolves, rabbits, and many other animals are born blind and helpless. They must nurse, and they need a long period of care. The mothers of these animals can leave their offspring alone for short periods while hunting for food. In contrast, hares, wildebeests, and zebras are relatively independent not long after they are born. Porcupines can walk when they are only a few minutes old. Cavies nibble on plants soon after birth.

Some mammals cooperate in caring for young. A female lion may nurse another's cubs. Cape hunting dogs share food with each other's pups.

Some kinds of mammals, such as chimpanzees, have complex social systems that shape the ways they behave. By copying the behavior of adults, the young of these species learn the skills they need to survive and to live in groups. The young learn how to find food, how to groom themselves and each other, how to build nests, and how to behave toward other members of their group.

▽ *After a meal, a female cheetah grooms her purring five-month-old cub by licking its face.*

△ Lending a helping trunk, an African elephant tugs a calf out of the water. Young elephants can walk soon after birth. But during the first months of their lives, they often need the help of adults.

Inside a lodge of sticks, stones, and mud, a female beaver △ nurses one of her furry twins.

Two female rhesus monkeys groom their young. This social ▷ activity helps keep hair and skin clean.

Sounds and Signals

△ *Twin pronghorn young bound after their mother. Their white rump patches serve as signals that danger lurks nearby. Other pronghorns that see the signal may also take flight.*

△ *Young hoary marmot touches noses with an adult. These rodents often greet each other this way.*

Head thrown back and body held erect, a black- ▷ *tailed prairie dog calls out shrilly, possibly to defend its home. Sometimes an excited prairie dog may jump into the air or even fall over backward. If this North American rodent spots danger, it barks an alarm.*

AS A PRONGHORN dashes across the prairie, the white hairs of its rump stand on end. This flash of white can be seen for a long distance. It serves as a signal to other pronghorns that danger is near. This kind of signal is only one of the many ways that mammals communicate with each other.

Communication does not mean that animals talk to each other as people do. Mammals communicate in several silent ways. For example, they use face and body positions to communicate. A chimpanzee lets others know how it feels by the expression on its face. The leader of a wolf pack usually carries his tail straight out. All the other members of the pack walk with their tails drooping. After a fight, one wolf indicates that it recognizes another as leader by lying down and showing its throat.

Many mammals communicate by the positions of their ears. Ears laid back may mean that an animal is annoyed or angry. Perked ears may show that an animal is alert.

Scent helps some mammals find each other, and it keeps others apart. Such animals as cats and dogs mark territories by spraying urine on trees and rocks. These marked places are called scent posts.

Many other animals also leave scent marks. Rabbits and hares produce a strong-smelling substance in glands under their jaws. They rub their jaws on the ground throughout their home areas. During the mating season, male pronghorns mark trees and bushes with scent from glands near their eyes. Both scent and claw marks on trees announce a bear's presence to other bears.

Some mammals use sounds to communicate. They make noises to frighten enemies, to attract mates, and to challenge rivals. They use sounds to call their young, to signal that danger has passed, or to gather others of their kind.

During the mating season, many mammals are noisier than usual. A bull elk has a strong, deep voice. His bugling sounds may attract females and keep rivals away.

To sound an alarm, a marmot whistles. A beaver warns of danger by striking the surface of the water with its tail. This loud whacking sound carries a long distance. A raccoon makes low throaty noises as it moves about. If danger threatens, the female's "churr churr" becomes louder and louder, until she screams—sending her young for cover.

Crossing snowy terrain in Michigan, a group of five gray wolves hunts for prey. The dominant wolf, or leader (second from last), walks with his tail held straight out. The tails of the other wolves droop. This may show that they recognize the dominant wolf as the most important member of the pack.

Season by Season

IN A FEW ENVIRONMENTS around the world—such as tropical rain forests—the climate changes very little from one season to the next. Food is usually available all year long. The lives of mammals that inhabit these areas also remain much the same whatever the season. Where the seasons do change, however, mammals must adapt their behavior. They must be able to get food and shelter in different kinds of weather.

Many mammals store food in the summer and fall. Rodents often put away nuts and seeds in their burrows. During the winter, when fresh food is scarce, they eat what they have saved. The pika builds haystacks. It gathers herbs and grasses and spreads them out to dry. Then it piles the dry food under rock ledges for use during the winter.

Some mammals, such as marmots and dormice, survive in cold weather by means of hibernation (hye-bur-NAY-shun). A hibernating animal eats a great deal in summer and fall and grows fat. When winter comes, it finds a burrow or den and drops into a kind of sleep called torpor. Its body temperature goes down; its breathing and heart rate get slower. It lives on the fat in its body and uses up very little energy.

△ *Curled nose to tail, a golden-mantled ground squirrel sleeps during the winter. While it hibernates, its temperature drops, and breathing and heart rate slow.*

◁ *Crew-cut summer coat appears as a mountain goat sheds its winter hair. New hair will grow out all summer, forming a long, thick coat by fall.*

Animals can survive harsh conditions in a state of torpor at any time of year. If they do so during the heat of summer, they are said to aestivate (ES-tuh-vate).

Mammals that live in cool climates usually have two different coats of hair. Their thick winter coat serves as insulation, keeping body heat in and cold out. This heavy coat is shed in warm weather. It is replaced by a thinner summer coat. This process is called molting.

A few mammals, such as the snowshoe hare and some weasels, change color as the seasons change. In summer, their hair is brown. Gradually, new white

△ *As spring arrives, male bighorn sheep feed on plant shoots in Glacier National Park in Montana. All winter, they nibbled plants on lower slopes. When summer comes, they will move higher.*

◁ *In summer, a short-tailed weasel's brownish coat (left) blends well with rocks. Some weasels change color with the seasons. A white-coated weasel (far left) is hard to see against the snow.*

hair grows in. By winter, the summer hair has been shed, and the coats are white. The color changes help camouflage the animals. Their white coats blend in with snow. Their brown coats are hard to see against rocks and dry grasses.

Some mammals escape harsh winters by migrating, or traveling, from one place to another. In the summer, for example, mountain sheep feed high in the mountains. They come down to lower areas during cold weather. Certain whales swim to warmer water in winter. They spend only the summer months in the polar regions.

Studying Mammals

Dr. Merlin Tuttle examines a frog-eating bat lured into a net by recorded frog calls.

WHY STUDY MAMMALS? What makes us want to learn more about this varied group? We share the earth with mammals. We use them as sources of food and clothing, as work animals, and as pets. We too are mammals. By studying other mammals we learn more about ourselves.

Scientists who study mammals are called mammalogists (muh-MAL-uh-justs). Mammalogists may be interested in certain specialized subjects. The study of anatomy (uh-NAT-uh-mee), for example, tells them how the bodies of mammals are put together. Physiology (fizzy-AHL-uh-gee) is the study of how mammals' bodies work. Taxonomy (tak-SAHN-uh-mee) classifies the many kinds of mammals and reveals how they are related. Some mammalogists learn about ethology (ee-THAHL-uh-gee), or the study of why mammals behave in the ways that they do. Ecology (ee-KAHL-uh-gee) teaches scientists how mammals interact with their environments.

Some scientists study mammals in laboratories. They may experiment with live animals in carefully controlled environments. Or they may use collections of mammal skeletons or preserved blood and tissue. By comparing measurements, biochemical features, and DNA, scientists can learn a great deal about how different species have developed. Other scientists may also study mammals that are living in the wild. They use many kinds of electronic equipment, tape recorders, cameras, and detailed journals. The scientists sometimes track animals' movements by radio and satellite.

But you don't have to be a mammalogist to study mammals in some way. Most of us would find it too hard to study such animals as giraffes and aardvarks in the wild. Squirrels, chipmunks, and raccoons, however, often live near people. We can see what they look like and how they behave. Pet dogs and cats also are easy to study. We can learn about mammals by looking at the animals around us and by watching those that share our lives.

Male caribou carries a radio transmitter through a ▷
park in Alaska. Signals from such collars permit
rangers to track the animal's movements.
▽ *Along a creek in South America, Dr. Nicole Duplaix,*
a mammalogist, measures waste left by giant otters. By
studying these traces, scientists can learn much about
mammals in the wild.

▽ *Artificial burrow in a laboratory lets*
scientists study naked mole rats.

Survival in Question

HUMAN BEINGS share the earth with all of the other mammals. People change their environment in many ways to suit themselves. They often do not think about how these changes affect other animals. They build houses for shelter, plow the land to plant crops, and use natural resources for energy. In many places, human activity destroys the homes of other kinds of mammals.

The mountain gorilla, for example, lives in a small area in Africa. Even though the area is part of a park, local people increasingly farm in the area. As the gorillas' habitat gets smaller and as the animals are killed by poachers, scientists worry that the species may die out.

In many parts of the world, such as Australia, people have introduced, or brought in, animals that had never lived there before. Many of the native animals could not compete with the newcomers for food—or they themselves became prey. Some of them died out completely.

Over long periods of time, other species have not been able to adapt to natural changes and have

also become extinct. As these animals have disappeared, other species have replaced them.

Species that are in danger of extinction now can be saved, or at least protected. One way to do this is to set aside special areas for wild animals. On wildlife preserves and in zoos, many endangered species have another chance for survival.

One animal that has been rescued in this way is the Arabian oryx. Once there were only a few of these graceful animals left in their desert homeland. In the early 1960s, some of them were captured and taken to

△ *Golden lion tamarins huddle in a tree. Destruction of their natural habitat in Brazil endangers these tiny animals. Some survived in preserves. Scientists bred others in captivity and returned them to the wild.*

◁ *Arabian oryxes live at San Diego Wild Animal Park. The animals had almost disappeared from their natural environment in the Middle East. These oryxes have bred so successfully that some are being returned to the wild.*

△ *Volcano rabbit crouches in the grass, which it uses as food and as nesting material. These rabbits, endangered by a shrinking habitat, live only on the slopes of a few volcanoes in Mexico.*

preserves in Africa and in the United States. There the oryxes have adapted to new environments, have bred, and have raised young. Now there are enough Arabian oryxes that some may be returned to their natural environment.

For many species of mammals, conservation in zoos and breeding in captivity offer the only hope of survival. Golden lion tamarins, sometimes called marmosets, are carefully monitored both in the wild—in remnant rain forests of a small area of Brazil—and in zoos worldwide. Some 25 countries cooperate with Brazil to reestablish them in the wild.

Scientists continue to study ways to ensure the survival of endangered mammals. Some governments and individuals help by taking an active interest in conservation. People can try to make sure that their descendants will see and enjoy the other mammals that inhabit earth's deserts and mountains, its seas and forests, its swamps and grasslands.

A

Aardvark

(ARD-vark)

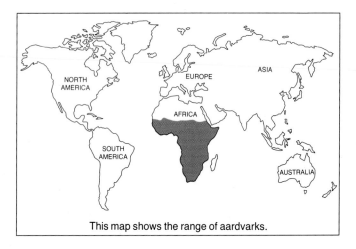

This map shows the range of aardvarks.

Long ears and piglike snout of an aardvark cast a shadow on a termite mound in Africa. Keen hearing and a sharp sense of smell help the animal find food and avoid danger. Above, strong claws make dirt fly as an aardvark burrows into the side of a mound in search of insects to eat.

THE SPELLING OF ITS NAME gives the aardvark its place at the beginning of most animal lists. Aardvark means "earth pig" in the Afrikaans language of South Africa. Its snout does look like a pig's. But this long-nosed, long-eared animal is not related to the pig or to any other mammal!

The aardvark's nighttime habits make the animal difficult to find and to study. Only after sunset does it leave its burrow in the grasslands or the forests to search for food. Outside the den, the stocky animal, which measures about 6 feet (183 cm) from head to tail, pauses. It listens and sniffs for danger. If all is safe, it trots away. The aardvark moves on its toes and claws, often following a zigzag path. Its tail drags behind, making a groove in the ground.

When the aardvark finds a termite mound, like the one in the picture at right, it digs a hole near the base. The sunbaked earth of a mound can dry as hard as concrete. But the aardvark is a strong burrower. With the thick, sturdy claws of its front feet, it can burrow through even hard-packed soil. The aardvark then pushes its blunt snout close to the opening in the mound. It catches the termites with its long, worm-shaped tongue.

Tough skin protects the aardvark from insect bites. The animal can even close its nostrils, so that termites, ants, and dust do not get into its snout.

After the aardvark has eaten from one mound, it may move on to another or dig into an underground ant nest. Aardvarks may travel several miles a night searching for food.

Although it is a timid animal, the aardvark can fight off attackers such as big cats and wild dogs. It sits on its rump and lashes out with its front claws. Sometimes the aardvark lies on its back and slashes at an enemy with all four feet. But rather than fight, the aardvark will try to escape from danger. It runs for its den or quickly digs a hole for cover.

By morning, the aardvark returns to its cool, tunnel-like burrow. All day, the aardvark sleeps there curled up in a circular room. There is just enough room for the aardvark to turn around—and leave its den headfirst.

A female aardvark usually has one offspring a year. The hairless newborn has tender, pinkish skin. It stays in the den for about two weeks. Then it begins to search for food with its mother. After six months, the young aardvark digs its own burrow. But it stays near its mother for several months more.

AARDVARK

LENGTH OF HEAD AND BODY: **43-53 in (109-135 cm); tail, 21-26 in (53-66 cm)**

WEIGHT: **110-180 lb (50-82 kg)**

HABITAT AND RANGE: **grasslands and woodlands of Africa south of the Sahara**

FOOD: **usually termites, ants, and some fruit**

LIFE SPAN: **up to 24 years in captivity**

REPRODUCTION: **1 or 2 young after a pregnancy of about 7 months**

ORDER: **tubulidentates**

Aardwolf

AARDWOLF

LENGTH OF HEAD AND BODY: 22-31 in (56-79 cm); tail, 8-12 in (20-30 cm)

WEIGHT: 20-31 lb (9-14 kg)

HABITAT AND RANGE: open woodlands and plains in eastern and southern Africa

FOOD: mostly termites

LIFE SPAN: 19 years in captivity

REPRODUCTION: usually 2 to 4 young after a pregnancy of about 3 months

ORDER: carnivores

△ *From ears to bushy tail, an aardwolf stands alert on the plains of Africa. If threatened, the animal will make itself look larger by raising its dark mane.*

AT NIGHT, IN THE WOODLANDS and on the dry plains of southern and eastern Africa, the aardwolf searches along the ground for termites. When it finds food, the animal quickly laps the insects up with its long, sticky tongue. Then the aardwolf may groom itself. It uses its tongue to clean its narrow muzzle and the inside of its mouth. It lies down and licks its striped, yellowish fur.

Though its name means "earth wolf" in the Afrikaans language of South Africa, the aardwolf is not related to the wolf. The seldom-seen animal belongs to the same family as the hyena. Aardwolves are sometimes mistaken for striped hyenas, though they are smaller. They grow only about 3 feet (91 cm) long from head to tail. Aardwolves are carnivores, that is, they are meat eaters. But their jaws and teeth are weaker than those of their relatives, and they have turned to a diet of insects. Find out more about hyenas on page 278.

During the day, aardwolves sleep in holes in the ground. Usually, they stay in old burrows left by aardvarks or other animals. Occasionally aardwolves dig dens of their own. They may leave them in the morning to lie in the sun. If the weather is bad, they may stay in their dens for days at a time.

A female aardwolf usually gives birth in a den. The newborn cubs—normally three in a litter—are blind and helpless. They are fully grown in about nine months.

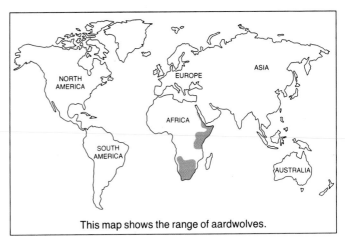

This map shows the range of aardwolves.

◁ *Aardwolf licks up termites with its sticky tongue. It quickly feeds on insects from one area and moves on. The animal can eat 40,000 termites in three hours!*

When threatened by other animals, an aardwolf raises its black-and-yellow mane. This ridge of hair extends down the neck and back. When the mane stands on end, the animal looks much larger than it usually does. The aardwolf also barks and roars ferociously. Though the aardwolf rarely fights, it will use its sharp, small teeth if it finds itself cornered. Usually it hides in its den.

Agouti (uh-GOOT-ee)

AGOUTI 🐾 **3 of 13 species**

LENGTH OF HEAD AND BODY: 16-24 in (41-61 cm); tail, about 1 in (3 cm)

WEIGHT: 2-9 lb (1-4 kg)

HABITAT AND RANGE: tropical forests in Mexico and in Central and South America

FOOD: fruit, leaves, roots, and stalks

LIFE SPAN: 13 to 20 years in captivity

REPRODUCTION: 1 or 2 young after a pregnancy of about 3 months

ORDER: rodents

Thirsty agouti heads for the water during the dry ▷ *season in Bolivia. Quick and alert, it freezes if it hears a noise. If seen by an enemy, it will dash for cover.*

SITTING UP AND LISTENING to the sounds of the forest, an agouti holds an avocado between its forepaws. It peels the soft fruit with its teeth and eats it. Suddenly, the agouti perks its short ears. Sensing danger, it freezes. A rustle of leaves warns of an approaching enemy—perhaps an ocelot.

With a call of alarm, the agouti dashes through the forest to escape its enemy. It swiftly zigzags among the trees. Using its strong legs, the large rodent tries to outrun the wild cat. Or the agouti tries to trick its pursuer. It darts into a hollow log and slips out the other end.

There are about 13 kinds of agoutis. The animals have short tails and small, rounded ears. Agoutis make their homes in the tropical forests of Mexico, Central America, and South America. Usually they live in sheltered spots under tree roots, between rocks, or in hollow logs.

During the day or in the evening, agoutis look for parts of plants to eat. Their coarse hair—pale orange, brown, or almost black—blends with the colors of the forest. Though an agouti's coat appears to be one shade, each hair has bands of color.

Female agoutis usually bear one or two young. The newborn are covered with hair and are more developed than the offspring of some other rodents. Able to see at birth, they often nibble on green plants an hour later. Like full-grown agoutis, they freeze when in danger.

A close relative of the agouti is the paca. You can read about the paca on page 420.

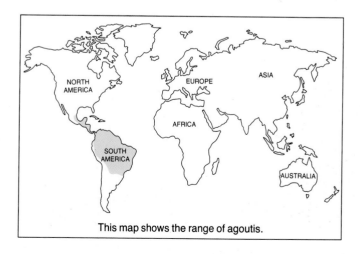

This map shows the range of agoutis.

Alpaca

The alpaca is a close relative of the llama. Read about alpacas and llamas on page 336.

Anteater

(ANT-eat-er)

Giant anteater: 49 in (124 cm) long; tail, 35 in (89 cm)

Holding onto its mother's back, a five-month-old giant anteater hitches a ride in the grasslands of Brazil. Broad, dark stripes on the animals' sides line up, helping to hide the young against the adult's fur.

DOES AN ANTEATER EAT ANTS? Yes, this remarkable animal with the long snout really lives up to its name. To reach its food, the anteater scratches a hole in an anthill with a sharp, curved claw. It darts its long tongue through the hole and inside the nest. With a flick, it jerks back its tongue, which is covered with ants. The insects are swallowed whole.

An anteater does not linger at an anthill. It may stay for less than a minute. The longer it feeds, the more chance the insects have to sting.

The anteater eats several kinds of insects. But ants and termites are the animal's main foods. In fact, an anteater can eat some 35,000 ants and termites in a single day.

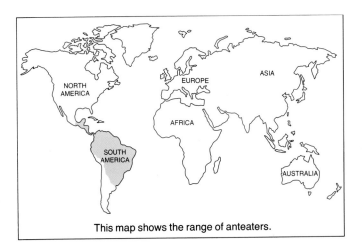

This map shows the range of anteaters.

ANTEATER 🐾 1 of 4 species

LENGTH OF HEAD AND BODY: 6-49 in (15-124 cm); tail, 7-35 in (18-89 cm)

WEIGHT: 6 oz-86 lb (170 g-39 kg)

HABITAT AND RANGE: tropical forests and grasslands from southern Mexico through northern Argentina

FOOD: mostly ants and termites

LIFE SPAN: up to 26 years in captivity, depending on species

REPRODUCTION: usually 1 young after a pregnancy of about 5 or 6 months

ORDER: xenarthrans

An anteater's mouth is not much more than a pencil-size hole at the end of its snout. The animal has no teeth, so it cannot chew the insects it eats. The ants and termites are crushed and digested in the anteater's stomach.

The anteater does not see very well. It depends on its nose to lead it to an insect nest. Its sense of smell is much better than a person's.

Anteaters live in tropical forests and grasslands of Central and South America. The squirrel-size silky anteater stays mostly in trees. It gets its name from its soft, silky fur. The raccoon-size tamandua (tuh-MAN-duh-wuh) divides its time between the trees and the ground. The tamandua is sometimes called a collared anteater because of the ring of light-colored fur around its neck.

At night, both the tamandua and the silky anteater look for food. They move slowly but easily through the branches, grasping them with their long tails and hooklike claws. During the day, they curl up into tight balls and sleep in tree forks.

The giant anteater measures as long as 7 feet (213 cm) including its tail. It rarely climbs trees. It spends most of its waking hours sniffing for food on the ground. It seems to shuffle along on its front knuckles. Actually, it is walking on the sides of its paws. Unlike a cat, the giant anteater cannot pull in its strong claws. To protect them and keep them sharp, it curves them under its body as it walks.

The giant anteater usually stays in its home territory. It takes to water easily, and sometimes it even swims across wide rivers in search of food. When it tires, the animal lies down and covers itself with its bushy tail. The tail serves as a blanket on cold nights and helps to hide the animal from its enemies.

Anteaters usually live alone, but females are sometimes seen with young. An anteater gives birth about once a year to a single offspring. A young anteater spends much of its time riding on its mother's back. A young giant anteater often becomes hidden in its mother's thick fur. When it is older, it occasionally will gallop alongside its mother.

A female silky anteater may leave her young hidden in a tree nest of dry leaves while she looks for food. When the young is asleep, it blends in with the branches, and enemies cannot easily see it.

Though anteaters never attack another animal first, they will defend themselves fiercely. When in danger, the giant anteater strikes out with its thick, strong claws. Sometimes it even rears up on its hind legs. The claws of a giant anteater can measure as long as 4 inches (10 cm). The animal is a match even for a mountain lion or a jaguar.

Long, tapered snout helps a giant anteater sniff for food. The animal has such poor eyesight that it probably could not see a person standing just a few feet away.

Anteater

Silky anteater: 6 in (15 cm) long; tail, 7 in (18 cm)

◁ *Carrying her offspring on her back, a female silky anteater walks along a branch in an Amazon forest. This anteater spends almost all of its time in trees.*

Up on its hind legs, an alarmed tamandua prepares ▷ to defend itself. The animal's sharp claws can cause serious wounds if an attacker gets too close. Its tail acts as a prop. Another tamandua (far right) uses its tail to hold on as it climbs down a tree in South America.

▽ *Giant anteater feeds on insects at a termite mound. The animal flicks its worm-shaped tongue in and out as many as 160 times a minute. It catches thousands of ants and termites every day.*

Tamandua: 21 in (53 cm) long; tail, 21 in (53 cm)

The tamandua uses its claws as weapons, too. When it is startled, the animal rises on its hind legs and spreads out its paws. If there is no real danger, it will drop back on all fours and move away. If attacked, however, the tamandua may strike with its razor-sharp claws. Or it may grab its enemy in a strong grip and hold it away from its body until the attacker is stunned or dead.

Like the other anteaters, a threatened silky may rise on its hind legs to defend itself. It braces itself with its tail. Then it raises its front paws above its head and strikes down hard, slashing at its enemy. But a silky anteater's best defense is camouflage. Its gray-brown fur is hard to see against the branches in which it lives.

Giant anteaters are declining in number throughout their range. Although laws protect them in some countries, they are still hunted by people. They are easy targets and can be seen from far away, lumbering across the grasslands.

51

Antelope

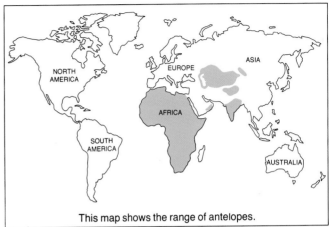

This map shows the range of antelopes.

ANTELOPE 🐾 **26 of 72 species**

HEIGHT: **10-71 in (25-180 cm) at the shoulder**

WEIGHT: **4-2,000 lb (2-907 kg)**

HABITAT AND RANGE: **many kinds of habitats in Africa, central and southern Asia, and southern Russia**

FOOD: **grasses, herbs, leaves, twigs, bark, buds, fruit, and insects**

LIFE SPAN: **3 to 25 years in captivity, depending on species**

REPRODUCTION: **1 to 3 young after a pregnancy of 4 to 9½ months, depending on species**

ORDER: **artiodactyls**

MANY PEOPLE THINK of antelopes as handsome, deerlike animals that bound gracefully across the wide plains of Africa. Some antelopes do fit this description. But this group of hoofed animals is amazingly varied. From the jackrabbit-size royal antelope to the oxlike eland (EE-lund), antelopes come in a wide range of shapes and sizes. A look at their horns gives a good idea of how different these animals can be. The horns may be straight, curved, twisted, spiraled, or ringed. Each of the nearly one hundred species, or kinds, of antelopes has a uniquely shaped set of horns.

Some kinds of antelopes are found in Asia—the saiga (SIGH-guh) and the black buck, for example. But most live in Africa. They are found in nearly every

Peaceful scene at water's edge: Several springboks share a water hole with wading birds. The rest of the herd grazes behind them. Dutch settlers in South Africa named these antelopes for their habit of jumping straight up into the air when startled.

Springbok: 30 in (76 cm) tall at the shoulder

Antelope

Horns crossed, two gemsboks in Namibia clash in ▷ battle while another watches. Gemsboks may fight for mates or to test their strength. Each twists and turns its head, as if trying to throw its rival to the ground. The stronger animal wins. Gemsboks, like most antelopes, rarely hurt each other when fighting. But they do use their swordlike horns as weapons against lions and other large predators.

▽ Female defassa waterbuck and their month-old young jump into a lake in Kenya. True to their name, these large antelopes seldom roam far from water.

Gemsbok: 48 in (122 cm) tall at the shoulder

Defassa waterbuck: 48 in (122 cm) tall at the shoulder

Saiga: 30 in (76 cm) tall at the shoulder

Bulky noses and bulging eyes identify saigas (above) of southern Russia and parts of central Asia. Their large nostrils may warm and moisten cold, dry air. Huge ears erect, a young female greater kudu (right) stands near a water hole in Namibia. Greater kudus can go several days without drinking.

54

Greater kudu: 59 in (150 cm) tall at the shoulder

Scimitar-horned
oryx: 47 in (119 cm)
tall at the shoulder

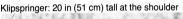

△ Graceful curving horns sprout from the heads of scimitar-horned oryxes. Both males and females grow horns about 3 feet (91 cm) long. People have almost hunted them to extinction in the wild.

Surefooted klipspringer perches on a rock. ▷ This small antelope lives in rocky and mountainous regions of eastern, central, and southern Africa. Dutch settlers named the animal "cliff springer" because it leaps easily from rock to rock. The antelope's rubberlike hooves help it land safely on rock ledges no bigger than a teacup. Like a dancer on tiptoe, it stands and walks on the tips of its hooves.

kind of habitat—deserts, swamps, and mountains. But most of the species are found in forests and on grasslands in Africa.

A small antelope like the duiker (DYE-ker) usually lives in forests or in thick brush. Duikers feed on the leaves and twigs of bushes and trees. They may live alone, in pairs, or in small family groups. A male often protects the territory in which he and a female live, perhaps with offspring. If other male duikers try to invade this area, he chases them away. Since only a few duikers live in a territory, there is plenty of food to go around. Other antelopes may not have this kind of territory. And they may have to roam great distances in search of food.

Large antelopes such as elands may travel in herds of as many as 700 animals. In the rainy season, herds gather on the plains. In the dry season, they scatter into brushy areas to find food and water.

Often several kinds of antelopes may roam the same area. Some graze, or eat only grass. Others browse, or eat only leaves and twigs. Still others do both. But the different kinds of antelopes do not compete for the same food. Smaller antelopes feed on the lower leaves of a plant. Larger antelopes eat the leaves higher up.

Most antelopes eat during the cool parts of the day—early morning and late afternoon. As they feed, the animals watch constantly for enemies. They eat quickly, swallowing their food nearly whole. Later, when resting, they bring up a mouthful of partly digested food—called a cud—and chew it thoroughly. Antelopes are related to other cud-chewing animals, such as camels, cows, deer, goats, and sheep. You can read about these animals under their own headings in this book.

Lions, cheetahs, hyenas, wild dogs, and about a

Red hartebeest: 49 in (124 cm) tall at the shoulder

△ *All four hooves off the ground, a red hartebeest gallops across a plain in Botswana. Hartebeests live in herds of five to twenty animals. If an enemy approaches, the antelopes speed away in single file.*

▽ *Young suni sniffs curiously at its mother's mouth. Young antelopes often learn what they can eat by imitating their mothers. These small antelopes live in dense brush in eastern and southern Africa.*

Suni: 14 in (36 cm) tall at the shoulder

Zebra duiker: 16 in (41 cm) tall at the shoulder

56

dozen other meat-eating animals are predators (PRED-ut-erz), or hunters, of antelopes. People, too, hunt them for their meat, hides, and horns.

Antelopes have keen senses, and they are always alert to enemies. Sniffing the air, antelopes may pick up the scent of a predator. Their large ears hear the slightest sound. With huge eyes on the sides of their heads, they keep a sharp lookout for danger. When threatened, a small antelope, such as a dik-dik, may hide. A big antelope—an eland, for example—may try to stand its ground. But for many antelopes the best defense is speed.

Most antelopes are fast runners and can escape a predator in long leaps. Antelopes are built for swift movement. They have long legs, strong hindquarters, and sturdy hooves that help them jump.

Hiding, protective coloring, and traveling in herds are useful defenses against enemies. A small antelope such as the suni (SOO-nee) usually lives in areas that offer thick cover. If a jackal or other predator approaches, the suni hides among the bushes and tall grasses. The little animal drops down and lies very still until the jackal passes. But if a jackal gets too close, the suni jumps up and runs away. When it gets far enough ahead of the predator, it drops down again and hides.

Springboks are too big to hide. They often rely on a different method to avoid enemies. When a predator comes close, these fleet-footed antelopes jump straight up into the air several times. As they leap, a patch of white hair flashes under their tails. This signal warns other springboks that danger is near. Then the animals run away.

Some antelopes, such as bongos and reedbucks, have coats that blend into their surroundings and act as camouflage.

Herds offer antelopes protection from predators because of the number of animals in one place. With so many eyes, ears, and noses alert, a lion or a cheetah has more difficulty sneaking up on a herd. Sometimes several members of a topi or a hartebeest herd act as guards. If they spot a predator, they snort in alarm and gallop away. *(Continued on page 60)*

◁ *After a chilly night, a zebra duiker warms itself in the sun. Duikers usually feed after dark. Some kinds grow only as big as hares. Others grow as tall as deer.*

"Are you mine?" a female topi asks with a sniff. A female knows her offspring by its scent. She can find her young even in a large herd. A newborn can walk soon after birth.

Topi: 48 in (122 cm) tall at the shoulder

Black buck: 32 in (81 cm)
tall at the shoulder

Bongo: 48 in (122 cm) tall at the shoulder

△ *Group of black buck chew grass on a preserve in India. There they live protected from hunters who want their meat and their horns.*

◁ *Broad stripe stretches across a young male bongo's face. The markings on its sides and back make the animal hard to see among forest shadows.*

▽ *Oxlike in size and appearance, an eland strides through the grass. Both male and female elands grow horns. The snapping muscles of an old bull's legs often make a clicking sound when walking. Scientists think the clicking lets other elands know of its presence.*

Eland: 70 in (178 cm) tall at the shoulder

Bohor reedbuck: 30 in (76 cm) tall at the shoulder

△ *Male bohor reedbuck in Kenya watches for danger. It will dash away if an enemy approaches.*

▽ *Male nyala drinks at a water hole. When the white hair on its back bristles, the animal is signaling a threat.*

Kirk's dik-dik: 14 in (36 cm) tall at the shoulder

Nyala: 45 in (114 cm) tall at the shoulder

△ *Tiny Kirk's dik-dik, about 14 inches (36 cm) tall, becomes hard to see among grasses. A dark spot at the corner of the eye produces a sticky substance. The dik-dik uses this to mark its territory.*

Beneath misty mountains, a herd of Uganda kobs grazes quietly on a game preserve in Africa. These animals feed mainly on grasses as they roam the plains. When food is plentiful, thousands of animals may gather. Much of the year, kobs live in three separate groups. Females and young form a nursery herd. The strongest males guard their own territories. Males without territories stay together in a bachelor herd.

Uganda kob: 36 in (91 cm) tall at the shoulder

Then the entire herd takes off. The slower-moving antelopes—the old, sick, or very young—often get caught by predators.

A few kinds of large antelopes, such as the gemsbok (GEMZ-bahk) and the eland, use their horns as weapons against predators. Hard, hollow horns grow around two bony cores on an antelope's head. The horns keep growing throughout the animal's life. They do not fall off every year as a deer's antlers do. Not all female antelopes grow horns, but all males do. Males often fight with their horns.

Fighting among male antelopes is a show of strength, a contest to prove which antelope is stronger. The fights rarely end in death. In fact, antelopes usually do not draw blood when fighting. Dik-diks, one of the smallest kinds of antelopes, battle without even touching. Instead, male dik-diks charge at each

other as if they were going to attack. Then they stop short. They do this over and over until one dik-dik is forced back into its own territory.

Some antelopes mate at any time of the year. Others mate only during a certain season. At that time, fighting among male antelopes increases. A male kob, for instance, stakes out a territory. If another male comes into this area, the holder of the territory will fight it. Locking horns, the two push and shove. They continue fighting until one kob tires and leaves. The winner remains in the territory and mates with any female kobs that enter it.

Female antelopes usually bear one young at a time. Scientists group these young antelopes into hiders and followers. Smaller antelopes often hide out after they are born. The female gives birth to her offspring in a secluded spot safe from predators. Usually the newborn lies hidden under a bush or in the grass for several weeks. The mother feeds as usual, but she returns to the hiding place several times a day to nurse her young. As the young grows bigger, it starts to wander with its mother. Within six months, it may become independent.

Offspring born to larger antelopes that roam in herds may be followers. The young can stand and walk shortly after birth. It stays close by its mother's side and goes with her everywhere. In a few days, it can run as fast as an adult antelope.

Read about some of the best-known antelopes under their own headings. You can find out about gazelles on page 212, gerenuks on page 220, impalas on page 292, and wildebeests on page 571.

Armadillo

Tough scales shield the body of a nine-banded armadillo, the only kind found in the United States. Thick skin and a few coarse hairs cover the unarmored parts of its head and legs.

Nine-banded armadillo: 18 in (46 cm) long; tail, 12 in (30 cm)

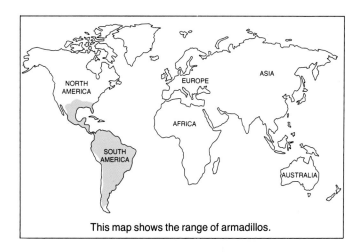

This map shows the range of armadillos.

△ *Young nine-banded armadillo and its mother sniff the ground in search of food. The young animal has soft leathery skin. As it grows, its skin will harden.*

▽ *With its snout in the soil, a nine-banded armadillo eats worms and insects. A keen sense of smell helps the armadillo find food, and a long tongue helps catch it. Armadillos often make grunting and sniffling noises as they search for a meal.*

ARMADILLO 🐾 **6 of 20 species**

LENGTH OF HEAD AND BODY: 5-37 in (13-94 cm); tail, 1-21 in (3-53 cm)

WEIGHT: 3 oz-120 lb (85 g-54 kg)

HABITAT AND RANGE: grasslands and open forests from the southern United States through most of South America

FOOD: ants, termites, worms, snails, beetles, roots, fruit, snakes, and dead animals

LIFE SPAN: up to 23 years in captivity, depending on species

REPRODUCTION: 1 to 12 young; pregnancy varies by species and is not known for all

ORDER: xenarthrans

LIKE A SUIT OF ARMOR, plates of skin-covered bone protect most of the armadillo's body. *Armadillo* means "little armored one" in Spanish. The large, solid plates are connected by overlapping bands that partly circle the animal's middle and allow it to bend. The armor protects the armadillo from thorns and branches and sometimes from its enemies.

Armadillos are well equipped for digging. The stocky animals have short front feet with powerful, curved claws. They use the claws to dig underground

Nine-banded armadillo cuts through a river. Armadillos swallow air as they swim. This helps them float. Sometimes an armadillo may cross a river by holding its breath and walking on the bottom.

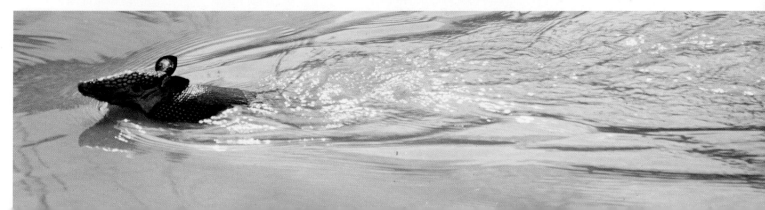

Armadillo

burrows where they sleep and raise young. Because an armadillo can hold its breath as long as six minutes, it does not breathe in dirt when it is digging. The nine-banded armadillo can even cross rivers by holding its breath and walking along the bottom.

There are twenty different kinds of armadillos. All of them live from Mexico through most of South America. And one kind is also found in the southern United States: the nine-banded armadillo. Actually, this long-nosed armadillo sometimes has only eight bands between its shoulder and hip plates.

Armadillos come in many sizes. The pink fairy armadillo is the smallest—6 inches (15 cm) from head to tail. The giant armadillo is ten times as long—measuring about 5 feet (152 cm).

Armadillos are timid animals. When frightened, they run for their dens. Inside their burrows they are safe. The pink fairy armadillo often blocks the opening of its den with its blunt, scaly hind end. The pichi (PEA-chee) armadillo wedges itself into a shallow burrow with the toothlike edges of its jagged scales. It is difficult for an enemy to drag it out.

An armadillo can also protect itself by digging a new place to hide. It rapidly makes a tunnel and vanishes before a predator's eyes. Finally, the three-banded armadillo can roll its body into an armored ball. Such enemies as foxes or wolves cannot get a grip on the smooth plates. Other armadillos curl up only partway to protect their soft bellies.

Most armadillos live alone, but some kinds live in pairs or in small groups. Armadillos may even share a burrow. Most dig their dens in open grasslands. But giant and nine-banded armadillos also live in forest underbrush.

Pichi armadillo: 11 in (28 cm) long; tail, 4 in (10 cm)

△ *Pichi armadillo runs quickly to escape from danger. Once the pichi reaches its grass-lined burrow, the toothlike edges of its armor will help wedge it inside.*

New kind of ball? No, it's a three-banded armadillo. ▷
When threatened, the animal curls up tightly and hisses. Its head, tail, and feet fit under the plates that cover its curved back. Enemies cannot bite its soft underparts.

Three-banded armadillo: 9 in (23 cm) long; tail, 3 in (8 cm); diameter rolled up, 4 in (10 cm)

Armadillos make snorting noises as they move about. Hikers near sand dunes in Florida—and in other dry parts of the southern United States—often hear armadillos sniffing for grubs in the tall grass. The animals probably depend on their sense of smell to find food. Some burrow into termite mounds and stay there all day, feeding on insects.

Ants and termites are an armadillo's favorite foods. The animal pushes its worm-shaped tongue far into an insect nest. Its tongue comes out covered with insects. These are quickly gobbled down. Armadillos also eat snakes, worms, snails, beetles, roots, fruit, and sometimes dead animals.

Most armadillos give birth to one offspring or to twins. But the nine-banded armadillo bears four identical offspring. The young in each litter are the same sex—all male or all female.

Pink fairy armadillo: 5 in (13 cm) long; tail, 1 in (3 cm)

△ *Which end points forward? Soft, white hair covers the tiny snout of a pink fairy armadillo. A short fringe flutters from its back end. This kind of armadillo—the smallest of all—weighs only 3 ounces (85 g). A giant armadillo (below) weighs 120 pounds (54 kg)—600 times as much—and measures ten times as long from head to tail. The claws on the larger animal's front feet grow as long as the body of the pink fairy armadillo.*

Giant armadillo: 37 in (94 cm) long; tail, 23 in (58 cm)

Ass

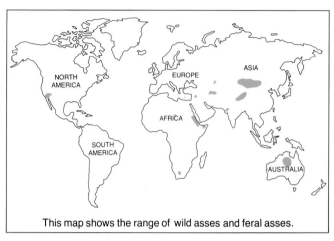

This map shows the range of wild asses and feral asses.

Female asses, called jennies, lead two-month-old foals to water. The young can run a few hours after birth.

ASS 🐾 **2 of 3 species**

HEIGHT: 38-63 in (97-160 cm) at the shoulder

WEIGHT: 300-1,200 lb (136-544 kg)

HABITAT AND RANGE: dry areas of Africa, the Middle East, Asia, Australia, and parts of North America; domestic asses are found in many parts of the world

FOOD: desert plants

LIFE SPAN: 10 to 25 years in the wild

REPRODUCTION: usually 1 young after a pregnancy of 11 or 12 months, depending on species

ORDER: perissodactyls

SUREFOOTED AND UNHURRIED, the ass trots along on small, tough, U-shaped hooves. This sturdy animal—a close relative of the horse—is well suited, or adapted, to the harsh, dry lands in which it lives.

Asses can make their way in rocky canyons and up steep hills. They can go without water for several days while searching for a drink. They can eat leaves, bark, twigs, and thistles, as well as grasses.

For centuries, people around the world have kept asses as pack animals. Tame asses—called burros or donkeys—probably carried supplies for the people who built the pyramids of Egypt thousands of years ago. Columbus brought donkeys with him to the New World. About a hundred years ago, burros carried the belongings of prospectors in the western United States. Some of these burros got away and ran off into the wild. Their descendants are called feral (FEAR-ul) asses.

The wild ass is smaller than most horses. It has large pointed ears that stick up into the air. A dark stripe usually runs down the animal's back, from its short, wiry mane to its tufted tail. Asses range in color from white to tan to black. The Nubian ass of Egypt has a stripe across its shoulders. Dark bands circle the legs of the Somali ass.

The gray coats of Somali asses blend into their desert environment. A group may travel for days without finding water, eating only tough grasses and

Long ears tilted to catch sounds, a male ass, called a ▷ jack, nibbles on thorny shrubs. Asses have adapted well to life in rugged places, like this island off California. ▽ Two jacks fight for a mate. Such battles test strength, but they rarely end in serious injury.

North American feral ass: 46 in (117 cm) tall at the shoulder

Ass

small, thorny bushes. To escape such enemies as hyenas, Somali asses climb steep hills and hide among the broken rocks. If attacked, they may bite and kick fiercely to defend themselves. When sandstorms blow, the animals lower their heads and turn their tails to the wind.

The khur (KUR), another kind of wild ass, lives in Asia. With its shorter ears and broader hooves, this animal looks more like a horse than other asses do. Sand-colored khurs live in dry, open country. These swift animals travel and graze in the cool evening and early morning hours.

Asses are known for their loud braying "hee-haw." The noise they make sounds like a rusty hinge of a door slowly opening. Scientists have found that each ass makes its own special braying sound. One animal can recognize another by its call. Wild asses have greatly declined; only a few hundred survive in Africa. Some 45 million are domesticated worldwide.

Somali ass: 49 in (124 cm) tall at the shoulder

△ *Like striped stockings, black markings cover the legs of a Somali ass feeding on bushes. People in Africa began taming such asses thousands of years ago.*
▽ *Hardy khurs roam a sun-scorched plain in India. In the early morning and in the evening, they travel widely, looking for food. The animals graze on islands of grass that spring up after rains.*

Khur: 46 in (117 cm) tall at the shoulder

Aye-aye

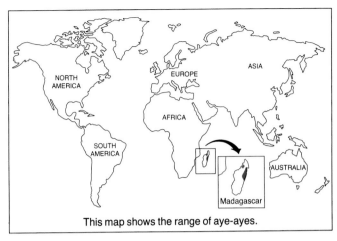

This map shows the range of aye-ayes.

AYE-AYE 🐾 1 of 1 species

LENGTH OF HEAD AND BODY: 14-17 in (36-43 cm); tail, 22-24 in (56-61 cm)

WEIGHT: 4 lb (2 kg)

HABITAT AND RANGE: rain forests of Madagascar

FOOD: insect larvae and fruit

LIFE SPAN: up to 23 years in captivity

REPRODUCTION: 1 young after a pregnancy of 5 to 6 months

ORDER: primates

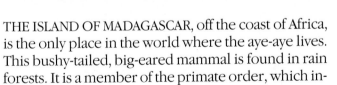

Sensitive ears alert, a male aye-aye (left) makes a nighttime search for food. An aye-aye eats insect larvae. It removes them from under tree bark with its long middle finger (right).

THE ISLAND OF MADAGASCAR, off the coast of Africa, is the only place in the world where the aye-aye lives. This bushy-tailed, big-eared mammal is found in rain forests. It is a member of the primate order, which includes monkeys, apes, and humans.

The aye-aye spends the day sleeping in a ball-shaped nest made of leaves and branches. The animal builds its nest in the fork of a large tree. Each round nest has a hole in the side through which the aye-aye enters and leaves. The nest is a closed, safe place for the animal to rest.

The aye-aye wakes up when the sun goes down. It climbs through the trees searching for food. Sometimes it dangles from a branch by its legs.

With its long, thin fingers, the aye-aye grooms itself. The animal's middle finger is even longer and thinner than the others. It looks like a dry, bent twig. Using this finger, the aye-aye can get insect larvae from under tree bark. The animal listens for the sounds of larvae, then quickly gnaws a hole in the bark with its sharp teeth. It reaches into the hole with its long middle finger and removes the larvae. Aye-ayes also use their middle fingers to scoop out the juice and meat of coconuts.

Female aye-ayes have one offspring at a time. They give birth to tiny young in their nests in the trees. Except for females with offspring, aye-ayes usually live alone.

B

Babirusa

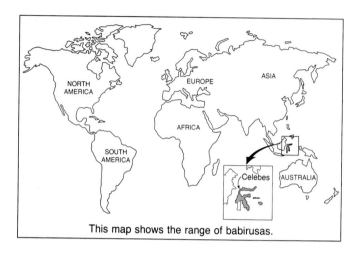

This map shows the range of babirusas.

ON SOME ISLANDS of Indonesia lives a kind of wild hog with curved tusks that grow right through the skin of its snout. Some people there think the tusks look like a deer's antlers. So they call the animal *babirusa,* which means "pig-deer."

Only the male babirusa has tusks. The lower tusks, like those of other wild hogs, are sometimes used for fighting. But its upper tusks are something of a mystery. The babirusa uses them as a shield for self-defense but not for rooting because they point in the wrong direction. Sometimes they grow as long as 17 inches (43 cm) and curve around in a circle! Scientists think the upper tusks may help to attract mates.

Dried mud cakes the curling tusks and wrinkled hide of a male babirusa, a wild hog of Indonesia.

△ *After a tropical rain, a male babirusa cools off with a roll in the mud. Like other pigs, babirusas often wallow in mud. They live in dense, swampy forests.*

▽ *Female babirusa towers over her one-month-old young. When danger threatens, she fiercely defends her offspring. A newborn measures 8 inches (20 cm) long. Within nine months, it grows to full size.*

The babirusa is a distant relative of the pig that lives on farms. Aside from its curious tusks, a babirusa looks much like a pig. But its legs are longer than a pig's legs. A full-grown babirusa can measure more than 3 feet (91 cm) long and almost 3 feet (91 cm) high. It can weigh as much as 220 pounds (100 kg). Its brownish gray hide looks hairless. The babirusa's skin may be either wrinkled or smooth.

Babirusas have small ears, but their hearing is sharp. This comes in handy, since the animals feed and move around in the dark. It is hard for scientists to study babirusas in the wild because of the animals' nighttime habits.

Babirusas live in moist forests and along the edges of rivers and lakes. Like other members of the pig family, they spend much of their time wallowing in the mud. Sometimes babirusas swim to nearby islands to feed on water plants, leaves, fallen fruit, and shoots. They also eat insect larvae found in rotting tree trunks.

Before a female babirusa gives birth, she prepares a nest in a hidden place. There she has her young. Usually one or two offspring are born after a pregnancy of about five months. Most other members of the pig family have larger litters. At birth, the babirusas are tiny—only about 8 inches (20 cm) long. Unlike many other young wild hogs, which have striped coats, newborn babirusas have smooth, unmarked skins. You can read more about other kinds of hogs on page 264.

People of the islands where babirusas live have a legend about the animals. They say that when a babirusa wants to sleep, it hangs itself up on a tree branch by its tusks. That way it is out of danger. Actually, the babirusa spends its sleeping hours safely hidden on the ground.

BABIRUSA   🐾 I of I species

LENGTH OF HEAD AND BODY: 35-43 in (89-109 cm); tail, 8-12 in (20-30 cm)

WEIGHT: as much as 220 lb (100 kg)

HABITAT AND RANGE: moist forests and edges of rivers and lakes on Celebes and on nearby islands of Indonesia

FOOD: water plants, leaves, shoots, fruit, and insect larvae

LIFE SPAN: as long as 24 years in captivity

REPRODUCTION: I or 2 young after a pregnancy of about 5 months

ORDER: artiodactyls

Baboon

The baboon is a kind of monkey. Read about monkeys on page 370.

Badger

(BADGE-er)

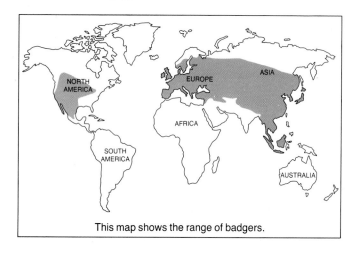

This map shows the range of badgers.

BADGER 🐾 **2 of 9 species**

LENGTH OF HEAD AND BODY: 13-31 in (33-79 cm); tail, 4-7 in (10-18 cm)

WEIGHT: 4-37 lb (2-17 kg)

HABITAT AND RANGE: dry open plains, woodlands, mountains, tropical forests, and prairies of Europe, Asia, and parts of North America

FOOD: rodents, small mammals, birds, snakes, frogs, insects and their larvae, worms, fruit, and roots

LIFE SPAN: up to 26 years in captivity, depending on species

REPRODUCTION: 1 to 4 young after a pregnancy of 2 to 10 months, depending on species or the season

ORDER: carnivores

WHETHER IT IS LOOKING FOR FOOD or for a safe place to sleep, the badger usually digs a hole. This strong, short-legged animal loosens the dirt with the long claws at the ends of its forefeet.

In North America, badgers usually live alone on dry plains and on open prairies. There they can easily dig holes to find their prey: mice, pocket gophers, ground squirrels, and insects. During warm months, some badgers dig a new hole every day. There they rest and escape from the hot sun. In very cold weather, they dig a burrow and remain inside for weeks at a time. They sleep most of that time, waking only occasionally to look for food.

In Europe and Asia, badgers live in woodlands and meadows, on mountains and plains. The animals usually dig in dry, loose soil. European badgers live in groups called clans. Together they make setts—underground networks of rooms and tunnels. Some setts are hundreds of years old. Many generations of badgers may have enlarged the same sett. European badgers eat more plants and worms than relatives in

Poking up through the sand, a North American ▷ *badger emerges from a new entrance to an old burrow. Badgers often snort and snuffle as they dig.*

Kicking up dirt, a North American badger (below, left) tunnels under a rocky cliff. Another pursues a mouse it chased out from underground. Badgers dig for food and shelter with their long claws.

North American badger: 29 in (74 cm) long; tail, 5 in (13 cm)

Badger

North America do. They eat earthworms, sucking them in like spaghetti. They feed on fruit, plants, and small animals.

Litters of one to four young badgers are born inside a burrow. A European badger gives birth to its offspring in a nest inside its sett. To make its nest, the mother badger clutches leaves and grass between its chin and forelegs. The animal shuffles backward into its sett. Most young badgers drink their mother's milk for four or five months. Then they begin to find food for themselves.

European badgers are playful. Both adults and young—called cubs—chase and tumble and even play a game that looks like King of the Mountain. These games are important in a badger's life. Cubs learn to defend themselves. And games make the ties between badgers stronger.

Badgers become fierce, even vicious, when cornered by such enemies as dogs and foxes. Facing attackers, badgers bristle their fur and look larger. Their skin is so tough that it is difficult for enemies to bite into them. With powerful jaws, strong teeth, and sharp claws, badgers are savage fighters.

Because European badgers live in groups, they

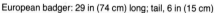

European badger: 29 in (74 cm) long; tail, 6 in (15 cm)

communicate with each other by various sounds and smells. A growl means a badger may attack. A mother calls her young with a high-pitched cry.

Badgers are relatives of skunks, weasels, martens, and polecats. All these animals have scent glands. By making a scent mark along its path, one badger can let another badger know it has passed by. Scent marks also show the way to feeding grounds. The stink badger of southeastern Asia can spray its enemies, just as a skunk does.

Read about another badger relative, the ratel, or honey badger, on page 481.

△ *Following a scent, a ferret badger sniffs out its prey. Hunting at dusk or during the night, this Asian badger eats worms, insects, rodents, and fruit. It can climb trees to find small birds and eggs. During the day, it may sleep in a rocky shelter or occasionally on the branch of a tree.*

◁ *European badger trots across the countryside to the safety of its burrow. It can move surprisingly fast on its short legs. These badgers travel well-worn paths from their setts, or burrows, to feeding grounds. They mark the way with scent.*

▽ *Resting on leaves, a hog badger of Asia finds roots and worms with its long, blunt snout. Hog badgers often hide in deep burrows during the day. Strong teeth and sharp claws help these animals defend themselves.*

Hog badger: 24 in (61 cm) long; tail, 7 in (18 cm)

75

Bandicoot

Rabbit-eared bandicoot: 15 in (38 cm) long; tail, 8 in (20 cm)

Barred bandicoot: 12 in (30 cm) long; tail, 4 in (10 cm)

△ *Barred bandicoot sniffs for insects in the soil. The pouch of this striped marsupial opens to the rear.*

◁ *Sand clings to a rabbit-eared bandicoot—or bilby— as it digs an underground home in a dry desert in Australia. The short-nosed bandicoot has the shortest pregnancy of any mammal—less than 12^1/$_2$ days.*

WHEN NIGHT FALLS in Australia, New Guinea, and neighboring islands, small sharp-nosed animals scurry from their nests and shallow burrows. These frisky animals are called bandicoots. After dark, they scamper about searching for food. With the sharp claws on their front feet, the animals scratch in the soil for insects and worms. Some kinds of bandicoots also feed on young mice and plants.

Bandicoots usually hunt and live alone. Most kinds make shallow burrows or grassy nests. These homes help protect them from their enemies. They also shelter bandicoots from the heat of the desert areas where the animals often live. The rabbit-eared bandicoot digs its den deeper than other kinds—as much as 5 feet (152 cm) underground.

Bandicoots—like koalas, kangaroos, and wallabies—belong to the group of pouched mammals called marsupials (mar-SOO-pea-ulz). There are 22 kinds of bandicoots.

Just two weeks after mating, a female bandicoot gives birth to as many as six tiny, underdeveloped young. Bandicoots spend their first two months of life in the safety of their mother's pouch. A bandicoot's pouch is different from a kangaroo's pouch. It opens to the rear! Inside the pouch, young bandicoots are shielded from flying dirt when their mother digs for food or shelter.

BANDICOOT 🐾 **5 of 22 species**

LENGTH OF HEAD AND BODY: 7-22 in (18-56 cm); tail, 4-10 in (10-25 cm)

WEIGHT: about 2 lb (1 kg)

HABITAT AND RANGE: plains, deserts, and forests of Australia, New Guinea, and neighboring islands

FOOD: mostly insects, but also lizards, mice, snails, worms, and some plants

LIFE SPAN: 3 to 7 years in captivity, depending on species

REPRODUCTION: 1 to 6 young after a pregnancy of 2 weeks

ORDER: marsupials

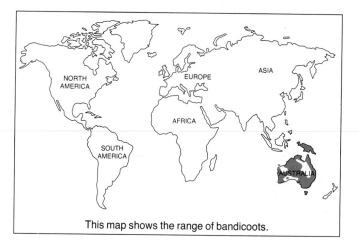

This map shows the range of bandicoots.

Barbary ape

The Barbary ape is a kind of monkey. Read about monkeys on page 370.

Bat

BAT 🐾 **231 of 975 species**

LENGTH OF HEAD AND BODY: **1-16 in (3-41 cm); tail, about 1-3 in (3-8 cm); wingspan, 6 in-6 ft (15-183 cm)**

WEIGHT: **less than ¼ oz-2 lb (7 g-1 kg)**

HABITAT AND RANGE: **all kinds of habitats worldwide, except in the Antarctic and in parts of the Arctic**

FOOD: **insects, fruit, nectar, pollen, flowers, small animals, fish, and blood**

LIFE SPAN: **as long as 30 years in the wild, depending on species**

REPRODUCTION: **usually 1 young after a pregnancy of 1½ to 8 months, depending on species**

ORDER: **chiropterans**

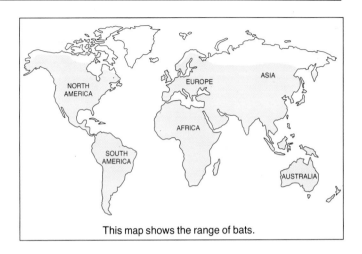

This map shows the range of bats.

IN GHOST STORIES, no haunted house is complete without a few bats flying around. And Halloween brings to mind scary images of witches, goblins, and bats. Bats seem frightening and mysterious. They dart around at night, hang upside down in caves, and roost in abandoned buildings. But most stories about bats aren't true. Bats don't get tangled in people's hair. And they are not blind.

All bats can see, but many do not use their eyes to find food. Instead, they use their ears. Even in the dark, a bat can find its way, can avoid obstacles, and can detect food by using echolocation (ek-oh-low-KAY-shun). When flying, a bat sends out a series of short, high-pitched beeping sounds through its mouth or its nose. It listens for the echoes that bounce back when *(Continued on page 80)*

Awakening at night, two bats circle at the entrance of the home they share in a hollow tree.

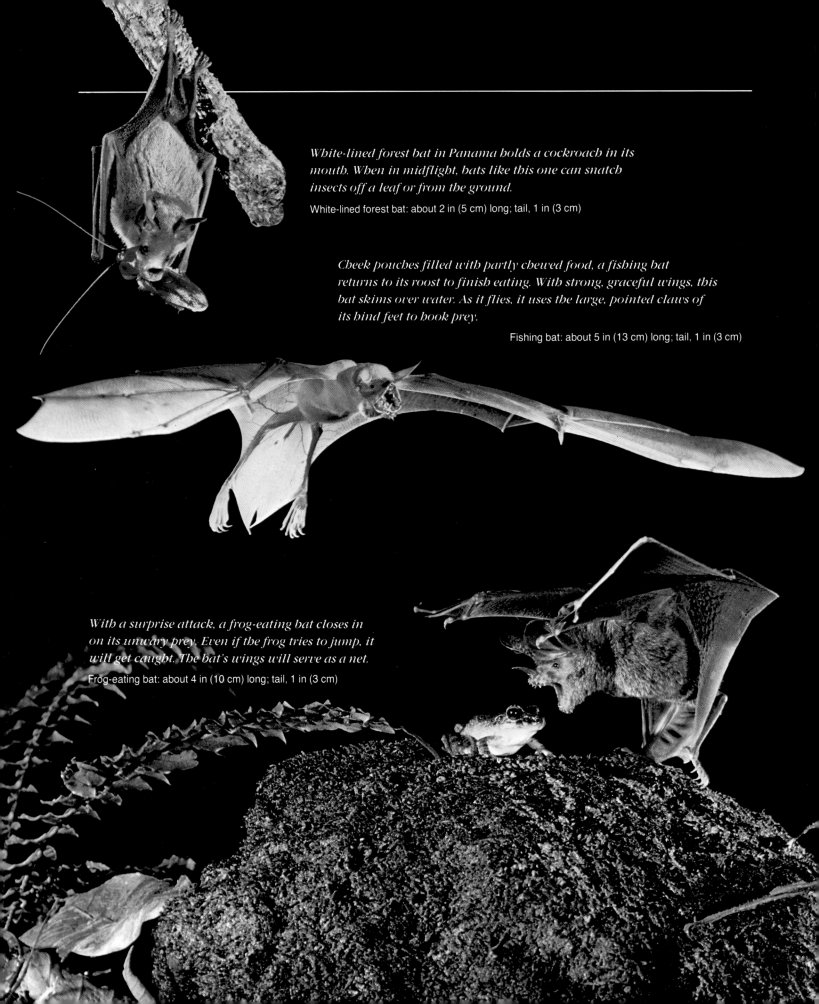

White-lined forest bat in Panama holds a cockroach in its mouth. When in midflight, bats like this one can snatch insects off a leaf or from the ground.

White-lined forest bat: about 2 in (5 cm) long; tail, 1 in (3 cm)

Cheek pouches filled with partly chewed food, a fishing bat returns to its roost to finish eating. With strong, graceful wings, this bat skims over water. As it flies, it uses the large, pointed claws of its hind feet to hook prey.

Fishing bat: about 5 in (13 cm) long; tail, 1 in (3 cm)

With a surprise attack, a frog-eating bat closes in on its unwary prey. Even if the frog tries to jump, it will get caught. The bat's wings will serve as a net.

Frog-eating bat: about 4 in (10 cm) long; tail, 1 in (3 cm)

Hummingbird of the night, a lesser long-tongued bat sips nectar from a tropical flower in Panama. Using its short, broad wings, the bat can hover at a flower while it feeds. This bat also eats fruit and insects.

Lesser long-tongued bat: about 3 in (8 cm) long; tail, 1 in (3 cm)

Sharp claws on its toes give a tube-nosed bat in Australia a good grip on a branch. This bat spends its day roosting upside down, wrapped in its wings.

Tiny suction cups on wrists and ankles help two sucker-footed bats walk on a smooth surface. These small bats live in partly opened leaves.

Tube-nosed bat: about 4 in (10 cm) long; tail, 1 in (3 cm)

Sucker-footed bat: about 2 in (5 cm) long; tail, 1 in (3 cm)

Bat

the beeps hit an object. From these echoes, a bat can tell where an object is and whether it is moving. The tones of the beeping sounds that each kind of bat produces are different. People don't notice the sounds that most bats make because they are beyond the range of human hearing.

Bats are the only mammals in the world that can fly. Flying lemurs and flying squirrels can move through the air, but they really only glide. Bats flap their wings and fly. Two delicate layers of skin stretch from the sides of a bat's body to the ends of its long finger bones. The wings are moved by powerful muscles that help the animal fly easily through the air. Some bats can fly 40 miles (64 km) an hour or more.

There are nearly a thousand kinds of bats—with wingspans that range from 6 inches (15 cm) to 6 feet (183 cm). Some bats have tails, and some bats do not. Scientists divide the animals into two main groups. In one group are the microchiropterans (my-crow-kye-ROP-tuh-runs). The bats in this group tend to be small. They have large ears and small eyes. The microchiropterans use echolocation. In the other bat group are the megachiropterans (meg-uh-kye-ROP-tuh-runs).

These bats are usually larger. They have small ears and large eyes. Most of the megachiropterans do not use echolocation.

Most bats are microchiropterans. These bats feed mainly on insects and other small animals. Some microchiropterans also feed on fruit and flowers. They live everywhere in the world, except in the Antarctic and in parts of the Arctic.

Some bats that live in colder areas may fly to warmer places before winter arrives and food becomes hard to find. Others sleep for months at a time. This kind of sleep is called hibernation (hye-bur-NAY-shun). When a bat hibernates, its body temperature drops. Its heart rate and breathing slow down. And it lives off fat stored in its body.

Most megachiropterans live in Africa, in Asia, and in Australia. They feed mainly on fruit and flowers. Most fruit- and flower-feeding bats—in either group—are very much alike. They use their keen sense of smell to detect flowers and ripe fruit. To lap nectar from inside a blossom, a flower-feeding bat uses its pointed snout and a tongue that may measure one-third the length of its body.

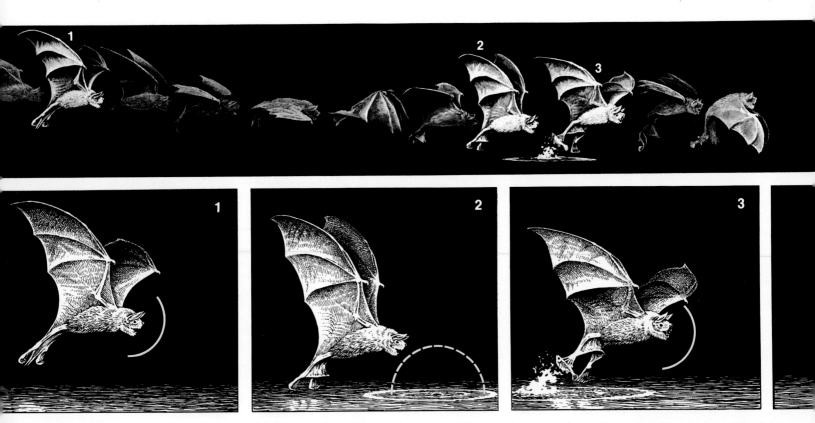

Two ways to look at a fishing bat catching prey: The top drawing shows the animal in motion. The bottom

△ *Wings flutter and flap in a cave in Trinidad. Even in crowded conditions, bats rarely collide. Bats usually begin to stir toward evening. As they wake up, they circle the cave in orderly flights. They then leave the cave to feed.*

◁ *Using echolocation to search for food and to find its way, a fishing bat approaches the water (1), beeping high-pitched sounds (each shown as a solid line). As a guppy's head breaks the surface (2), it reflects a sound, causing an echo (shown as a broken line). Beeping again, the bat hooks the fish with its curved claws (3). As it brings the prey to its mouth (4), the bat remains silent. Chewing on the fish in midair (5), the bat sends out another signal. The bat actually would produce about 14 beeps during this hunt, although the drawing shows only 3 of them. From start to finish, the action takes just half a second!*

one freezes the movement at certain points in the hunt.

Bat

Vampire bat: about 4 in (10 cm) long

Blossom bat: about 3 in (8 cm) long

◁ *Attic of a house in France provides a roost for a group of long-eared bats. Huge ears help the animals find insects by echolocation.*
Long-eared bat: about 2 in (5 cm) long; tail, 2 in (5 cm)

△ *Razor-sharp teeth of a vampire bat (above, left) in Trinidad make a painless cut on a donkey's foot to get at blood. After a meal of nectar and pollen, a blossom bat (above, right) in Australia grooms one of its wings.*

Insect eaters use echolocation to find their prey. These bats feast on insects that fly through the night air. A bat may catch a big insect with its mouth. It may scoop a small insect up with a wing and pull its victim to its mouth. Some bats can gobble 12 or more mosquito-size insects in a minute.

Fishing bats also hunt by echolocation. They use their huge claws to catch fish. Flying low over water, these bats can detect a fish breaking the surface. Then they reach down and hook their catch with their sharp, curved claws.

A vampire bat has razor-sharp teeth that it uses to make a shallow, painless cut in the skin of its prey. With rapid movements of its tongue, it laps up blood from the cut. This bat is only about 4 inches (10 cm) long—about the size of a mouse. It may drink over half its weight in blood—about half an ounce (14 g)— each night and yet remain nimble on the ground and in flight. A bat may drink so much that it becomes too full to fly! Vampire bats rarely bite people. They often feed on the blood of chickens, cattle, donkeys, and deer. Vampires and other bats may carry a disease called rabies, but people rarely catch it from them.

Most bats have only one offspring a year. Many kinds give birth in nurseries where large numbers of bats are found. A nursery may contain fewer than a hundred or as many as several million females and their young. A newborn bat clings to its mother or to the ceiling of the nursery. Within two to twelve weeks, the young bats will begin to fly.

Bats benefit people in several ways. Some feed on harmful insects. Others pollinate flowers as they fly from blossom to blossom sipping nectar. Seeds dropped by fruit bats may sprout into plants.

Scientists are studying echolocation. They would like to perfect a similar system that would allow blind people to detect objects with sound.

◁ *Two hoary bats cling to the belly of their mother, hanging upside down in a spruce tree. The hoary bat usually gives birth to twins—or sometimes even triplets.*
Hoary bat: about 3 in (8 cm) long; tail, 2 in (5 cm)

Pink and naked, thousands of young bent-winged bats squeak and squirm in a cave in Australia. Huddling together keeps these young bats warm. Two mothers (with fur) have returned from hunting to nurse their young. After about three weeks, the young bent-winged bats will have fur and will begin to practice flying.

Bent-winged bat: about 2 in (5 cm) long; tail, 2 in (5 cm)

Wrapped in its wings, a greater horseshoe bat (below) in France wakes up from hibernation.

With specially shaped noses and ears, the bats below get food and find their way. Large eyes and a sensitive nose help a bat called a black flying fox (below, right) find food. The large ears of a yellow-winged bat (below, center) pick up sounds from its prey. Flaps on the snout of a hammer-headed bat may help it call and attract mates.

Greater horseshoe bat: about 3 in (8 cm) long; tail, 1 in (3 cm)

Hammer-headed bat: about 11 in (28 cm) long

Yellow-winged bat: about 3 in (8 cm) long

Black flying fox: about 10 in (25 cm) long

Bear

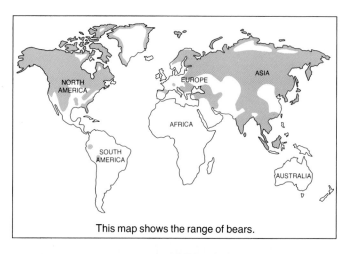

This map shows the range of bears.

"GRIZZLY!" JUST THE WORD could frighten settlers in the Old West. Pioneers often lived in wild regions where grizzly bears roamed. And they knew that a disturbed or wounded grizzly could kill a person with one swipe of its paw. American Indians also feared and respected the grizzly. As a test of bravery, young men of some tribes had to kill a bear using only a bow and arrows. Its claws were strung into a necklace and worn with great pride.

Grizzlies are a type of brown bear—the most wide-ranging of the seven different kinds of bears. The animals are called grizzlies because their thick brown fur is tipped with lighter-colored hairs. The

animals' coats look grizzled, or streaked with gray.

Once, grizzly bears lived throughout western North America. But now they are found mainly in mountainous areas of Wyoming, Montana, Alaska, and western Canada. Grizzlies grow very large. Males reach a length of about 8 feet (244 cm) from head to rump and weigh about 800 pounds (363 kg).

Another, much larger, brown bear is found on the Alaskan coast. These giant bears measure as long as 10 feet (305 cm) and weigh as much as 1,700 pounds (771 kg). Alaskan brown bears and polar bears are the largest meat-eating land mammals in North America.

Alaskan brown bear: 10 ft (305 cm) long

Grizzly bear: 8 ft (244 cm) long

△ *Grizzly bear in Alaska stands in a meadow and looks around. Grizzlies have a keen sense of smell. As they search for food, they stop often to sniff the air.*

◁ *After a nap, a female Alaskan brown bear and her cub head for a river to catch fish.*

Bear

◁ *Grizzlies feed on wild berries. In the summer and fall, these brown bears eat large amounts of rich food and grow fat. The fat will nourish them through the winter.*

Bears are very adaptable animals: That means they can fit into many kinds of environments. Bears will eat whatever food is available or in season. Though some bears are huge animals, they feed mainly on plants, fruit, and insects. Some use their long, curved claws to dig for roots. Bears also eat small mammals and the remains of dead animals.

Bears are loners and usually wander by themselves in search of food. Usually only females with cubs feed together. But in summer, when salmon swim up coastal rivers to lay eggs, as many as eighty Alaskan brown bears may gather together to fish. A bear waits on shore until it spots a salmon. Then, with a leap, it belly flops into the water and pins the fish to the bottom with its paws or mouth. A bear may catch six to eight salmon before it has eaten enough and lumbers off to rest.

In summer and autumn, brown bears—like other bears that live in cold or moderate climates—eat

---

BEAR 🐾 **3 of 7 species**

LENGTH OF HEAD AND BODY: 43 in-10 ft (109-305 cm)

WEIGHT: 55-1,700 lb (25-771 kg)

HABITAT AND RANGE: mountains, forests, swamps, and grassy plains in parts of North and South America, Europe, and Asia

FOOD: grasses, roots, berries, insects, fruit, eggs, birds, fish, and other animals and their remains

REPRODUCTION: usually 1 to 4 young after a pregnancy of 7 to 9 months

LIFE SPAN: up to 50 years in the wild, depending on species

ORDER: carnivores

▽ *In late summer, Alaskan brown bears gather at a river to fish for salmon swimming upstream to lay eggs. The biggest males take the best fishing spots. Mothers with cubs usually take the next best. In the small picture, a bear eats its meal shoulder-deep in water. Some bears carry their catch to land.*

large amounts of rich food and grow very fat. As the weather turns colder, their fur becomes thick. They start to prepare dens where they will sleep during the winter, when food is hard to find. Brown bears dig their dens in hillsides. Black bears may find places in caves, under dead trees, or anywhere they will be sheltered from bad weather. They bring in leaves, branches, and grasses to line the den. Some bears return to the same area every year.

When winter arrives, bears retreat to their dens. Their fat nourishes them throughout the cold months, and their heavy coats keep them warm. Bears sleep through the winter. Their sleep is a kind of hibernation (hye-bur-NAY-shun), but their body temperatures do not drop sharply. Bears can be awakened easily during the winter. They may even leave their dens for short periods of time.

In North America and in Europe, a female bear—called a she-bear—gives birth to young in her den. A litter of two or three bear cubs is usually born in midwinter. The blind, helpless cubs weigh about a pound (454 g) at birth. Their mother may nurse them for several months. If little food is available, she may nurse them much longer.

In the spring, bears come out of their dens and start looking for food. The adults may weigh much

△ American black bear looks out from a tree branch. Good climbers, black bears live mainly in forests.
▽ Black bear walks through a meadow in Montana. The most common bear in North America, the black bear lives from Canada through northern Mexico.

less than when they entered their dens. The cubs now have soft, fluffy fur. They are playful and curious, but they stay close to their mother. If a she-bear thinks that her cubs are in danger, she will move quickly to protect them. She will charge an animal that threatens her young.

Bear cubs stay with their mother for about two years. They follow her and learn to search for food and to defend themselves. The cubs spend the next winter with their mother in the den. Then, when they are old enough to care for themselves, they wander off on their own.

A young bear would have little chance of surviving without its mother's protection. But one orphaned black bear cub became famous. Most people know him as Smokey Bear. The cub was rescued after

American black bear: 5 ft (152 cm) long

◁ *Black bear nibbles on a branch. Except for females with cubs, bears usually live and hunt alone. They eat almost anything—insects, berries, roots, small mammals, and dead animals they find.*

▽ *Born in a winter den, black bear cubs only a few months old begin to explore the world outside with their mother. Newborn cubs weigh less than a pound (454 g). They nurse for a few months, or perhaps longer. Cubs stay with their mother for about two years.*

Bear

△ *Powerful swimmer, a polar bear paddles with its front paws and steers by moving its back legs. People have seen polar bears hundreds of miles from land. The animals float much of that distance on ice. But they swim strongly in search of prey—usually seals.*

Something moves against the arctic landscape! Coal black eyes and nose mark an approaching ▷ *polar bear. Its white coat blends well with the snowy terrain.*

a forest fire when he was only a few months old. A game warden named him Smokey and cared for the badly burned cub. Smokey recovered and became a living national symbol for fire prevention.

Black bears are the most common bears in North America. They live mainly in the mountains, forests, and swamps of the United States, Canada, and northern Mexico. They often wander through the woods, breaking off branches and eating acorns or berries. Skillful climbers, black bears can quickly go up tree trunks by gripping the bark with sharp, curved claws. Some even make winter dens in holes in trees, as high as 60 feet (18 m) above the ground.

Although the animals are called black bears, the color of their fur can range from black to brown to a rarer blue-gray or white. These medium-size bears weigh about 300 pounds (136 kg) and reach about 5 feet (152 cm) in length.

Many black bears live in national parks, and they sometimes become tourist attractions. Although visitors are warned not to feed the bears, they often do. These bears may seem tame, but if one of them is irritated—watch out! All bears can be dangerous if they are angered or bothered by someone. But when they

are left alone, bears usually will not harm anyone.

Some black bears are known as campsite thieves because they are always searching for something to eat. Bears love honey. Finding a bee tree, a bear will sit down and eat its fill, despite the stings of angry bees. But its sweet tooth can lead to a problem: The

▽ *Curled into a cradle, a female polar bear in Alaska naps and shelters her cub. Dense fur and a thick layer of fat protect polar bears from the icy temperatures of their arctic home.*

Bear

Short, sleek fur covers the body of a Malayan sun ▷
*bear. Smallest of all bears, these animals get their name
from the light fur on their chests. They spend some of
their time in trees, sleeping by day and feeding by night.*

▽ *V-shaped marking looks like a collar around the
neck of an Asiatic black bear, or moon bear. These
animals live in mountain forests. Like all bears in Asia,
they feed mainly on plants, insects, and fruit.*

Malayan sun bear: 43 in (109 cm) long

Asiatic black bear: 4 ft (122 cm) long

bear is one of the few mammals in the wild that can get cavities!

Bears look awkward and slow moving. Their bodies are bulky, and they shuffle along on flat feet. But don't be fooled! Bears can run quickly to chase prey or to escape danger.

The polar bear lives in the icy wilds of the Arctic. Polar bears prey mainly on seals. Floating on pack ice, they travel great distances in search of food. Polar bears have been spotted hundreds of miles from land as they hunt seals. These huge bears take naturally to the water. The toes on their front paws are slightly webbed. And they have broad feet for paddling. By moving their back legs, they can control the direction they are swimming.

Polar bears are well adapted, or suited, to their icy home. A thick layer of fat and a coat of dense fur keep them warm. Fur on the bottom of their paws prevents them from slipping on ice. Their white coats help them blend into the snowy landscape. Males grow as long as 10 feet (305 cm) and weigh as much as 1,700 pounds (771 kg).

Polar bears build their dens in snowbanks. They tunnel down into the drifts and dig out a small room. A female usually gives birth to twin cubs in these winter dens. The male bears will continue hunting throughout the winter.

Bears that live in warmer climates normally stay active most of the year. The Malayan sun bear lives in tropical forests in Southeast Asia. It spends some of the day resting in a nestlike bed of branches in a tree. Plants and insects are its main foods.

The sloth bear of India and Sri Lanka also feeds on insects and plants. With its long, curved claws, it

△ *European brown bear climbs a tree in its forest home. People sometimes capture these bears and train them to perform in circuses.*

tears open termite mounds. Then it sucks up the insects, using its lips and long, flexible snout.

The Asiatic black bear roams mountain forests. It sometimes sleeps during the day in caves. At night, the animal climbs trees in search of nuts, fruit, and honey. Because the V-shaped marking on its chest looks a little like a crescent moon, it is sometimes called a moon bear.

The rarely seen spectacled bear of South America gets its name from the whitish circles around its eyes. It looks like it is wearing glasses! In its mountainous home, it climbs trees to find fruit to eat. It often sleeps high among the moss-covered branches.

△ *Young spectacled bear stays almost out of sight high in the trees (top) in South America. In a closeup view (above), the bear hangs from a branch and looks for figs and other fruit to eat. Few people have seen these animals—the only bears in South America. They roam parts of the Andes. As the mountain forests in which they live disappear, the bears may become even rarer.*

△ Home for perhaps a dozen beavers, a lodge built of sticks, mud, and stones rises from a mountain pond in Wyoming. The lodge shelters the beavers and protects them from such enemies as bears, wolves, and coyotes. Holding forepaws against its chest, a beaver darts toward an underwater ▷ entrance to its lodge. Webbed hind feet work like swim fins. The broad tail acts as a rudder. It helps the beaver steer left or right, up or down.

94

Beaver

North American beaver: 3 ft (91 cm) long; tail, 12 in (30 cm)

BEAVER

LENGTH OF HEAD AND BODY: about 3 ft (91 cm); tail, about 12 in (30 cm)

WEIGHT: 30-70 lb (14-32 kg)

HABITAT AND RANGE: rivers, lakes, and streams near woodlands in North America and in parts of Europe and Asia

FOOD: bark, twigs, leaves, roots, and aquatic plants

LIFE SPAN: up to 24 years in the wild, up to 50 in captivity

REPRODUCTION: usually 2 to 4 young after a pregnancy of 3 or 4 months

ORDER: rodents

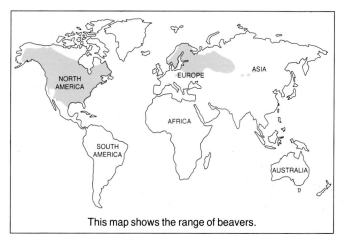

This map shows the range of beavers.

◁ *Sleek, whiskered beaver emerges from the water to repair its lodge. With its forepaws, the animal can hold sticks and stones, roll logs, and scoop up mud.*

THE BUSY BEAVER is one of the few animals—other than man—that can alter its environment. Sometimes beavers dig burrows in the banks of lakes and large rivers. But where the water is not deep enough for their way of life, beavers change the landscape. They build dams across streams. Soon the water deepens behind the dams, turning fields and forests into a watery world of beaver ponds.

On land, the beaver moves awkwardly. The bulky animal—about 3 feet (91 cm) long—cannot escape easily from bears and wolves as it waddles

through the woods. In water, however, the beaver is a strong and graceful swimmer. It often builds its home in the middle of a pond. In this island home, or lodge, the beaver family usually is safe.

A beaver is well suited for life in the water. Long hairs—called guard hairs—protect its thick underfur. This heavy coat helps a beaver stay warm, even in icy water. With two split claws on each hind foot, a beaver can comb the fur and keep it clean. The beaver combs in oil produced by glands in its body. This helps to make its coat sleek and waterproof.

The animal's hind feet serve as swim fins. These large webbed feet can push a beaver through the water at speeds of 5 miles (8 km) an hour. Its broad, scaly tail acts as a rudder. The beaver uses it to steer right or left, up or down. Sometimes a beaver signals with its tail, too. It slaps the water, warning other beavers when danger threatens.

A beaver can stay underwater for as long as 15 minutes without coming up for air. It holds its breath, and its nose and ears shut tightly when it dives. A beaver has a set of transparent eyelids that slide across its eyes. These serve as goggles, protecting the animal's eyes underwater.

A beaver can close its mouth by pressing together flaps of skin behind its front teeth. The beaver can then chew on wood underwater without getting wood or water down its throat.

Beavers live throughout forested areas in North America and in parts of Europe and Asia. There they can find the trees they need for food and for building lodges and dams. As a beaver cuts down a tree, it usually stands on its hind legs and leans back on its tail. Tilting its head to one side, the animal bites into the tree with its sharp teeth. Chipping deeper and deeper, it cuts through the trunk. As the tree falls, the beaver scampers out of the way.

The beaver then trims off the branches and bark

Inside their lodge, young beavers—called ▷ kits—greet their mother with high-pitched cries. The kits stay with the family for two years, even after the birth of another litter.

▽ Holding its dinner in its paws, a beaver nibbles on a young, tender plant. The kit at its side chews on a leaf. In late summer and early fall, beavers anchor branches near an underwater entrance to their lodge. They use these for food during the winter.

Kits cling to a parent on one of their first outings. The ▷ young float easily in the water soon after birth. As they grow heavier, the kits learn to swim and to dive.

and cuts the trunk into smaller pieces. It takes most of the wood to a stream by dragging it or by floating it down canals it has dug. It uses some of the logs to build a dam. With stones and mud, the beaver anchors the logs and branches to the muddy bottom of a stream. It wedges sticks in between the logs. More stones and brush go on top.

As the dam gets bigger, a deep pond forms behind it. The pond must be deep enough so that the water at the bottom does not freeze, even in the coldest weather. In the winter, under a layer of ice, a beaver still continues its underwater life. It swims into and out of its lodge and brings in pieces of branches it keeps near the entrance of its home.

Beavers often build lodges near the middle of their ponds. They anchor sticks in the muddy bottom. They pile stones and more wood on top until the dome-shaped lodge shows above water. They gnaw underwater openings into the lodge and hollow out living quarters, just above the water level. A platform provides a place for drying off and for eating. Shredded wood covers the sleeping area.

▽ *Underwater tunnels lead to the living quarters of a beaver lodge. This drawing shows how a lodge looks on the inside. On a platform, a beaver munches bark on a stick. In this dry area, beavers also sleep and raise their young. Outside, another beaver repairs the lodge with more sticks and mud.*

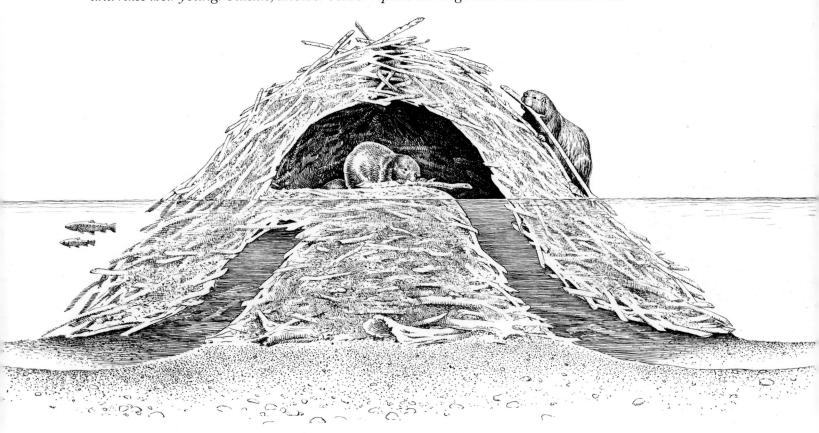

Beaver

Beavers seal their lodge with mud. They fill almost all the cracks so that winter wind and rain cannot get in. But beavers always leave vents in the roof. On frosty days, you might see the warm air from inside the lodge rising through the vents.

A beaver family lives together in the lodge: the mother and father, the young of the year before, and the recent litter. Usually from two to four young—called kits—are born each spring or summer.

◁ *Tim-ber! A beaver cuts down a small tree by gnawing its way around the trunk. It uses logs of willow, poplar, and alder to build a dam or a lodge.*

▽ *Gigantic beaver dam dwarfs a woman in Alaska. Some beaver dams rise 12 feet (4 m) high and stretch longer than a football field. It takes several generations of beavers to build and maintain them.*

Binturong

Stiff whiskers curve out from the face of a binturong, a rarely seen mammal of southern and southeastern Asia.

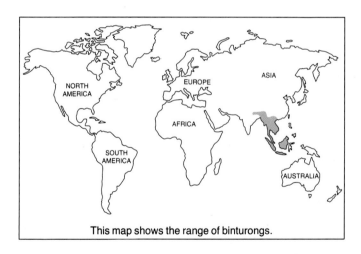

This map shows the range of binturongs.

BINTURONG 🐾 I of I species

LENGTH OF HEAD AND BODY: 24-38 in (61-97 cm); tail, 20-33 in (51-84 cm)

WEIGHT: 20-44 lb (9-20 kg)

HABITAT AND RANGE: dense forests of southern and southeastern Asia.

FOOD: fruit and small animals

LIFE SPAN: up to 26 years in captivity

REPRODUCTION: I to 4 young after a pregnancy of 3 months

ORDER: carnivores

FROM ITS TUFTED EARS to the end of its muscular tail, a binturong is covered with thick fur. The black hairs of the animal's coat are often tipped with white or dark red. The binturong uses its strong, heavy tail almost like an extra hand as it moves through the trees. The tail often grips a branch tightly as the animal reaches for food with its front feet. Young binturongs can even hang by their tails.

During the day, binturongs rest. But at night they look for food. Their keen sense of smell leads them to fruit and small animals.

The female binturong bears from one to four offspring. After about seven weeks, the young begin to climb out of their nest and explore. They will reach their full size—about 5 feet (152 cm) from head to tail—in about a year and a half.

Binturongs communicate with each other by scent. Each animal has a special gland under its tail that produces a strong-smelling oil. As a binturong travels, it sometimes stops and rubs its hindquarters against a branch. This makes a scent mark and lets other binturongs know it has passed by. The binturong is a kind of civet. All civets communicate with scent. Read about other civets on page 154.

*Wading through fresh snow, a herd of bison looks for food in Wyoming's Grand Teton National Park.
To reach the grass, bison push snow aside with their muzzles. Bison once roamed most of North America.
Later, settlers hunted them nearly to extinction. Bison now live on preserves and on ranches.*

Bison

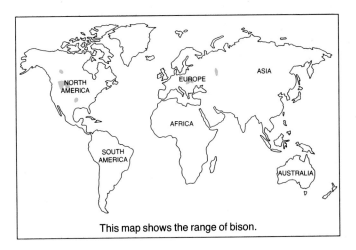

This map shows the range of bison.

DID YOU KNOW that Buffalo Bill never shot a single buffalo? Or that the "home where the buffalo roam" is not part of the United States? The large, shaggy animals pictured on coins and described in folklore are really bison—though the animals are sometimes called American buffaloes.

In the past, many herds of bison roamed North America from Oregon to New York State and from Canada to Mexico. Today these animals live mainly in parks and on wildlife preserves on the Great Plains

Bison: 6 ft (183 cm) tall at the shoulder

Light snow dusts the shaggy winter coat of a bison ▷ feeding on prairie grasses in South Dakota. Its sharp, curved horns may grow more than 2 feet (61 cm) long.

and in the Rocky Mountains. Their buffalo relatives are found in Asia and in Africa. Find out more about buffaloes on page 106.

The bison—the heaviest land animal in North America—can weigh a ton (907 kg) or more. An adult male, called a bull, measures about 6 feet (183 cm) tall at the shoulder. A female, known as a cow, is smaller. Both males and females have short, curved horns and large humps on their shoulders. In spite of their size and weight, bison can move surprisingly fast. When danger threatens, the animals can run at 30 miles (48 km) an hour.

In winter, matted, woolly hair covers most of a bison's body. A longer, darker mane hangs from the animal's head, neck, and shoulders. This heavy hair protects the animal. A bison begins to shed its winter coat as the weather gets warmer. It rubs its body against a tree, a rock, or even another bison to help remove the hair. The bison stops this scratching by summer, when its outer coat has dropped off. In warm weather, insects often bother the bison. It gets rid of the pests by rolling in the dust.

Bison usually graze in the morning and in the evening and rest during the day. Like many hoofed animals, bison do not chew their food fully before swallowing. Later, when resting, they bring up wads of food, called cuds. After chewing these cuds thoroughly, they swallow them and digest the food.

For most of the year, cows and adult bulls live separately. With the approach of the mating season in the summer, they come together and form large herds. Restless males begin to grunt and paw the

Bison plunge into a river in Montana to drink and to cool off. The calves at far left and at far right wear only stubby horns. Their small humps will grow to full size in a few years.

Male bison rolls in dust before challenging a rival. Bulls also wallow to rid their coats of pests.

Young calf nurses on a prairie in Nebraska. Darker hair will grow in to replace its reddish brown coat.

ground. Ramming their heads together, two bulls fight to see which is stronger. But rivals rarely battle to the death. Usually the weaker bull signals surrender by turning its head to one side.

In spring, after a nine-month pregnancy, a cow bears one young. The calf, reddish in color, is born without horns or a hump. Within two months, horns sprout and a hump begins to form. Gradually, dark brown hair grows in.

At one time, more than fifty million bison lived in North America. The Great Plains held the largest number. Indians there depended on the bison for survival. They ate bison meat and used the hides to make clothes, tepees, and canoes. Bison also were important in the religions of these Indians.

Settlers who moved west, however, viewed the bison as a nuisance. Shooting the animals became a favorite sport on the frontier. And traders killed the

bison for their hides and tongues. By 1889, fewer than 600 bison survived in the United States.

Several years later, the government outlawed bison hunting. Lands were set aside especially for the animals' protection. Slowly the bison population began to recover. Today there are more than 200,000 animals on preserves and on ranches.

The wisent (VEE-zent), or European bison, is a taller relative of the North American animal. The chestnut-colored wisent lacks its American relative's long, shaggy hair and massive shoulders. The wisent once was also in danger of becoming extinct. Cities and towns had replaced many of the woodlands where it made its home. Now the wisent lives in zoos and on preserves.

Wisent nibbles on twigs on a preserve in Scotland. ▷
The wisent, a European bison, lacks the bulky mane and hump of its North American relative. The wisent lives in forests instead of on plains.

Wisent: 6$\frac{1}{2}$ ft (198 cm) tall at the shoulder

BISON 🐾 **I of 2 species**

HEIGHT: 5-6$\frac{1}{2}$ ft (152-198 cm) at the shoulder

WEIGHT: 930-2,200 lb (422-998 kg)

HABITAT AND RANGE: prairies, plains, forests, and woodlands in North America and in Europe; most bison now live on preserves

FOOD: grasses, herbs, leaves, shrubs, and twigs

LIFE SPAN: 12 to 20 years on preserves, 40 years in captivity

REPRODUCTION: I young after a pregnancy of about 9 months

ORDER: artiodactyls

Black buck
The black buck is a kind of antelope. Read about antelopes on page 52.

Boar
Boar is a name for a type of hog. Read about hogs on page 264.

Bobcat
(BOB-cat)

Perched on a rock, a bobcat warms itself on a winter day in Colorado. People rarely see these animals because they hunt at night. During the day, bobcats usually stay hidden among rocks or thick brush.

THROUGHOUT FORESTS, mountains, swamps, and deserts, the bobcat roams and hunts. Wherever prey is plentiful in North America, this shy, strong animal can live and find food. Though only about twice as large as an ordinary house cat, a bobcat can kill an animal that is several times its own size. Perhaps that is why it is also known as a wildcat. Usually, the bobcat goes after smaller prey. It hunts rabbits, hares, mice, and squirrels. Crouching low to the ground, the bobcat slowly creeps toward its victim. Then, swiftly, it pounces. It may leap as far as 10 feet (305 cm) to catch an animal.

A bobcat's soft, tan fur is spotted with black. Fringes of long side-whiskers grow out from beneath its tufted ears. The bobcat's tail—with its black tip and white underside—is only about 6 inches (15 cm) long. In fact, the cat is named for its stubby tail, which seems to be cut off, or bobbed!

Bobcats usually live alone. They make their homes among rocks and bushes and in caves and hollow logs. The female bobcat chooses a hidden spot to use as a den. There she will give birth to her litter of one to six young.

After nursing her kittens for two months, the mother will begin bringing meat back to the den for them. A month or two later, she will begin to take them on nighttime hunts. As she leads her young around rocks and bushes, the mother raises her tail. Her kittens can see the white fur in the darkness.

After 9 to 12 months, the kittens are ready to leave the den and live alone. In the wild, they may survive about 10 to 12 years. Raised in a zoo, however, they might live to be 25 years old.

BOBCAT

LENGTH OF HEAD AND BODY: 26-41 in (66-104 cm); tail, 4-7 in (10-18 cm)

WEIGHT: 11-30 lb (5-14 kg)

HABITAT AND RANGE: forests, mountains, swamps, and deserts throughout most of North America

FOOD: hares, rabbits, rodents, and birds

LIFE SPAN: 10 to 12 years in the wild

REPRODUCTION: 1 to 6 young after a pregnancy of about 2 months

ORDER: carnivores

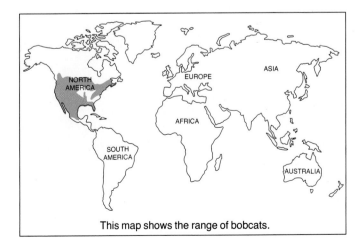

This map shows the range of bobcats.

Fluffy seven-day-old bobcat kittens (above) snuggle together in a den in a hollow log. The young have not yet opened their eyes. But in about two more days they will be able to see. Soon they will be climbing trees, like the two-month-old bobcat below. Full-grown bobcats are about twice as large as house cats. They can weigh as much as 30 pounds (14 kg).

▽ *Nine-month-old bobcat leaps as if pouncing on its prey. Actually it is only playing in the snow. Still as frisky as a young kitten, this bobcat soon will leave its mother. It will begin to live and to hunt on its own.*

Bongo

The bongo is a kind of antelope. Read about antelopes on page 52.

Brocket

The brocket is a kind of deer. Read about deer on page 170.

Buffalo

(BUFF-uh-low)

SWIMMING IN A RIVER cools a buffalo on a hot afternoon. Sometimes this large, cowlike animal even wallows neck-deep in a mudhole. Because the buffalo has few sweat glands in its skin, it cannot cool off by sweating. It lowers its body temperature with a swim or a mud bath. These activities also keep pesky insects off the buffalo's tough hide.

A buffalo never strays far from rivers, creeks, or water holes. After its swim, it finds a shady spot in the underbrush and settles down to rest. During the night or in the early morning, buffaloes drink and graze. When feeding, an animal bites off blades of grass and swallows the partly chewed food. The food goes into its stomach, where it is formed into wads that are called cuds. After eating, the animal brings up a cud and chews it slowly. After chewing the cud thoroughly, the buffalo again swallows and finally digests it. Antelopes, camels, cows, deer, goats, and sheep also

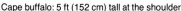

Cape buffalo: 5 ft (152 cm) tall at the shoulder

△ Huge horns curve from the head of a Cape buffalo. The contented animal ignores the tiny hitchhiker perched near its eye. The small bird—known as an oxpecker—eats ticks and insects from the buffalo's coat. If an oxpecker chirps and flies away, a buffalo becomes alert and watches for an approaching enemy.

chew cuds. You can read about these animals under their own headings.

Buffaloes have adapted, or become suited, to many environments. Buffaloes in Africa live on open grassy plains and in dense forests. Other kinds of wild buffaloes live in southern Asia, Indonesia, and the Philippines. Most of these animals are diminished, however, and very much endangered.

No wild buffaloes live in North America, however. The animal that is sometimes called the American buffalo is actually the bison. Find out more about the bison on page 100.

Not all buffaloes look alike. One kind of buffalo

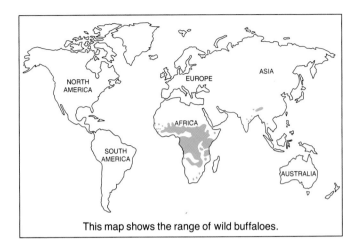

This map shows the range of wild buffaloes.

Cape buffaloes drink at a water hole in Africa. Buffaloes can drink their fill of about 7¹/₂ gallons (34 L) in six minutes. They drink at least once a day, usually between noon and sunset.

Buffalo

may differ from another in height, weight, or color. But most of these animals have short, thick necks, broad heads, and long tails. Stout legs support their stocky bodies. Heavy, pointed horns curve outward from the heads of both males and females.

The Cape buffalo of Africa is well known among hunters. It has a reputation as the most dangerous big-game animal. This huge, coal-black buffalo measures more than 5 feet (152 cm) tall at the shoulder and weighs as much as 1,300 pounds (590 kg). When it charges, it may run 30 miles (48 km) an hour!

Lions sometimes prey on adult Cape buffaloes. Other hunters such as leopards and hyenas seek out wounded animals or the very young or old. When a Cape buffalo is under attack, however, another member of the herd may come to its rescue. Charging at top speed, a stronger male or female buffalo tries to drive off the enemy. The buffalo's thick, sharp horns—perhaps 4 feet (122 cm) from tip to tip—make dangerous weapons. By twisting and charging,

Two-month-old Cape buffalo strolls with three ▷ oxpeckers on its back. The calf's woolly brown coat will grow darker and coarser with age. Its stubby horns will not reach their full size for five years.

▽ Standoff! A male Cape buffalo defends another buffalo by confronting three lions. One buffalo often comes to the rescue of another. Huge horns—4 feet (122 cm) from tip to tip—can pierce the hide of an attacker. A herd of wildebeests grazes in the distance.

a buffalo can easily gore the body of an attacker with its horns.

In the past, Cape buffaloes were far more abundant than they are now. In the late 1800s, however, a widespread cattle disease began to kill many African buffaloes. Until recently, herds were much smaller than those of a century ago. Today scientists have controlled the disease, but the buffaloes are threatened by loss of habitat.

Another kind of African buffalo, the forest buffalo, lives in smaller herds of about fifty animals. The forest buffalo makes its home in rain forests near the Equator. Smaller and lighter than the Cape buffalo, it measures nearly 4 feet (122 cm) tall at the shoulder

Resting in the midday heat, a Cape buffalo peacefully shares a mud bath with a group of hippopotamuses. Because the buffalo's skin has few sweat glands, the animal cannot cool off by sweating. Instead, it lowers its body temperature by wallowing in the mud.

and weighs about 660 pounds (299 kg). The forest buffalo has a thick, reddish brown coat. Its short horns sweep back, ending in sharp points.

Both the Cape buffalo and the forest buffalo wander free in their African homelands. In Asia, however, few buffaloes roam wild. People began to domesticate, or tame, these animals about 5,000 years ago. Domestic buffaloes pull plows and carts. Often they carry heavy loads on their backs. Some also are raised for their milk or meat.

The best known buffalo living in Asia is the

BUFFALO 👣 **4 of 5 species**

HEIGHT: 3-5 ft (91-152 cm) at the shoulder

WEIGHT: 450-1,500 lb (204-680 kg)

HABITAT AND RANGE: forests, woodlands, grasslands, swamps, and mountains in Asia and in Africa south of the Sahara; domestic buffaloes live on every continent except Antarctica

FOOD: grasses and leaves of shrubs

LIFE SPAN: 16 to 20 years in the wild

REPRODUCTION: 1 young after a pregnancy of 9 to 11 months

ORDER: artiodactyls

Buffalo

stocky water buffalo. This barrel-shaped animal measures about 5 feet (152 cm) tall at the shoulders. Its enormous, curved horns—the largest of any buffalo—may reach 5 feet (152 cm) from tip to tip. A water buffalo's nearly hairless coat is usually dull gray or black. Some breeds that live on islands in the Pacific Ocean have white coats.

True to its name, the water buffalo often lies in a river or a creek from morning until evening. Only its head and horns show above the water's surface. Often a water buffalo will roll and wallow in mud at the water's edge. It covers its skin with the mud, protecting itself from insects.

Thai boy balances on a female water buffalo's ▷
back while her year-old calf wades nearby. Small children often tend these obedient animals.

▽ *Herders drive water buffaloes through high water in Brazil. These hardy animals, originally from Asia, now live in many parts of the world.*

△ *Two-month-old calf huddles near its mother among a herd of water buffaloes in India. A few small herds roam wild in parts of Asia.*

Neck-deep in a river, a pair of Asian water ▷ buffaloes takes a swim after a morning spent plowing rice fields. Asians have used buffaloes as work animals for thousands of years. Buffaloes also work in many other parts of the world.

Water buffalo: 5 ft (152 cm) tall at the shoulder

Another kind of Asian buffalo, the small tamarau (tam-uh-RAU), lives in swampy areas of mountain forests on one of the Philippine Islands. It measures about 3½ feet (107 cm) tall at the shoulder. The tamarau's coat is dark gray with white marks on its head, neck, and legs. The animal's horns are ridged and slightly curved.

The smallest kind of Asian buffalo, the anoa (uh-NO-uh), makes its home in Indonesia. This brown buffalo grows only about 3 feet (91 cm) tall. Its small, straight horns point backward from the top of its head. The anoa lives in wooded mountains. The rare-ly seen animal stays in thick underbrush, and little is known about its habits.

A female buffalo—African or Asian—may bear a single calf each year or two. A pregnancy varies in length from nine to eleven months, depending on the kind of buffalo. The newborn stands within thirty minutes of its birth. For two years, it stays close to its mother in the herd. But it may join other calves to play. The frisky calves chase one another, tease their mothers, or run after their own tails. Although the calves grow rapidly during their first year, they do not reach adult size until about the age of five.

Burro The burro is a domestic ass. Read about asses on page 66.

Bush baby

(BUSH BAY-bee)

THE LOUD, SHRILL CRIES of the tiny bush baby helped earn the animal its name. When it calls out, this member of the primate order sounds surprisingly like a human baby. Other primates include monkeys, apes, and humans.

Bush babies live in Africa, in forests and in open shrubby areas called the bush. The largest kinds are about the size of cats. Others are only as big as chipmunks. All have long tails. Pads on their fingers and toes help them cling to trees.

Smaller bush babies are expert jumpers. They seem to fly among the branches, but actually they are leaping. Using their muscular legs, bush babies spring from tree to tree. On the ground, they can hop like tiny kangaroos.

Bush babies spend the day resting. Sometimes they sleep in nests made of leaves and twigs. Or they may curl up in hollow trees or in tree forks. At night, the furry animals move about searching for food. Bush babies eat tree gum, insects, lizards, mice, and small birds. Larger kinds of bush babies eat fruit to fill out their diet.

With its big eyes, a bush baby can spot prey in the dark. Sensitive hearing alerts it to the approach of another animal. The bush baby moves its ears in the direction of a noise. Even the slightest sound will not escape its keen hearing. Before sleeping, the animal folds up its ears like fans.

Females usually give birth to one or two young after a pregnancy of about four months. The offspring are raised in nests made of leaves. Frequently a mother will move her young to another nest. She carries them in her mouth, or they cling tightly to her fur. Sometimes she will leave, or "park," her infants in different spots for a short time. The mother may even park them for most of the night while she searches for food. But she always brings them back to the nest before dawn.

Bush babies are popular pets in some parts of the world. Tame ones may lick their owners' faces and ride about in their pockets.

Another name for the bush baby is galago (guh-LAY-go). Find out about its close relatives the loris on page 342 and the potto on page 453.

Seeking security, young Senegal bush babies huddle in a tree. These animals often sleep clustered together.

Senegal bush baby: 6 in (15 cm) long; tail, 9 in (23 cm)

Senegal bush baby peers from a tree. Big eyes help this animal see well in the dark. Keen hearing alerts it to the approach of prey. The bush baby can move its ears in the direction of a sound. It also can fold them like fans. The animal sleeps with its ears curled shut.

Thick-tailed bush baby: 13 in (33 cm) long; tail, 15 in (38 cm)

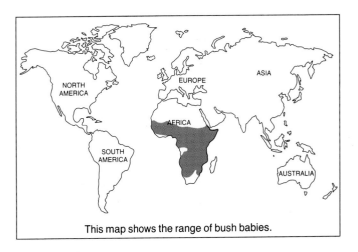

This map shows the range of bush babies.

BUSH BABY

LENGTH OF HEAD AND BODY: 5-14 in (13-36 cm); tail, 7-16 in (18-41 cm)

WEIGHT: 11 oz-4 lb (312 g-2 kg)

HABITAT AND RANGE: forests and brushy regions of Africa

FOOD: tree gum, fruit, insects, and other small animals

LIFE SPAN: up to 19 years in captivity

REPRODUCTION: usually 1 or 2 young after a pregnancy of about 4 months

ORDER: primates

Thick-tailed bush baby crouches on a branch. Pads on the tips of its fingers and toes help it grip the branch. When this animal senses danger, it scampers away.

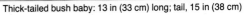

Expert broad jumper, a Senegal bush baby takes a flying leap to travel from tree to tree. It uses strong leg muscles to push off. It holds its arms up to go farther. In the air, it tucks its arms and legs to its body. As it lands, the animal brings its legs and arms forward and grabs with its hands and feet. It can jump as far as 15 feet (5 m)!

113

C

Cacomistle
The cacomistle is a close relative of the ringtail. Read about ringtails on page 488.

Camel
(KAM-ul)

UNDER THE DESERT SUN, merchants lead a caravan of camels across hot sand. The camels will drink no water until they reach the next oasis—perhaps three or four days later. Yet these hardy animals keep up a steady pace. They may travel 100 miles (161 km) without water.

Camels do not easily sweat. Therefore they lose the moisture in their bodies slowly. They get the moisture they need by drinking water and by eating desert plants. In winter, plants provide enough moisture for camels to go without drinking for several weeks!

Even when water is available at wells and at water holes, camels drink only if necessary. They take in just enough to replace the water used since their last drink. Sometimes, however, they have used up quite a lot of water. A thirsty camel can gulp down as much as 30 gallons (135 L) of water in just 13 minutes! That would be like drinking 480 cups of water in the same length of time.

Arabian, or one-humped, camels are found mainly in the hot deserts of North Africa and Asia.

Bearing bags of salt to market, a caravan of Arabian camels winds across the Sahara in Africa. These hardy pack animals can carry heavy loads about 25 miles (40 km) a day. Some desert peoples measure wealth by the number of camels a person owns.

These camels live in regions where temperatures rise above 120°F (49°C). Their short coats help to block out the heat of the sun. With broad, thickly padded feet, they walk easily on shifting sands. Arabian camels stand more than 7 feet (213 cm) tall at the hump and weigh as much as 1,600 pounds (726 kg). People sometimes call Arabian camels dromedaries (DRAH-muh-dare-eez).

Bactrian (BACK-tree-un) camels have two humps. They also have tough feet for crossing the rocky deserts of East Asia. Temperatures range there from a low of –20°F (–29°C) in winter to more than 100°F (38°C) in summer. The thick, shaggy coats of these

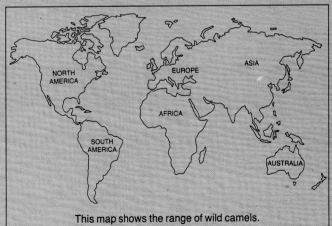

This map shows the range of wild camels.

Protected from the blistering heat by short hair and padded hooves, Arabian camels cross a ridge of sand in a desert in Africa. The animals range in color from brown to "camel's-hair" tan to white.

camels protect their bodies from the cold weather. When temperatures soar, the animals shed their heavy winter coats. Stockier and slightly shorter than their Arabian relatives, Bactrian camels measure about 7 feet (213 cm) tall at the hump and weigh about 1,800 pounds (816 kg).

Well suited to life in harsh deserts, both Arabian and Bactrian camels have bushy eyebrows and double rows of eyelashes. Their ears are lined with hairs. Special muscles allow them to close their nostrils and lips tightly for long periods. These features help protect them from blowing sand or snow.

Camels' humps help the animals survive in the desert. Many people think that camels store water in their humps, but the humps are really masses of fat. This fat nourishes the animals when food is scarce. With this energy supply on their backs, the animals can go several days without eating. Camels store about 80 pounds (36 kg) of fat in their humps. As camels use this fat, their humps shrink. If camels do not eat, their humps get flabby. The humps become firm again after the camels eat and drink.

Camels nibble at whatever plants they can find. Like cows, they do not chew food completely before

At a camp in the Sahara, a girl baby-sits for a young Arabian camel while its mother grazes nearby. When hungry or frightened, a calf calls for its mother with a lamblike "baa." A camel begins to learn its owner's commands when it reaches a year old.

CAMEL 🐾 1 of 2 species

HEIGHT: 6-7½ ft (183-229 cm) at the hump

WEIGHT: 1,000-1,800 lb (454-816 kg)

HABITAT AND RANGE: the Gobi in Asia; domesticated camels live in Africa, Asia, the Middle East, and Australia

FOOD: grasses, juicy plants, leaves, branches, grains, and dates

LIFE SPAN: up to 50 years in captivity

REPRODUCTION: 1 young after a pregnancy of about 12 or 13 months

ORDER: artiodactyls

Bactrian camel moves quickly across a plain. One of its humps has flopped sideways, because the animal has used the fat stored inside it for energy.

swallowing it. After eating, they bring up the partly digested food, called a cud, and chew it thoroughly. Then they swallow the cud and digest it.

Camels' mouths are so tough that even the sharp thorns of desert plants do not hurt them. If they cannot find food, camels nibble on ropes, on sandals, and sometimes on their owners' tents!

A female camel may give birth to a calf every other year. The newborn can stand shortly after birth and can walk within a few hours. It stays with its mother until it is almost two years old. It is not fully grown, however, until the age of five.

People first domesticated, or tamed, camels at least 3,500 years ago. Today almost all of them are domestic. Of the millions of camels in the world, probably fewer than a thousand roam wild.

For desert peoples, camels are strong and dependable work animals. Camels carry goods to market or carry riders. The animals also provide their owners with food, clothing, and fuel. Camel milk is thick and rich, and people sometimes eat camel meat. The fat inside their humps can be melted down and used for cooking.

When the animals shed their coats, their owners gather up the woolly hair. They weave it into clothing, blankets, and tents. From the tough hide, they make shoes and saddles. They burn dry camel waste as fuel for cooking and heating.

Bactrian camel: 7 ft (213 cm) tall at the hump

Capybara

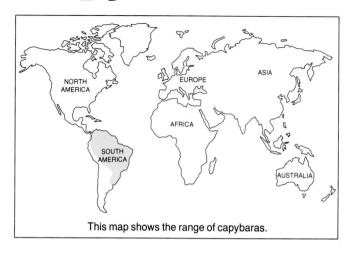

This map shows the range of capybaras.

WORLD'S LARGEST RODENT, the capybara is at home on land or in the water. If an enemy like a jaguar or a person chases it, the animal can run or leap away. It is an able swimmer. In the face of danger, capybaras will plunge into water. Only their eyes, ears, and nostrils show as they paddle away. Their webbed toes act a little like swim fins. The animals can also stay underwater for several minutes.

Capybaras look somewhat like giant, long-legged guinea pigs. They grow more than 4 feet (122 cm) long and weigh as much as 110 pounds (50 kg). Their coarse hair is so thin that their skin can dry out in the hot sun of Central and South America where

In a muddy river in Brazil, a capybara provides a hairy perch for a cattle tyrant bird. Capybaras often wallow in water. This keeps their skin from drying out in the hot sun.

they live. So capybaras often spend time wallowing in the mud. They also rest in the shade of swampy woods. In the morning and evening, they stand in water up to their stomachs and feed on plants. The front teeth of capybaras, like those of all rodents, keep growing. Capybaras must chew and gnaw all their lives to wear down their teeth.

Capybaras live in groups of about twenty adults. A female capybara has a litter of one to eight young each year. These offspring—born with hair and able to see—weigh about 2 pounds (1 kg). The young follow their mother for a year.

Capybaras do not dig burrows. Instead they hollow shallow beds in the ground. When they live near gardens and ranches, the animals sometimes eat melons, squash, corn, and other crops. For this reason—and for their meat—people in South America often hunt capybaras.

CAPYBARA

LENGTH OF HEAD AND BODY: 40-52 in (102-132 cm); height at the shoulder, 20 in (51 cm)

WEIGHT: 60-110 lb (27-50 kg)

HABITAT AND RANGE: marshes, swamps, and wooded areas near rivers and lakes in Central and South America

FOOD: aquatic plants, grains, and fruit

LIFE SPAN: 8 to 10 years in the wild

REPRODUCTION: 1 to 8 offspring after a pregnancy of about 5 months

ORDER: rodents

◁ *Dripping wet, a young capybara climbs onto a riverbank in Brazil. Capybaras weigh about 2 pounds (1 kg) at birth. The newborn have hair and can see.*

▽ *Capybaras gather near water during the dry season. At other times the animals live in smaller groups. The animals communicate with grunts and whistles.*

Caracal

The caracal is a kind of cat. Read about caracals and other cats on page 126.

Caribou

(CARE-uh-boo)

AS SNOW MELTS IN EARLY MAY, most of the caribou of Alaska and Canada start to travel, or migrate, to their summer feeding grounds. Female caribou—called cows—may move about 600 miles (965 km) north along trails worn smooth by former migrations.

Day and night, the herd flows along. Thousands of caribou feed, rest, and move on again. Male caribou—called bulls—follow a few weeks later, along with yearlings, calves born the year before.

Broad hooves help caribou cross the harsh land. The hooves act like snowshoes in deep snow and like paddles in water. Sharp edges help caribou get good footing on rocky hillsides and on slick ice. With the scoop-shaped undersides of their hooves, caribou can dig through the snow to find food. Each animal clears many feeding holes every day.

As they travel, caribou shed hair from their thick winter coats. Heaps of matted grayish brown hair mark places where many animals have passed.

By June, the cows and their calves, which were born along the way, have arrived at summer pastures.

Crowned with sharp-tipped antlers, a male caribou— ▷ *called a bull—rests in Alaska's September sunshine.*

▽ *With month-old calves nearby, female caribou—called cows—graze in a summer feeding ground.*

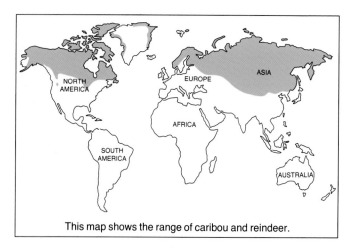

This map shows the range of caribou and reindeer.

△ *Shreds of velvet, a covering of soft skin, hang from a caribou bull's antlers in early fall. Though the pieces look bloody, shedding them does not hurt the animal.*

On the slopes of Mount McKinley, caribou bulls ▷ *roam their summer grounds. They feed in one valley after another, wandering all the time.*

A cow usually has one offspring a year. Wolves, wolverines, lynxes, and bears often prey on the newborn animals. But the calves develop quickly. A young caribou can stand on its feet only a few minutes after it is born. The next day it can follow its mother as she looks for food.

New calves nurse often at first. But after six months, they eat only plants, as adults do. In cool summer pastures, they feed on grasses and on the leaves of shrubs and other plants. An adult eats about 12 pounds (5 kg) of food each day.

Summer brings huge swarms of insects. Mosquitoes and flies bite the animals' bodies. Some flies lay eggs under their skins. The frantic caribou splash in ponds or climb to breezy hilltops to ease the itching and to escape from the insects.

Caribou

By July, the bulls have grown new sets of antlers covered with a soft skin called velvet. Bulls grow and shed their antlers every year. The new antlers begin as bumps. These grow and branch out.

In early fall, the velvet begins to fall off. To help remove it, a bull rubs his antlers against bushes. This exposes the sharp points of bone. During the fall mating season, bulls use their antlers to jab and to wrestle with each other as they fight for mates. Just before winter, their antlers fall off.

Caribou cows have smaller and thinner antlers. They begin to grow in late summer, and they drop off the next June. Deer, elk, and other close relatives of caribou also grow and shed antlers—but only the males. Read more about antlers on page 170.

With the first snowfall, the entire herd—bulls, cows, and calves—begins to head south to spend the winter in sheltered woodlands. Then, in early May, caribou begin their migration north again.

For centuries, the Eskimo have depended on caribou meat for food. They have used the hides for clothing, tents, and kayaks. They have made needles and fishhooks from caribou bones and antlers.

In northern Europe and Asia, people herd a kind of caribou called reindeer. They follow their herds with skis, boats, and snowmobiles. Their meat, cheese, and butter all come from the reindeer. One subspecies, the arctic caribou, is endangered.

Caribou move across a snowfield in Alaska. Sharp ▷ *hooves help them cross the terrain, still icy in late spring.*

CARIBOU   🐾 I of I species

HEIGHT: 4-5 ft (122-152 cm) at the shoulder

WEIGHT: 240-700 lb (109-318 kg)

HABITAT AND RANGE: tundra, northern forests, and mountain uplands from western Alaska through Canada to western Greenland, northern Europe, and northern Asia

FOOD: mostly grasses and tiny plants, and some leaves

LIFE SPAN: about 15 years in the wild

REPRODUCTION: I young after a pregnancy of about 8 months

ORDER: artiodactyls

△ *With bare antlers, two young bulls spar. They practice for the time when they will fight for a mate. Each animal tilts its head sideways and jabs with the sharp points. After the mating season, the antlers will fall off.*

◁ *Caribou cross the chilly Kobuk River on their yearly migration. The hollow hairs of their outer coats trap air, helping the animals float. Bulls wear heavy antlers. Cows, with delicate sets, swim alongside and behind. Caribou migrate as many as 1,600 miles (2,574 km) each year.*

CATS ARE FULL OF CONTRASTS. Their soft, padded paws hide sharp, hooked claws. At rest, cats stretch out lazily. On the move, they glide silently through the grass. Their glossy fur covers powerful muscles. A cat can freeze, still as a statue, then explode in a savage attack.

There are 38 different species, or kinds, of cats. All the different breeds of house cats make up only one of these species. The rest are wild cats. You can find out about some well-known big cats—bobcat, cheetah, jaguar, leopard, lion, lynx, and tiger—under their own headings.

Cats vary in size—from a dainty pet calico cat to a huge Siberian tiger. They vary in color—from a pure white Persian cat to a velvety black leopard.

Regal and watchful, two young mountain lions rest in a cave in Utah. The mother of the cubs relaxes in the shadows. Mountain lions often sleep during the day and hunt at night.

This map shows the range of wild cats.

But members of the cat family are not hard to recognize. Most cats have rounded heads with rather flat faces. Their sleek, streamlined bodies move gracefully on muscular legs.

Cats live in almost every kind of environment throughout the world. The snow leopard pads along the cold, rocky slopes of the Himalaya, the highest mountains on the earth. The ocelot (AH-suh-lot) prowls through steamy South American rain forests. The caracal (CAR-uh-kal) roams dry, desert country in Africa and Asia. And the rare Iriomote (ear-ee-uh-MO-tay) cat lives deep in a forest on only one small Japanese island.

Cats and people have lived together for centuries. At first, wild cats probably hunted the mice and rats that lived where food was stored. People began to like these mousers and treated them well. Gradually, cats moved into people's homes.

Cats probably were first tamed in Egypt about 4,000 years ago. The ancient Egyptians worshiped a cat goddess. When a family cat died, people would cut their hair to show how sad they were. Thousands of the dead cats were made into mummies. They were even supplied with mouse mummies for food in the next world!

Most cats are good at running, jumping, climbing, and even swimming. Some of them are star performers. The rippling muscles in a mountain lion's hind legs can send it soaring through the air to pounce on its prey or to sail over an obstacle in its

◁ *Roaming the hills of Idaho, a young mountain lion looks over its home range. These cats often live in remote, dry areas with deep canyons and steep cliffs. There they prey mainly on deer, elk, and hares.*

▽ *Male mountain lion (below) carefully licks his claws to clean them and to remove bits of meat, bone, and hair. When not in use, the animal's claws retract into protective coverings in its paws. At bottom, another mountain lion prowls through the snow on padded feet. A long, graceful tail helps it keep its balance while stalking, running, leaping, and climbing.*

path. As a serval (SIR-vul) hunts, it moves through tall grass in fantastic flying leaps. A fishing cat uses the weblike skin between its toes to help it swim. Sometimes it even dives underwater.

A cat walks on pads that are under the toes and the sole of each foot. It seems to walk on tiptoe. When its claws are not in use, they retract into protective coverings. The long, curved, retractable claws always stay needle-sharp.

All cats, tame or wild, are effective hunters. In the wild, cats prey on almost anything that moves, from insects to buffaloes. A caracal can leap up and snatch a bird right out of the air. With a swift move of its paw, a fishing cat can scoop fish, crabs, and frogs out of a stream. Smaller cats feed mostly on mice, rats, and birds. Big cats eat antelopes and other larger animals, as well as small prey.

Arching leaves surround a frosty-looking Pallas's cat. ▷
These animals have the longest and thickest fur of all wild cats. Coats of white-tipped hairs protect them from the harsh weather of their homeland in central Asia.

▽ *With a swift and sure leap, a serval pounces toward its prey. The tall grass of eastern Africa hides small animals. So servals hunt often by sound rather than by sight. They usually eat snakes, birds, mice, and rats.*

No matter what they hunt, all cats get their food in a similar way. Usually they hunt alone. Sometimes they hide and wait for an animal to pass by. More often they silently creep up on their prey.

When they stalk another animal, cats move swiftly at first. Then they suddenly stop and watch intently. They stay flat against the ground and under cover. They creep again and stop again. As they get closer, they move even more slowly. Some cats crouch so

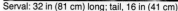
Pallas's cat: 22 in (56 cm) long; tail, 10 in (25 cm)

Serval: 32 in (81 cm) long; tail, 16 in (41 cm)

Ocelot: 40 in (102 cm) long; tail, 12 in (30 cm)

△ *Surefooted ocelot tiptoes along a dead branch in Venezuela. Ocelots usually hunt on the ground. But sometimes they stalk birds or monkeys in the trees.*

Pampas cat: 25 in (64 cm) long; tail, 12 in (30 cm)

△ *Spots and stripes mark the fur of a pampas cat. These markings help it blend into its many habitats: grasslands, mountains, and forests of South America.*

◁ *Stalking jungle cat barely disturbs the morning calm. Jungle cats live in the Middle East and Asia. They feed on hares, rats, mice, and lizards. Centuries ago, Egyptians trained jungle cats to hunt birds for them.*

Jungle cat: 26 in (66 cm) long; tail, 11 in (28 cm)

131

Quick and skillful, a fishing cat wades into the water to catch its dinner. On a sandbank in a river in India, this rarely seen cat arches its back and pounces on a fish. It pins its prey to the streambed with its front paws.

low that their shoulder blades and hip bones stick up above their backs. When they are very close to their prey, cats spring. They seize prey with sharp teeth and strong claws.

Cats kill their prey with a well-aimed bite of their powerful jaws. An ancient relative of modern cats was the saber-toothed cat. Its long fangs could pierce the toughest hides. Today cats still have pointed fangs. They use these teeth to bite prey. Their sharp-edged back teeth cut through meat like scissors. Cats have no flat-topped teeth for chewing food, so they cannot grind their meat. Cats swallow their food without chewing it.

A cat's tongue is rough, like sandpaper. It can lick

CAT 🐾 **13 of 30 species**

LENGTH OF HEAD AND BODY: 13 in-6 ft (33 cm-183 cm); tail, 6 in-3 ft (15 cm-91 cm)

WEIGHT: 4-500 lb (2-227 kg) from house cat to Siberian tiger

HABITAT AND RANGE: every kind of habitat worldwide, except in Antarctica, Australia, Madagascar, the West Indies, and some oceanic islands; domestic cats are found almost everywhere

FOOD: animals and sometimes plants

LIFE SPAN: 12 to more than 20 years in captivity, depending on species

REPRODUCTION: 1 to 8 young after a pregnancy of about 2 to 4 months, depending on species

ORDER: carnivores

a bone clean of the last shred of meat. Cats also use their tongues to clean themselves. By bending and stretching, a cat can reach almost every hair on its body with its tongue.

Of all the senses, cats depend most on their sight and hearing. A cat's ears turn to catch the slightest sound. The serval has enormous oval ears. It is hard for this cat to see prey in the tall grass of the African plains where it lives. But the serval's huge ears pick up every chirp, squeak, and rustle nearby.

The Pallas's (PAL-us-ez) cat lives in the cold, harsh areas of central Asia. Its ears are very short. They are low on its head and wide apart. The eyes of this cat are very near the top of its head. This arrangement may help the cat hunt where there are few bushes to hide behind. It can peer over rocks and still not show much of itself.

Cats do most of their hunting in the dark. Their eyesight at night is good. Like other nighttime hunters, they can see when it is dark, because inside a cat's eye there is a special surface that reflects light. This surface is what makes a cat's eyes shine in the dark. Many cats have pupils that become tall, narrow slits in bright light. In the dark, these pupils open wide to let in light.

Cats also find their way in the dark with their whiskers. These long, stiff hairs on their faces have no

Then it rears up on its two back legs, gripping the struggling fish in the air. After killing it, the cat again places the fish underwater. Many cats do not like the water, but the fishing cat usually lives near streams or rivers.

real feeling. But if the tips of the whiskers brush something, a cat feels the movements at the roots of its whiskers.

Cats use their sense of smell to communicate. They mark trees or lookout points by scratching them with their claws and by leaving their waste. These places are called scent posts. By their odor, they show where a cat's home range is.

A long, graceful tail helps a cat keep its balance as it leaps and climbs. The movement of the tail can indicate a cat's mood—excitement, anger, fright, relaxation. On some cats, markings make the tail easier for others to see. Tails of jungle cats and pampas (PAM-pus) cats are ringed and tipped with black.

Most cats have coats of dark spots on lighter fur. A snow leopard's spots look a little like large roses. An ocelot's spots resemble links in a chain. The background color of most wild cats is light brown or golden yellow. But the snow leopard has gray fur. And the serval's fur may be reddish.

A cat's color and markings help it hide while creeping up on prey. The snow leopard blends into its rocky background. The brown Iriomote cat seems to disappear among forest shadows. The spots and stripes of the pampas cat help it hide in tall grass. And the tan caracal matches its sandy home.

Cats that live in warm climates generally have

The cat moves the fish to a safer hold in its mouth. It carries its prize this way as it crosses a sandbank and then goes through deeper water to shore.

shorter fur. In cool climates, fur is longer. The Pallas's cat lives in high, cold regions. Some people think that the extremely long, thick fur on the underside of its body protects it when it lies on the frozen ground. But short, thin fur on its back may let this cat soak up heat from the sun.

House cats have been bred to suit different people. So their fur may be long, short, or even curly!

133

◁ *Female snow leopard, prized for its spotted coat, peers over a ridge in the rugged mountains of Pakistan. The cat roams widely looking for such prey as wild sheep. It comes down from the high, treeless slopes only in winter.*

Snow leopard: 41 in (104 cm) long; tail, 35 in (89 cm)

It may be striped, spotted, marbled, or plain. And besides the more common shades of tan, brown, and black, their fur may be silver, blue, or ginger.

Different kinds of cats mew, purr, snarl, growl, grunt, hiss, yowl, scream, and roar. But no cat makes all these noises. Only some of the big cats can roar. And the bigger the cat, the louder the noise. Smaller cats can purr for a long time. When a big cat purrs, it has to stop to catch its breath. Cats' piercing yowls and screams often can be heard for long distances. These sounds, along with scents, help cats mark their ranges and find partners at mating time.

In cool climates, wild cats mate in winter or in early spring. The young are then born two to four months later. In warm climates, the young may be born at any time of year.

The female chooses a hidden spot for a den. A mountain lion may find a cave. An ocelot looks for a hollow tree. A serval may take over a porcupine's burrow. A jungle cat may hide among dry reeds.

Some cats have only one or two young at a time. Others have three or four. Tame cats sometimes have eight or more helpless little balls of fur. Young cats are called cubs or kittens. They are born with their eyes closed, and they are barely able to move.

The mother feeds her kittens, cleans them, and protects them. If danger threatens, she may move her litter to a new nest. A female cat carries her kittens, one at a time, in her mouth. She holds them gently by the neck and shoulders. Females almost always care for their young alone. Most mothers will not let males get near the young.

Cubs soon start exploring the world around their den. They play at hunting right away. On wobbly legs, one cub follows the trail of a fluttering leaf. Another rears up to catch its mother's twitching tail. From a rock, one cub leaps onto the back of another, and the two go tumbling in the dust. Cats often play games of stalk-and-pounce. As they grow older, they join their mother on hunting trips, learning the skills they will need later. Then most cats leave to find hunting grounds of their own.

▽ *Long ears perked to catch sounds, a caracal watches its desert surroundings. The cat can move its ears to show confidence, anger, or alertness. Caracals roam from India through the Middle East and into Africa.*

Caracal: 28 in (71 cm) long; tail, 9 in (23 cm)

Iriomote cat: 23 in (58 cm) long; tail, 8 in (20 cm)

△ *Iriomote cat in Japan creeps through the nighttime shadows. It cocks its ears to catch a rustle in the forest. This rare cat hunts birds, snakes, and lizards. Until 1967, no scientists knew that such a cat existed!*

Seal Point Siamese: 18 in (46 cm) long; tail, 12 in (30 cm)

Bi-color Persian: 18 in (46 cm) long; tail, 12 in (30 cm)

Red Tabby Shorthair: 18 in (46 cm) long; tail, 12 in (30 cm)

HOUSE CATS *have lived with people for centuries as popular and useful pets. More than thirty different breeds of tame cats exist. They vary a great deal—in color, markings, and length of fur. But all house cats belong to a single species, or kind, of cat.*

◁ *One of the most popular breeds of house cats, a Seal Point Siamese nestles among forget-me-nots.*

Scottish Fold: 18 in (46 cm) long; tail, 12 in (30 cm)

◁ *Pure white Scottish Fold cat shows off its eyes of different colors—one blue and the other deep coppery orange. Many white cats have these "odd eyes." A pink nose also often appears in light-colored cats. Cat shows provide good places to see how widely cats vary.*

▽ *Proud Abyssinian cat gazes at the world with large, almond-shaped eyes. This cat's fur looks grayish brown. But actually each hair in its coat has bands of black, brown, and white. People call this coloring "ticking."*

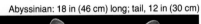

Abyssinian: 18 in (46 cm) long; tail, 12 in (30 cm)

Cream Persian: 18 in (46 cm) long; tail, 12 in (30 cm)

△ *Fiery orange eyes blazing, a champion Cream Persian cat scowls. This breed of popular show cat has a flat muzzle and long, soft hair.*

Colorful patchwork of black, orange, and white covers ▷ *the coat of this Calico Rex. Its short hair grows in rippling waves from the top of its head to the tip of its tail.*

◁ *Black-and-white Bi-color Persian (far left) displays the long glossy fur and large round eyes typical of its breed. A Red Tabby Shorthair (left) stalks along the branches of a plum tree. Like their wild relatives, house cats hunt well. Kittens even pounce on insects and balls of dust.*

Calico Rex: 18 in (46 cm) long; tail, 12 in (30 cm)

Cavy

The cavy is a close relative of the guinea pig. Read about both animals on page 247.

Chamois

Read about both animals on page 247.

(SHAM-ee)

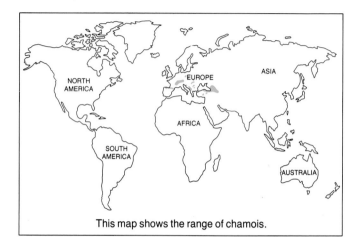

This map shows the range of chamois.

CHAMOIS 🐾 **2 of 2 species**

HEIGHT: 28-33 in (71-84 cm) at the shoulder

WEIGHT: 53-110 lb (24-50 kg)

HABITAT AND RANGE: mountains of Europe, southwestern Asia, and New Zealand

FOOD: grasses, herbs, flowers, evergreen shoots, woody plants, and dry leaves

LIFE SPAN: as long as 24 years in the wild

REPRODUCTION: 1 or 2 young after a pregnancy of about 6 months

ORDER: artiodactyls

LEAPING FROM ONE NARROW LEDGE to another, a chamois quickly climbs a steep mountain slope. It jumps gracefully across a 20-foot (6-m) ravine and lands lightly on the other side. The chamois is at home in the rugged mountains of Europe and of Asia. People have taken the animal to New Zealand, and it now lives in the wild there. It is so surefooted that it can balance on a small knob of rock.

The scientific, or Latin, name for chamois means "rock goat." In fact, the chamois looks like a goat, and it is closely related to the goat family. A male chamois measures about 30 inches (76 cm) tall at the shoulder and weighs about 90 pounds (41 kg). Both males and females have black, ringed horns. The chamois usually grows a new set of rings on each of its horns in the summer. If it has five sets of rings on each horn, it is probably five years old.

In summer, chamois feed on grasses, wild herbs, and flowers high in the mountains where no trees grow. When winter comes, chamois may come down to the forests below. There they feed on shoots, woody plants, and dry leaves.

Female chamois, called does, roam together with their young in herds of ten to thirty animals. Mature males, called bucks, usually wander alone. During the late spring and summer, the bucks pick out the best feeding areas for themselves. They eat a great deal and grow strong and fit. Groups of younger males and groups of females feed elsewhere.

At mating time in the late fall, the bucks join the females. Glands on each buck's head, near the base of his horns, produce a waxy substance. The buck rubs this substance on trees, bushes, and tall grasses to announce his presence. Chamois bucks fight over the females. They chase each other wildly along mountain slopes. As they race, they may try to jab each other with their hooked horns. The battle lasts until one buck runs off. The winner then looks for mates among the females.

About six months after mating, a female chamois gives birth, usually to one kid. Sometimes she may bear twins. The kids can walk almost immediately after birth. Young chamois play much of the time, running and jumping and sliding down snow-covered hills. A kid follows its mother everywhere and stays close by her side.

If an enemy comes near a herd of grazing chamois, several members will warn the rest of the herd with high-pitched whistles and stamping of hooves. The chamois quickly disappear among the rocks.

Eagles, lynxes, and wolves prey on chamois. People hunt them as game. Chamois skins are made into a very fine, soft leather. In most areas, laws now protect the chamois. Even so, four subspecies are threatened with extinction.

Warm in its winter coat, a male chamois climbs a ▷ snowy slope in Italy. A long, thick layer of hair protects the chamois from cold mountain winters. In summer, it sheds this coat for a shorter, lighter-colored one.

Cheetah

(CHEE-tuh)

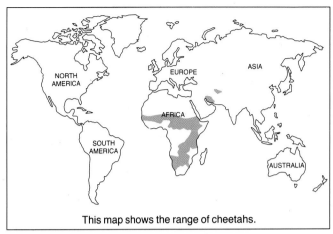

This map shows the range of cheetahs.

FASTEST MAMMAL ON LAND, the cheetah can reach speeds of 60 or perhaps even 70 miles (97-113 km) an hour over short distances. It usually chases its prey at only about half that speed, however. The cheetah can make sudden, sharp turns. With its long, muscular legs and flexible spine, it is the champion sprinter among land mammals.

Standing on a fallen acacia tree in Africa, a cheetah searches for prey. Because of its keen eyesight, this cat can see long distances across the grasslands. A short mane on the neck of the cheetah below marks the animal as young. The mane will disappear as it ages.

△ *Sprawled atop a termite mound, a mother cheetah watches over her playful cubs. They stalk, run, and pounce. The games prepare them for the time when they must hunt alone for the animals they eat.*

Like other wild cats, the cheetah hunts to survive. Its excellent eyesight helps it find such prey as hares and antelopes during daylight hours. Though it rarely climbs trees, it sometimes perches on high places—a fallen tree, a hilltop, or a termite mound—and watches for prey.

When it sights prey, the cheetah usually begins to stalk. It creeps as close as possible before the attack. It may lift its head high to keep the prey in sight. But it keeps its body hidden. The cheetah is hard to see because its spotted coat blends with the tall, dry grass of the plains.

Suddenly, the cheetah makes a lightning dash. With a paw, it knocks its prey to the ground and then bites its throat. Usually, the cheetah drags the kill off to a shady spot. There it eats its meal.

Because it tires quickly, the cheetah does not always catch its victim. The cheetah can run at top speed

▽ *Cubs huddle close to their mother for protection from enemies and for shade from the sun. She will nurse them for several months, until they can eat meat.*

Lapping at a water hole, a cheetah drinks after a kill. ▷
Cheetahs drink only once every three or four days.

for only about 300 yards (274 m)—the length of three football fields. An antelope may be able to zigzag and get away from a cheetah.

A cheetah has claws on all four feet. Unlike other cats, the cheetah has no protective coverings for its claws. Only one claw on each front foot is sharp. This dewclaw is higher than the other claws and never touches the ground. Cheetahs use their dewclaws to knock down prey.

△ Fastest mammals on land, cheetahs make a lightning dash after a gazelle. They can briefly reach speeds of 60-70 miles (97-113 km) an hour. As they run, they knock their prey to the ground.

◁ Successful hunter, a cheetah drags a gazelle to the shade. It tries to keep its prey away from hyenas and vultures.

Cubs eat their meal while ▷ their mother rests from the chase. Young cheetahs often watch their mother hunt. After about a year of watching and playing games of stalk and chase, they begin to hunt with her or on their own.

Female cheetahs generally live with their cubs. Males sometimes live alone but often form small groups of two or three animals. The cats communicate by marking tree trunks, bushes, and termite mounds with their waste. By the smell, other cheetahs know that an animal has passed by.

Female cheetahs usually bear three cubs in a litter. Cubs have blue-gray fur on their heads and backs until they are about three months old. To clean their fur, they lick themselves and each other. Often after eating, the cubs and mother groom each other with their long, pink tongues. They close their eyes, lick each other, and purr loudly.

Cheetahs do not roar as lions or tigers do. When alarmed, a cheetah may whine or growl. A cub makes chirping sounds to call its mother.

For thousands of years, cheetahs were kept by royalty as hunting companions. In the 16th century, emperors of India used trained cheetahs to bring down antelopes. But today cheetahs are extinct in India. A few are left in the Middle East, and some remain in Africa. They have little land to roam because the grasslands on which they live have been broken up for farms and ranches. People still hunt the animals for their spotted skins. To help protect cheetahs from hunters, the United States has laws against importing their fur.

CHEETAH   🐾 **I of I species**

LENGTH OF HEAD AND BODY: **44-59 in (112-150 cm); tail, 23-31 in (58-79 cm)**

WEIGHT: **77-143 lb (35-65 kg)**

HABITAT AND RANGE: **grasslands and open woodlands in Africa and the Middle East**

FOOD: **antelopes, sheep, and smaller animals**

LIFE SPAN: **10 to 12 years in the wild**

REPRODUCTION: **I to 6 young after a pregnancy of 3 months**

ORDER: **carnivores**

▽ *Always alert, cubs and their mother watch for gazelles in the distance, even when resting.*

Chimpanzee

(chim-pan-ZEE)

NOISY AND CURIOUS, intelligent and social, the chimpanzee is the wild animal that is most like a human. Maybe that's why visitors to zoos seem to love chimps so much. Chimpanzees—like orangutans, gorillas, and gibbons—are apes. And apes belong to the primate order, a group that also includes lemurs, monkeys, and humans.

Chimps have long arms and short legs. Long black hair covers much of their bodies. Their faces, ears, fingers, and toes are bare. A full-grown male chimp usually measures about 4 feet (122 cm) long and weighs about 100 pounds (45 kg). Females are slightly shorter and lighter. The pygmy chimp is a smaller kind of chimpanzee.

Chimpanzees are found in the dense rain forests, in the open woodlands, and on the broad grasslands of Africa. Chimps spend much of their time on the ground, traveling on all fours. They may walk upright

for a short distance, especially if they are carrying something. They climb into trees to sleep and sometimes to find food.

Chimps are active during the day, searching for food and eating. They feed on fruit, leaves, seeds, buds, bark, stems, and insects. Scientists have also seen chimps catch and eat other small mammals such as young baboons.

Chimpanzees have hands that can grip firmly.

This allows them to pick up and use objects for special purposes. Sometimes the animals use leaves for sponges. They chew on the leaves, which makes them absorbent. Then the animals soak the leaves in water and suck on them to get moisture.

Chimps have been seen using sticks to drive intruders away. Chimps also use a blade of grass or a twig to fish termites or ants out of the ground. A chimp will push a twig into an insect nest, and the ants or

◁ *Chimpanzee finds a comfortable perch on a tree branch. The rain forests and open woodlands of Africa provide places for chimpanzees to play, feed, and sleep. The animals may also travel through grasslands.*

Anything there for me? A female chimp peers at ▷ *another female's mouth as she eats. Chimpanzees often share such foods as leaves, fruit, and small animals.*

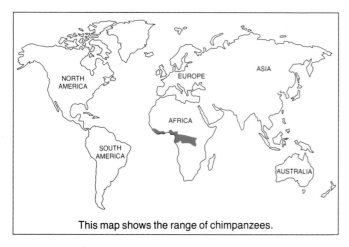

This map shows the range of chimpanzees.

CHIMPANZEE   🐾 **2 of 2 species**

***STANDING HEIGHT:* 3-5 ft (914-1,524 cm)**

***WEIGHT:* 55-110 lb (25-50 kg)**

***HABITAT AND RANGE:* rain forests, open woodlands, and grasslands of Africa**

***FOOD:* fruit, leaves, bark, stems, seeds, buds, insects, and other small animals**

***LIFE SPAN:* 35 to 40 years in the wild**

***REPRODUCTION:* usually 1 young after a pregnancy of about $8\frac{1}{2}$ months**

***ORDER:* primates**

Female chimp cradles her eight-month-old offspring ▷ *—a rare set of twins. Mothers nurse their young for several years. At times, other females help baby-sit.*

termites will cling to it. The chimp then pulls the twig out and picks the insects off with its lips.

Chimps live in communities of about fifty animals that share the same area. Within these large communities, chimps form smaller groups of three to six animals. The chimps in these groups travel together for a while. But they do not always stay together. Groups are always changing as chimps choose new companions. Most groups are a mixture of males,

▽ *Napping in a day nest in the trees, a chimp stretches out lazily. At night, the chimp will build another sleeping nest. It bends branches and twigs into a comfortable, leafy pad in a tree fork.*

females, and young. At times, however, only females and young remain together. At other times, a chimpanzee may travel alone.

When there is a large amount of food, chimps gather to have a feast. They bark loudly to announce the find. When other chimpanzees hear the call, they rush over to join in the eating. Chimps beg each other for some food by holding out their hands with the palms up.

Chimpanzees use a complicated system of sounds to communicate with each other. For example, a loud call like "wraaaa" warns of something that is unusual or disturbing. The calls can be heard 2 miles (3 km) away. To express contentment, a chimp grunts softly.

Touch is also important in the lives of chimpanzees. A nervous animal will reach out to touch another chimp. Chimps may kiss when they meet, and they also hold hands. An adult chimp sometimes has a special companion. The two chimps spend time together and comfort each other.

Another way a chimp communicates is by the expression on its face. When a chimpanzee bares its teeth, it lets others know that it is excited or frightened. If the animal grins with its lips covering its teeth, it means that it is in a friendly mood. If it puckers up its lips and looks as if it's about to give someone a big, smacking kiss, the chimp is worried. Another expression—lips pressed together—means the chimp may be about to charge or to attack.

Female chimps give their offspring a great deal of care. The young are born after an eight-and-a-half-month pregnancy. During the first months of a newborn's life, its mother carries it everywhere. The female cradles the tiny chimp carefully as it clings to

◁ *Like a small jockey, a two-year-old chimp rides on its mother's back. The youngster joins in her hooting call. Copying the behavior of an adult animal forms an important part of a chimp's education.*

Can you find the chimp hidden in the trees? Only his ▷ *head shows among the leaves. In the small picture, a mother chimp eats as her offspring clings to her belly. She uses her long, strong arm to hang from a branch. Chimps sometimes use their arms and hands to swing short distances in the trees.*

Chimpanzee _____

▽ *Young male chimpanzee picks through his mother's hair as she grooms her daughter. Grooming helps keep a chimp's skin and hair clean. It also provides important social contact for chimps in a group.*

△ *Using a blade of grass, a chimp fishes into a termite mound in search of food. The insects inside cling to the grass. Then the chimp pulls the grass out and gobbles up the termites. Chimps also use other objects found in the forests. They may use sticks as weapons. Or they may chew leaves and use them as sponges to soak up water.*

◁ *Two adult chimps open their mouths wide during a series of pants and hoots. Silent, a young chimp clings to its mother. Chimps sometimes pant-hoot when they find food. Chimps communicate many things by their calls. A soft bark means a mild warning. During grooming sessions, animals may grunt as they pick at one another's hair and skin.*

the hair on her belly. At about five months, the young chimp begins to ride on its mother's back. It perches there like a little jockey. Chimpanzee mothers play with their young, grooming and tickling them and sharing their sleeping nests with them at night. Female chimps help each other with baby-sitting chores. Older females will often look after their younger sisters and brothers.

Like humans, chimpanzees grow up slowly. When about nine years old, they begin adolescence. By the time they are 12 years old, they may have offspring of their own.

As young chimps grow and become better able to care for themselves, they play with other young chimps. Older chimpanzees in the community usually are patient with the energetic youngsters. They allow them to do pretty much as they please. And the young chimps do! They climb trees, wrestle with each other and their elders, and play with sticks, food, and other objects.

Play helps young chimpanzees learn about their world. By wrestling, they learn how strong they are and what they can do. They learn which branches are big enough to hold them. Young chimps also learn by trying to do what adults do. They make leafy sleeping nests. And they practice making the expressions their elders make and the calls they give. All of these activities are important to a young chimp's development.

They help the chimpanzee learn to take care of itself as an adult.

The intelligence of the chimpanzee has enabled scientists to teach captive animals many things. By studying how these primates react, experts can find out more about the learning process.

In the wild, the number of chimpanzees has become smaller. The wilderness in which the animals live is gradually disappearing. In recent years, scientists have studied chimps in Africa. What they have learned may make the difference between survival and extinction for chimpanzees.

Chinchilla

(chin-CHILL-uh)

COLD WINDS whip through the high Andes of South America. Few plants cover the rugged mountains. The wild chinchilla moves easily among the rocks in search of food. The cold does not bother the small rodent because it is covered with thick fur.

The chinchilla's head and body measure only about 10 inches (25 cm) long, and its fur is about 1 inch (3 cm) long. The soft, fine hairs range in color from bluish gray to brownish gray. Each hair may be tipped with black.

Wild chinchillas feed in the morning and in the evening, coming out of hiding places among the rocks to eat bark, grasses, and herbs. Sitting up, they hold their food in their forepaws as they gnaw on it. They do not drink much water. Chinchillas get most of the moisture they need from plants.

Chinchillas are born in litters of one to four young. They have fur at birth.

Long ago, Indians of South America used the chinchilla's soft fur for blankets and clothes. Today people still prize the fur, and wild chinchillas have been hunted until few are left. Most chinchillas now are raised on farms in several parts of the world. Their fur is used in making coats and jackets.

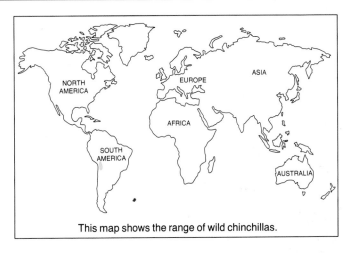

This map shows the range of wild chinchillas.

▽ *Chinchilla nibbles a plant with its sharp teeth. Like all rodents, a chinchilla must gnaw on hard substances to wear down its front teeth, which never stop growing.*

CHINCHILLA   🐾 **2 of 2 species**

LENGTH OF HEAD AND BODY: 9-15 in (23-38 cm); tail, 3-6 in (8-15 cm)

WEIGHT: 18-28 oz (510-794 g)

HABITAT AND RANGE: parts of the high Andes in South America; chinchillas are raised for their fur in several parts of the world

FOOD: bark, grasses, and herbs

LIFE SPAN: 15 to 20 years in captivity

REPRODUCTION: 1 to 4 young after a pregnancy of about 4 months

ORDER: rodents

Chipmunk

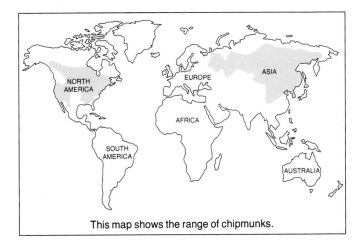

This map shows the range of chipmunks.

CHIPMUNK 🐾 4 of 25 species

LENGTH OF HEAD AND BODY: 4-7 in (10-18 cm); tail, 3-5 in (8-13 cm)

WEIGHT: 1-5 oz (28-142 g)

HABITAT AND RANGE: forests, open woodlands, and brushy areas in North America and Asia

FOOD: nuts, berries, seeds, fruit, grain, and insects

LIFE SPAN: about 2 or 3 years in the wild, 10 years in captivity

REPRODUCTION: 2 to 8 young after a pregnancy of about 1 month

ORDER: rodents

Least chipmunk: 4 in (10 cm) long; tail, 3 in (8 cm)

△ *Least chipmunk rests on a tree stump on a spring day. Smallest of about 17 kinds of chipmunks, the least chipmunk lives in parts of North America.*

SITTING UP, TAIL TWITCHING, forepaws clasped to its chest, a chipmunk sings to its neighbors. "Chip, chip," pipes the little striped rodent. When it spies an enemy—a weasel, a fox, a hawk, or a snake, for example—a chipmunk calls out a sudden warning and dashes for cover.

There are about 25 kinds of chipmunks. They range throughout North America and Asia. They are at home in forests, in open woodlands, and even in city parks. Some chipmunks dig burrows. Others build nests in bushes or logs. You have probably seen one of these grayish or brownish animals on the ground or on a branch.

Chipmunks spend the summer eating plants and insects. Then, in early fall, they begin to gather nuts and seeds for winter. They tuck the food under rocks and logs or inside their burrows. As cold weather sets in, most chipmunks move underground to sleep. From time to time, they wake up and eat the food they have stored.

When spring arrives, chipmunks emerge from their burrows and find mates. Females bear two to eight young about four weeks later. For two months, the parents care for their offspring. Then the young chipmunks begin putting away their own food for the winter ahead.

Cheek pouches packed with food, a watchful eastern chipmunk (left) pauses on a limb. It can stuff several acorns at a time into its mouth. Gathering nuts and seeds takes up most of a chipmunk's time. At right, another eastern chipmunk emerges from its burrow.

Eastern chipmunk: 7 in (18 cm) long; tail, 4 in (10 cm)

Civet

Fanaloka, a small civet of Madagascar, balances on a rock. This rare animal usually lives in forests.

FORESTS, GRASSLANDS, AND MARSHES—lean, long-tailed civets roam through them all. Civets live in a variety of habitats and are known by many names. Genets, linsangs, and binturongs all are kinds of civets. You can read about them under their own headings in this book.

Civets live in parts of Asia, in central and southern Africa, and on the island of Madagascar. They make their homes in trees, in piles of brush, among roots, and between rocks.

Palm civets spend most of their time in trees. They sleep curled up on a branch or in a tangle of tree limbs. Palm civets eat small animals as well as fruit they find among the leaves and on the ground.

The African civet stays on the ground. It sleeps in a grassy bed or in a rocky shelter. When it wakes, it pads softly through the underbrush in search of such food as insects, rodents, birds, and fruit.

The otter civet is adapted, or suited, to life in the water. This strong swimmer gets its food by catching frogs and fish in rivers of southern Asia.

Most civets sleep through the tropical heat of the day and awake to hunt at night. Their striped and spotted fur blends in well with their shadowy surroundings. Though they usually live alone, civets have a way to communicate with each other. They use their sense of smell.

Civets have many scent glands in their bodies. As a civet travels, it makes scent marks along its path. These marks let others know that a civet has passed by. By sniffing, a civet can tell whether the civet that left the mark is looking for a mate.

Some civets have glands under their tails that produce a strong-smelling oil. For centuries, people have used this oil from captured civets to make perfume. People have been familiar with some kinds of civets for a long time. But not much is known about these animals in the wild.

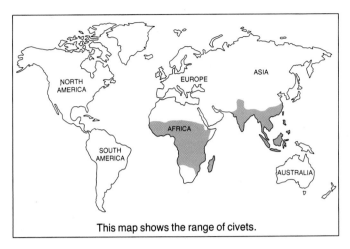

This map shows the range of civets.

CIVET 🐾 **9 of 17 species**

LENGTH OF HEAD AND BODY: **16-35 in (41-89 cm); tail, 7-26 in (18-66 cm)**

WEIGHT: **2-44 lb (1-20 kg)**

HABITAT AND RANGE: **forests, woodlands, and grasslands of Madagascar, southern and southeastern Asia, and central and southern Africa**

FOOD: **fruit and small animals, including rodents, birds, reptiles, shellfish, and insects**

LIFE SPAN: **up to 28 years in captivity**

REPRODUCTION: **1 to 4 young after a pregnancy of 2 or 3 months**

ORDER: **carnivores**

Small-toothed palm civet: 18 in (46 cm) long; tail, 21 in (53 cm)

△ *Small-toothed palm civet clutches an egg in its front paws. Although palm civets eat mostly fruit, they sometimes vary their diet by raiding birds' nests. The animal's grayish coloring blends well with its surroundings in the forests of Asia.*

▽ *Nose to the ground, an African civet follows a scent. Like some other civets, this animal produces oil in a gland under its tail. By pressing its rump against trees, bushes, and rocks, it makes a scent mark.*

African civet: 33 in (84 cm) long; tail, 18 in (46 cm)

Coati

THEY SNORT AND SNUFFLE along the ground, looking for something to eat. As coatis wander through a tropical forest, they rustle through the leaves. They grunt softly to one another.

A member of the raccoon family, the coati is a very social animal. About four to twenty female coatis travel with their young in a group called a band. The band spends most of the day searching for food. From time to time, coatis stop moving around. As they rest, they groom each other by nibbling at one another's fur. At night, they sleep in the trees. Male coatis live alone, except during the mating season.

Yawning after a nap, a coati bumps its nose ▷
on a tree branch. Because of the coati's long snout,
people sometimes call the animal the hog-nosed coon.

▽ *Bushy brown-and-white tails wave in the air as*
ring-tailed coatis in Brazil look for food. Because of
the animals' tails, people sometimes mistake coatis for
monkeys. Coatis really belong to the raccoon family.

Coati: 25 in (64 cm) long; tail, 25 in (64 cm)

Ring-tailed coati: 25 in (64 cm) long; tail, 25 in (64 cm)

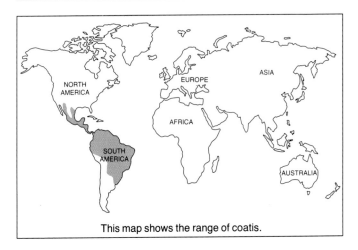

This map shows the range of coatis.

▽ *Extending its long tail for balance, a coati climbs a tree in Arizona. Coatis feed on fruit and insects in trees. To get the food, they may hang upside down.*

COATI 🐾 **1 of 2 species**

LENGTH OF HEAD AND BODY: 13-27 in (33-69 cm); tail, 13-27 in (33-69 cm)

WEIGHT: 7-15 lb (3-7 kg)

HABITAT AND RANGE: dense forests, grasslands, and brushy areas from the southwestern United States through northern Argentina

FOOD: insects, snails, small reptiles, rodents, fruit, and nuts

LIFE SPAN: 14 years in captivity

REPRODUCTION: 2 to 6 young after a pregnancy of about 2½ months

ORDER: carnivores

Females leave their bands to bear young—usually two to six. They have their young in nests that they build in trees. In five or six weeks, they return to the group, bringing their offspring with them.

Young coatis join their mothers in search of food as soon as they leave the nest. But they play much of the time, wrestling or chasing one another among the trees. The young will be full grown when they are two years old.

The coati is sometimes called the hog-nosed coon because of its long snout. Its nose is very sensitive. Coatis find food by sniffing until they detect an animal or a piece of fruit. When a coati smells prey underground, it uses strong claws to dig it out.

Each band of females and young has a home area where it searches for food. Each male coati has its own territory. At certain times of the year, coatis travel more widely to find food. When fruit is in season, coatis might make a special trip to a place where many fruit trees grow.

Most coatis are found in dense, wet forests from Mexico into South America. Since the beginning of the century, they have moved into the southwestern United States, even where there are few trees. The coatis that live in the Southwest often sleep in caves and rock piles, instead of on branches.

▽ *Coati drinks from a small pool in Arizona. Most coatis live in wet forests in Central and South America, but their range has spread north to drier areas.*

Colobus

The colobus is a kind of monkey. Read about monkeys on page 370.

Cougar

Cougar is another name for mountain lion. Read about it and other wild cats on page 126.

Cow

Texas Longhorn: 58 in (147 cm) tall at the shoulder

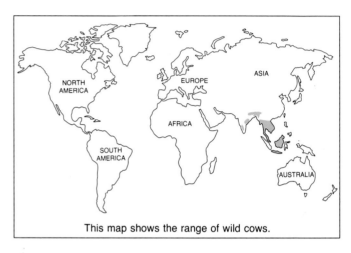

This map shows the range of wild cows.

◁ On a grassy prairie, a Texas Longhorn bull chews his cud. His horns measure about 4 feet (122 cm) from tip to tip. During the 1800s, cowboys herded millions of Longhorns on cattle drives north from Texas.

WE SEE THEM—and hear them mooing—when we visit a farm. Some cows are brown and white, some are tan, some are red, and some are black and white. Others are pure black or pure white with large humps on their shoulders. Cows are some of the most familiar farm animals in the world. We also use the word "cow" to refer to a female. The male animals are bulls, and the young are calves. Cows in general are often called cattle.

Cows have been domesticated—tamed and raised by people—for thousands of years. Cows are native to Europe, Asia, and Africa. They are now found in many other parts of the world. In some places in Africa, a person's wealth may be judged by the number of cows he owns.

All cows have long, tufted tails. They use them as switches to help keep pesky insects off their backs and sides. You probably have seen cows standing in fields, swinging their tails back and forth to keep flies away. As they stand there, they calmly chew wads of food called cuds.

A cow has a special stomach with four compartments that digest the huge amount of grass the animal eats. A cow swallows its food after chewing it only a little. In the first and second parts of its stomach, the food combines with liquid and forms into cuds. Later, the cow brings up a cud and chews it more completely. Then it swallows the cud, which ends up in the third and fourth parts of the stomach to be further digested. Some other animals that chew cuds are antelopes, deer, goats, and sheep.

On farms around the world, cows are raised for two important kinds of food: milk and meat. Milk cows are called dairy cows. In many parts of the world today, dairy farms have modern milking equipment. Machines squeeze the milk from a cow's udder—the baglike part of her body where the milk collects. But cows are still milked by hand in many places. Someone will sit beside the animal and gently squeeze the milk into a pail.

The large, black-and-white Holstein-Friesians (HOLE-steen FREE-zhunz) are the most common dairy

Hereford: 52 in (132 cm) tall at the shoulder

Hereford cows and calves, raised for beef, huddle against November winds in a Montana pasture.

Highland: 54 in (137 cm) tall at the shoulder

Holstein-Friesian: 58 in (147 cm) tall at the shoulder

△ *Coarse, shaggy coat of a Highland bull protects it from harsh weather in Scotland. People have raised these hardy animals for centuries for their meat.*

△ *Newborn Holstein-Friesian calf stands for the first time. Its mother watches her unsteady offspring. Cows usually bear one young every year.*

159

cows in the United States. Some other widespread dairy breeds are brown Jerseys and tan-and-white Guernseys (GURN-zeez). Both Jerseys and Guernseys are famous for their creamy yellow milk, which is rich in butterfat.

Herefords (HER-ferdz) are a popular beef breed. You can recognize them by their white faces and reddish coats. Sometimes their coats are quite curly. The Hereford breed came from England originally, but these cattle now are found on farms and on ranches all over the United States. Aberdeen Angus, beef cattle originally from Scotland, are thickset animals with black bodies. Unlike many other breeds, Aberdeen Angus cattle have no horns.

Besides providing milk and meat, cows give us hides for leather as well as substances used in medicine, soap, and glue. In some parts of the world, domestic cattle are still used to pull carts and plows. Cows are useful—most of the time. There are 1.3 billion cows in the world, and nearly all of them belong to farmers or herders.

Most cows give birth to one calf after a pregnancy of about nine months. The calves may nurse for as long as eight months. During this time, they will also eat grass.

Modern breeds of cows can be traced back to wild European cattle called aurochs (OW-rocks). Aurochs are now extinct. But we know what the animals looked like. Thousands of years ago, people painted pictures of aurochs on the walls of caves.

Several kinds of wild cattle—sometimes known as oxen—live in Asia. Bantengs (BON-tengz) roam the forests of Southeast Asia. They have brown coats and white rump patches. Marks that look like white stockings cover their legs. Bantengs live in herds and are often active at dawn, at dusk, and sometimes even at night. Some of them have been domesticated and live on farms.

Gaur, large dark brown cattle, live in forests in

▽ *Herd of gaur—females and young—graze in a grassy clearing in India. The largest wild cattle, gaur live in forested hills. They usually move around and feed between dusk and dawn.*

Gaur: 72 in (183 cm) tall at the shoulder

Zebu: 56 in (142 cm) tall at the shoulder

◁ *Zebus wander through a meadow in Brazil. These humpbacked cattle, originally from India, survive easily in hot climates. Ranchers often breed them with other cattle to produce even hardier animals.*

COW 👣 **3 of 4 species**

HEIGHT: 46-75 in (117-191 cm) at the shoulder

WEIGHT: 325-3,000 lb (147-1,361 kg)

HABITAT AND RANGE: grassy plains, open and dense woodlands, rain forests, and hilly areas in India, Nepal, Burma, and Southeast Asia; domesticated cows live in many parts of the world

FOOD: grasses, herbs, leaves, twigs, and bamboo shoots

LIFE SPAN: 12 to 26 years in captivity, depending on species

REPRODUCTION: usually 1 young after a pregnancy of about 9 months

ORDER: artiodactyls

India and Southeast Asia. They often feed in the evening and in the early morning on grasses, herbs, and leaves. They are the largest of all wild cattle. Like bantengs, gaur have stockinglike white marks on their lower legs. Their horns curve in a half-moon shape toward each other. In spite of their size, gaur can move quickly in times of danger. They make a snorting sound as they speed away.

In India, people of the Hindu religion consider cows sacred. They do not kill or eat the animals. Indian cows—or zebus (ZEE-booz)—are often grayish white, though some zebus may be black or red. The zebu has a hump on its shoulders. A fold of skin, called a dewlap, hangs down from its neck. Sometimes the dewlap almost reaches the ground. Zebus give milk and are used to pull plows. Some zebus wander freely in cities and towns. They often cause trouble, stopping traffic and eating food from open-air markets.

Banteng bull in Java (below) swishes his tufted tail and tosses his slender horns. In the wild, bantengs roam in herds of as many as 25 animals. Two Ankole cattle in Africa chew their cuds (below, left). A female's horns can measure 5 feet (152 cm) across. But a bull's horns do not grow as big. Can you recognize the female here?

Ankole: 52 in (132 cm) tall at the shoulder

Banteng: 59 in (150 cm) tall at the shoulder

Coyote

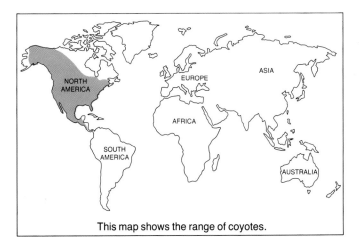

This map shows the range of coyotes.

◁ *Alone and watchful, a coyote sits among golden grasses in Yellowstone National Park. People have nicknamed this sly animal "prairie wolf" after its larger relative, the wolf.*

▽ *Lone coyote sings to the sky. By sending its call across the prairie, it lets other coyotes know where it is. In the evening, many animals may join the chorus.*

IN SOME INDIAN STORIES, the trickiest creature of all is Coyote. And in real life, coyotes *are* clever animals. They quickly take advantage of changes around them. Once coyotes lived mainly on the prairies and in the deserts of North America. But as people settled across the land, coyotes learned to survive in mountains and in forests, too. Now they roam throughout much of the continent.

The coyote's tan coat is usually mixed with hairs of rusty brown and gray. This helps the coyote hide in grasses, among rocks, or in underbrush.

As it hunts, the coyote uses its sharp eyesight, keen hearing, and sensitive nose. It trots long distances in search of prey.

Coyotes will eat almost anything. In the summer, they usually feed on mice, rabbits, and insects. Coyotes also catch fish and frogs. They pounce on snakes and lizards. They even feed on grasses, nuts, and fruit—including watermelon! Coyotes eat dead elk and deer that they find—especially in winter.

Coyotes and badgers sometimes help each other when they hunt. Chased by a coyote, a rabbit or a mouse may run into a hole. There a badger can dig it out. At other times, a badger may dig for a ground squirrel, only to have it pop out of another entrance and escape. When the ground squirrel emerges, a waiting coyote can grab it.

△ *Coyote pounces on its prey—perhaps a mouse scurrying through the grass. Coyotes use their keen senses when they hunt for food.*

163

△ Winter snow does not stop a coyote. Its thick fur protects it in even the harshest weather. The colors in its coat help it blend into many kinds of surroundings.

Defending its food, a coyote growls at an intruder. ▷ Bold magpies join in the feast. Coyotes often find dead animals to eat by watching the sky for circling birds.

Some coyotes kill lambs and calves. So, for a century, many people have tried to get rid of coyotes—with guns, poisons, and traps. Still, coyotes continue to thrive in North America.

Coyotes may live in family groups of parents and young. Each family guards its own area. The animals mark the area with urine to show that it is occupied. They defend their area fiercely, especially in spring. The pups are born then. And the coyotes need to protect the young and to make sure there is enough food for a growing family.

A coyote may dig its den in a hidden spot, often under a hollow tree or on a bushy hillside. There the female bears three to twelve pups.

Both parents care for the pups. They chew food partially and swallow it. Later they bring it up again for the pups to eat.

Pups learn to hunt by chasing insects. A parent may also bring home a live mouse for them to practice on. By fall, the pups are ready to hunt on their own or with their parents.

Coyotes woof softly to warn their young. A bark tells their enemies to keep away. In the evening, several coyotes may "sing" in chorus. One of them starts off with a string of sharp yips. Then it gives a howl. Other coyotes join in. Soon their song echoes across the hills.

COYOTE

LENGTH OF HEAD AND BODY: 32-37 in (81-94 cm); tail, 16 in (41 cm)

WEIGHT: 20-50 lb (9-23 kg)

HABITAT AND RANGE: forests, prairies, deserts, and mountains of North America

FOOD: rodents, lizards, snakes, fish, grasses, fruit, and grain

LIFE SPAN: up to 14½ years in the wild, 22 years in captivity

REPRODUCTION: 3 to 12 young after a pregnancy of 2 months

ORDER: carnivores

▽ *Peeking over a snowdrift, a coyote perks its ears and listens for other animals. Coyotes communicate by the positions of ears, tails, and the rest of their bodies.*

Coypu

WHEN IT HEARS A NOISE, the shy coypu perks its small ears and wiggles its long whiskers. Then this furry, groundhog-size rodent runs to the water's edge and jumps in. Clumsy on land, the coypu moves gracefully in the water. Paddling with its webbed hind feet, it swims quickly to safety.

The coypu digs a burrow in the soft earth of a riverbank. Or it may build a nest of reeds in a marsh or along a lakeshore. In these wet places, the coypu searches for plants, mussels, and snails to eat. With its forepaw it skims the water for food or reaches underwater to yank out a reed or a root.

Coypus live in pairs or in large colonies. Females give birth to two or three litters every year. Usually a litter has five to seven young. When the newborn are only five days old, they are able to survive on their own. Usually, though, they stay with their mothers for six to eight weeks.

Trappers have long hunted the coypu for its thick, valuable fur. Beneath the coarse, reddish

brown outer hair is an undercoat of brown or dark gray. This soft fur, called nutria (NYU-tree-uh), is sometimes made into winter jackets and overcoats. Nutria is also another name for the coypu.

Coypus originally were found only in southern South America. Today they are raised in many parts of the world for their fur. Sometimes coypus escape from the fur farms, and many of the animals now live wild in North America. In some areas, they are pests because they destroy crops.

COYPU

LENGTH OF HEAD AND BODY: 17-25 in (43-64 cm); tail, 10-16 in (25-41 cm)

WEIGHT: 15-22 lb (7-10 kg)

HABITAT AND RANGE: near rivers and lakes in North and South America

FOOD: water plants, mussels, and snails

LIFE SPAN: about 6 years in captivity

REPRODUCTION: usually 5 to 7 young after a pregnancy of about 4 months

ORDER: rodents

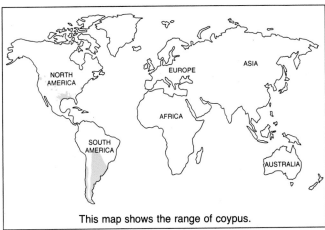

This map shows the range of coypus.

◁ *Curving its long tail under its chin, a coypu suns itself on a post. It feeds on the plants floating nearby.*

▽ *Orange teeth gleaming in the sun, a coypu paddles through the water with its webbed hind feet. The animal can dive underwater and stay for five minutes.*

Spotted cuscus: 20 in (51 cm) long; tail, 17 in (43 cm)

Cuscus

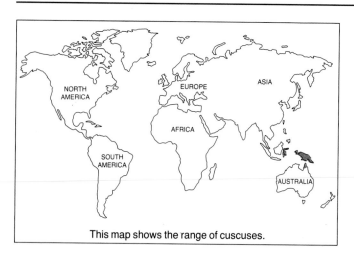

This map shows the range of cuscuses.

ALL DAY LONG, the furry cuscus sits in a treetop overlooking its dense forest home. The cuscus eats and often sleeps in a sitting position. In fact, this animal spends so much time sitting that it often rubs a bare place on its rump!

A good climber, the cuscus hardly ever comes down from the trees. To help keep a firm grip on the branches, the cuscus uses its hind paws as well as its front paws. The animal wraps its strong, thick tail around tree limbs for more security.

During the night, the cuscus moves along tree branches looking for food. Occasionally, it quietly creeps up on a lizard or a bird and grabs it with its front paws. This adds variety to the leaves, fruit, and insects that it usually eats.

Cuscuses rarely hurry. They are usually safe in the treetops. The animals have few enemies where they live on the northeastern tip of Australia, in New Guinea, and on nearby islands. If another animal does threaten or annoy a cuscus, the animal will strike with its front paws. It barks and snarls sharply, frightening away the intruder.

Some people consider the cuscus one of the most colorful mammals in the world. Many cuscuses have bright yellow noses and bulging yellow, orange, or red eyes. Their fur comes in many colors—from white or yellow, to black or grayish green. Patterns often decorate their woolly coats.

◁ *High-wire artist, a spotted cuscus creeps along a branch by gripping with all four paws. For extra support, the cuscus can curl its tail around a tree limb.*

▽ *Big eyes stare out from the face of a spotted cuscus. Keen sight helps this animal move about the trees at night in search of lizards, birds, insects, and fruit.*

△ *Quiet during the day, a "spotless" spotted cuscus nestles in the branches. Cuscuses wear coats of many colors and patterns. An animal's fur may change color several times as it grows older.*

The cuscus's fur often grows so thick that it covers the animal's small ears. The cuscus grooms its fur by combing it with its claws.

The cuscus is about the size of a monkey, and some people mistake it for one. However, cuscuses belong to the group of pouched mammals called marsupials (mar-SOO-pea-ulz). The marsupials give birth to very small, underdeveloped young. These offspring stay in their mother's protective pouch for several months, until they are bigger. A female cuscus bears one or two young each year. Find out about other marsupials by reading the entries on kangaroos on page 304 and koalas on page 312.

CUSCUS 🐾 **4 of 17 species**

LENGTH OF HEAD AND BODY: 13-26 in (33-66 cm); tail, 10-25 in (25-64 cm)

WEIGHT: as much as 11 lb (5 kg)

HABITAT AND RANGE: forests of northeastern Australia, New Guinea, and neighboring islands

FOOD: leaves, fruit, insects, lizards, small birds, and eggs

LIFE SPAN: 3 to 11 years in captivity, depending on species

REPRODUCTION: 1 or 2 young after a pregnancy of about 2 weeks

ORDER: marsupials

D

Powerful hind legs of a white-tailed deer buck swing forward in a bounding stride. White-tailed deer can run for several

Deer

EVERY SPRING, new sets of antlers begin to sprout from the heads of male deer in many parts of the world. Antlers are not the same as horns. Antlers are bones that develop and usually fall off each year. Horns grow out of the skin, just as hair and fingernails do. They never stop growing.

When antlers first begin to develop, they look like two bumps on the top of a deer's head. They grow quickly and branch out. But the antlers remain soft and tender for the first few months, until they reach their full size. Velvet, a layer of soft skin and fine hairs, covers the antlers. Late in the summer, when the antlers have stopped growing, the velvet dries up. The male deer rubs it off on trees and bushes, revealing the hard, sharp points of the antlers.

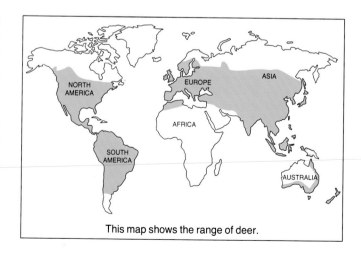

This map shows the range of deer.

miles at speeds of 30 miles (48 km) an hour.

△ *Shielded by its mother, a young white-tailed deer watches wood ducks in Florida. The young stays with its mother for one or two years. Deer often feed on plants near ponds and streams.*

◁ *Spotted coat of a six-week-old white-tailed deer blends well with grass and bushes. Because the newborn have no scent, even enemies with keen senses of smell cannot easily find them.*

171

Deer

Of the many kinds of deer, only two do not have antlers. Musk deer and Chinese water deer have tusks, or long teeth, instead. Both of these kinds live in Asia. Other deer, the Asian muntjac (MUNT-jack) and the South American guemal (GWAY-mul) have both tusks and antlers. The female deer of most species do not develop antlers.

A male deer, often called a buck, carries his

Red deer: 45 in (114 cm) tall at the shoulder

△ *Antlers clash as young male red deer in Scotland test their strength. These close relatives of North American elk live in many parts of Europe.*

Antlers come in a ▷ variety of shapes. A sambar deer of India (right) has thin, branching antlers. But the antlers of a fallow deer (far right) are shaped like hands with the fingers spread. Older males usually have larger antlers.

172

Sambar deer: 54 in (137 cm) tall at the shoulder

Fallow deer: 37 in (94 cm) tall at the shoulder

antlers for several months. In winter, after the mating season, the bony branches fall off. First one antler and then the other drops to the ground. The buck has no antlers until the following year. Smaller animals like mice, squirrels, and porcupines gnaw on the old antlers. The bones are rich in the minerals that these animals need.

During the mating season, the bucks strut and show off their antlers. They use them to keep their rivals away and to attract the attention of female deer—often called does. Two bucks threaten each other by snorting loudly and by shaking their heads. If the bucks spar, they shove and wrestle with their antlers and tear up the earth with their hooves. Their antlers may crash together, but the sharp tips seldom reach the bodies of the bucks. Such a match may last for two hours, until one buck gives up and dashes off. Usually neither deer is seriously hurt. The winner and the doe stay together for several days. Then the buck leaves her to find another mate.

Most female deer give birth to one or two young each spring, six to nine months after mating. The fawns, or offspring, of many kinds of deer have spotted coats. But the patterns disappear after a few months, when the fawns grow their winter coats. In a few kinds of deer—the fallow deer of Europe and the axis deer, hog deer, and sika deer of Asia—adult animals have spotted coats too. *(Continued on page 176)*

Every spring, a male white-tailed deer begins to grow new antlers. First, knobs appear (1). By late summer, antlers have formed (2) under a cover of skin called velvet. The velvet peels off in strips (3), revealing sharp points. In winter, the antlers fall off, usually one at a time (4). They leave small wounds that heal quickly.

Short, hooked antlers of an Asian muntjac (below, left) sprout from bony ridges on its face. Instead of antlers, a male musk deer of Asia (below, center) has sharp tusks that measure 2 inches (5 cm) long. A brocket deer in Mexico (below, right) has short, spiky antlers. Antlers of brocket deer can be present any time of year.

Muntjac: 21 in (53 cm) tall at the shoulder

Musk deer: 22 in (56 cm) tall at the shoulder

Brocket deer: 26 in (66 cm) tall at the shoulder

Deer

△ Pawing the soft snow, a mule deer buck searches for food. Large ears give the mule deer its name. It lives in mountains, plains, and deserts of the western United States. Bucks usually roam alone or in small groups.

Guemal fawn copies its mother's alert pose. Guemals live in the rugged Andes of ▷ South America, from Ecuador through Chile. In winter, Chilean guemals leave the mountains to find shelter in the forests below.

Golden coats of swamp ▷ deer gleam in the sunshine after an April shower in India. A group of male and female adults and young feeds on lush grasses that grow in the rainy season. The hooves of these deer spread out to support their weight on soft, wet ground.

Swamp deer: 45 in (114 cm) tall at the shoulder

174

Guemal: 33 in (84 cm) tall at the shoulder

Hog deer: 28 in (71 cm) tall at the shoulder

△ Heavyset, short-legged body of a hog deer gives the animal its name. The hog deer does not run gracefully as most deer do. Instead it dashes through tall grass like a wild pig. Called the paddy-field deer in Sri Lanka, it feeds on growing rice.

175

Deer

The spotted coats of the fawns blend with forests and grasslands and make the young hard to see. Newborn fawns are also protected from danger because they have no scent. Even a dog, with its sensitive nose, may not smell a nearby fawn.

When the fawn is strong enough, its mother takes it to join a group of other does and their young. Fawns play together. They stand on their hind legs and box with their forelegs. Or they butt and chase each other. Their safety from enemies may depend on the lessons that they learn during such play. Many animals prey on deer. In North America, the deer's natural enemies include coyotes, wolves, bears, and mountain lions.

Elsewhere, deer are hunted by big cats like tigers, leopards, and jaguars.

Deer feed early in the morning and again in the evening. They tear off bites of grass, bark, leaves, and twigs and then swallow the food almost whole. After eating, when a deer lies hidden, it brings up a wad of partly digested food—called a cud—from its stomach. The deer chews the cud thoroughly, swallows it, and digests it completely.

Because they have so many enemies, deer must be alert. They rely mostly on their keen senses of sight, smell, and hearing to warn them when enemies are nearby. When danger first threatens, deer may freeze. Then they run away. White-tailed deer can gallop for about 4 miles (6 km) at 30 miles (48 km) an hour. They usually run much shorter distances, however. They try to find a hiding place in a grove of trees or just over a hill from danger.

Today deer are found on all continents except Antarctica. The smallest deer, the pudu, is the size of a raccoon. It weighs about 20 pounds (9 kg). The moose, the largest member of the deer family, can measure 7 feet (213 cm) tall at the shoulder. It can weigh 1,800 pounds (816 kg).

In North America, most deer are white-tailed deer. About 14 million of them live in the United States, making them the most common of the country's large mammals. White-tailed deer may grow more than 4 feet (123 cm) tall at the shoulder and weigh as much as 300 pounds (136 kg). West of the Mississippi River, the most common deer are mule deer. They get their name from long, mulelike ears.

For centuries, people have hunted white-tailed deer for food, for sport, and for their skins. The skins often were used for jackets and other clothing and for moccasins. Many years ago, people who lived on the frontier even used deer hides, known as buckskins, as a kind of money. That's why people sometimes call a dollar bill a "buck."

Find out about other members of the deer family by reading about caribou on page 120, elk on page 198, and moose on page 386.

Pudu: 15 in (38 cm) tall at the shoulder

△ *Pudu doe picks her way through the grass. The smallest of all deer, the raccoon-size pudu makes its home in forests and mountains in South America.*

DEER   🐾 **18 of 43 species**

HEIGHT: 15 in-7 ft (38-213 cm) tall at the shoulder

WEIGHT: 20-1,800 lb (9-816 kg)

HABITAT AND RANGE: woodlands, mountains, forests, grasslands, and deserts in Europe, Asia, northern Africa, the Middle East, North and South America. People brought them to New Zealand, Australia, and some Pacific Islands.

FOOD: grasses, bark, twigs, and leaves

LIFE SPAN: up to 20 years in the wild

REPRODUCTION: 1 to 3 young after a pregnancy of 5 to 10 months, depending on species

ORDER: artiodactyls

Like mirror images, male sika deer in Japan rear up ▷ and prepare to box. With their antlers still soft and sensitive in velvet, the males settle disputes by fighting with their forelegs.

Sika deer: 35 in (89 cm) tall at the shoulder

Dik-dik

The dik-dik is a kind of antelope. Read about antelopes on page 52.

Dingo

(DING-go)

◁ *Male dingo, a wild dog of Australia, watches the grasslands. Dingoes sometimes howl like wolves.*

DENSE FORESTS and open, dry plains provide homes for the dingo of Australia. Dingoes are thought to be related to other primitive dogs of southern Asia. Some scientists think that they were brought to Australia by traders about 3,500 years ago. Only partially tame, the animals soon escaped from human control and ran wild again.

Dingoes hunt at night, alone or in family groups. They eat rats, rabbits, lizards, birds, and kangaroos. Sometimes they prey on farm animals.

Dingoes make their dens in underground burrows or in hollow logs. There a pair has a litter of four or five pups each year. Pups may stay with their parents for two years and help raise the next litter.

Sometimes Aboriginals, the native people of Australia, train dingoes as hunting dogs. They capture and raise wild pups. Dingoes once even served as living blankets. A chilly night was a "three-dog night." A really cold one was a "six-dog night."

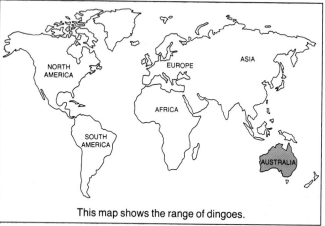

This map shows the range of dingoes.

DINGO

LENGTH OF HEAD AND BODY: 46-49 in (117-124 cm); tail, 12-13 in (30-33 cm)

WEIGHT: 22-33 lb (10-15 kg)

HABITAT AND RANGE: forests, open plains, deserts, and rocky mountains in Australia; close relatives in New Guinea

FOOD: rabbits, rodents, lizards, birds, fruit, marsupials, sheep, and cattle

REPRODUCTION: 4 or 5 pups a year after a pregnancy of 2 months

LIFE SPAN: up to 15 years

ORDER: carnivores

Dog

"MAN'S BEST FRIEND," the dog was probably the first animal ever to be tamed. Today domestic, or tame, dogs are our companions at work and at play, in the city and in the countryside, in North America and all over the world.

All domestic dogs make up only one of the 36 species, or kinds, of dogs. All of the other kinds of dogs live in the wild.

Wild dogs, like wild cats, are carnivores (CAR-nuh-vorz). That means they are mainly meat-eating hunters. But dogs and cats hunt in different ways. Dogs usually run down their prey. Most cats lie in wait for prey or creep up on their victims. Cats almost always hunt alone. Dogs may hunt alone or in pairs to find small prey. Larger dogs can bring down animals much bigger than they are by hunting together in packs. Smaller wild dogs eat small mammals, insects, fruit, and birds.

Long legs and deep chests give most dogs the speed and the strength they need to catch swift prey. Pads on the bottoms of their paws cushion their feet as they run.

When they have chased their prey to exhaustion, wild dogs attack and kill with powerful jaws. Front teeth bite flesh. Back teeth cut the meat into large chunks. Dogs do little real chewing. They simply swallow their food.

Wild dogs have keen senses. Most find prey by sniffing the air or the ground. A dog's sense of smell is much better than that of a human being. On open plains, sharp-eyed dogs can spot the movement of distant prey. In brushy areas, their ears catch sounds of small, scurrying animals.

Some wild dogs mate for life. A female has one

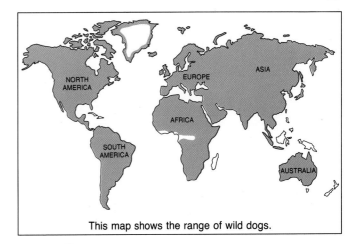

This map shows the range of wild dogs.

DOG 🐾 **3 of 4 species**

LENGTH OF HEAD AND BODY: 14-57 in (36-145 cm); tail, 5-20 in (13-51 cm); domestic dogs are measured in height at the shoulder—6-33 in (15-84 cm)

WEIGHT: 3-175 lb (1-79 kg)

HABITAT AND RANGE: all kinds of habitats almost everywhere in the world; domestic dogs live in many parts of the world

FOOD: animals and plants

LIFE SPAN: 12 to 20 years in captivity, depending on species

REPRODUCTION: 2 to 12 pups after a pregnancy of about 2 months, depending on species

ORDER: carnivores

▽ *Lean and hardy, a dhole listens for danger. People sometimes call this animal the red dog of Asia.*

▽ *Stocky and short-legged, a bush dog of South America can scurry easily through dense underbrush.*

Dhole: 35 in (89 cm) long; tail, 17 in (43 cm)

Bush dog: 25 in (64 cm) long; tail, 5 in (13 cm)

litter a year. There are usually four to six furry, help-less pups in a litter. Both parents help care for the young. Some pups go off on their own before they are a year old. Others stay with their parents and help rear the next litter.

You can read about some of the better known wild dogs—coyotes, dingoes, foxes, jackals, raccoon dogs, and wolves—under their own headings in this book. Other wild dogs include the dhole (DOLE) of Asia, the bush dog of South America, and the Cape hunting dog of Africa.

Dholes usually hunt in packs of five to twelve ani-mals. In the forests of India, dholes run down axis deer and sambar deer. High in the mountains of Chi-na and Tibet, packs of dholes hunt wild goats and mountain sheep.

Bush dogs roam grassy swamps and tropical for-ests near rivers in South America. They probably live in family groups of as many as ten animals. During the daytime, these bands hunt such rodents as pacas. The stocky bodies, short legs, and webbed paws of bush dogs are well suited to swimming. If their prey runs away and jumps into a river, bush dogs will dive in af-ter it. Some dogs may already be waiting in the water for the prey.

Cape hunting dogs search for herds of antelopes and zebras on the plains and in the woodlands of east-ern, central, and southern Africa. They usually travel in packs of ten to twenty dogs. Before they hunt, the dogs jump around, make twittering calls, and lick each other's faces. It looks as if they are having a pep rally. Because they cooperate, Cape hunting dogs are successful pack hunters.

All the adults in a pack of Cape hunting dogs help care for the pups. Pups beg for food from returning hunters. The adults then bring up meat they have

Cape hunting dog: 40 in (102 cm) long; tail, 14 in (36 cm)

◁ *Young wildebeest staggers as a pack of Cape hunting dogs closes in for the kill. When they hunt, these African wild dogs go after a slow animal. The pack chases the animal until it cannot go any farther.*

▽ *Pausing during its meal, a Cape hunting dog watches for hyenas that might try to steal its kill.*

△ *In friendly play, Cape hunting dogs rear up and lunge at each other's throats. When excited, the dogs utter twittering, birdlike cries.*

swallowed and carried back in their stomachs. Old and lame animals and those that stayed behind to watch the pups are fed in the same way. Sadly, people have nearly exterminated the fascinating Cape hunting dogs.

Domestic dogs are relatives of wild dogs. Scientists think all dogs may have descended from small south Asian wolves. Thousands of years ago, people began to tame the wild dogs that came prowling around their camps, probably in search of food. Later some tame dogs may have become wild again.

Today there are several hundred breeds of domestic dogs. They range in size from the tiny Chihuahua to the huge Irish Wolfhound. Their coats can be smooth and short or thick and shaggy. Some domestic dogs could not survive in the wild now. But domestic dogs and wild dogs still share many of the same traits.

Most dogs defend their territories fiercely. A pet

Two Cocker Spaniels lounge on a ▷
tree stump. Popular family pets, these
animals were once used to hunt birds.

Old English Sheepdog: 22 in (56 cm) tall at the shoulder

Cocker Spaniel: 15 in (38 cm) tall at the shoulder

△ *Shaggy hair nearly hides the eyes of an Old English Sheepdog.*
Domestic dogs can vary greatly—from the tiny, smooth-haired
Chihuahua to the huge, hairy Irish Wolfhound. Despite the
differences among the several hundred breeds, all domestic dogs
belong to a single species, or kind, of dog.

▽ *Long legs of a Pharaoh Hound help it chase down animals.*
The rulers of Egypt may have used this kind of sleek racer to hunt
gazelles more than 3,000 years ago.

Pharaoh Hound: 25 in (64 cm) tall at the shoulder

Golden Retriever: 24 in (61 cm) tall at the shoulder

△ *Ears flying and eyes squinting,*
a Golden Retriever hits the water.
A retriever accompanies a hunter and
retrieves birds shot by its master. The
dog grasps the birds gently in its mouth.

dog's territory may be only its owner's house and yard. A dog marks its territory by leaving urine on trees and rocks. By sniffing these scent posts, other dogs can tell that the territory is occupied. Many wild dogs bury meat from a kill and return to eat it later. Many pet dogs have the same habit. They bury bones. Domestic dogs often turn around several times before lying down. Some wild dogs do this, perhaps to trample down grass and form a bed.

Dogs communicate with each other by scent, by the positions of their bodies, by the expressions on their faces, and by the sounds they make. Dogs that live and hunt in groups have different ways of communicating than dogs that live and hunt alone.

Dogs growl, snarl, and whine. Most dogs bark as a warning. Domestic dogs may yelp in fear or in pain. Dogs howl to communicate over long distances. Bared teeth and bristling fur are clear threatening signs. A pup begs for food or for attention by rolling over, whining, and nuzzling. When greeting another pack member—or a member of a pet's human family—an excited dog wags its tail.

Komondor: 25 in (64 cm) tall at the shoulder

△ *Thick, matted coat covers a Komondor, a guard dog of Hungary. Many kinds of fierce, loyal dogs work as police dogs or watchdogs. Some kinds of domestic dogs serve as guide dogs for blind people.*

"Keep it moving!" From its perch on a fence, a sheep dog directs traffic at a New Zealand sheep farm. Sometimes it even climbs on the backs of sheep. Other dogs round up the animals on the open range.

Mixed-breed sheep dog: 18 in (46 cm) tall at the shoulder

Dolphin

Dolphin is another name for porpoise. Find out about porpoises on page 446.

Donkey

The donkey is a domestic ass. Read about asses on page 66.

Dormouse

(DOOR-mouse)

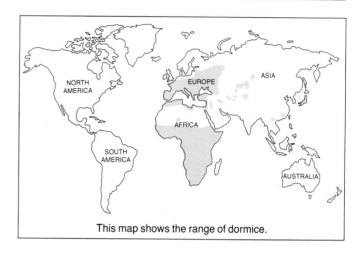

This map shows the range of dormice.

Common dormouse: 3 in (8 cm) long; tail, 3 in (8 cm)

Snug in its nest and fast asleep, a common dormouse looks like a tiny ball of fur. As it hibernates through the winter, its body temperature falls. Its heart rate and breathing slow down. In spring, the animal will wake up and build another nest in thick shrubbery. Because the common dormouse often lives in hazel bushes and fattens itself on the nuts, people sometimes call it the hazel mouse.

BEFORE ITS "LONG WINTER'S NAP," the dormouse fattens up its body on such food as nuts and fruit. Then, as the cold weather sets in, this furry, squirrel-like rodent curls up in a burrow, a hole in a tree, or a space between rocks. There it hibernates (HYE-bur-nates), or sleeps, for several months. The dormouse probably gets its name from a French word that means "to sleep."

In cold climates, dormice hibernate for nearly eight months—from late September to early May. Usually they hibernate alone. But sometimes several animals huddle together. From time to time, they wake up to eat seeds and nuts they have stored.

There are about 28 kinds of dormice. These rodents live in Europe, Asia, and Africa. They are found in forests, grasslands, gardens, and parks. At night, the small animals scurry up and down bushes and trees, using their sharp claws to cling to branches. In the darkness, they search for such food as insects, snails, and young birds.

Dormice also nibble at the fruit and nuts on trees. Farmers often wake to find their orchards damaged by these hungry animals.

Fat dormice, the largest of all dormice, are well known for their big appetites. In early summer, the

184

Garden dormouse: 5 in (13 cm) long; tail, 4 in (10 cm)

animals weigh between 3 and 6 ounces (85-180 g). Then they begin stuffing themselves with food. By winter, they have nearly doubled in weight.

As they hibernate, dormice use up their stored fat. When they wake up in the spring, they immediately set about searching for food.

Soon the females are ready to give birth. They make nests out of grass and leaves. After a three- or four-week pregnancy, they bear two to nine offspring. Although the newborn nurse for only three or four weeks, they often stay with their mothers during the following winter.

DORMOUSE 🐾 **8 of 28 species**

LENGTH OF HEAD AND BODY: 2-8 in (5-20 cm); tail, 2-6 in (5-15 cm)

WEIGHT: up to 6 oz (180 g)

HABITAT AND RANGE: bushes and brushy forests in Africa, Asia, and Europe

FOOD: fruit, nuts, insects, snails, young birds, and eggs

LIFE SPAN: up to 6 years

REPRODUCTION: 2 to 9 young after a pregnancy of 3 or 4 weeks

ORDER: rodents

◁ *Black mask around its eyes identifies a garden dormouse. Despite its name, this kind of dormouse sometimes nests in woods as well as in gardens.*

▽ *Stretching out its tail for balance, a fat dormouse scampers along a branch in search of figs. In summer, it eats so much that it nearly doubles its weight.*

Fat dormouse: 6 in (15 cm) long; tail, 5 in (13 cm)

Douroucouli

A douroucouli is a kind of monkey. Read about douroucoulis and other monkeys on page 370.

Dugong

Read about douroucoulis and other monkeys on page 370.

(DOO-gong)

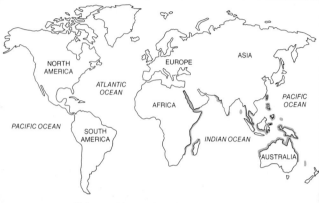

This map shows the range of dugongs.

DUGONG   🐾 I of I species

LENGTH OF HEAD AND BODY: 8-10 ft (244-305 cm)

WEIGHT: 510-1,100 lb (231-499 kg)

HABITAT AND RANGE: warm, coastal waters scattered throughout the Indian Ocean and the western Pacific Ocean

FOOD: sea grasses

LIFE SPAN: 73 years in the wild

REPRODUCTION: usually I young after a pregnancy of about 14 months

ORDER: sirenians

Dugong calf shadows its mother as they swim in shallow waters off the coast of Australia. The calf's smooth, cream-colored skin will become rusty brown as it grows older. Dugongs usually bear one young after a 14-month pregnancy. The mother guards her calf closely during its first year and a half. She even carries the calf on her back from time to time.

PUSHED BY THE STRONG, WAVING MOTION of its tail and body, the torpedo-shaped dugong swims gracefully through the water. This huge animal— measuring about 9 feet (274 cm) long and weighing almost 600 pounds (272 kg)—lives in warm, coastal seas from Africa to Australia. Eating is the dugong's main activity, and sea grasses are its main food.

A dugong feeds alone or in a herd, day or night. It nibbles on sea grasses that grow underwater. Using its flat, hairy snout, it roots for plants that are anchored on the sea bottom. The animal grasps the food with its coarsely bristled lips.

Then it gives the plants a powerful shake that cleans off clinging grains of sand. Sometimes a dugong uses its flippers to scratch its face, to rub its gums, or to guide a young calf.

A dugong looks and acts much like its relative, the manatee. But its flat tail has a notch in the center, like a whale's tail. The manatee's tail is rounded. Dugongs and manatees also live in different parts of the world. Read about manatees on page 346.

Like all mammals, dugongs breathe air. They surface to take a breath every few minutes. But they can stay submerged for about six minutes.

For centuries, these marine mammals have been hunted for their skin, oil, and meat. Yet scientists do not know much about their habits. Today many countries have laws to protect dugongs.

Duiker

A duiker is a kind of antelope. Read about duikers and other antelopes on page 52.

Long-nosed echidna: 24 in (61 cm) long; tail, 4 in (10 cm)

Echidna

(ih-KID-nuh)

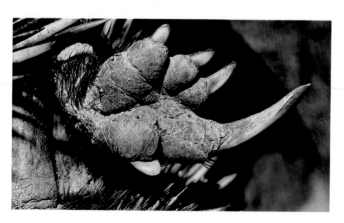

Long-nosed echidna (above) searches the forest floor in New Guinea for soft soil in which to burrow. Tips of its sharp spines poke through thick hair. With a long hind claw (left), the short-nosed echidna can reach among its sharp spines and groom itself.

IS THERE A MAMMAL that lays eggs? Actually, there are two! One kind is the echidna, or spiny anteater, of Australia and New Guinea. The other is the platypus. Both these animals belong to the monotreme (MON-uh-treem) order. You can read about the platypus on page 438.

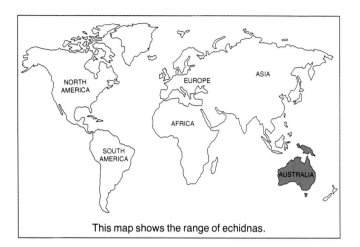

This map shows the range of echidnas.

ECHIDNA 🐾 **1 of 2 species**

LENGTH OF HEAD AND BODY: 14-39 in (36-99 cm); tail, 4 in (10 cm)

WEIGHT: 11-22 lb (5-10 kg)

HABITAT AND RANGE: forests, mountains, valleys, and plains of Australia and New Guinea

FOOD: earthworms, ants, termites, and other insects

LIFE SPAN: more than 50 years in captivity

REPRODUCTION: usually 1 young hatched from an egg after an incubation period of about 10 days

ORDER: monotremes

Short-nosed echidna: 16 in (41 cm) long; tail, 4 in (10 cm)

The female echidna carries a single leathery egg in a pouch that forms on her belly at the beginning of the breeding season. After about ten days, the egg hatches. The blind and hairless offspring, no bigger than a raisin, sucks milk from glands that are inside the pouch. The young grows quickly. After several weeks, sharp spines develop. Then it can no longer remain in its mother's pouch. After several years, the young is fully grown.

There are two species of echidnas—long-nosed and short-nosed. Both have long spines. They also have heavy claws and sensitive snouts. The animals use them to search for food. The short-nosed echidna looks for insects. It tears open logs and underground nests and can easily push over stones twice its weight to get to food. Its sticky tongue darts in and out, catching ants and termites.

The long-nosed echidna of New Guinea eats mostly earthworms. It hooks a worm on a row of tiny spines along a groove in its tongue. Then the echidna pulls the worm inside its beaklike snout.

When threatened, an echidna burrows straight down, sinking rapidly into the ground. Or it may squeeze into a hiding place. With only its spiny back showing, it is safe from danger.

Short-nosed echidna (above, right) digs a hiding place. After a few moments, only its prickly back will remain above ground. A young short-nosed echidna (right) waits in a sheltered spot for its mother. Spines have begun to appear on its back. Unlike all other mammals, except the platypus, newborn echidnas hatch from eggs. But an offspring still drinks its mother's milk.

Eland

The eland is a kind of antelope.
Read about antelopes on page 52.

Elephant

(EL-uh-funt)

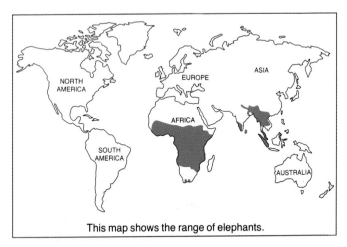

This map shows the range of elephants.

△ *Broken and worn, the tusks of an African elephant show the effects of years of heavy use. With their tusks, elephants dig for roots and move tree branches. They also use them to pry bark off tree trunks.*

Huge African elephant strides through the grass ▷ *with a cattle egret riding on its back. As they walk, elephants stir up insects, which the egrets eat.*

190

African elephant: 10 ft (305 cm) tall at the shoulder

LAZILY STRETCHING ITS TRUNK down to a stream, an elephant sucks up some water. It curls its trunk toward its mouth and squirts in the drink. Despite its usefulness in drinking, an elephant's trunk is more than a straw. The animal breathes through two nostrils at the end of its trunk. With the help of a fingerlike part at the tip, it can grasp small objects.

Elephants use their trunks mostly to drink and to bring food to their mouths. But they also can use them to nudge their calves or to pluck berries from a bush. If threatened, elephants may trumpet a warning through their trunks.

The largest of all living land animals, elephants may weigh more than 6 tons (5,443 kg). Thick skin crisscrossed with wrinkles covers their huge bodies. The animals have very little hair, just small clumps around their ear openings, on their chins, and at the ends of their tails.

Most elephants have tusks—huge, pointed, ivory teeth that grow all during an animal's life. Elephants use their tusks as tools. A tusk can help dig up a bush so the elephant can eat the roots. A tusk can pry bark from a tree. Often, one of an elephant's tusks is shorter than the other. The animal wears down that tusk by using it more than the other, just as people use one hand more than the other.

Until about 10,000 years ago, relatives of our elephants roamed most of the earth. Scientists believe

Reaching high with its trunk, an African elephant ▷ pulls branches from an acacia tree. Elephants use their trunks to gather food and to get drinks of water.

△ *Sparring with their tusks, two elephants battle on an open plain in Africa. Adult male elephants often fight to test their strength.*

192

that Ice Age people hunted these shaggy animals, called mammoths and mastodons. Drawings of these animals have been found in caves in Europe. Today wild elephants live only in Africa and in Asia.

The easiest way to tell the difference between an African elephant and an Asian elephant is by the ears. African elephants have much larger ears than their Asian relatives do. Their ears are shaped somewhat like the continent of Africa.

African elephants also are slightly taller and heavier than Asian elephants. Male African elephants often measure about 10 feet (305 cm) tall at the shoulder—slightly taller than male Asian elephants. Both male and female African elephants have tusks that grow several feet long. Among Asian elephants, only the males grow tusks.

Although African and Asian elephants do not look exactly alike, their habits are similar. Both kinds of elephants feed mainly on roots, leaves, fruit, grasses, and sometimes bark. After pulling a bunch of grass from the ground with its trunk, an elephant may beat

ELEPHANT   🐾 **2 of 2 species**

HEIGHT: **6-12 ft (183 cm-4 m) at the shoulder**

WEIGHT: **5,000-14,000 lb (2,268-6,350 kg)**

HABITAT AND RANGE: **woodlands, grasslands, and forests in parts of Asia and Africa**

FOOD: **roots, leaves, fruit, grasses, and sometimes bark**

LIFE SPAN: **about 70 years in the wild**

REPRODUCTION: **usually 1 young after a pregnancy of 18 to 22 months**

ORDER: **proboscideans**

In an elephant-style hug, two African elephants show affection by wrapping their trunks together.

Elephant

◁ *Eye-deep in water, an African elephant bathes in a river. The animal can stand underwater and breathe— as long as its trunk reaches above the surface.*

▽ *At a river in Kenya, African elephants cool off by taking a muddy bath. Elephants bathe often, because the hot sun dries their skin. During the hottest part of the day, they usually stay in the shade of trees. On very hot days, they cool themselves by flapping their huge ears, thus allowing heat to escape from their bodies.*

the grass against its leg to shake the dirt off before eating. An adult elephant eats as much as 300 pounds (136 kg) of food a day!

To find that much food, these huge animals must roam wide areas. Females—called cows—travel together in herds with their young, called calves. Adult males—or bulls—usually travel alone or with other bulls. They join the group of females for mating and occasionally at other times.

An elephant cow usually gives birth to one calf

▽ *Stirring up a cloud of dust, African elephants powder themselves after bathing. First they suck dirt up with their trunks. Then they blow it over their wet bodies. The dirt helps protect their skin.*

△ *"Let's play!" a young African elephant seems to say to a resting friend. Young elephants often pull older elephants' tails or snatch food from their mouths.*

every two to four years. Elephants have the longest pregnancy of any mammal in the world—nearly 22 months. A newborn calf stands about 3 feet (91 cm) tall and weighs about 200 pounds (91 kg). It nurses for three or four years. About six months after birth, however, the calf begins to eat some solid food. Sometimes a calf sucks its trunk, just as a human baby sucks its thumb!

drink and bathe. Elephants travel to several water holes daily, and they sometimes spend hours rolling around in the mud and water. Surprisingly, elephants swim very well.

With their strong legs, elephants move around easily on land. They have been used as work animals for thousands of years. More than 2,000 years ago, they carried soldiers and weapons into battle. In Asia,

Asian elephant: 8 ft (244 cm) tall at the shoulder

Small herd of Asian elephants travels with young in the middle and adults on either side. Few Asian elephants remain in the wild. Governments have passed laws to protect them.

The youngster is looked after by other cows in the herd as well as by its mother. Young calves are often kept together in groups called kindergartens. One adult baby-sits while other adults feed.

Elephant calves play much of the time. They splash in the water, chase small animals, and fight each other with their trunks. When the calves stop playing they often lean against each other and nap.

Adult elephants need little sleep. They spend most of their time feeding or visiting water holes to

◁ *Drenching itself with its built-in hose, an Asian elephant takes an afternoon shower. Asian elephants are about 2 feet (61 cm) shorter than African elephants.*

people still train elephants to lift and carry logs. Some elephants perform in circuses.

Because of their size, elephants have few enemies. Lions, tigers, crocodiles, and other meat-eating animals occasionally prey on small calves that have become separated from the herd. But these hunters rarely attack adult elephants. People are the elephant's only real enemies.

For centuries, people have killed elephants for sport and for their valuable ivory. In Asia, most wild elephants live on preserves. In Africa, some elephants still roam wild through grasslands and forests. Illegal hunting goes on today, even though laws have been passed in some places to prevent it.

Elk

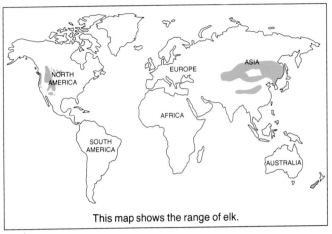

This map shows the range of elk.

IN WINTER, herds of elk feed in mountains and valleys throughout parts of western North America. Elk can paw through snow 2 feet (61 cm) deep to find grass, their favorite food. When the snow is deeper or encrusted with ice, elk must browse, or nibble at shrubs. The cold temperatures do not harm a healthy animal. Beneath an elk's heavy winter coat lies a layer of warm underfur. This woolly undercoat helps to hold in the animal's body heat.

Elk once roamed most of North America. But over the years hunters have killed off many of the animals. The spread of farming meant that elk had fewer places in which to live. Today the largest herds are found in Wyoming—on the National Elk Refuge and in Yellowstone National Park. Another kind of elk is found in central Asia.

Some people call elk *wapiti* (WOP-ut-ee), an American Indian word meaning "light-colored deer." Elk are members of the deer family. Find out about deer on page 170.

Elk are larger than most other kinds of deer. Full-grown male elk, called bulls, weigh as much as 1,100 pounds (499 kg) and measure 5 feet (152 cm) tall at the shoulder. Female elk, called cows, weigh less and are shorter than bulls.

Only bulls have antlers. These large, heavy, bony growths develop from the top of an elk's head. They may measure 4 feet (122 cm) from base to tip. Every

In a land blanketed by fresh snow, an elk feeds near hot springs in Yellowstone National Park. The bull paws at the soft snow to clear patches of grass.

199

March, bulls shed their antlers. In May, new sets begin to grow. Rounded bumps start to swell on the bulls' heads, pushing up about half an inch (13 mm) each day. The antlers are covered with soft skin called velvet. New antlers develop each year.

As the weather becomes warm, elk begin to lose their long winter coats. Sleek, reddish coats replace their heavy gray-brown ones.

Soon the elk migrate, or travel, from the lower slopes to high mountain meadows. Some travel as far as 40 miles (64 km). Cows and their offspring move together. Bulls travel separately.

At their summer feeding grounds, cows give birth to young. A cow usually bears a single calf. The wobbly, spotted calf can stand up when it is about twenty minutes old. Within an hour, it begins to nurse. The calf follows its mother in three days and joins the herd of cows some weeks later.

Late summer signals the mating season. Restless bulls thrash at bushes with their full-grown antlers to remove the velvet. As they search for mates, bulls make bugling sounds. They start on low notes that become high pitched and end in grunts. Sometimes bulls parade side by side. Often they fight over the

Resting in the grass, a bull chews his cud. Soft skin called velvet covers his branching antlers.

Male elk swims behind two cows and their calves at ▷ mating time. If rivals come near, he may fight them with his sharp-tipped antlers, now bare of velvet.

cows. Pushing and shoving with their antlers, they begin to wrestle. Their powerful neck muscles bulge. The battles usually do not end in injury. The weaker bull trots away.

The winning bull becomes master of a group of cows. He herds the cows together and fights off rival bulls. He has little time to eat or sleep. After a few weeks, he becomes exhausted, and another bull may take over the group.

The mating season lasts from late August into November. Then the leaders of the herds give up control of their cows, and all the elk gather once more into large groups. As the snow begins to fall, the elk again head for their pastures in the valleys.

▽ *Four-month-old calf nuzzles against its mother in a mountain meadow. The female grooms her calf's coat.*

ELK

HEIGHT: 4-5 ft (122-152 cm) at the shoulder

WEIGHT: 325-1,100 lb (147-499 kg)

HABITAT AND RANGE: mountain forests and grassy valleys of western North America and central Asia

FOOD: grasses, herbs, shrubs, and trees

LIFE SPAN: 8 to 12 years in the wild

REPRODUCTION: usually 1 young after a pregnancy of 8 or 9 months

ORDER: artiodactyls

Ermine
The ermine is a kind of weasel. Read about weasels on page 558.

F

Ferret

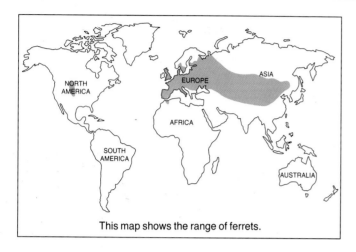

This map shows the range of ferrets.

FERRET 🐾 1 of 3 species

LENGTH OF HEAD AND BODY: 15-18 in (38-46 cm); tail, 5-7 in (13-18 cm)

WEIGHT: about 3 lb (1 kg)

HABITAT AND RANGE: prairies, forests, and meadows of Europe, Asia, North Africa, and the western United States

FOOD: prairie dogs, ground squirrels, and other rodents, as well as amphibians, reptiles, birds, and fish

LIFE SPAN: 8 to 14 years in captivity, depending on species

REPRODUCTION: 2 to 12 young after a pregnancy of 6 weeks, depending on species

ORDER: carnivores

RAREST OF ALL NORTH AMERICAN MAMMALS, the black-footed ferret has nearly disappeared from the plains of the central United States.

With a black band across its eyes, the sleek black-footed ferret looks like a masked bandit. Its fur is tan,

Sniffing with its sensitive nose, a domestic ferret ▷ *prepares to leave the nest it shares with its mate. People in Europe once used ferrets to hunt other small animals. Now they sometimes keep ferrets as pets.*

but black hair covers its feet and legs and the tip of its tail. Shaped like its relative the weasel, the ferret has a long, slender body. When it hunts prairie dogs, it easily slides into a burrow.

Though the ferret also eats mice, rabbits, and ground squirrels, prairie dogs are its main food. Ferrets usually live in prairie dog towns. These are large areas where prairie dogs dig networks of burrows in which they live and raise young. There, the black-footed ferret can find and kill its prey. It also finds shelter in abandoned burrows.

During the twentieth century, the number of prairie dogs has plummeted. Some farmers and ranchers have tried to get rid of prairie dogs because they burrow holes in fields and pastures. With far fewer prairie dogs, black-footed ferrets nearly disappeared. Luckily a few were captured and bred in captivity. Now efforts are being made to restore them to their natural habitat.

The surest sign of a ferret is a long trench extending from a burrow entrance. During the day, while a ferret sleeps underground, a prairie dog may close up the entrance to the burrow in which its enemy is resting. It kicks dirt into the opening and pushes it down with its nose. At night, the ferret can dig itself out, often leaving the telltale trench.

Black-footed ferret seeks its prey in a prairie dog town in South Dakota. Slinking up to a burrow, the ferret sniffs carefully. Smelling a prairie dog, it enters the burrow and searches the tunnels.

202

Domestic ferret: 18 in (46 cm) long; tail, 5 in (13 cm)

Relatives of the black-footed ferret live in Europe and in Asia. The black-footed ferret's closest relative is the steppe polecat. It makes its home on the plains of central Asia and of eastern Europe. The steppe polecat hunts at night. It eats mainly rodents, especially ground squirrels. If it kills more than it can eat, it stores the extra food in its burrow.

Another relative, the European polecat, is found in Europe. It often lives near farms, hunting mice and rats during the night. This animal has dark fur with a light-colored undercoat.

Some people raise domestic, or tame, ferrets for their soft fur—called fitch. It is used in making coats. For centuries, people in Europe also used ferrets to hunt small animals. The ferret was sent down a burrow to chase out the inhabitant. From this practice comes the expression "to ferret out," which means to uncover something hidden.

After a successful hunt, the ferret pops its head out, holding a prairie dog firmly by the throat. Then it crawls out of the burrow and carries off its prize across the prairie.

Black-footed ferret: 16 in (41 cm) long; tail, 6 in (15 cm)

Fisher
The fisher is a close relative of the marten. Read about both animals on page 357.

Flying lemur

(FLY-ing LEE-mur)

Malayan flying lemur: 15 in (38 cm) long; tail, 9 in (23 cm)

HIDDEN FROM VIEW and sheltered by a roof of leaves, the flying lemur spends most of its life high among the tree branches. The flying lemur is rare and is hard to find in its habitat—forests and coconut plantations in parts of Southeast Asia. And since the flying lemur does not live long in captivity, not much is known about the animal's way of life. Another name for the flying lemur is colugo (kuh-LOO-go). The flying lemur is not related to the lemur, which is a member of the primate order.

During daylight hours, most flying lemurs rest. Some of them hang from branches and from huge palm leaves, gripping firmly with their sharp, curved claws. Others curl up in holes in tree trunks. Their brownish gray fur—speckled with white—blends in with the bark of the trees, so the animals are difficult to see.

At dusk, flying lemurs begin to eat. Trees are their main source of food. The animals feed on leaves, buds, and flowers. They probably get water by licking rain from the leaves.

A flying lemur travels from tree to tree by gliding. Spreading its limbs, the flying lemur stretches folds of skin that extend from the sides of its neck to all four feet and its tail. Then it leaps into the air and glides down to another tree. From below, the animal looks like a kite. Some flying lemurs may cover more than 330 feet (100 m) in a single leap!

Cradled in the folds of its mother's silky fur, a young flying lemur stays warm and dry. When its mother glides to another tree, the youngster clings to her belly.

FLYING LEMUR   🐾 **1 of 2 species**

LENGTH OF HEAD AND BODY: 13-17 in (33-43 cm); tail, 7-11 in (18-28 cm)

WEIGHT: 2-4 lb (907-1,814 g)

HABITAT AND RANGE: forested areas and coconut plantations in parts of Southeast Asia

FOOD: leaves, buds, and flowers

LIFE SPAN: unknown

REPRODUCTION: usually 1 young after a pregnancy of about 60 days

ORDER: dermopterans

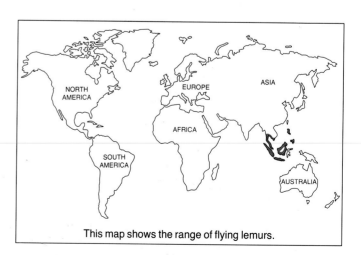

This map shows the range of flying lemurs.

Fossa

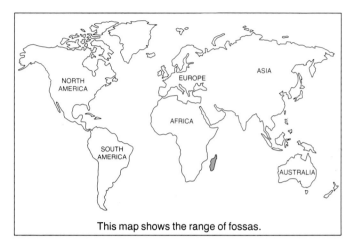

This map shows the range of fossas.

FOSSA 👣 I of I species

LENGTH OF HEAD AND BODY: 24-31 in (61-79 cm); tail, 24-31 in (61-79 cm)

WEIGHT: 15-26 lb (7-12 kg)

HABITAT AND RANGE: forests of Madagascar

FOOD: small mammals and birds

LIFE SPAN: 15 years in captivity

REPRODUCTION: 2 to 4 young after a pregnancy of about 3 months

ORDER: carnivores

CREEPING NOISELESSLY along a tree branch, a fossa stalks its prey. It hunts at night, catching birds and lemurs by surprise.

The fossa is the largest predator, or meat-eating hunter, on Madagascar, an island off the southeastern coast of Africa. This sleek animal is about twice as large as a house cat. With sharp teeth and curved claws, the muscular fossa can overpower almost any animal it attacks.

Whether it is looking for food or resting in the fork of a tree, the fossa spends much of its time high above ground. Its claws and the hairless pads on its feet give the fossa a secure grip in the trees. Its long, heavy tail helps the animal keep its balance.

Like their close relatives the civets, fossas communicate with scent. A fossa has glands that produce a strong-smelling oil. As it moves about, the fossa occasionally leaves some of this oil along its trail. During September and October, the oily patches serve as scent signals as fossas look for mates. During most of the year, however, fossas avoid each other. Read about civets on page 154.

Three months after mating, a female fossa finds a hollow tree or a small cave in which to give birth. Her litter may contain two to four offspring. The young are full grown in about four years.

Catlike fossa rests on a tree limb. This strong meat eater hunts on the ground and in the trees.

Fox

THE THICK, BUSHY TAIL of a fox has many uses. When a fox curls up in cold weather, it curls its tail—sometimes called a brush—to cover its feet and its nose. The tail looks like a long, woolly scarf. When a fox runs, its tail streams out behind. This helps the fox keep its balance as it zigzags across the land. By moving its brush in certain ways, a fox can send messages to other foxes. But it is not true that a fox uses its brush to sweep away its tracks in snow.

Foxes live nearly everywhere in the world. The arctic fox stays in the treeless regions of the Far North. Another kind of fox, the fennec (FEN-ick), makes its home in the deserts of Africa and in the Middle East.

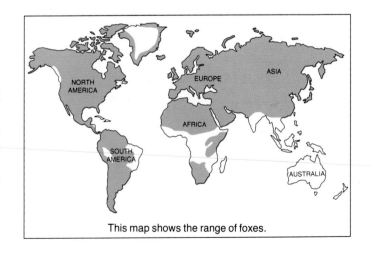

This map shows the range of foxes.

FOX 🐾 1 of 22 species

LENGTH OF HEAD AND BODY: 14-39 in (36-99 cm); tail, 7-20 in (18-51 cm)

WEIGHT: 3-29 lb (1-13 kg)

HABITAT AND RANGE: almost every kind of habitat worldwide, except for Antarctica (brought to Australia by people)

FOOD: small mammals, birds, eggs, insects, reptiles, amphibians, fish, grasses, berries, nuts, roots, and the remains of dead animals

LIFE SPAN: up to 15 years in captivity

REPRODUCTION: 2 to 12 young after a pregnancy of 1 1/2 to 2 1/2 months, depending on species

ORDER: carnivores

◁ *Extending its tail, a red fox in Maine follows the track of its prey. Foxes hunt mostly at night.*

Red fox: 31 in (79 cm) long; tail, 15 in (38 cm)

△ *Female red fox nuzzles her two-month-old pup. Most adult foxes care for their young for about six months. Then the offspring go off to live alone. Newborn red foxes have soft brown or gray fur. Their colorful red coats do not begin to grow in until they are about four weeks old.*

◁ *Up on a stump, a red fox sniffs for traces of other foxes. Foxes make scent posts by marking trees, rocks, or patches of ground with their urine. From the smell, a fox knows that another fox has passed by.*

◁ Swift fox pauses on a prairie in Colorado. This animal lives up to its name. It can escape from a coyote by sprinting to a burrow. It often catches jackrabbits.

▽ Enormous ears make a tiny fennec look even smaller. The ears help the animal hear prey as well as approaching enemies. Thick fur insulates this fox from the desert's nighttime cold.

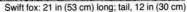

Swift fox: 21 in (53 cm) long; tail, 12 in (30 cm)

Fennec: 15 in (38 cm) long; tail, 10 in (25 cm)

The chilla (CHILL-uh) roams dry plains in South America. The red fox lives in Europe, Africa, and Asia, as well as in North America.

Not all red foxes are red. They vary in color from pale rosy gold to deep rusty brown. Some of the animals have pure black fur. When their fur is black and frosted with white, red foxes may be called silver foxes. Cross foxes have red coats with black crosses on their backs and shoulders. Hunters sometimes trap foxes for their soft, thick fur. Foxes are also raised on fur farms. Silver fox fur is especially prized, as is the fur of the arctic fox.

Arctic foxes can be white or "blue." Both kinds change color with the season. Like the land around them, white foxes turn brown in summer. They blend

◁ Chilla stretches for a mouthful of berries. This yellow-gray fox roams the dry plains of South America.

Chilla: 31 in (79 cm) long; tail, 13 in (33 cm)

◁ *Rare Simien fox of Ethiopia stands alert, searching for prey. It feeds mainly on rodents. This fox lives on plateaus and in mountains as high as 10,000 feet (3,048 m). Although these foxes hunt alone, they live in groups and may play and romp together.*

Simien fox: 31 in (79 cm) long; tail, 13 in (33 cm)

▽ *Litter of bat-eared foxes in Africa basks in the sunshine. Their mother will use a high-pitched whistle to call them. Bat-eared foxes feed mainly on insects, especially termites, which they dig from the ground.*

Bat-eared fox: 22 in (56 cm) long; tail, 12 in (30 cm)

Gray fox explores a log. It searches for insects to ▷
eat or for a place to make a den. Gray foxes roam dense, brushy forests in North and South America.

Gray fox: 28 in (71 cm) long; tail, 13 in (33 cm)

April sun bathes an arctic fox resting on a snowy hillside in Alaska. Prey can be hard to find during the long, northern winter. The foxes often follow polar bears onto pack ice and eat scraps left from the bears' kills. In spring, the foxes catch rodents, birds, and fish.

Fox _____

in so well with their surroundings that it is hard to spot the animals against the golden grass and bare ground. Blue foxes change from a light blue-gray coat to a darker one in summer.

Other foxes match their backgrounds, too. The sand-colored kit fox fades into the desert terrain of the western United States. The tan swift fox matches the color of dry prairie grasses. The gray fox almost disappears among the rocks and leaves of shadowy

forests in North and South America. Foxes are adapted, or suited, to their surroundings in other ways. Long fur on the bottoms of the arctic fox's broad paws protects its feet from the cold. Sharp claws help the arctic fox keep its footing on icy ground. The fennec and other desert foxes also have furry feet to help them run in soft sand.

The ears of the fennec and of the bat-eared fox are very different from those of the arctic fox: They are enormous, and they help the desert animals hear prey burrowing in the sand. Because their ears are so big, these foxes lose body heat through them. This helps the animals to keep cool. In contrast, the small, round ears of the arctic fox barely poke above its long, thick coat. Because its ears are only slightly exposed to the cold, this animal loses very little body heat through them.

Red foxes often live where forests and farmlands meet. Woodlands offer good sites for foxes to build dens. In fields, foxes can find rabbits, mice, and birds for food. Red foxes also eat lizards, frogs, and fish. If farms are nearby, the foxes may raid hen houses for chickens and eggs. In summer, they feast on blackberries and plums. They gobble down grapes and nuts in the fall.

Most foxes hunt alone and live together only when they are raising young. But some foxes live in pairs or in groups all year round. Although some foxes dig their own dens, others may take over abandoned burrows. Or they may creep under thick bushes or into hollow logs. With the help of sharp, curved claws, gray foxes can climb straight up a tree until they find a hollow place in which to hide. Desert foxes dig networks of tunnels under the sand. Their dens remain quite cool even in the hottest weather. During a blizzard, arctic foxes may dig into the snow for shelter.

Once a year, a female fox bears two to twelve helpless pups. The mother nurses the pups for about two months. The father also helps to care for them. As long as the pups are too young to be left alone, he carries prey to the den for the mother. Later both parents go hunting to feed their pups.

Fox pups are playful. They race and tussle. They bark and yap. They crouch, then jump on one another—or on anything that wiggles, hops, or flies. The parents bring home live rodents for the pups to chase and to pounce on. This gives the little animals practice in hunting.

Soon the pups tag along as their parents search for food. At about six months of age, young foxes leave to seek hunting grounds of their own.

A fox hunts different animals in different ways. It catches mice by pouncing when it hears rustling sounds in the grass. A kit fox may stand on its hind legs and turn in a circle, ready to leap the instant a mouse gives itself away. Bat-eared foxes dig for insects in the sand. To catch a bird, a red fox creeps up silently until it is close enough to spring. It can run down a rabbit in a wild, zigzag chase.

To outwit its own enemies, a red fox doubles back on its tracks. Bat-eared foxes listen for danger, then scurry under a rock or into their sandy burrows in the desert. An arctic fox always keeps a sharp lookout for wolves as it feeds.

▽ *Poking its head out of its den, an arctic fox pup in Alaska shows its brown summer coat. The animal's fur will become thick and white before winter. An arctic fox digs out a new chamber in its den once a year for each new litter of pups.*

Arctic fox: 24 in (61 cm) long; tail, 12 in (30 cm)

G

Galago
Galagos are bush babies. Read about them on page 112.

Gazelle
(guh-ZELL)

Thomson's gazelle: 25 in (64 cm) tall at the shoulder

△ *Less than a day old, a gazelle nuzzles against its mother to nurse. The female Thomson's gazelle licks her offspring to clean it.*

Crowned with slightly curved, ringed horns, a male ▷ Thomson's gazelle chews a blade of grass on an African plain. Of all the gazelles, only the Thomson's gazelle has jet-black stripes on its sides.

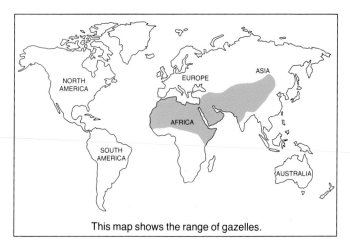

This map shows the range of gazelles.

ALERT TO DANGER, a herd of Thomson's gazelles grazes on an open plain. The animals look up from time to time while feeding. Suddenly, a few members of the herd sight enemies—a pack of wild dogs. The gazelles jump into the air. Bouncing up and down with their stiff, straight legs, they signal an alarm to the rest of the herd. Soon the whole herd is bouncing in this way. Then the gazelles run off, scattering in all directions. One gazelle may be caught by the dogs, but most of the herd will escape. To get away from a cheetah, the fastest land mammal, gazelles usually gallop away without bouncing. By running at speeds of about 40 miles (64 km) an hour, they can sometimes avoid lions, leopards, hyenas, wild dogs, and other meat eaters.

Thomson's gazelles are one of about 19 species,

or kinds, of gazelles—a group of medium-size antelopes. Gazelles are found in Asia and in Africa. Some live in mountainous regions. Others make their homes in the desert or in open shrubby areas called the bush. Most gazelles live on grassy plains.

Gazelles grow ringed horns that may be straight or curved. In most species, both males and females have horns. A female's horns are shorter and thinner than those of a male. Their coats range from grayish white to orange to brown. Some gazelles have a dark band that runs along each side of their bodies. Bellies and rumps are usually white.

Gazelles roam in herds numbering from a few animals to several hundred. They graze on grasses or nibble on leaves and shoots of bushes and other

plants. During the rainy season, when food is plentiful, herds of gazelles may come together to form groups of thousands of animals. In the dry season, some gazelles migrate, or travel, from the plains to the bush in search of food and water. Certain other gazelles that are able to survive without drinking water remain behind.

At certain times of the year, an adult male of some species leaves the herd and marks a territory, or

---

GAZELLE   🐾 **11 of 20 species**

HEIGHT: 20-43 in (51-109 cm) tall at the shoulder

WEIGHT: 26-165 lb (12-75 kg)

HABITAT AND RANGE: grasslands, treeless plains, shrubby areas, deserts, and mountainous regions of parts of Africa and Asia

FOOD: grasses, herbs, leaves, buds, and shoots

LIFE SPAN: up to 18 years in captivity

REPRODUCTION: 1 or 2 young after a pregnancy of about 5 or 6 months, depending on species

ORDER: artiodactyls

◁ *Watchful Grant's gazelles stare across dry grass in Kenya. These animals need little moisture to survive. In the dry season, they may remain on the plains long after other animals have left in search of water.*

Grant's gazelle: 35 in (89 cm) tall at the shoulder

◁ *With heads lowered, two male Grant's gazelles prepare to test their strength. The animals may fight often, but they rarely hurt each other.*
▽ *Dorcas gazelles race across a rocky hill. These rare animals live in desert areas of northern Africa.*

Dorcas gazelle: 24 in (61 cm) tall at the shoulder

area, of his own. He may fight to keep rival males out of his area. He tries to mate with the females that wander into his territory. Females and young stay together in groups. Males without territories roam in bachelor herds.

About six months after mating, a female leaves the herd and gives birth to one or two young. For several days or even weeks, the young gazelle lies hidden in the grass. Its mother goes off to feed as usual, returning several times a day to nurse her offspring. When the young gazelle is old enough, it begins to follow its mother and to graze with the herd. If the offspring is a female, she will stay with a herd of females. Male offspring will join a bachelor herd.

Gemsbok

The gemsbok is a kind of antelope. Find out about antelopes on page 52.

Genet

(JEN-ut)

SLEEK AND SLENDER, the genet glides through thickets and between rocks on dry grassy plains. In dense forests, the animal darts up trees and leaps nimbly among the branches. Several species, or kinds, of genets live in Africa. One kind is also found in the Middle East and in southern Europe.

GENET 2 of 11 species

LENGTH OF HEAD AND BODY: 16-23 in (41-58 cm); tail, 13-21 in (33-53 cm)

WEIGHT: 2-7 lb (1-3 kg)

HABITAT AND RANGE: forests and grasslands of Africa and parts of southern Europe and the Middle East

FOOD: small animals and fruit

LIFE SPAN: less than 10 years in the wild

REPRODUCTION: 2 to 4 young after a pregnancy of 2½ months

ORDER: carnivores

This map shows the range of genets.

People know little about these animals because they rarely see them in the wild. Genets sleep during the day. They curl up in hollow trees, under bushes, or in tall grass. Their tan fur with light-and-dark markings blends into their surroundings.

After dark, genets prowl in search of food. Slinking through the forest, they eat insects, fruit, and birds. On the plains, they catch lizards and snakes. They also feed on mice and rats. People in ancient Egypt kept genets in their homes just to catch these small rodent pests.

Except for their pointed noses and short legs, genets look like small cats. Actually they are a kind of civet. Find out more about other civets on page 154.

The genet uses scent to communicate with other genets. It has a scent gland under its long, ringed tail. It marks its path with sweet-smelling oil from this gland. By the odor one genet leaves, other genets know it has passed by.

In captivity, female genets can have two litters of two to four offspring each year. The young nurse for a couple of months. When they are six weeks old, they begin to eat solid food. In the wild, genets probably live less than ten years. In zoos, they may survive twice as long.

Markings on a common genet's body and tail stand out against the darkness. Although experts believe there are many genets in Africa, people rarely see these shy animals. Sometimes only the gleam of its large eyes, caught in the beam of a flashlight, gives the genet away.

Common genet: 20 in (51 cm) long; tail, 18 in (46 cm)

Gerbil

Gerbil's tufted tail sweeps across desert sand in Africa. The animal's coloring blends with its surroundings.

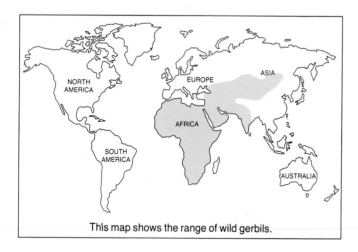

This map shows the range of wild gerbils.

NOT LONG AGO, most Americans had never heard of the small, frisky gerbil. In the 1950s, a scientist in New York got several Mongolian gerbils for his work. Today most of the pet gerbils in the United States trace their ancestors back to his nine animals!

Mongolian gerbils are actually jirds, close relatives of about a hundred other kinds of wild gerbils.

Most of these rat-size animals are not kept as pets. They usually live in dry parts of Asia and Africa. Their gray or sand-colored fur blends well into their environment. Gerbils often hop across the sand at night, using their long, thin tails for balance. Or they scurry about, looking for seeds, leaves, roots, flowers, and insects. Their food supplies them with almost all of the water they need.

Gerbils look for hard foods to gnaw on. This keeps their teeth from getting too long. Like other rodents' teeth, their front teeth never stop growing.

During the day, most gerbils escape the heat by staying in their underground homes. Some live in small, simple burrows. Others dig complex tunnel systems. Often several gerbils form a colony by building their burrows close together.

In nests inside their burrows, females give birth to litters of one to eight young. Because a pregnancy lasts less than a month, gerbils are able to have several litters a year. The newborn stay underground for about three weeks after birth. Then they begin to search for food on their own.

Round entrance (above) leads to the tunnels of a gerbil burrow in Africa. Underground, two sleeping gerbils nestle (right), away from the daytime heat. At night, they will look for insects, seeds, and other plant foods. They will carry some of their finds back to their burrows and store them there to eat later.

GERBIL 🐾 **20 of 110 species**

LENGTH OF HEAD AND BODY: 3-7 in (8-18 cm); tail, 3-9 in (8-23 cm)

WEIGHT: 1-7 oz (28-198 g)

HABITAT AND RANGE: mostly dry, sandy areas of Asia and Africa; some kinds of gerbils are kept as pets

FOOD: seeds, roots, leaves, flowers, and insects

LIFE SPAN: about 4 years in the wild

REPRODUCTION: 1 to 8 young after a pregnancy of about 3 weeks

ORDER: rodents

Gerenuk

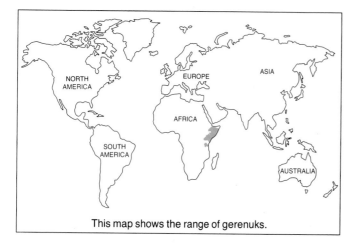

This map shows the range of gerenuks.

GERENUK

HEIGHT: 35-41 in (89-104 cm) at the shoulder; about 7 ft (213 cm) when standing

WEIGHT: 75-110 lb (34-50 kg)

HABITAT AND RANGE: dry brushy areas of eastern Africa

FOOD: leaves, shoots, flowers, and fruit of woody plants

LIFE SPAN: up to 14 years in captivity

REPRODUCTION: 1 young after a pregnancy of about 7 months

ORDER: artiodactyls

WANDERING SLOWLY among thornbushes, a gerenuk searches for food. The animal rises gracefully on its hind legs. Standing straight and tall, it rests its forelegs against a bush. It chooses a leaf and plucks it with its flexible lips. By stretching its long neck, it can feed on the leaves of high branches that smaller animals cannot reach.

Gerenuks live in dry brushy areas of eastern Africa. During the day, they browse, that is, they nibble on leaves and shoots of woody plants. Occasionally, they feed late at night.

Gerenuks seem to get most of the moisture they need from the plants they eat. Some scientists think that gerenuks never drink water at all!

A male gerenuk weighs about 100 pounds (45 kg). It measures more than 3 feet (91 cm) tall at the shoulder. But when standing upon its hind legs, the animal reaches a height of about 7 feet (213 cm). Its curved, ringed horns grow to a length of about 14 inches (36 cm). A female gerenuk is smaller and has no horns.

Gerenuks are closely related to gazelles. The

△ Up on its hind legs, a male gerenuk nibbles leaves from a thorny shrub. For support, the animal leans its front legs lightly against the branches.

Like living statues, female gerenuks in Kenya freeze ▷ and watch for danger. With their long, slender necks, they can see over tall bushes and shrubs. Their name in an African language means "giraffe-necked."

gerenuk's long neck, however, reminds people of a giraffe. So the gerenuk is sometimes called a giraffe gazelle. Read more about gazelles on page 212.

Gerenuks have keen senses. Looking and listening, they stay alert to enemies such as lions and leopards. If startled, gerenuks freeze. They stand perfectly still for several minutes. Their thin legs are difficult to see among trees and bushes. Their reddish brown coloring sometimes blends with their surroundings. If an enemy approaches, the animals dash away. They may try to escape their pursuer by dodging around trees and bushes.

An adult male gerenuk holds a territory, or area, about a square mile in size. The male animal marks bushes and trees in this area with a substance that comes from glands in the corners of his eyes. A small group of females and their young usually lives and feeds in this territory. Sometimes the male stays apart from them. Occasionally females also wander on their own.

A male usually mates with the females in his territory. Gerenuks may mate at any time of year. About seven months later, a female gerenuk gives birth to one young. The newborn animal stays hidden in a sheltered place for a month or more. During the day, its mother goes off to feed. When she returns, she nurses her offspring.

If the young gerenuk is a female, she might remain with her mother. But if the offspring is a male, he will leave his mother after about a year. Then he may roam with a few other young males. When he is fully grown, he will try to find a territory of his own.

Gibbon: 24 in (61 cm) long

Long-armed gibbon hangs lightly between two small branches. These apes spend most of their time in trees.

GIBBON 🐾 **4 of 11 species**

LENGTH OF HEAD AND BODY: 16-36 in (41-91 cm)

WEIGHT: 9-29 lb (4-13 kg)

HABITAT AND RANGE: tropical forests of southern and southeastern Asia

FOOD: fruit, flowers, leaves, insects, birds' eggs, and young birds

LIFE SPAN: up to 44 years in captivity

REPRODUCTION: usually 1 young after a pregnancy of about 7 months

ORDER: primates

Gibbon

(GIB-un)

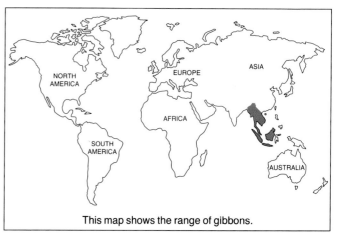

This map shows the range of gibbons.

GRACEFUL, ACROBATIC APES, gibbons live high in the trees of tropical forests in southern and southeastern Asia. Like other apes—gorillas, orangutans, and chimpanzees—gibbons have no tails. But these hairy animals are smaller than their relatives. So gibbons are called lesser apes. Most full-grown male gibbons measure less than 3 feet (91 cm) long. They weigh about 15 pounds (7 kg). Female gibbons are slightly smaller and lighter.

A gibbon is well equipped for life in the trees. Its bones do not weigh much. And its long, strong arms are twice the length of its body. The animal has very long fingers and shorter thumbs. When the gibbon swings through the branches, the thumb is out of the way. A gibbon uses its fingers almost like hooks.

Gibbons travel through the trees with a hand-over-hand movement called brachiation (bray-kee-AY-shun). Most of the time, gibbons move along at a leisurely pace. But when necessary, they can swing at an astonishing speed.

Sometimes gibbons are known to walk upright along branches. To keep their balance, they stretch their arms out to the sides. Gibbons look a little like tightrope walkers. They can cross large gaps between the branches—sometimes covering as much as 30 feet (9 m) in a single leap! Occasionally, gibbons come down to the ground.

Gibbons usually eat fruit, flowers, and leaves.

White patches of dense, woolly hair highlight the ▷ face, hands, and feet of a gibbon. Strong flexible fingers give the animal a hooklike grip.

Gibbon _____

Throat sac inflated like a balloon, a siamang roars a warning to other gibbons: "Stay out of my territory!" A siamang's booming cry can be heard more than a mile away.

other kinds of gibbons. A male weighs about 22 pounds (10 kg). The siamang has a special throat sac to make its voice carry over long distances. The animal puffs up the sac until it is about the same size as its head. Then it makes an amazingly loud "hoo-hoo-hoo" sound. The siamang's calls can be heard more than a mile away.

Within their own territories, gibbons have favorite trees in which to sleep. They return to the same trees night after night. There they huddle together. Or they may sleep alone, wedged in a tree fork. Unlike other apes, gibbons do not build sleeping nests. Special pads of tough skin on their hind ends serve as built-in cushions.

◁ *Young siamang imitates its parent by dangling between tree branches. Adult siamangs are larger and darker than other kinds of gibbons. They have dense black hair.*
▽ *Hanging carefully just above the water's surface, a siamang reaches to get a drink. The animal dips in its hand, then licks the water from its fingers.*

But they also eat insects, birds' eggs, and probably young birds. They live in family groups that include a male, a female, and two to four offspring.

A gibbon usually has only one mate during its lifetime. About seven months after mating, females give birth to a single young. The newborn travels with its mother soon after birth, clinging to the hair on her belly. Young gibbons stay with their parents about six years. They go off by themselves when they are ready to start families of their own.

Each gibbon family occupies a well-defined area in the forest. The adults defend this territory against other gibbons. Every morning when the gibbons wake up, they sing loudly to remind other animals that this is their area. Other gibbons should stay away! If they do come near, the family challenges the intruders by hooting loudly.

The kind of gibbon that makes the loudest noise is the siamang (SEE-uh-mang). It is also larger than

Siamang: 30 in (76 cm) long

Giraffe

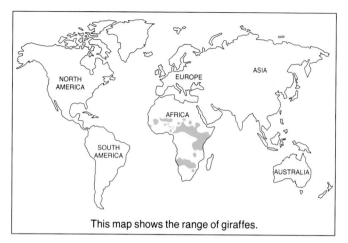

This map shows the range of giraffes.

IT'S IMPOSSIBLE TO CONFUSE the long-legged, long-necked giraffe with any other mammal. Giraffes are the tallest animals on earth. Adult males, called bulls, grow to a height of nearly 19 feet (6 m). Their legs are about 6 feet (183 cm) long. And their necks can be even longer than that!

Giraffes live on the savannas, or grasslands, of Africa. The animals wander in small groups of about five members. Giraffes live together peacefully most of the time. But sometimes bulls have contests to see which animal is stronger. During these "necking" bouts, bulls slam their necks and heads together until one gives up.

Stretching its long neck, a giraffe can eat leaves from the tops of thorny acacia trees. The animal pulls the leaves from a branch with its tongue, which can measure 21 inches (53 cm) long. Because of stinging ants among the branches, the giraffe does not linger at a tree.

Giraffes can go for several days without drinking water. They get moisture from the juicy leaves of the plants they eat. When a giraffe does try to drink from a stream or a water hole, it usually spreads its front legs far out to the sides. Then the animal stretches its long neck down as far as it can and takes a drink of water. In this awkward position, it is hard for a giraffe to watch for danger.

Towering above acacia trees, three giraffes move to a new feeding area on the grasslands of Africa. Giraffes often travel many miles every day to find food. Each animal eats hundreds of pounds of leaves a week.

Giraffe: 17 ft (5 m) tall

Giraffe

Even though a giraffe's neck is very long, it has only seven neck bones—the same number that most mammals have. A stiff, brushlike mane runs the length of the neck. On its head, the giraffe has two short horns and sometimes two or three knobs. The horns and knobs are covered with skin.

Legs spread and head down, a giraffe stretches to reach the water. This awkward position makes the animal easy prey for big cats. Giraffes do not drink often. They get much of the moisture they need from their food.

Head high in a treetop, a giraffe feeds on the leaves of a thorny acacia. The animal avoids the largest thorns, and small ones cannot prick its tough lips.

Most giraffes have tan coats with irregular dark brown spots. But the reticulated (rih-TICK-you-lay-ted) giraffe has large brown spots outlined in white. No two giraffes have the same pattern, but all giraffes have larger spots on their bodies than they do on their heads and legs. Giraffes from different areas have different kinds of patterns.

Some scientists think that a giraffe's spots may help hide the animal when it is standing in a shadowy grove of trees. The spots blend in with the shadows. And the giraffe's legs look like tree trunks. Its head is hidden in the leaves.

Even in the open, a giraffe has ways to protect itself from such enemies as lions. Its good eyesight allows the animal to see for long distances. And its height helps it see things that are far away, just as a person can see better from a lookout tower.

When a giraffe spots an enemy, it often has a good chance to gallop away before the attacker gets too close. A giraffe can run as fast as 35 miles (56 km) an hour. But it can't keep up that speed for very long.

Two bulls slam their necks together (below, left) in a "necking" bout that tests each animal's strength. They shove and push (below, center). And sometimes they even wrap their necks together as they spar (below, right). The fighting may look dangerous, but the bulls seldom get badly hurt.

Usually a giraffe lopes along at about 10 miles (16 km) an hour. Young giraffes can run faster than their parents because they weigh less. Adult giraffes can weigh as much as 2,800 pounds (1,270 kg).

Most of a giraffe's day is spent eating. Like a cow, a giraffe first swallows its food and then later brings it up to chew in the form of a cud—a wad of partly digested food. A giraffe has a four-chambered stomach like that of a cow.

Giraffes chew their cuds for hours at a time. The rest of the day, they wander and doze briefly. Giraffes nap standing up. Sometimes they lie down at night, but they never sleep deeply for more than a few minutes at a time.

After a 15-month pregnancy, a female giraffe gives birth—while standing—to one young. The offspring drops more than 5 feet (152 cm) to the ground when it is born! Then its mother turns and licks it. About half an hour later, the young giraffe can stand on its long, wobbly legs. It begins to nurse. After only

Necks swaying back and forth as they run, a small herd of young and adult giraffes lopes across a dry plain in Kenya. Giraffes can run as fast as 35 miles (56 km) an hour for short distances.

Giraffes at a water hole take turns drinking and watching for danger.

about ten hours, it can run alongside its mother. The newborn giraffe is tall—6 feet (183 cm)—and it weighs about 150 pounds (68 kg). The animal grows fast during its first year of life, adding almost 4 feet (122 cm) to its height. A giraffe is full grown after five to seven years.

For many years, it was thought that giraffes were completely silent. But by watching and listening, scientists have now learned that the animals do have voices—very quiet ones.

GIRAFFE

HEIGHT: 14-19 ft (4-6 m)

WEIGHT: 1,750-2,800 lb (794-1,270 kg)

HABITAT AND RANGE: grasslands in central, eastern, and southern Africa

FOOD: leaves, twigs, and bark, especially from acacia trees

LIFE SPAN: about 25 years in the wild

REPRODUCTION: usually 1 young after a pregnancy of 15 months

ORDER: artiodactyls

Full-grown female licks an infant giraffe as a younger female stands by. Coats of brown spots outlined with thin bands of white identify these animals as reticulated giraffes.

Reticulated giraffe: 17 ft (5 m) tall

Gnu
Gnu is another name for wildebeest. Read about this animal on page 571.

Goat

AT HOME in rocky terrain, wild goats roam some of the most rugged mountains in the world. The hardy animals scramble through barren, bone-dry mountains of the Middle East. In Europe, they climb steep cliffs and peaks. In Asia, on cold and windy slopes of the Himalaya, wild goats range where few trees dot the landscape.

In North America, mountain goats live in a rocky, snowy world—high in the Rockies and in the mountains along the northwestern coast. Mountain goats are not really goats. But these shaggy-haired, sure-footed climbers are close relatives. They are called goat-antelopes.

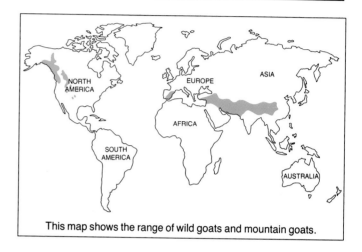

This map shows the range of wild goats and mountain goats.

Thick white coat protects a female mountain goat, or nanny, from icy winds high in the Rocky Mountains. With her split hooves and padded toes, she can keep her balance on snowy slopes.

Mountain goat: 42 in (107 cm) tall at the shoulder

Perched at the very edge of a cliff, two male mountain goats, called billies, rest in the sun. Mountain goats live in high country from Alaska through western Canada into the United States.

Goat

The hooves of mountain goats each are split into two toes. Rough pads on the bottom grip the surface of the ground. For an even better hold on slick slopes, a mountain goat's toes can spread wide.

A mountain goat's long outer coat protects it from wind, rain, and snow. This coat is shed in summer, leaving a layer of thick, fluffy wool. Both males, called billies, and females, called nannies, have beards and sharp black horns.

During most of the year, nannies and their young, called kids, travel in herds of as many as twenty animals. Billies live alone or occasionally in groups of two or three. They join the nannies and young at mating time. Then rival billies threaten each other. If a serious fight develops, they will lunge at each other's rumps with their daggerlike horns. Toward a female, a male acts differently. He crawls on his belly and bleats softly like a kid.

Young are born in late spring. A nanny usually

Balanced on a steep slope, a nanny feeds on tender ▷ new leaves that cover a hillside. Her days-old kid stays close to her. A billy (in the small picture) nibbles tiny plants from the surface of a rock.

▽ Bath time for a billy means a roll in the dust. The spray of soil helps keep his coat free of oil and insects. Powerful shoulders and stocky legs give a mountain goat the strength a good climber needs.

Toggenburg goat: 32 in (81 cm) tall at the shoulder

◁ *Mountain goats scramble at a dizzying height above Lake Ellen Wilson in Glacier National Park in Montana.*
▽ *Like many other domestic— or tame—goats, this nanny has no horns. Goats provide people with milk, cheese, and meat. And for centuries people have prized the fine wool of Angora and Kashmir goats.*

Mixed-breed domestic goat: 32 in (81 cm) tall at the shoulder

△ *Sleek and healthy, a Toggenburg goat of Switzerland grazes in a meadow. Swiss goats are champion milk producers. Easy and inexpensive to raise, goats are often called "the poor man's cow."*

has one kid. But she may have twins. Within minutes, a newborn kid struggles to its feet. Soon it is nursing, guzzling its first meal. Before long, it may try climbing its first steep slope.

Nannies keep careful watch over their young. Kids are frisky and often get into trouble. They might scramble up on a boulder and leap off. A frightened kid may run to its nanny for safety. The kid tucks itself between its mother's legs.

Kids stay with their mothers for almost a year— longer if she doesn't have another kid. During that time, they learn where to find the tender plants they eat. They learn where to seek shelter from storms. They learn where bears or wolves might prowl. They learn how to survive in their rugged world.

No real goats are native to North or South America. The common wild goat lives in dry, rocky parts of Asia and on some of the islands in the Mediterranean Sea. The Spanish goat lives in southern Spain. The markhor (MAR-kor) and the tur (TOUR) roam parts of

the high mountain ranges that cover the heart of central Asia.

Goats were domesticated, or tamed, in what is now Iran at least 10,000 years ago. Today domestic goats provide people throughout the world with milk, cheese, meat, leather, and fine wool.

Goats can live in steep, bare places where domestic sheep and cattle cannot roam or find enough to eat. Often nothing grows in such areas because

---

GOAT 🐾 **5 of 6 species**

HEIGHT: 17-42 in (43-107 cm) at the shoulder

WEIGHT: 26-280 lb (12-127 kg)

HABITAT AND RANGE: mountainous regions of western North America and parts of Europe and Asia; domesticated goats live in many parts of the world

FOOD: grasses, herbs, trees, shrubs, and other plants

LIFE SPAN: 9 to 12 years in the wild

REPRODUCTION: 1 to 3 young after a pregnancy of 5 or 6 months

ORDER: artiodactyls

Goat

goats have already eaten all the plants. Tame or wild, goats feed on almost anything that grows. They nibble plants down to the ground and even uproot them. They snap twigs off bushes and peel bark off trees. Goats do not chew their food completely before swallowing it. After eating, they bring up a cud—a wad of partly digested food—and chew it thoroughly. Then they swallow and digest it.

Goats are closely related to sheep. One common difference between the two is the shape of their horns. A sheep's horns grow out to the side, then down and up again. A goat's horns usually grow straight up and then curve back.

The horns of the Kashmir markhor sweep up in graceful spirals. The Turkmen markhor's horns twist up in tight corkscrew curls. The tur and the bharal (BUH-rul) have thick, rounded horns. Male wild goats have much larger horns than females have. They may also have flowing beards and manes. In addition, male goats give off a strong odor.

At mating time, the males fight with each other and show off

for the females. Wild goats fight head to head. Sometimes two bucks lock horns and pull sideways.

To learn more about goats and their relatives, read about chamois, ibexes, serows, sheep, and tahrs under their own headings.

Female Kashmir markhor leads the way across a ▷ slope in Pakistan. Large, spiraling horns identify the male in the middle. Twin kids bring up the rear.

▽ Bharal, or blue sheep, bask in winter sunshine high above the tree line in Nepal. Despite their name and appearance, they are more like goats than like sheep. The heavy horns of male bharal keep growing throughout their lives. The bigger the horns, the older— and probably the stronger—the animal.

Bharal: 36 in (91 cm) tall at the shoulder

Kashmir markhor: 40 in (102 cm) tall at the shoulder

Turkmen markhor: 40 in (102 cm) tall at the shoulder

△ *Elegant swirling horns crown a regal Turkmen markhor. Its magnificent flowing mane sweeps down from its neck. Such goats make their homes in the high mountains of central Asia.*

▽ *Popping out from behind a rock, a Spanish goat shows its impressive horns. Hunters have long prized as trophies the curving horns of this rare animal.*

Spanish goat: 28 in (71 cm) tall at the shoulder

Gorilla

◁ *Face framed by leaves, a gorilla stares from a tropical thicket in Africa. The crest of hair on its huge head shows that this animal is an older male. Traveling on all fours, a group* ▷ *of gorillas moves from one lush feeding spot to another. The forest offers food at their fingertips —from roots and bamboo shoots to the bark and pulp of trees.*
▽ *Young gorilla rides on its mother's back through dense underbrush. A gorilla begins to travel in this way at about four months of age. Some continue for two years or more.*

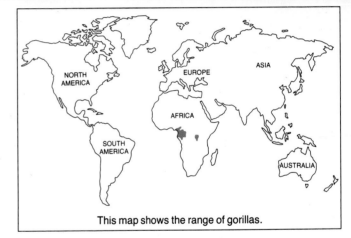

This map shows the range of gorillas.

"HU-HU-HU." Standing up and thumping his chest, an adult male gorilla can be an incredible sight. But don't let his looks scare you. The huge ape is quite peaceful most of the time.

A full-grown male gorilla can measure 6 feet (183 cm) long and weigh as much as 400 pounds (181 kg). Females are smaller and weigh only about half as much. Like the other apes—chimpanzees, orangutans, and gibbons—gorillas have no tails.

Gorillas roam the dense, moist forests of Africa. There they live in groups of two to thirty members. One kind of gorilla—the lowland gorilla—is found in west-central Africa. Scientists know little about the animal's habits in the wild. Another kind—the mountain gorilla—makes its home in forests in east-central Africa. Though they sometimes climb trees, adult gorillas spend most of the time on the ground. They usually travel along on all fours with their weight on their feet and on the knuckles of their hands. They can walk upright for short distances.

A mature male guides each group of mountain gorillas. He is called a silverback because he is older and the hair across his lower back has turned a silver color. The other gorillas follow his lead when it is time to feed, to travel, or to build night nests.

Silverbacks sometimes show off by hooting, standing up, and wildly throwing plants around. They beat their chests, *(Continued on page 244)*

Gorilla

Broad-shouldered male gorilla—called a silverback—surveys his range in a mountain forest in east-central Africa. He gets his name from the saddle of silver-colored hair across his lower back. A silverback often acts as the leader of a gorilla group. He guides other gorillas in their daily activities, determining when a group will move and when it will eat. The others also follow his example in building leafy nests in which to sleep. Sometimes, in a show of leadership, a silverback will stand upright and beat his chest. At right, a frisky young gorilla plays in a tree. Between the ages of three and six, gorillas often slide down trunks and climb and swing on branches.

△ *Soft tree pulp makes a snack for a female gorilla. Behind her, other gorillas rest in the underbrush.*

Fuzzy young gorilla plays with a leaf. Gorillas start ▷ *eating plants several months after birth.*

making hollow sounds that can be heard far away. The display shows a silverback's position as leader. It also is used to scare away intruders.

Gorillas have no trouble finding food in the lush forests where they live. Because of their size, these animals need a large amount of food every day. Their diet includes wild celery, roots, and the pulp and bark of trees. They also eat bamboo shoots and fruit in certain seasons.

After feeding, a group of gorillas settles down for a rest. Occasionally the animals pile together leafy plants for a day nest. Later the group again searches for food. As evening approaches, the gorillas make night nests, usually on the ground.

A female gorilla gives birth to only one young after a pregnancy of about eight and a half months. The newborn is helpless and tiny, weighing less than 4 pounds (2 kg) at birth. At first, the young gorilla clings to its mother's chest. Later, it learns to ride on her back. By two years of age, a gorilla has begun to move about on its own. But it may share its mother's nest until it is five.

Between the ages of three and six, gorillas act much like children. They spend their time playing. They climb trees, swing on branches, slide down tree trunks, chase each other through the forest, and even play a game that looks like tug-of-war. They also imitate adult gorillas.

 Gorilla

GORILLA 🐾 1 of 1 species

STANDING HEIGHT: **4-6 ft (122-183 cm)**

WEIGHT: **150-400 lb (68-181 kg)**

HABITAT AND RANGE: **dense, moist lowland and mountain forests in west-central and east-central Africa**

FOOD: **wild celery, roots, tree bark and pulp, fruit, and bamboo shoots**

LIFE SPAN: **up to 54 years in captivity**

REPRODUCTION: **usually 1 young after a pregnancy of about 8½ months**

ORDER: **primates**

◁ *Dangling in midair, a female gorilla hangs by her long, strong arms. As gorillas jump down from trees, they may break branches simply to make noise.*

▽ *Mossy fork of a massive tree provides a comfortable sun deck for an adult gorilla. More often, adults sunbathe on the ground. Gorillas frequently bask for an hour or two at a time.*

Lesser grison: 17 in (43 cm) long; tail, 7 in (18 cm)

Grison

(GRIZ-un)

This map shows the range of grisons.

GRISON

LENGTH OF HEAD AND BODY: 16-23 in (41-58 cm); tail, 6-8 in (15-20 cm)

WEIGHT: 2-7 lb (1-3 kg)

HABITAT AND RANGE: tropical forests, woodlands, and grasslands from Mexico through South America

FOOD: rodents, young birds, eggs, and fruit

LIFE SPAN: 10 years in captivity

REPRODUCTION: 2 to 4 young after a pregnancy of 39 days

ORDER: carnivores

Common grison: 20 in (51 cm) long; tail, 7 in (18 cm)

Headband of white fur highlights a common grison (above) as it pokes its head out of a hole. At top, a lesser grison sits in a tree. These animals usually search for food on the ground.

A HOLLOW LOG or a rocky shelter may serve as a den for the long, slender grison of Mexico and Central and South America. Or this member of the weasel family may take over a large rodent's burrow. Grisons make their homes in forests, on grasslands, and sometimes near towns. Grisons are thought to live in pairs or small groups. There are usually two to four offspring in a litter.

Moving briskly along the ground, grisons hunt

both by day and by night. They feed on small animals. When a grison goes after a rodent like a vizcacha, it may follow the prey into its burrow. Grisons also catch birds on the ground.

Like its relative the badger, the grison has a black-and-gray coat with white markings. A white stripe goes across its forehead and down to its shoulders. Grisons also have scent glands. These give off a strong-smelling odor when the animals are excited or threatened. Read about badgers and other relatives of grisons—ratels, skunks, and zorillas—under their own headings.

Groundhog
Groundhog is another name for the woodchuck. Learn about woodchucks and other marmots on page 352.

Guanaco
The guanaco is a close relative of the llama. Read about both animals on page 336.

Guenon
The guenon is a kind of monkey. Read about guenons and other monkeys on page 370.

Guinea pig
(GINN-ee pig)

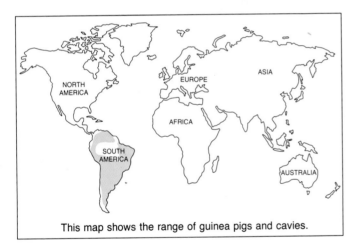

This map shows the range of guinea pigs and cavies.

Long-haired guinea pig: 10 in (25 cm) long

ONCE YOU HAVE HEARD the sound it makes, you can guess why this little animal has "pig" in its name. When the guinea pig gets excited, it often squeals like a pig.

The guinea pig is not related to the pig. This

Guinea pigs may differ greatly in the kinds of coats they have. A short-haired guinea pig (right) climbs over toadstools. The coat of the multicolored long-haired guinea pig (top, right) sweeps the ground. Although one guinea pig may look very different from another, there is only one kind, or species, of guinea pig.

Short-haired guinea pig: 10 in (25 cm) long

plump, short-legged animal is really a rodent. Guinea pigs are much smaller than real pigs. They measure only about 10 inches (25 cm) long.

A guinea pig may be black, white, yellow, brown, or a combination of these colors. Its hair may be short or long, straight or curly. Though one guinea pig may differ from another, there is only one species of domestic guinea pig.

Female guinea pigs usually bear one to four offspring after a pregnancy of about two months. Young guinea pigs nurse for about three weeks. But, if necessary, they can survive without their mothers after about five days.

The guinea pig developed from a small wild animal called the cavy (KAY-vee). Many hundreds of years ago, people in South America began to capture cavies and to raise them for food. Explorers saw these animals and took some of them back to Europe. After years of breeding, the wild cavy became the tame guinea pig we know today.

GUINEA PIG AND CAVY

LENGTH OF HEAD AND BODY: 6-16 in (15-41 cm)

WEIGHT: 11-50 oz (312-1,418 g)

HABITAT AND RANGE: rocky areas, grasslands, open woodlands, swamps, and dry plains in parts of South America; guinea pigs are kept as pets in many parts of the world

FOOD: grasses, herbs, and other plants

LIFE SPAN: about 8 years in captivity

REPRODUCTION: usually 1 to 4 young after a pregnancy of about 2 months

ORDER: rodents

Desert cavy: 8 in (20 cm) long

△ *Wild relative of the guinea pig, a desert cavy stretches to pluck a berry from a bush. These cavies live on dry plains in southern Argentina. The color of their coats blends well with the sandy soil.*

◁ *Female desert cavy nurses her young, even though they can eat some plants soon after birth. These newborn—like newborn guinea pigs—have hair and teeth. A desert cavy usually gives birth to two young in a litter.*

The guinea pig still has many wild relatives in South America. All of them are members of the cavy family. Of about fifteen species of cavies, most are the same size as the guinea pig. The desert cavy, for instance, measures only about 8 inches (20 cm) long. It lives on dry plains in southern Argentina.

Other species of cavies live in different parts of South America and in many kinds of terrain—rocky areas, grasslands, open woodlands, and swamps. Cavies, like many rodents, eat grasses, herbs, and other plants. They have sharp front teeth for cutting and gnawing and strong back teeth for grinding. Their teeth grow all their lives. Unless a rodent gnaws a great deal, its front teeth become so long that it cannot close its mouth. Then it is not able to chew or to swallow its food.

Gymnure

(JIM-nur)

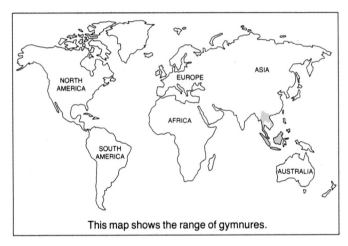

This map shows the range of gymnures.

Moonrat: 17 in (43 cm) long; tail, 8 in (20 cm)

Pointed teeth and bristling fur warn intruders to leave this gymnure—called a moonrat—alone. When threatened, the moonrat, largest of several kinds of gymnures, opens its mouth wide and hisses loudly.

WADDLING ALONG THE FOREST FLOOR at night, the gymnure noses through leaves and underbrush, searching for worms, insects, and snails to eat. There are several kinds of gymnures. One kind, the moonrat, lives near water and catches frogs and fish. As a gymnure travels about, glands at the base of its tail produce an unpleasant-smelling substance. The gymnure leaves this scent along its path. At dawn, it curls up in a hollow log to sleep.

With its small round ears, whiskered snout, and nearly hairless tail, the gymnure looks almost like a rodent. But it is not—it is in the same family as the hedgehog. Because it has a fuzzy coat, this animal of Southeast Asia is often called a hairy hedgehog. Find out about hedgehogs on page 256.

The gymnure was not known to scientists until about 150 years ago. Although experts now have identified at least four kinds of gymnures, they still know little about the animals.

GYMNURE 🐾 **4 of 6 species**

LENGTH OF HEAD AND BODY: 4-17 in (10-43 cm); tail, 1-8 in (3-20 cm)

WEIGHT: 2-49 oz (57-1,389 g)

HABITAT AND RANGE: forests and mangrove swamps in Southeast Asia

FOOD: insects, worms, plants, and small water animals

LIFE SPAN: more than 7 years in captivity for moonrat; unknown for other species

REPRODUCTION: 2 young after a pregnancy of 35-40 days

ORDER: insectivores

H

Hamster

ALTHOUGH THEY ARE FAMILIAR as household pets, several kinds of hamsters also live in the wild. There these rat-size rodents dig burrows along riverbanks, in desert areas, in fields, and sometimes on mountain slopes. These underground homes usually have storerooms, a nest area, and several entrances. Burrows also have separate areas that serve as toilets for the animals.

Hamsters range in length from 2 to 11 inches (5-28 cm). They usually have very short tails, but a few kinds have longer ones. Most hamsters have large pouches in their cheeks. They use these to carry food back to their burrows.

Female hamsters give birth several times a year. The young—usually 4 to 12 in each litter—are born blind and helpless. They grow to full size quickly.

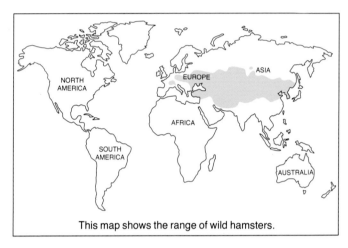

This map shows the range of wild hamsters.

HAMSTER 🐾 **2 of 18 species**

LENGTH OF HEAD AND BODY: **2-11 in (5-28 cm); tail, as long as 4 in (10 cm)**

WEIGHT: **as much as 32 oz (907 g)**

HABITAT AND RANGE: **fields, riverbanks, mountains, and desert areas in parts of Europe and Asia; hamsters are kept as pets in some parts of the world**

FOOD: **fruit, grain, seeds, roots, and small animals**

LIFE SPAN: **2 or 3 years in captivity**

REPRODUCTION: **usually 4 to 12 young after a pregnancy of 2 or 3 weeks**

ORDER: **rodents**

Shiny black eyes of a golden hamster stare out from the animal's round face. Cheek pouches stuffed with food give this hamster a well-fed look.

Golden hamster: 7 in (18 cm) long

Hare

FROM A STANDSTILL, the hare can explode in a powerful jump straight into the air. This furry, long-eared animal can run at speeds of about 40 miles (64 km) an hour. Some hares can also leap forward as far as 10 feet (305 cm) with their long legs and large hind feet. These are impressive feats for an animal that is only about 2 feet (61 cm) long from its twitchy nose to its stubby tail.

Most people cannot tell the difference between a hare and a rabbit. The animals are close relatives, and both live almost everywhere in the world. Hares and rabbits look very much alike. Even their names are

Stretching its powerful hind legs forward, a white-tailed jackrabbit races across a snow-covered field.

confusing. A jackrabbit is really a hare. A Belgian hare is really a rabbit. Usually a hare is larger than a rabbit, and it has longer hind legs. The ears of a hare are also longer than the ears of a rabbit and are often tipped with black.

There are about thirty kinds of hares. They can survive in almost any climate and in any terrain, as long as they can find shelter and low-growing plants to eat. The animals live in open country and in forests, in mountains and in deserts.

In North America, most hares live alone. They generally do not live in burrows. Their dens, called forms, are often in the open and are not much more than shallow places in the ground. A hare digs this kind of resting place with its forefeet. A single hare may have several forms. Some may use the empty dens of foxes and marmots. Others may seek shelter in caves or under rocks.

A hare's life can be very dangerous. Coyotes, lynxes, foxes, eagles, hawks, and owls prey on hares. Hares are hunted by people, too. For centuries, they have killed hares for their meat, for their fur, and for sport. The animals can be pests to farmers, eating garden vegetables and other crops.

HARE 🐾 **4 of 31 species**

***LENGTH OF HEAD AND BODY:* 14-28 in (36-71 cm); tail, 2-4 in (5-10 cm)**

***WEIGHT:* 3-12 lb (1-5 kg)**

***HABITAT AND RANGE:* forests, grasslands, tundra, deserts, and mountains worldwide, except for Antarctica and some oceanic islands (brought to South America and Australia)**

***FOOD:* grasses, herbs, shrubs, twigs, and bark**

***LIFE SPAN:* as long as 7 years in captivity**

***REPRODUCTION:* 2 to 8 young after a pregnancy of about 1½ months**

***ORDER:* lagomorphs**

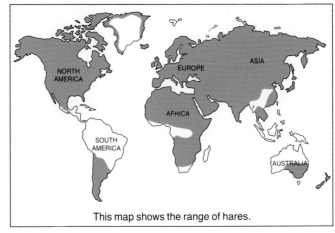

This map shows the range of hares.

Blue hare: 21 in (53 cm) long; tail, 3 in (8 cm)

Most kinds of hares are in no danger of dying out, however, because there are so many of them. Some female hares have as many as four litters a year. Each litter may include from two to eight young. A newborn hare, called a leveret (LEV-uh-rut), has its eyes open and is covered with fur. It can hop just minutes after it is born. A female hare spends little time taking care of her young.

Hares eat only plants. They feed alone, usually in the morning and in the evening. The animals nibble mainly grasses and herbs. When food is scarce in winter, they eat shrubs, twigs, and even bark. The little water they need comes mostly from the plants they eat. Hares cut or nip plants with their sharp front teeth. Hares grow two pairs of upper front teeth, one set right behind the other. The front pair continues to grow as long as the animals live, just as a rodent's front teeth do. Hares are not rodents, though. Scientists put them in a separate group with pikas and rabbits. Read about pikas on page 436 and rabbits on page 466 of this book.

As they hop around their home range, hares often mark the land with their scent. They even mark

◁ Protected by its coloring, a blue hare pauses at the entrance of its resting place high in the Alps of Switzerland. When the snow melts, this hare's coat will change to brown.

▽ From winter to summer, the color of a snowshoe hare gradually changes. In winter, the hare's fur is light colored (below, left) and grows in long and thick. In late spring (below, center), its fur coat shows a mix of white and brown. A hare's summer coat (below, right) grows in darker and shorter. Smallest of the more than 20 kinds of hares—a snowshoe hare weighs less than 3 pounds (1 kg).

Snowshoe hare: 15 in (38 cm) long; tail, 2 in (5 cm)

Hare

Cape hare freezes, ▷
sitting perfectly still
among plants in South
Africa. The lack of
movement helps hide
the animal from its
enemies. Eyes on the
sides of its head give
a hare a wide angle
of vision. It sees best
at dusk.

△ *Black-naped hare,*
named for the dark patch
of fur on the back of its
neck, feeds on grasses in
Sri Lanka. This kind of
hare may take shelter in
caves or in hollow logs.
◁ *Antelope jackrabbit*
skims the ground with all
four feet in the air. These
large hares, the fastest of
all, can reach speeds of 40
miles (64 km) an hour.
They may cover 10 feet
(305 cm) in a single leap.
Their ears measure about
7 inches (18 cm) long—
about one-third the length
of their bodies.

Antelope jackrabbit: 21 in (53 cm) long; tail, 3 in (8 cm)

Young European hares, barely one week old (below, left), nestle together for warmth in an English
marsh. Two adults (below, right) stand ready to fight during the mating season.

European hare: 22 in (56 cm) long; tail, 4 in (10 cm)

Arctic hare: 21 in (53 cm) long; tail, 2 in (5 cm)

◁ *Well camouflaged in its coat of white, an arctic hare in northern Canada fluffs up its fur for warmth. In the Far North, hares stay white all year. Farther south, some arctic hares change to a grayish color in summer.*

▽ *In early evening, a black-tailed jackrabbit sniffs for food or for the scent of other hares. This North American hare often takes shelter near bushes.*

Black-tailed jackrabbit: 19 in (48 cm) long; tail, 3 in (8 cm)

themselves. Special glands on a hare's lower jaw put out a strong-smelling liquid. A hare rubs its jaw on the ground or on a twig to mark the area as its own. When a hare grooms itself, it spreads some of this liquid over its body. Because of other scent glands near its tail, a hare can leave its scent while sitting. This strong smell lets other hares know that it has been there. Scent also helps males and females find each other at mating time.

To protect themselves, hares rely on their senses of hearing, smell, and sight. When its senses alert it to danger, a hare may react in one of several ways. If the enemy is far away, the hare may sneak away, keeping its ears low and running close to the ground. It often hides among shrubs that are growing nearby. If an enemy is close by, though, the hare may freeze. It sits still, with its head down, ears back, and nose twitching. It is difficult to see the hare—even on bare ground. If the enemy comes closer, the hare may pop into the air in a mighty leap. It dashes away with its ears up and tail down. The hare can outrun many animals that chase it.

When a hare is being chased, it tries to stay within its home range. At first, it runs in a straight line. If the enemy gets too close, however, the hare may run in a zigzag pattern. Running zigzag helps throw its pursuer off balance. A hare may even swim a short distance to escape.

A hare runs by moving its forefeet first. Then it jerks its rear end forward. Its hind feet hit the ground in front of its forefeet. When moving slowly, a hare curves its tail along its back. When the animal runs fast, its tail moves up and down.

All hares molt, or gradually shed their hair. Some molt twice a year. For most of these animals, summer hair is short and dark. Winter hair is usually thick, long, and light. Some North American hares grow white hair in autumn. This coloring helps hide them during snowy winters. The snowshoe hare changes from white in winter to grayish brown in summer. The change explains its other name, varying hare. Most arctic hares stay white all year round, but a few molt to a grayish color in summer. Hares in desert areas are almost red. Some of the hares in Asia are completely black.

Hares have lived near people for centuries. They often appear in stories and folklore around the world. More than 2,000 years ago, the Greek storyteller Aesop created the fable of the speedy hare that lost a race to the slow-but-steady tortoise. And one of the most famous characters in *Alice in Wonderland* is the March Hare.

Hartebeest

The hartebeest is a kind of antelope. Read about antelopes on page 52.

Hedgehog

(HEDGE-hog)

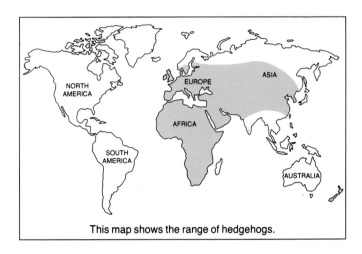

This map shows the range of hedgehogs.

HEDGEHOG 🐾 I of 15 species

LENGTH OF HEAD AND BODY: 5-12 in (13-30 cm); tail, 1-2 in (3-5 cm)

WEIGHT: 14-39 oz (397-1,106 g)

HABITAT AND RANGE: forests, plains, and deserts of Europe, Asia, and Africa (brought by people to New Zealand)

FOOD: insects, snails, mice, birds, frogs, lizards, and snakes

LIFE SPAN: about 10 years in captivity

REPRODUCTION: I to 7 young after a pregnancy of I or 2 months, depending on species

ORDER: insectivores

European hedgehog: 11 in (28 cm) long; tail, 1 in (3 cm)

△ *Soft, white spines stick out from the backs of five-day-old hedgehogs in a grassy nest. As the animals grow, their spines will become stiffer, sharper, and longer. At about two weeks of age, young hedgehogs open their eyes. Soon after, they begin to follow their mother as she hunts for food. After several months, they can live on their own. A full-grown European hedgehog (top) sits by a mountain stream before jumping in.*

SMALL ENOUGH TO FIT IN YOUR HANDS—but too prickly to hold—the hedgehog has armor that resembles needles in a pincushion. Thousands of stiff, sharp spines stick out from the animal's back.

By curling up and tucking in its head and legs, the hedgehog can turn its body into a spiked ball. A rounded shield of spines almost completely encloses its hairy face and underparts. In this position, the hedgehog is usually safe from attackers. It even sleeps curled up.

Only a few animals—such as badgers and foxes—can pry open a rolled-up hedgehog. Because most other animals leave it alone, the hedgehog does not need to keep silent to avoid discovery. When angry, it screams. It often snorts, coughs, and wheezes as it pokes about in the dirt for food.

Hedgehogs feed on cockroaches, snails, young mice, birds, frogs, and lizards. Some people keep hedgehogs as pets because they eat garden pests. Hedgehogs also feed on bees and wasps. The stings seem to have no effect on the hardy little mammals. Sometimes a hedgehog will even attack a poisonous snake for food. Usually its spiny coat will protect it from the fangs.

Hedgehogs can live in many kinds of climates and terrains. They are found in parts of Europe, Africa, and Asia. Settlers took them to New Zealand about a hundred years ago.

A hedgehog roams within its own small territory. Each night, it trots along the same pathways looking for food. It sleeps during the day in a grass-lined nest hidden by rocks, hedges, or underbrush.

If food is scarce, a hedgehog may sleep for weeks at a time. In cool climates, the animal's long sleep takes place in winter. Its breathing and heart rate slow down, and its temperature falls. Scientists call this hibernation (hye-bur-NAY-shun).

In desert regions, a hedgehog sleeps through the driest summer weather. This hot-weather slumber is called aestivation (es-tuh-VAY-shun). An animal that aestivates does not sleep as deeply as an animal that hibernates.

Female hedgehogs give birth to as many as seven young in a litter. The newborn are covered with soft, white spines. Their spines become stiffer, sharper, and longer as the offspring grow.

◁ *African hedgehog scampers across sandy soil hunting for food. Usually it stays in its nest during the day.*

African hedgehog: 10 in (25 cm) long; tail, 1 in (3 cm)

△ *Prickly as a pincushion full of needles, an African hedgehog rolls into a tight ball to defend itself.*

◁ *Wiggling snake makes a meal for a long-eared hedgehog. The hedgehog's spiny armor usually protects it from bites.*

Long-eared hedgehog: 9 in (23 cm) long; tail, 1 in (3 cm)

Hippopotamus

△ *Ears, eyes, and nostrils above water, a bull river hippo rests its muzzle on another's back. In water, a hippo usually keeps most of its body under the surface.*

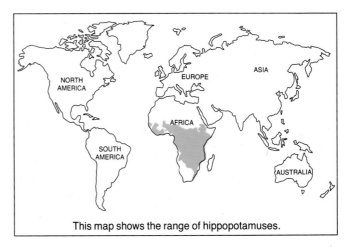

This map shows the range of hippopotamuses.

DESPITE ITS SIZE and awkward looks, the river hippopotamus moves lightly through the water. This huge animal walks like a dancer in slow motion on the bottom of a calm river. As it rises to take a breath, its great head breaks the surface. Bulging eyes pop open. Ears unfold and wag, sending up a shower of water droplets. "Un-n-nk," grunts the hippo loudly. Other hippos answer.

The hippopotamus is one of the largest land mammals in the world. A bull hippo can measure 15 feet (5 m) long and can weigh 8,000 pounds (3,629 kg). A female is usually smaller.

People have known about the hippopotamus for thousands of years. Ancient Egyptians made models of hippos and glazed them blue. Greeks named the animal *hippopotamus,* which means "river horse." Hippos are more closely related to pigs than to horses, however. Romans exhibited captured hippos in their arenas.

Until recent times, hippos ranged throughout most of Africa. They could be seen in lakes, streams, and rivers. Because of hunting and the spread of farms, hippos have now disappeared from many areas. Today these barrel-shaped animals live mostly in central and southern Africa. In a few places, there still may be as many as 2,000 hippos in a 20-mile (32-km) stretch of a river.

The hippo is well adapted, or suited, to its life in the water. With eyes, ears, and nostrils on the top of its head, it can see, hear, and breathe even when most of its body remains underwater. A good swimmer, the animal stays in water much of the day.

From time to time, a hippo may sink from sight beneath the surface. An adult hippo may stay on the bottom for as long as five minutes. Its heart rate slows down. The animal may walk along the bottom, following underwater trails that it and other hippos have made. The hippo's great weight keeps it from floating to the surface.

A hippo's skin is thick and almost hairless. Oily red drops ooze from its pores. People once thought that the animal was sweating blood. But this thick, red

◁ *Female hippos and young rest in the calm waters of an African river. Some sun themselves on the sandy bank. Others cool off in the shallows at the river's edge.*

HIPPOPOTAMUS 🐾 **2 of 2 species**

LENGTH OF HEAD AND BODY: 12-15 ft (4-5 m); tail, 16-22 in (41-56 cm). Pygmy: 59-69 in (150-175 cm); tail, 6-7 in (15-18 cm)

WEIGHT: 5,000-8,000 lb (2,268-3,629 kg). Pygmy: 400-600 lb (181-272 kg)

HABITAT AND RANGE: rivers, lakes, and streams of central and southern Africa. Pygmy: wet forests in parts of western Africa

FOOD: grasses and water plants. Pygmy: leaves, shoots, grasses, and fruit

LIFE SPAN: up to 61 years in captivity. Pygmy: as long as 44 years in captivity

REPRODUCTION: 1 young after a pregnancy of 7 or 8 months, depending on species

ORDER: artiodactyls

River hippo: 13 ft (4 m) long; tail, 20 in (51 cm)

Hippopotamus

away neatly. As they munch the grass, hippos make a lot of noise. Mothers and their young feed close together. Others feed alone. An adult hippopotamus may eat 150 pounds (68 kg) of grass in a night. That may seem like a lot, but it's not very much for such a huge animal.

A hippo's front teeth keep growing throughout the animal's life. The teeth used for chewing are worn down as the animal grows older. In its lower jaw are two tusks, which may grow more than 1 foot (30 cm) long. These tusks wear against a hippo's upper teeth and stay sharp.

Strong male hippos control territories, or

△ *Open w-i-d-e! A female hippo yawns, flashing pink gums and pointed tusks. An open mouth may mean excitement, or it may signal a threat. Hippos also open their mouths wide before they leave the water to feed.*

Rearing up with a splash and a roar, a male and a ▷ female hippo slam their jaws together in a courtship display. Other females surround them.

liquid actually keeps the hippo's skin moist. It also may help to kill germs and to heal wounds.

After sundown—earlier on cloudy days—hippos leave the water to feed on land. A hippopotamus may look fat and awkward, but its body is muscular. Hippos easily climb steep banks using well-worn footholds. Out of the water, hippos walk in line on narrow paths to grazing grounds as far as 5 miles (8 km) away. If danger threatens, hippos will hurry back to the safety of the water. The animals can run as fast as a person can over short distances.

Although hippos sometimes eat water plants, grass is their main food. A hippo closes its huge, tough lips around a mouthful of grass, then tears the food

mating areas, in the water and on the nearby land. The territory can measure about 1,000 feet (305 m) long and 165 feet (50 m) wide. A bull hippo is master of his territory. But he allows other male hippos in as visitors. He may challenge them by opening his enormous mouth and displaying his tusks. The visitors must show their respect or he will chase them away. Sometimes two bull hippopotamuses challenge each other at the boundary of their territories. With mouths open, they rush at each other and meet jaw to jaw. The clash continues until one animal gives up and both of them retreat.

If one hippo tries to take over another's territory, the two fight in a different way. Facing in opposite directions, the animals stand side by side. They swing their heads sideways and up. Each one tries to drive his sharp tusks into the other's sides and rump. The fights may last more than an hour. The blows strike where the hippo's hide is more than 2 inches (5 cm) thick, but the tusks still stab deeply. Scars mark the bodies of many bulls.

Hippos mate in shallow water. Their young are born in the water or on land. After a pregnancy of eight months, a female hippo gives birth to a single grayish pink calf that weighs 100 pounds (45 kg). Sometimes a calf nurses on land, lying like a piglet

the calves are strong enough to keep up on the trips to the grazing grounds. The female walks very close to her offspring. When danger threatens, she defends her young furiously.

A young hippo's first year is a dangerous time. Lions, leopards, hyenas, crocodiles, and wild dogs prey on small hippos. Adults are rarely attacked by other kinds of animals. Hippos may live for more than forty years in the wild.

Another kind of hippo lives in swampy forests in a small area of western Africa. The pygmy hippopotamus, a hog-size animal, is not simply a small copy of its huge relative. Its eyes are set in the sides of its head instead of on top. Its skin is kept moist by a clear liquid instead of a red one.

Not much is known about this rare animal in the wild, though its habits seem to be different from those of the river hippo. The pygmy hippo spends most of its time on land. There it travels along tunnel-like paths in search of food.

Pygmy hippos feed on leaves, shoots, grasses, and fruit. Scientists think that adult pygmy hippos live alone or perhaps in pairs. A calf weighs about 10 pounds (5 kg) at birth.

▽ *Pygmy hippo looks like a hog and weighs only about one-tenth as much as its larger relative. This animal spends most of its time on land rather than in the water. It feeds on leaves, shoots, grasses, and fruit.*

Pygmy hippo: 5 ft (152 cm) long; tail, 7 in (18 cm)

△ *Like islands in a stream, river hippos provide motionless perches for a group of snow-white cattle egrets. When the hippos leave the water for land, the birds follow and catch insects that fly up.*

◁ *Beneath an arch of plants, a young male hippo walks gracefully on the bottom of a shallow pool. Scientists think the fish swimming nearby clean the hippo's skin of bits of plants.*

beside its mother. At other times it may nurse underwater. But in either case, the calf sucks with its nostrils closed and its ears folded shut. It must stop drinking from time to time to breathe.

A young hippo may scramble onto its mother's back and rest while she lies in the water. That way it does not have to struggle to stay afloat.

After a few days, a female hippo and her newborn join the other mothers and calves in a nursery herd. The little ones chase each other and play at fighting. Mothers will stay near the water to feed until

Hog

Wild boar sniffs the air in a forest in France. Despite its shaggy coat, the animal resembles its tame relatives. Adaptable animals, hogs can eat many kinds of food and live in many kinds of terrain.

IF YOU COULD CLIMB aboard a time machine and travel back millions of years, you might find a familiar animal: the hog. Scientists think that hogs have existed for at least 45 million years. And in all that time their stocky, round body and flat snout have changed very little. Hogs go by many names. They are known as swine and as pigs. Male hogs and some kinds of wild pigs are called boars. Females are sows. Young hogs are called piglets.

Domestic, or tame, hogs are important food animals on every continent except Antarctica. Wild pigs roam forests, meadows, and swamps around the world. Africa is home to the giant forest hog and the fierce-looking warthog. The bearded pig lives in Indonesia. In the southern foothills of the Himalaya in Asia, rust-brown pygmy hogs live in the underbrush. Wild boars were brought by people to North America and Hawaii.

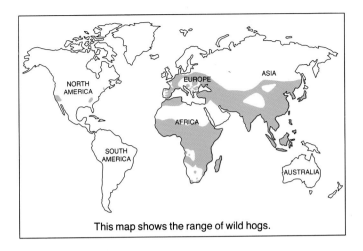

This map shows the range of wild hogs.

HOG 🐾 **7 of 15 species**

HEIGHT: 12-40 in (30-102 cm) at the shoulder

WEIGHT: 13-800 lb (6-363 kg)

HABITAT AND RANGE: forests, grasslands, meadows, and swamps in Africa, Asia, Europe, and North America; domestic hogs live in many parts of the world

FOOD: small animals and all kinds of plants

LIFE SPAN: 15 to 20 years in the wild

REPRODUCTION: 2 to 12 young after a pregnancy of about 3½ to 5 months; domestic hogs may have many more young

ORDER: artiodactyls

Hogs will eat just about anything they can get their snouts on: roots, grasses, fruit, nuts, herbs, mushrooms, worms, and even snakes. Hogs have been able to live successfully in so many different places because they can find food almost anywhere. To find food, the animals often root, or dig into the ground with their snouts. Pigs hardly ever overeat, even though we call a person who stuffs himself with food a "pig."

Because hogs like to wallow in mud, people sometimes think of them as dirty animals. But when they have a choice hogs stay in clean water, rather than in mud. Lying in water helps hogs cool off on a hot day. The animals have few sweat glands in their skin so they cannot cool off by sweating. They take frequent cool baths to keep their body temperatures low and to escape from insects.

Hogs are intelligent animals. Like dogs, they can learn to sit up and to roll over on command. Some hogs even appear in circus acts, dancing and doing tricks. Hogs used in experiments have learned how to switch on heat lamps to warm up their cages. Centuries ago, some people in England trained hogs as hunting companions. Because of their sensitive noses and keen hearing, the hogs made good helpers for the hunters.

In the wild, most pigs live in groups called sounders, although some older boars live alone. Hogs stay close to each other most of the time. Piglets pile close together when they sleep. Since they have little hair, this helps keep them warm.

Hogs communicate with each other by making different noises. High-pitched squeals signal danger. Low grunts mean contentment. Hogs often grunt quietly as they eat. The animals produce a variety of other sounds. They use them during courtship and while searching for food.

Hogs come in many sizes. The smallest member of the pig family, the pygmy hog, grows only about 1 foot (30 cm) tall at the shoulder. It weighs about 13 pounds (6 kg). The giant forest hog is about 40 inches (102 cm) tall and weighs 600 pounds (275 kg). Some domestic hogs are even heavier. Farmers fatten some of their breeding hogs until they weigh as much as 900 pounds (450 kg)!

Also large—and much hardier than domestic

Wild piglet about two weeks old stands unsteadily in a field in Malaysia. The light stripes on its coat will begin to fade within three months. After a year, the animal will grow thick, bristly hair.

Southeast Asian pig: 33 in (84 cm) tall at the shoulder when fully grown

Hog

▽ *Warthog sow and her piglet wallow in mud along a river in South Africa. Such mud baths keep the warthogs cool and help them escape from biting insects. Warthog piglets do not have striped coats like those of other young hogs. Instead, they have thick, reddish hair.*

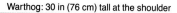
Warthog: 30 in (76 cm) tall at the shoulder

Giant forest hog: 40 in (102 cm) tall at the shoulder

△ *Giant forest hogs, marked by crescent-shaped growths under their eyes, head for a water hole in Kenya. Scientists discovered this kind of hog in 1904.*

hogs—are European wild boars. These bristly animals have massive bodies and large heads and can weigh as much as 700 pounds (318 kg). Males have long, sharp tusks, which they use in fights over females. But males have some protection from each other's tusks. Just before mating season, when the battles occur, the skin on boars' flanks grows especially thick. Female wild boars also have tusks. But they use them for digging rather than for fighting.

Wild boars wander through the forests of many European countries, including Germany, Spain, Belgium, Holland, and France. In England, they died out more than 200 years ago. Wild boars also live in many Asian countries. Domestic hogs are descendants of the wild boar.

The bushpig is another wild member of the pig family. Bushpigs live in most parts of Africa south of the Sahara. Like many wild swine, they are active after dark. Bushpigs spend much of their time rooting in the ground trying to find food. These wild pigs grow about 30 inches (76 cm) tall, and they have short, very sharp tusks. Some kinds are colorful. The red river hog, for example, has bright white markings on its rust-colored coat.

The warthog is one of the fiercest-looking mammals in the world. The male's long, flat head is dotted with bumps that look like huge warts. Four pointed tusks stick out from the sides of the animal's large snout. Its face is long, and tiny eyes shine from the top of its forehead.

In spite of its appearance, the warthog is a peaceful animal. Rather than fight, it will turn and run away from an enemy. With its tufted tail sticking straight up into the air, the animal gallops along at 30 miles (48 km) an hour.

A warthog often protects itself by hiding in an

◁ *Hightailing it across the grasslands of Africa, a group of warthogs runs for cover. The animals point their tufted tails straight into the air as they go. Warthogs can move as fast as 30 miles (48 km) an hour.*

▽ *Yellow-billed oxpecker perches on a warthog's shoulder. The bird searches for ticks on the skin of the fierce-looking animal. The oxpecker also may signal danger. If another animal comes near, the bird will fly off. This alerts the warthog to watch out for trouble.*

Hog

empty aardvark den. When a group of warthogs is in danger, the young animals scurry quickly into the den. Then an adult backs in, blocking the entrance and protecting the young behind it. Any animal that tries to follow runs right into the adult warthog's sharp tusks.

Female warthogs also use abandoned aardvark dens to raise their young. Other kinds of wild pigs prepare nests for their offspring. Before giving birth,

Chester White hog: 36 in (91 cm) tall at the shoulder when fully grown

◁ *Three-week-old Chester White piglets snuggle for warmth on a hog farm. People throughout the United States raise these hogs for their meat.*

▽ *Colorful coat of a female red river hog in Africa shows why people sometimes call this animal "the dandy of the pig family."*

△ *Indian women in Ecuador herd hogs in a mountain*

a pregnant sow will go off by herself to make the nest. She builds a mound of leaves and grasses and hides her young inside.

Both wild and domestic sows are careful about raising their young. A mother hog will fiercely defend her offspring from danger. She will fight anything that dares to approach her litter. A wild sow gives birth to 2

Red river hog: 30 in (76 cm) tall at the shoulder

South American domestic hog: 30 in (76 cm) tall at the shoulder

pasture. The dark woolly coats of the hogs protect them from cool temperatures and heavy rains.

to 12 piglets. Domestic hogs may have even larger litters: On a hog farm in the Midwest, one sow gave birth to 27 piglets.

Usually piglets in the wild try to eat solid food soon after birth. But they continue to nurse for about three months. Even when they have become quite large, the piglets will chase their mother and butt against her side until she lets them drink her milk.

Pigs are familiar animals, not only because we see them on farms, but also because they turn up in stories, sayings, and rhymes. Just about everyone knows the tale of "The Three Little Pigs." And most people have had their feet tickled as someone recited, "This little piggy went to market. . . ."

Horse

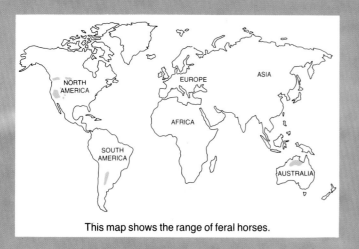

This map shows the range of feral horses.

MANE FLYING AND HOOVES THUNDERING, a galloping horse inspires images of wildness and freedom. For centuries, people have admired horses for their strength, their beauty, their spirit, and their speed. Horses probably were first tamed by nomadic peoples in Asia about 4,000 years ago. They captured wild horses with thick coats that roamed the treeless plains. They used the horses as work animals and drank the milk of the mares. Gradually, the practice of taming and breeding horses spread into Europe. From there, explorers brought the animals to North and South America.

Horses are well equipped for running. With

Mustang mares and their long-legged foals gallop across a rolling prairie in Wyoming. These wild descendants of tame horses roam in scattered bands in parts of the western United States.

Mustang: 55 in (140 cm) tall at the withers — the ridge between the shoulders

their strong, muscular bodies, they can run for many miles at a time. Their nostrils flare wide to let air into their large lungs. Though a horse pounds the ground with tremendous force as it runs, its feet are protected by hard hooves. The foot is actually a single toe, and the hoof is like a very thick toenail.

Horses spend most of the day grazing. They bite grasses and other plants with sharp front teeth. Then they grind the food with large, ridged back teeth. Though a horse's teeth keep growing, their surfaces slowly wear away over many years of use. By looking at a horse's teeth, an expert can usually tell the animal's age.

Ears laid back, a gray mustang mare fights off a stallion. Stallions often nip and chase mares to keep their bands moving and grazing together.

Horse

Clydesdale: 65 in (165 cm) tall at the withers

In many parts of the world, bands of feral (FEAR-ul) horses roam free. These animals are the descendants of tame horses. In western North America, feral horses called mustangs descended from animals that were brought by explorers and settlers as long as 400 years ago.

Wild horses travel in bands of three to twenty animals. A male—called a stallion—guards the females—called mares—and the young foals from such enemies as mountain lions. As his band drinks and

◁ *Long leg hairs fluttering, a Clydesdale prances in a corral. Harnessed in teams, Clydesdales and other draft horses once commonly pulled heavy wagons in cities.*

As a horse moves faster and faster, it changes its gait—or the order in which its feet hit the ground. A horse walks at about 4 miles (6 km) an hour. The hoofbeats are slow and even. Some people think that they sound like the words "knick-er-bock-er, knick-er-bock-er." At a trot, a horse moves at about 9 miles (14 km) an hour. The hoofbeats

WALK

CAN

GAL

Peppy and alert, a Morgan horse, the first American ▷
breed, waits with ears erect. All Morgan horses trace
their ancestry to a stallion owned by Justin Morgan.

grazes, a stallion stands alert. A horse's eyes are
placed near the sides of its head. It can see almost in a
circle without turning its head. A horse also can turn
its ears separately. The position of its ears often shows
its mood. When a horse flicks one ear forward and the
other ear back, it is alert. Both ears pinned back usually means that the animal is angry.

A stallion keeps his band grazing and moving together. He chases off rival stallions that may try to steal
the mares. Stallions *(Continued on page 276)*

Morgan horse: 61 in (155 cm) tall at the withers

sound like "pop-corn, pop-corn." At a canter, a horse travels at about 12 miles (19 km) an hour. The hoofbeats
sound like "ap-ple pie (pause) ap-ple pie." The gallop is the fastest gait. Racehorses can reach 42 miles (68 km) an
hour. The sounds of the hoofbeats blur together.

T R O T

T   E   R

L   O   P

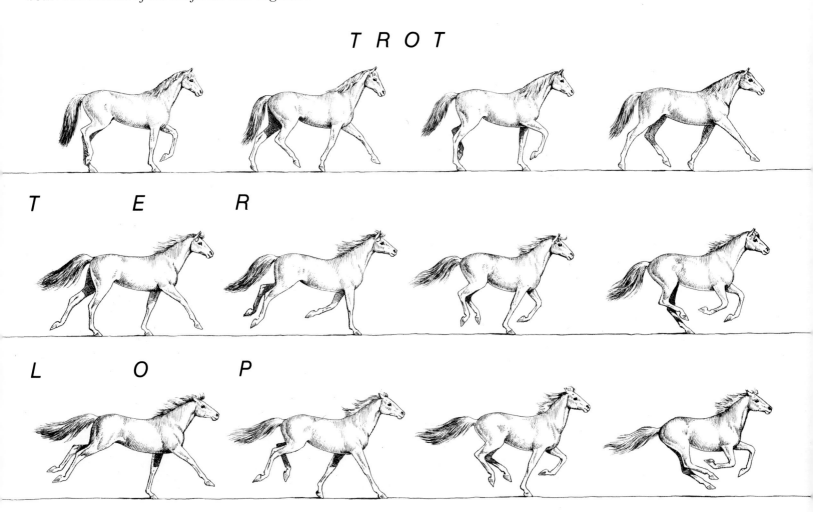

Horse

Camargue horse: 56 in (142 cm) tall at the withers

△ *Egret stands motionless on the back of a pregnant Camargue mare. These small, white horses have roamed the marshy areas of southern France since Roman times. Swift and agile, they move easily through the marshlands. Nipping and squealing, Chincoteague pony foals play at ▷ fighting. The ponies belong to a band that lives on a lonely, windblown island off the coast of Maryland and Virginia. Each year, people round up some of the ponies. The animals swim across the narrow bay and are sold on the mainland.*

Chincoteague pony: 53 in (135 cm) tall at the withers

Arabian horse: 59 in (150 cm) tall at the withers

△ Arabian horses race across a field in Sweden. The slender, elegant appearance of these horses has made the breed popular for riding the world over.

◁ Stiff manes identify a Przewalski's mare and her foal. Unlike mustangs, Przewalski's horses have no tame ancestors. The stocky animals once roamed central Asia. Today, about a thousand live in captivity.

Przewalski's horse: 50 in (127 cm) tall at the withers

275

Horse

challenge each other by arching their necks and tucking in their chins. They rear, biting and kicking. Finally, one stallion gives up and gallops away.

In the spring, mares give birth—usually to a single foal. The newborn, wobbly on its spindly legs, is up and nursing in an hour.

When the young males, or colts, are about two years old, the stallion drives them away. For a few years, they roam with other young males. Then they are ready to gather bands of their own.

Unlike feral horses, Przewalski's (per-zhih-VAHL-skeez) horses have no tame ancestors. Named for the Russian explorer who was the first Westerner to study them, these stocky, short-legged horses have stiff

manes and a black stripe down their backs. Przewalski's horses once roamed central Asia, but none have been seen in the wild since 1968. About a thousand have been bred in captivity.

Most of the horses in the world are domesticated, or tamed. There are now about four hundred breeds of horses. These animals may vary in size, in

Iceland pony: 51 in (130 cm) tall at the withers

HORSE

HEIGHT: **30-69 in (76-175 cm) at the withers—the ridge between the shoulders**

WEIGHT: **120-2,200 lb (54-998 kg)**

HABITAT AND RANGE: **grassy areas in parts of North and South America, Europe, and Australia; domestic horses live in many parts of the world**

FOOD: **grasses and other plants, including fallen fruit**

LIFE SPAN: **25 to 35 years in captivity**

REPRODUCTION: **usually 1 young after a pregnancy of about 11 months**

ORDER: **perissodactyls**

△ *Iceland pony mares groom one another. They nibble at each other's summer coats with their teeth. In winter, shaggy hair covers these hardy, short-legged horses. The coats protect them in the cold, harsh climate of their island home.*

◁ *White muzzle and eye patches highlight the dark coat of an Arkansas mule, the long-eared offspring of a female horse and a male ass. Mules are tougher and more surefooted than most horses.*

Mule: 58 in (147 cm) tall at the withers

color, or in the kinds of jobs they can do. Draft horses such as Belgians and Clydesdales are the largest and strongest of all horses. They have muscular bodies and thick, short legs.

Arabian horses are smaller animals with slender necks, high-set tails, and silky coats. Thoroughbreds, another breed, are famous for their speed at racing.

Quarter Horses, which can stop and turn quickly, are used as working horses on ranches. Ponies are the smallest horses. They often have broad chests and strong, sturdy bodies.

Mules are the offspring of a female horse and a male ass. Tough and surefooted, mules often are used for farm work.

Hutia

(oo-TEE-uh)

This map shows the range of hutias.

Bahamian hutia: 12 in (30 cm) long; tail, 3 in (8 cm)

Bahamian hutia rests on a rocky ledge. This kind of hutia survives on only one island in the Bahamas.

HUTIA 🐾 **9 of 14 species**

LENGTH OF HEAD AND BODY: 10-20 in (25-51 cm); tail, 1-12 in (3-30 cm)

WEIGHT: 2-15 lb (1-7 kg)

HABITAT AND RANGE: remote forests, swamps, and rocky regions in parts of the West Indies

FOOD: plants and a few small animals such as lizards

LIFE SPAN: about 12 years in captivity

REPRODUCTION: 1 to 3 young after a pregnancy of 2 to 4 months

ORDER: rodents

THOUGH ONCE COMMON in the West Indies, hutias have been heavily hunted by other animals and by people. For centuries, hutias had few enemies, except for the local peoples who killed them for food. Later, European settlers began to arrive and to bring with them animals that preyed on hutias. Today these large rodents have disappeared from a great many parts of the islands.

Hutias look a little like rats, with broad heads, small eyes and ears, and grayish or brownish hair. The hutias on one island usually are different from those on another island. The Bahamian hutia, for example, has short hair and a short tail. It feeds at night on leaves, bark, and twigs. During the day, it usually sleeps in caves or in small openings between rocks. It survives on only one island in the Bahamas.

Some Cuban hutias feed during the day. They eat fruit, leaves, and bark as well as such small animals as lizards. Cuban hutias are covered with coarse hair. Although they live in holes in the ground, they often climb trees and sun themselves on the branches. One kind of Cuban hutia can even wrap its tail around branches for balance.

Hutias have one to three young after a pregnancy of two to four months. The offspring are born with hair and with their eyes open.

Hyena

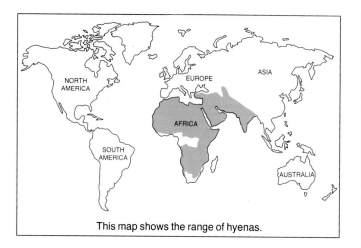

This map shows the range of hyenas.

Two spotted hyenas drink at a water hole. ▷
Spotted hyenas live on the plains of Africa.
They can go for several days without drinking.

▽ *Female spotted hyena takes an afternoon nap (below), as one of her offspring snuggles close and another peeks from their den. Spotted hyenas usually give birth to two cubs in a hole in the ground. For the first few weeks, the female stays close by her cubs. If her young wander from the den, she carries them back by the napes of their necks (lower right, top). Furry and black at birth, cubs grow lighter coats after about ten weeks. Spots begin to appear later. Hyena cubs often play (lower right, bottom). They chase each other and splash in water holes. They stay with their mother more than a year.*

AFTER DARK, eerie giggles, yells, and growls drift across the Serengeti Plain of Africa. Spotted hyenas have killed a wildebeest. As they feed, they squabble among themselves over the meat. The biggest hyenas take the best parts of the kill. Younger and weaker animals get the scraps.

A spotted hyena looks like a very large dog. It has a blunt muzzle, rounded ears, and long front legs. The yellow-gray fur on its sloping back is covered with dark spots. But hyenas are not part of the dog family. Their closest relatives are aardwolves.

Until recently, people thought hyenas mainly scavenged for food, that is, they fed on any dead animals they could find. Now scientists have discovered that spotted hyenas are skillful hunters.

As many as eighty hyenas may live together in a group called a clan. The animals often hunt in smaller

Spotted hyena: 45 in (114 cm) long; tail, 13 in (33 cm)

Hyena

packs—usually ten to thirty hyenas. Keen senses of hearing and eyesight help them track animals at night. Spotted hyenas can run for miles without getting tired. They often catch what they are chasing. Muscular shoulders and bodies allow them to overpower their prey easily.

Spotted hyenas hunt different animals in different ways. When a pack goes after wildebeests, for example, one hyena will charge into a herd and startle the animals. As the herd runs off, the hyenas watch for a slow or sick wildebeest. Then they all join the chase

In a tug-of-war, spotted hyenas and a lioness fight ▷
for the meat of a wildebeest that the hyenas killed. When the lioness heard the giggling calls of the feeding hyenas, she came to help herself to an easy meal. Several lions can chase hyenas away from their kill. But a group of hyenas can usually keep a single lion away.

▽ *Warming itself in the afternoon sun, a young hyena in Kenya looks as friendly as a puppy. But hyenas have jaws and teeth that can shred meat and splinter bones.*

to bring down the victim. When hunting alone, a spotted hyena looks for smaller prey such as a gazelle. It may circle a lake and then wade in to try to attack birds in the water. Or it may stand in the shallows and snap at fish.

Once the kill is made, and after a pack of hyenas begins to feed, the animals make their laughing sounds. Because of these noises, they are often called laughing hyenas. From the sounds, other hyenas know that the hunting pack has found food.

Spotted hyenas can eat almost all of their prey.

Their teeth and powerful jaws can even crush large bones. Their stomach juices can digest bone as well as skin. Hyenas come to some villages in Ethiopia at night and feed on garbage. After the hyenas have eaten, almost nothing is left.

Spotted hyenas often play in pools of water. They may wallow in mud. Sometimes hyenas even store food by dropping it in shallow water. Later, when they are hungry, the animals poke their heads underwater until they find the food.

Clans, led by females, hunt in their own areas.

Members of a clan mark their territory by scratching the ground and leaving waste. They mark the grass with a smelly substance from glands under their tails. The scent marks warn hyenas from other clans that the territory is occupied. Groups of spotted hyenas may also patrol the borders of the territory. If a hyena from another clan does try to invade, the patrol chases it away. At times two clans of hyenas may meet and battle over a kill.

Clan members often meet at a large den near the middle of the territory. The den is made up of many

Hyena

Brown hyena: 34 in (86 cm) long; tail, 10 in (25 cm)

△ *Shaggy-haired brown hyena lopes across scrubby dry plains in southern Africa. Brown hyenas usually travel alone. They may go long distances in search of such food as small mammals, fruit, or dead animals.*

burrows, connected by tunnels. When they arrive at the den, hyenas often greet each other by sniffing like dogs. In this way they recognize members of their clan. Hyenas have many ways of communicating. One animal may walk on its wrists in front of another hyena that is more important. Or a hyena may raise its whisk-broom tail to show excitement. Hyenas also use other calls besides laughter. Loud grunts often signal a threat.

Female hyenas give birth to twin cubs in shallow holes a short distance from the clan den. About two weeks later, a female hyena carries her cubs to the den. There all the cubs live together. The young stay with their mothers and nurse for more than a year. After a few months, however, they follow along on hunts and snatch scraps.

Another kind of hyena, the striped hyena, roams parts of Africa and Asia. Striped hyenas usually stay by themselves, but the animals may live together when they are raising young. During the day, they rest in holes in the ground. At night, they wander great distances in search of food. The striped hyena is mainly a scavenger of dead animals. But it may hunt for small mammals. It also likes to eat fruit and insects. Unlike the spotted hyena, the striped hyena does not laugh or whoop.

The rare brown hyena of southern Africa also lives by itself. The brown hyena is smaller than its spotted relative, but it has longer hair. Dark stripes circle its legs. It roams widely looking for live or dead animals. Sometimes it feeds on melons and ostrich eggs. The brown hyena also lives in clans, but they are led by males and are smaller than the clans of the spotted hyena.

HYENA

LENGTH OF HEAD AND BODY: 34-59 in (86-150 cm); tail, 10-14 in (25-36 cm)

WEIGHT: 82-190 lb (37-86 kg)

HABITAT AND RANGE: dry plains and brushy areas in parts of Africa and southwest Asia

FOOD: mammals, fruit, and insects

LIFE SPAN: as long as 25 years in the wild

REPRODUCTION: usually 2 young after a pregnancy of about 3 or 4 months

ORDER: carnivores

▽ *Striped hyena stretches its long, thick neck. Smaller than its spotted relative, this hyena has the typical powerful shoulders and sloping back of the hyena family. Striped hyenas live in parts of Africa and Asia.*

Striped hyena: 40 in (102 cm) long; tail, 11 in (28 cm)

Hyrax

Rock hyrax: 19 in (48 cm) long

Young rock hyraxes, watched over by an adult, huddle together on a boulder. Hyraxes often cooperate in caring for young. One adult tends the offspring while other adults feed.

STRANGE AS IT SEEMS, the tiny hyrax and the huge elephant may be related. Some scientists believe these animals had a common ancestor that lived about 55 million years ago. Their feet suggest that they are relatives. On their toes, the elephant and the hyrax both have flat nails that are almost like hooves. Scientists say that 30 million years ago, some hyraxes were almost as big as elephants.

The hyrax looks like a guinea pig. But the hyrax is not a rodent. It is so different from all other animals that scientists have placed it in an order, or group, all by itself.

There are three kinds of hyraxes. The rabbit-size rock hyrax is the largest. The tree hyrax and the bush hyrax are smaller.

Colonies of rock hyraxes and bush hyraxes live in rocky areas in parts of Africa and the Middle East. Sometimes rock hyraxes and bush hyraxes live side by side. During the day, the animals search for food. Some scientists think that the animals can live together because they usually do not eat the same foods. Rock hyraxes nibble mostly grasses. Bush hyraxes climb into trees and bushes and feed on leaves. While they eat, one of the hyraxes watches for enemies—leopards, eagles, and snakes.

Tree hyraxes live in the forests of Africa. These shy little animals become active at night, feeding on leaves and buds. They climb easily. Like the other hyraxes, tree hyraxes have rubbery pads on the soles of their feet that give them a good grip.

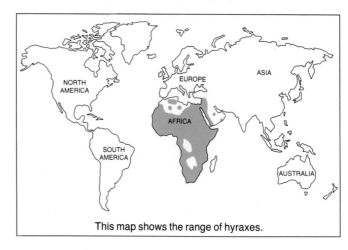

This map shows the range of hyraxes.

283

Bush hyrax: 17 in (43 cm) long

Tree hyrax: 17 in (43 cm) long

△ *Sound the alarm! A rock hyrax warns others of danger. If an enemy such as an eagle, a snake, or a leopard comes near, the hyrax will give a shrill cry.*

Little is known about the habits of the tree hyrax. But many people in Africa have heard the animal's call. Just after dark, a tree hyrax begins to make a soft, ringing sound. It repeats this call several times, getting louder with each cry. Finally, the hyrax gives a piercing scream. Then there is silence until other hyraxes begin their calls. Their cries are heard throughout the night. Scientists think that the male tree hyrax uses its call to find a mate or to say, "This part of the forest belongs to me."

Hyraxes usually have litters of one to four young after a pregnancy of about seven and a half months. The young can run and jump soon after birth. They nurse for as long as six months. Rock hyraxes and bush hyraxes sometimes eat grasses or leaves when they are only two days old.

△ *Termite mound offers a spot for several bush hyraxes to sun themselves. If danger threatens, they will dart into the holes in the mound and hide.*

◁ *Rock hyrax (far left) nibbles on a plant. Though these animals prefer grass, they will eat fruit, flowers, buds, and leaves, too. During the dry season, rock hyraxes use their curving front teeth to strip bark from bushes and small trees. Young tree hyraxes (left) in Africa peer out from among leaves. Hyraxes nurse for as long as six months. But some can eat grasses and leaves soon after birth. Young hyraxes scamper, jump, and climb as easily as adults do. Rubbery pads on the soles of their feet help them cling to rocks and branches.*

HYRAX   🐾 **4 of 7 species**

LENGTH OF HEAD AND BODY: 16-22 in (41-56 cm)

WEIGHT: 4-11 lb (2-5 kg)

HABITAT AND RANGE: rocky areas and forests in parts of Africa and the Middle East

FOOD: grasses, leaves, buds, stems, bark, and fruit

LIFE SPAN: as long as 12 years in captivity

REPRODUCTION: 1 to 4 young after a pregnancy of about 7½ months

ORDER: hyracoids

I

Ibex

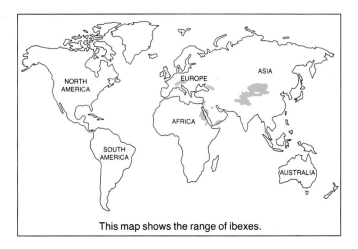

This map shows the range of ibexes.

IBEX   🐾 **4 of 6 species**

HEIGHT: 26-41 in (66-104 cm) at the shoulder

WEIGHT: 70-275 lb (32-125 kg)

HABITAT AND RANGE: mountainous and rocky regions of Europe, Asia, and northeastern Africa

FOOD: grasses, herbs, shrubs, and other plants

LIFE SPAN: as long as 22 years in captivity

REPRODUCTION: 1 or 2 young after a pregnancy of 5 or 6 months, depending on species

ORDER: artiodactyls

HIGH IN THE MOUNTAINS, the ibex climbs among rocky crags and cliffs. It grips the slopes with the soles of its split hooves. A kind of wild goat, the surefooted ibex seldom slips or falls—even though it carries a heavy weight on its head.

The male ibex has a pair of ridged horns that curve as much as 5 feet (152 cm) into the air. The horns can weigh 20 pounds (9 kg). The female has horns too, but they are shorter and lighter. The horns of an ibex keep growing year after year. Each year, a new ridged section is added. The older an ibex is, the longer its horns are. People can count the sections and find out how old an ibex is.

Ibexes have short, brownish coats. Males have heavy beards. Except for the horns and beards, ibexes look much like their relatives, bighorn sheep. Ibexes live in mountainous and rocky regions of Europe, Asia, and northeastern Africa.

One kind of ibex lives high on treeless mountain slopes of the Alps in Europe. In winter, these Alpine ibexes often come partway down the mountainsides to avoid the deep snows higher up. The animals seek out slopes facing south. It is sunnier and warmer there than on other slopes. Ibexes also try to find places where the wind blows the snow off grasses and other plants.

Alpine ibexes graze on grass when they can find it. But they also eat herbs, shrubs, and other plants. In the spring, before they return to higher ground, the ibexes sometimes go down the slopes to areas where trees grow. There they feed on green shoots.

Ibexes normally spend about half of each day filling their stomachs with partially chewed plants. Later, while they rest, they bring up wads of this food—called cuds—from their stomachs. They chew the cuds thoroughly and swallow the food again so that it can be further digested. Some other animals that chew cuds are antelopes, cows, goats, and sheep. Read about these animals under their own headings. When it is very windy, ibexes sometimes go to sheltered spots to spend the night.

Except during the mating season in late fall and early winter, adult male and female Alpine ibexes usually live apart from each other. Most males roam together in groups. Sometimes they gather in herds of not more than about ten animals. Old males often remain alone. Females and their kids form herds of about a dozen animals.

The herds of males break up during the mating season. The biggest and strongest male ibexes mate with more females. Smaller and weaker males rarely challenge the larger ones. But males of the same size sometimes fight to find out which is the stronger. Two male ibexes cross their massive horns and push against each other. They rise on their hind legs and butt their heads. The crash of their horns can sound like rocks banging together. The clash can be fierce

High on a snow-covered ridge in Italy's Gran Paradiso National Park, male Alpine ibexes graze. The animals use their hooves to uncover grass beneath the snow.

Alpine ibex: 34 in (86 cm) tall at the shoulder

Ibex

enough to break a horn. In May or June, about five months after mating, female Alpine ibexes give birth to their young. Usually only one kid is born, but sometimes a female ibex has twins. After giving birth, a mother ibex will lick her kid. She soon becomes familiar with its smell, so she will be able to identify her kid in the herd.

Newborn ibexes weigh about 8 pounds (4 kg). They develop quickly and can walk by the end of their first day. Soon after, they can run and jump. Within a few weeks, young ibexes can balance on the edges of rocky cliffs. They also eat small pieces of plants. The frisky kids take turns pushing each other off rocks. Sometimes they even playfully jump on their mothers' backs.

Female ibexes keep watch over their young. If a mother loses sight of her kid, she may "baaa" like a sheep. Her kid answers with a "baaa" of its own. When she finds her young, the female may sniff it to make sure it is hers.

In the Alps, golden eagles still prey on young ibexes. In other areas, leopards, bears, and wolves

Lone male ibex watches from a mountainside in ▷ *Italy. Old males often do not roam with a herd. They travel by themselves, except at mating time.*

▽ *Female Alpine ibex and two kids graze on a slope in the Gran Paradiso park. Alpine ibexes usually give birth to one young at the end of May or in June.*

Male Nubian ibexes pause on a rocky trail. Ridged sections on their massive horns show their age.

Nubian ibex: 33 in (84 cm) tall at the shoulder

hunt these horned animals. People too have hunted Alpine ibexes. Though the animal once was common, by the early 1800s it was almost extinct.

One reason the Alpine ibex became so rare is that some people believed that parts of the animal could cure various diseases. One bone near its heart was shaped like a cross and much desired as a good luck charm.

In 1854, King Victor Emmanuel II began to protect the few remaining Alpine ibexes. He set up a preserve for the ibexes in a part of the Italian Alps known as the Gran Paradiso. This preserve later became a national park. Ibexes survived and multiplied. Animals from the Gran Paradiso were sent to the mountains of other European countries. Today thousands of ibexes roam the Alps again.

Ibex

Nubian ibexes carefully pick their way along the side ▷ of a steep cliff on a preserve in Israel. Much of the land these animals once roamed has been taken over for grazing by domestic sheep and goats.

▽ Young Nubian ibexes (below) push and shove as they play among rocks. Ibex kids may play much of the time. Adult ibexes spend the day feeding and resting. An adult male (bottom) points his face toward the sun and leans back on the tips of his horns. While resting, ibexes often chew cuds—partly digested wads of food brought up from their stomachs.

The Alpine ibex is one of several kinds of ibexes. All ibexes look and behave alike, but there are a few differences. For example, the Nubian ibex is smaller than the Alpine ibex, and its horns are longer and thinner. The Nubian ibex lives in rocky desert regions around the Red Sea, in other parts of Egypt, in Jordan, and in other countries. In Israel, the Nubian ibex also lives protected on preserves.

Walia ibexes live in Ethiopia. They are larger

than Nubian ibexes. Walia ibexes have suffered as their range has been turned into farmland. Domestic sheep and goats also have taken over more and more of the land where these ibexes feed. Now the Walias are close to extinction.

The Siberian ibex, largest of all ibexes, is found in the mountains of central Asia. It can live as high as 16,000 feet (4,877 m). This animal is well adapted, or suited, to the cold weather of its home. Female Siberi-

an ibexes bear their young after six months—almost a month longer than other ibexes. This means Siberian ibex kids are born in June or July, when the weather is warm enough for them to survive.

In ancient times, ibexes were often kept by kings in Persia and in Egypt. Small statues of ibexes have been found in the tombs of Persian royalty. And images of ibexes have even been found in the tomb of King Tutankhamun.

Impala

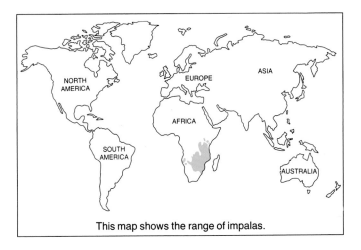

This map shows the range of impalas.

SENSING A LION NEARBY, an impala barks a sharp alarm that warns the herd. In a flash, fifty antelopes scatter in several directions across a plain in Africa. The startled and confused enemy hesitates. In that instant, the graceful, reddish brown animals disappear into the cover of shrubs and bushes.

When frightened, impalas spring into action. In a series of racing strides and long-distance jumps, the animals dash for safety. Soaring upward as high as 10 feet (305 cm), they clear tall grass and bushes—and even jump over other impalas. Their long, slender legs and muscular thighs enable them to travel as far as 30 feet (9 m) in a single leap.

Impalas are medium-size antelopes, lightly built for speed and jumping. Male impalas have sharp, curving horns that sweep backward and then turn upward. Females have no horns. Learn about other kinds of antelopes on page 52.

Impalas range over parts of eastern, central, and southern Africa, although one subspecies, the black-faced impala of southwestern Africa, has now become very rare. Impalas live on open grasslands, in brushy areas, and in open woodlands. Throughout the rainy season, impalas in some regions may graze in large herds of hundreds of animals. In the dry season, they must browse, or nibble on leaves and shoots of bushes. With food in short supply, the herd usually

---

IMPALA　🐾 I of I species

HEIGHT: 33-39 in (84-99 cm) at the shoulder

WEIGHT: 88-165 lb (40-75 kg)

HABITAT AND RANGE: grasslands, shrubby areas, and open woodlands of eastern and southern Africa

FOOD: grasses, herbs, bushes, and shrubs

LIFE SPAN: as long as 17 years in captivity

REPRODUCTION: usually I young after a pregnancy of about 7 months

ORDER: artiodactyls

◁ *Trade-off! Birds known as oxpeckers find a comfortable roost and also keep an impala free of ticks and insects. The young male appears undisturbed by his passengers. Face-to-face, two male impalas (far left) meet before a battle that will test their strength. Males of the same age and size may fight frequently, pushing at each other with their horns.*

breaks up into smaller groups. The animals roam in search of water holes. At other times of the year, water is usually available nearby.

In a few places, impalas mate at any time of the year. Older males mark out territories, or areas, and defend them from rivals. When females wander into a male's territory, he rounds them up. By herding them with a honking sound, he may keep them for days before they move on.

Adult males that have no territories often join younger males in groups known as bachelor herds. Bachelors frequently fight one another to find out which is stronger. The strongest bachelors then challenge the males with territories.

A battle for territory usually begins slowly. At first, the rivals parade about, horns held high. Sometimes a male will be able to force a challenger out of

Exploding into action, impalas leap away from ▷ danger. Swiftly, the herd flees across a grassy plain in Tanzania. An impala will jump over almost any object in its path—including another impala.

▽ Looking for mates, a male impala uses honking noises to round up females. Despite his efforts, females may leave his territory for that of a neighbor.

Dark stripes on its rump flash as a male impala springs gracefully into the air. Strong, slender legs equip the animal for long, high leaps.

his territory without a real fight. In more serious battles, the males meet head to head. They lunge forward and try to jab each other with their sharp horns. They also lock horns, pushing and twisting their heads. But they seldom get badly hurt. The layer of skin covering a male's head and neck is especially thick and protects him. When one of the male impalas can no longer keep up the struggle, he runs away. The winner may pursue him. Eventually the loser returns to the bachelor herd.

Holding a territory can be tiring for a male impala. He must fight off intruders, chase bachelors, herd the females, and mate with them. During this time, he may eat little.

About seven months after mating, a female leaves the herd for a secluded place. There she gives birth—usually to one young. After a few days, the mother and her young join a herd of females and offspring. A young female will remain with the females. A young male will join a bachelor herd.

Jackal

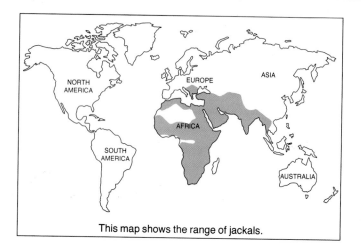

This map shows the range of jackals.

Golden jackal: 32 in (81 cm) long; tail, 10 in (25 cm)

△ *Keeping watch over a pup, golden jackals groom each other. Young sometimes roll over so parents can groom their bellies.*

SOON AFTER SUNSET, the howls of golden jackals echo across the plains of northern Africa. Jackals hunt mainly at night. With loud calls, these members of the dog family signal the beginning of their hunt. At sunrise, after a night of hunting, jackals again begin their eerie howls. Jackals also communicate with many other kinds of sounds. For example, they bark softly to warn that lions are nearby. Pups whine when they greet their parents.

Golden jackals roam the grassy plains of Africa and the brushy woodlands of India. Other kinds of jackals are found only in Africa. The silver-backed, or black-backed, jackal is at home in brushy woodlands.

The tan-and-red fur of this bold animal is topped with a saddle of black-and-white hairs on its back. The side-striped jackal often lives in brushy areas where the animal can find cover more easily. But it may hunt for food on the plains.

Jackals usually hunt alone for small mammals and insects. When they pair up or hunt in small groups, they can bring down bigger game, such as a young gazelle. Jackals often feed on the remains of dead animals or on kills that have been made by other

◁ *Fur bristling and ears laid back, a golden jackal stands its ground against a Cape hunting dog. The jackal tried to steal the wild dog's kill. Jackals often feed on the prey of other meat eaters.*

Glassy surface of a water hole ▷ mirrors a silver-backed, or black-backed, jackal as it sniffs the ground. The animal can find out about recent visitors to the area by scent. Its keen senses help this hunter find food.

Silver-backed jackal: 28 in (71 cm) long; tail, 14 in (36 cm)

Jackal

△ *Sitting up, two nine-week-old silver-backed jackals nurse on their mother's milk. The female watches the grasslands as her pups drink. She will fiercely defend them against such enemies as hyenas and eagles.*

Flying leap after a rat takes a silver-backed jackal ▷ *high above the grass.*

▽ *Ready for solid food, a young silver-backed jackal carries a rat killed by the pup's mother. Like most wild dogs, jackals feed their young by swallowing food and taking it back to the den in their stomachs. There they bring it up for the pups to eat.*

meat eaters. After a lion has fed from a kill, jackals gather round to eat the scraps.

A pair of male and female jackals stays together for years, or even for life. Before giving birth to her young, the female takes over a den, often an abandoned aardvark burrow. One to eight helpless pups are born in a litter. Both parents help care for the young. At two weeks of age, the pups begin to explore their world. At three months of age, they tag along on hunting trips. Young silver-backed jackals and golden jackals often stay with their parents for a year and help raise the next litter.

JACKAL

LENGTH OF HEAD AND BODY: 26-42 in (66-107 cm); tail, 8-16 in (20-41 cm)

WEIGHT: 14-33 lb (6-15 kg)

HABITAT AND RANGE: plains, brushy woodlands, and deserts in parts of Africa, Asia, and southern Europe

FOOD: rodents, small antelopes, birds, reptiles, insects, fruit, berries, grasses, and remains of dead animals

LIFE SPAN: as long as 16 years in captivity, depending on species

REPRODUCTION: 1 to 8 young after a pregnancy of about 2 months

ORDER: carnivores

Jackrabbit

Jackrabbits are hares. Read about them on page 250.

Jaguar

(JAG-wahr)

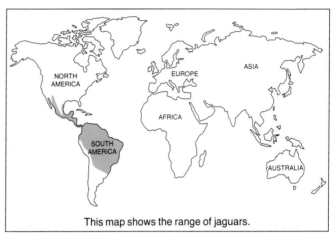

This map shows the range of jaguars.

FOR HUNDREDS OF YEARS, the mysterious jaguar has played an important role in the religions of Indians from Mexico into South America. For some, the Jaguar God of the Night was a ruler of the underworld. Its spotted coat represented the stars in the night sky. In spite of all the stories, though, scientists still know little about this big cat.

The jaguar is the largest cat in the Western Hemisphere. It prowls rain forests, marshes, dry scrublands, and grasslands from Mexico into Argentina. An expert swimmer, the jaguar wades into water to catch a fish or to chase a caiman—a small relative of the alligator. The jaguar also stalks prey in high grass or bushes. There it catches such animals as capybaras, peccaries, deer, and tapirs. The cat creeps close to its prey and then swiftly pounces. It seizes the animal with muscular forelegs and kills it with a bite in the neck or head. The jaguar is extremely strong. It may drag even heavy prey to a sheltered spot some distance away.

The jaguar has a broad head, very powerful jaws, large shoulders, and sturdy legs. Its short, stiff fur is usually golden or reddish orange. Rings of small black dots pattern its coat. Because these rings are

Powerful muscles rippling under brilliantly patterned fur, a jaguar guards its realm. Even a faint rustle of leaves or a snapped twig puts the cat on the alert.

301

Jaguar

rose-shaped, they are called rosettes. A jaguar's rosettes often have dark spots in the centers.

Jaguars usually weigh between 100 and 250 pounds (45-113 kg) and measure about 6 feet (183 cm) from head to rump. On the average, they are smaller than lions and tigers but larger than leopards. Scientists group all four kinds of animals together as big cats. Find out about leopards, lions, and tigers under their own headings.

All four big cats can roar, but their roars do not sound alike. The jaguar's roar resembles a loud cough, repeated several times. Jaguar hunters in Brazil imitate this sound by grunting into a hollow gourd. The jaguar is attracted to the sound.

A jaguar lives alone in a home range—an area it marks out for itself. Home ranges are often large, covering many square miles. Although the ranges of two or more jaguars may overlap, the cats rarely meet. They signal their whereabouts by scratching trees and leaving waste.

Male and female jaguars meet at mating time. About three months after mating, a female bears her cubs—usually two or three in a litter. The young jaguars are born blind and helpless. For about two years, they stay and hunt with their mother. Then, gradually, they spend more and more time on their own. Finally, they leave their mother's home range and find a range of their own. At about three years of age, jaguars are fully grown.

No one knows exactly how many of these cats still roam in the wild. Although jaguars once lived in the southern United States, they were hunted to extinction there. Farmers and ranchers thought the cats were a threat to livestock. Today ranchers in South America still kill jaguars to protect their cattle. The cats also are hunted for their fur.

Jaguars sun themselves high on a tree limb. From their lofty perch, these skilled climbers scan the ground below. In the wild, jaguars have little contact with one another. These cats, however, share their grounds with other jaguars in a zoo in Brazil. No one knows the number of jaguars left in the wild. Hunters kill many of the cats each year for their richly spotted fur.

JAGUAR

LENGTH OF HEAD AND BODY: 5-6 ft (152-183 cm); tail, 20-31 in (51-79 cm)

WEIGHT: 100-250 lb (45-113 kg)

HABITAT AND RANGE: rain forests, marshes, scrublands, and grasslands from Mexico into Argentina

FOOD: rodents, peccaries, deer, tapirs, fish, and cattle

LIFE SPAN: as long as 20 years in captivity

REPRODUCTION: 1 to 4 young after a pregnancy of 3 or 4 months

ORDER: carnivores

Jerboa

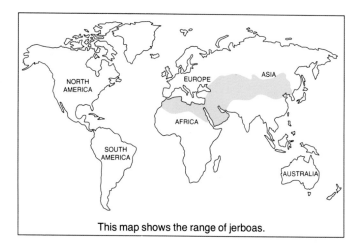

This map shows the range of jerboas.

JERBOA 🐾 **6 of 33 species**

LENGTH OF HEAD AND BODY: 2-6 in (5-15 cm); tail, 3-10 in (8-25 cm)

WEIGHT: 2-4 oz (57-113 g)

HABITAT AND RANGE: deserts and dry plains in parts of Asia and Africa

FOOD: plants, seeds, and insects

LIFE SPAN: about 6 years in captivity

REPRODUCTION: 2 to 6 young after a pregnancy of 1 month

ORDER: rodents

Standing on its long hind legs, a desert jerboa listens for danger. Its ear may have been nicked in a fight with another jerboa. Usually the animal escapes its enemies by leaping away. When jumping, the jerboa uses its long tail for balance.

Desert jerboa: 6 in (15 cm) long; tail, 10 in (25 cm)

LOOKING LIKE A TINY KANGAROO, the sand-colored jerboa springs across bare ground. Using its strong hind legs and feet to push off, this rodent can leap as far as 10 feet (305 cm). Such long-distance jumps are amazing for an animal that may measure only 6 inches (15 cm) long!

There are about 33 species, or kinds, of jerboas. They live in deserts and on dry plains in parts of Asia and Africa. Jerboas are active at night. They look for plants and seeds. Some jerboas also feed on beetles and other insects.

With their short front legs and their strong teeth, jerboas dig burrows in the ground. These underground homes protect them from both hot and cold weather. The burrows also help keep the animals safe from enemies such as owls and foxes. From inside their burrows, jerboas sometimes block the entrances with sand or soil. Using their snouts, they shove loose dirt into the openings.

Some jerboas curl up in their burrows during the winter. There they hibernate (HYE-bur-nate), or sleep. Their heart rates drop, and their breathing slows down. Some jerboas escape the heat of summer by sleeping this way. Summer sleep is called aestivation (es-tuh-VAY-shun).

Females give birth to two or three litters a year. Each litter contains two to six young.

K

Kangaroo

(kang-guh-ROO)

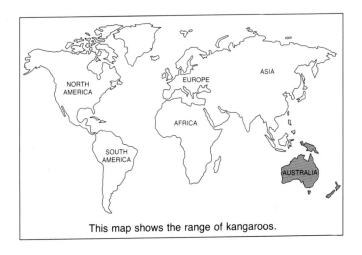

This map shows the range of kangaroos.

WHEN IT COMES TO CARRYING YOUNG, the kangaroo has an easy solution. It keeps its offspring in a pouch on its belly. Kangaroos are probably the best known of all pouched mammals, or marsupials (mar-soo-pea-ulz). But few people realize that there are more than 70 kinds of kangaroos. These furry gray, brown, or reddish brown animals live in Australia, New Guinea, and on nearby islands. Some kinds live in New Zealand. Their ancestors were taken there from Australia in the 1800s.

Kangaroos come in many sizes. Two kinds, gray kangaroos and red kangaroos, may stand taller than most people and weigh almost 150 pounds (68 kg).

Red kangaroo: 57 in (145 cm) long; tail, 37 in (94 cm)

△ *Droopy-eyed and relaxed, a red kangaroo rests on a plain in Australia. More than 70 kinds of kangaroos live in Australia and on islands in the region.*

◁ *With a graceful takeoff, a red kangaroo springs into action. Using its powerful hind legs, it can reach heights of 6 feet (183 cm) and cover 25 feet (8 m) in one jump.*

Red kangaroos drink from a sheep rancher's pond. ▷ *In dry weather, these hardy animals get the moisture they need from the plants they eat.*

Another kind, the wallaroo (WOLL-uh-roo), is slightly shorter and stockier. Red kangaroos, gray kangaroos, and wallaroos are known as the great kangaroos. They are the largest of all marsupials. Some other kinds of kangaroos seem tiny in comparison. The smallest kangaroo—the musky rat kangaroo—is only about the size of a rat.

Many kinds of small and medium-size kangaroos are called wallabies. Read about wallabies on page 548. Another member of the kangaroo family, the quokka, is described on page 464.

Kangaroos are found in many kinds of surroundings. Gray kangaroos live in forests. Red kangaroos roam plains. Wallaroos live in hilly, rocky regions. Most kinds of kangaroos feed only on grass. Some, though, nibble on other plants as well. The musky rat kangaroo eats insects and worms.

When grazing, a kangaroo moves slowly. First, it bends forward and balances on its front paws and tail. Then it swings its hind legs forward, following with its tail and front legs.

To cover short distances rapidly, a kangaroo hops. It pushes off with *(Continued on page 308)*

*With joeys—young kangaroos— ▷
tucked safely in their pouches, two
gray kangaroo mothers look up
from grazing. The adults use their
muscular tails as props when they rest.
The heads and feet of the joeys hang
out because the young are almost too
large for the pouches.*

*▽ To beat the heat, a young gray
kangaroo licks its paws. The moisture
evaporates, and helps cool the animal.*

Gray kangaroo: 48 in (122 cm) long; tail, 39 in (99 cm)

Kangaroo

◁ *Imitating its mother, a young joey hops to it! Bounding at a steady pace, the two gray kangaroos head for new feeding grounds. The kangaroos can keep up a speed of as much as 15 miles (24 km) an hour over long distances. About a year old, this youngster no longer returns to the pouch.*

▽ *Kangaroo mob scene: A mob—the name Australians give to groups of kangaroos—grazes in a clearing. The large adult male, second from right, probably leads these gray kangaroos. Red kangaroos also gather in mobs. Other kinds usually live alone or in pairs.*

Kangaroo

△ *Sheltered by ferns, vines, and other underbrush, a rufous rat kangaroo searches for food. At night, the tiny marsupial feeds on beetles and on woodland plants.*

Though awkward on the ground, a tree kangaroo ▷ *balances gracefully on a fallen limb. This tree dweller has long forelegs, unlike other kangaroos.*

its strong hind legs and feet. As it sails through the air, its outstretched tail helps it balance. Larger kangaroos can travel 25 feet (8 m) in a single jump!

Females move very fast. Smaller and lighter than males, they can keep up a quick pace over a long distance. Female red kangaroos—called blue fliers because of their bluish fur—may travel more than 30 miles (48 km) an hour in short spurts.

A male kangaroo does not move quite so swiftly as a female does. With his broad, muscular chest and strong forelegs, however, he is better equipped to fight. Sometimes his enemy is the wild dog called the dingo. Rival kangaroos may fight for mates. But they rarely injure each other seriously. Some people think that a male kangaroo defends himself by boxing. He is really grabbing his rival with his forelegs. Rearing back on his tail, he kicks the foe with his hind feet.

Sometimes he bites his opponent's throat or uses his sharp claws to tear at the enemy.

Kangaroos mate at any time of year. Just a little more than a month after mating, a female bears one young. The tiny newborn, called a joey, is only about the size of a lima bean. Moments after its birth, the joey crawls into the safety of its mother's pouch. There it continues to grow and develop.

KANGAROO 🐾 11 of 23 species

LENGTH OF HEAD AND BODY: 10-65 in (25-165 cm); tail, 5-42 in (13-107 cm)

WEIGHT: 18 oz-150 lb (510 g-68 kg)

HABITAT AND RANGE: all kinds of habitats throughout Australia, New Guinea, New Zealand, and neighboring islands

FOOD: grasses, leaves, twigs, insects, and worms

LIFE SPAN: as long as 23 years in the wild

REPRODUCTION: 1 young after a pregnancy of about 1 month

ORDER: marsupials

After several months, the joey tumbles out of the pouch for the first time. If danger threatens, the young kangaroo dives headfirst back into the pouch. There a quick somersault turns it right side up. Red kangaroo young give up the pouch at about eight months of age. Gray kangaroos remain for two or three months longer. Some rat kangaroos leave the pouch after only about three months.

Kangaroo rat

(kang-guh-ROO RAT)

Desert kangaroo rat: 5 in (13 cm) long; tail, 7 in (18 cm)

Cheek pouches full, a desert kangaroo rat stands on a patch of grass in California. It uses the fur-lined pockets on the sides of its face to carry seeds to its burrow.

This rnap shows the range of kangaroo rats.

KANGAROO RAT 🐾 **8 of 22 species**

LENGTH OF HEAD AND BODY: **4-7 in (10-18 cm); tail, 5-9 in (13-23 cm)**

WEIGHT: **1-6 oz (28-170 g)**

HABITAT AND RANGE: **deserts and dry, brushy regions in parts of North America**

FOOD: **seeds, leaves, stems, and insects**

LIFE SPAN: **as long as 9 years in captivity**

REPRODUCTION: **1 to 6 young after a pregnancy of about 1 month**

ORDER: **rodents**

HOPPING ACROSS DESERT SAND, the kangaroo rat moves like a tiny kangaroo. A long, tufted tail helps the animal steer and keep its balance.

About twenty kinds of kangaroo rats live in parts of North America. Like many other desert rodents, kangaroo rats are well adapted, or suited, to their environment. Large hind feet keep them from sinking into the sand. The animals drink little or no water. They get moisture from the plants, insects, and seeds they eat.

When a kangaroo rat finds food, it may stuff some of it into its fur-lined cheek pouches. Then it carries the food to its burrow for storage.

Kangaroo rats spend most of the day underground. They live in burrows with several openings. These may serve as escape hatches when the animal is chased out by a fox, a coyote, or a snake.

A female kangaroo rat may have three litters a year. There are one to six young in each litter.

Kinkajou

△ At home in the trees, a kinkajou moves swiftly along a narrow branch in a rain forest in Costa Rica. Because it can turn its hind feet backward, a kinkajou can scamper headfirst down a tree trunk with ease. The animal can hold on to a limb with its strong tail.

Nose buried in a hole, a young kinkajou sniffs for ▷ insects. When eating fruit, the kinkajou uses its front paws and sharp claws to hold on to its meal.

ITS TAIL TWINED AROUND A BRANCH, a golden-brown kinkajou hangs upside down in a tree. Like some kinds of monkeys, a kinkajou can hold on to a tree with its strong, slender tail. As the animal moves about the forests of Mexico and Central and South America, its tail serves as another paw, gripping a tree limb tightly. The 20-inch (51-cm) tail—about as long as the kinkajou's body—is useful in other ways. Running along a branch, a kinkajou swings its tail for balance. The animal wraps its tail snugly around its body when it sleeps.

310

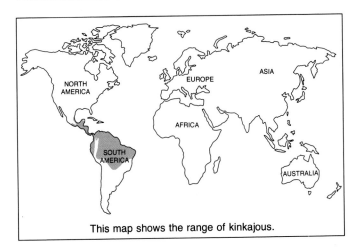

This map shows the range of kinkajous.

Kinkajous are members of the raccoon family. Find out about raccoons on page 471. Like their raccoon relatives, kinkajous have nimble front paws. They can easily pluck fruit while hanging by their hind feet and tails. They clutch the food in one paw and break it into small pieces with the other.

As they feed, kinkajous often use their long, narrow tongues. The tongues can slide into bees' nests to lick out honey, one of the kinkajou's favorite foods. Kinkajous are even nicknamed honey bears because of their fondness for the sweet food. They also eat fruit and small animals.

The kinkajou is difficult to study in the wild. It spends most of its life among the branches. During hot tropical days, a kinkajou naps in a hollow tree. At night, it wakes up and scampers about. Usually it travels alone. But sometimes two or more kinkajous gather in a tree full of ripe fruit. Though the animals are rarely seen, people sometimes hear them growling and barking as they feed.

Kinkajous communicate by scent as well as by sound. Each animal has scent glands at the corners of its mouth and on its throat and belly. These produce a substance that the animals rub off on tree branches throughout the area where they live. Scientists think that kinkajous keep track of each other by means of these scent marks. The scents may also help the animals find mates.

A female kinkajou usually gives birth to one offspring. With its soft, tan fur and tightly shut eyes, the tiny animal looks like a newborn kitten. Its tail can already grip objects lightly, though it is not yet very strong. About one month later, the young kinkajou is

△ *Hungry kinkajou feasts on termites from a nest in Colombia. With its long, thin tongue, it scoops out the insects. The animal also uses its tongue to lick nectar from flowers and honey from bees' nests.*

able to see. It can hang head down by its tail at about two months of age. The animal is fully grown within a year.

KINKAJOU

LENGTH OF HEAD AND BODY: **17-22 in (43-56 cm); tail, 16-22 in (41-56 cm)**

WEIGHT: **3-7 lb (1-3 kg)**

HABITAT AND RANGE: **forests in southern Mexico, Central America, and parts of South America**

FOOD: **honey, fruit, nectar, insects, birds, and small mammals**

LIFE SPAN: **as long as 24 years in captivity**

REPRODUCTION: **usually 1 young after a pregnancy of 3½ months**

ORDER: **carnivores**

Klipspringer
The klipspringer is a kind of antelope. Read about antelopes on page 52.

Koala

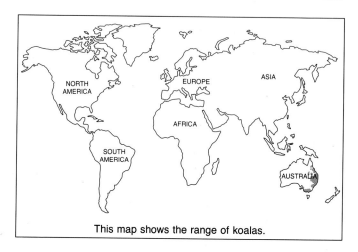

This map shows the range of koalas.

△ Nibbling on a leaf, a koala feeds in a eucalyptus tree in Australia. A strong-smelling oil in the leaves gives the animal an odor similar to cough drops.

KOALA

LENGTH OF HEAD AND BODY: 24-33 in (61-84 cm)

WEIGHT: about 20 lb (9 kg)

HABITAT AND RANGE: forests of eastern Australia

FOOD: primarily eucalyptus leaves and shoots

LIFE SPAN: about 20 years in the wild

REPRODUCTION: usually 1 young after a pregnancy of about 1 month

ORDER: marsupials

MOVING SLOWLY among the branches of a tree, the koala looks like a teddy bear come to life. It measures about 2½ feet (76 cm) long. Small, brown eyes stare out from its wide, round head. Soft fur covers its chubby body and fringes its ears. Its large nose is smooth and leathery.

Although the koala looks like a bear, this animal is not a bear at all. It is a pouched mammal called a marsupial (mar-SOO-pea-ul).

Koalas live in parts of eastern Australia. Eucalyptus trees there provide the koalas with food and homes. The animals rarely leave the branches of these trees. The koala climbs well. It spreads its toes and grasps the sides of a small branch. Its sharp claws dig into the bark.

Even when the koala moves to a different tree, it does not always come down to the ground. In thick forests, for example, it climbs along a branch toward a nearby tree. When it is close enough to the other tree, the koala jumps.

Koalas spend the day dozing high in the trees. Sometimes they curl up in a tree fork. Or they may sit on a limb with their legs hanging down. Toward evening, koalas become more active. They climb along

Clinging fast to its mother's soft fur, a young koala ▷ *rides piggyback up a limb. Female koalas carry their offspring in pouches for the first six months.*

the branches as they feed on eucalyptus leaves and bark. Each koala eats about 2½ pounds (1 kg) of leaves a day, and drinks very little water. The leaves supply most of the moisture a koala needs.

Though they eat a lot for their size, koalas are careful feeders. They may pass up several leafy branches before stopping to eat. At certain times of the year, eucalyptus leaves contain a poisonous acid. Koalas avoid these deadly leaves.

Because koalas need so much food, it is hard to keep them in zoos. A hundred tall eucalyptus trees are needed to provide food for each animal. With fewer trees, koalas soon would strip every branch bare. Neither the trees nor the koalas would survive. Outside Australia, the only place in the world where koalas breed is at the San Diego Zoo in California. Many eucalyptus trees have been planted there.

In the wild, koalas usually live alone. During the mating season, however, they often form small groups. One male and several females may stay together. Koalas are generally quiet animals. But during mating season males are very noisy. Their calls sound like saws cutting wood in a forest.

A female koala gives birth to one offspring, usually in the spring or summer. The newborn koala is hairless and no bigger than a grape. It climbs blindly into the protective pouch on its mother's belly. There the tiny koala attaches itself to a nipple and nurses for several months.

Bandicoots, kangaroos, and wombats also bear very small young that develop in pouches. Read about these marsupials under their own headings.

At six months of age, a young koala is strong enough to leave the pouch. But even then it travels everywhere with its mother. The small animal rides on her back, clinging to her fur with its claws. When resting, it hugs her belly. If the young becomes separated from its mother, it cries out for her.

After a young koala has left the pouch, it still returns there for food. For a few more months, it drinks only its mother's milk. Then it begins to eat leaves. By the time a koala is a year old, it no longer needs its mother. Soon it will go off and live alone. When it is

Koala

Wide yawn and sleepy eyes signal nap time. A koala ▷ spends as much as twenty hours a day dozing and resting in the trees. It wakes from time to time to eat a leafy snack. But the animal feeds mainly after dark.

△ *Snug in a double-deck bunk, two koalas curl up for a nap. Even swaying treetops will not disturb a sleeping koala nestled between two branches.*

three or four years old, it will begin to have offspring of its own.

Koalas once were common in many parts of Australia. But over the years hunters killed large numbers of the animals for food and for their thick, warm fur. Australians became concerned that the species would soon be extinct. Strict laws were passed to protect the animals, and koalas increased in number.

Meanwhile, however, people were cutting down the trees where koalas lived to get lumber for building and other uses, and to clear the land for farms. Fire also destroyed some of the forests.

Today, many people are again worried about the future of the koalas as they lose their habitat.

Kob
The kob is a kind of antelope. Learn about antelopes on page 52.

Kudu
The kudu is a kind of antelope. Read about antelopes on page 52.

L

Langur
The langur is a kind of monkey. Read about monkeys on page 370.

Lemming

(LEM-ing)

▽ *Tall grass shelters a southern bog lemming in an Ohio field. Lemmings make runways, or paths, by tunneling through grass or under snow.*

Southern bog lemming: 4 in (10 cm) long; tail, less than 1 in (3 cm)

PEOPLE HAVE TOLD MANY TALES about the thousands of lemmings that every so often march into the sea and die. Though the storytellers are exaggerating, they are not simply spinning yarns.

According to scientists, some lemmings do migrate, or travel, long distances. Approximately every 30 years, the population of Norwegian lemmings vastly increases. Then the animals leave their homes and scatter in all directions. Many of them soon die from exhaustion or starvation. Some become the prey of larger animals. Others at last make their way to the ocean's edge. Strong swimmers, some might be able to cross a small body of water. In the ocean, however, they drown.

Experts still do not fully understand why the furry animals make such journeys. Lack of food and of space for the huge numbers of lemmings may force some of the rodents to move elsewhere.

Norwegian lemmings are one of about a dozen kinds of lemmings. Most live in the cold northern areas of Europe, Asia, and North America. Some live in the northeastern and midwestern United States. Lemmings measure about 5 inches (13 cm) from their short snouts to the tips of their stubby tails. Most lemmings have gray or brown fur.

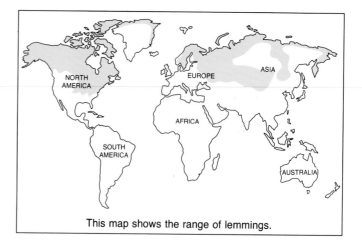

This map shows the range of lemmings.

Norwegian lemming: 5 in (13 cm) long; tail, less than 1 in (3 cm)

▽ *Well hidden by its light winter coat, a collared lemming digs in the snow in Alaska. In summer, the rodent's fur turns grayish brown.*

◁ *Furry, colorful ball, a Norwegian lemming sits on green moss. A thick coat hides its small ears and short tail.*

▽ *Carrying her offspring in her mouth, a collared lemming in Canada moves her young from her grassy nest. A female lemming usually has three to seven young in a litter. She may give birth several times a year.*

Collared lemming: 5 in (13 cm) long; tail, less than 1 in (3 cm)

Lemmings feed mostly on plants. In summer, these rodents live in burrows under mosses and other plants. They make paths called runways through the grass or under roots. In winter, the animals often live in tunnels under the snow. There they find food as well as shelter from cold temperatures. And they have better protection from such enemies as weasels and foxes.

A female lemming usually gives birth to three to seven young. A pregnancy lasts about three weeks, and females may have several litters a year.

LEMMING 🐾 **1 of 19 species**

LENGTH OF HEAD AND BODY: 3-6 in (8-15 cm); tail, less than 1 in (3 cm)

WEIGHT: $\frac{1}{2}$ oz-4 oz (14-113 g)

HABITAT AND RANGE: meadows, woods, marshes, and tundra in parts of North America, Europe, and Asia

FOOD: mostly plants such as mosses and grasses

LIFE SPAN: usually less than 2 years in the wild

REPRODUCTION: usually 3 to 7 young after a pregnancy of about 3 weeks

ORDER: rodents

Lemur

△ Hooking its legs over and under the branches, a sifaka, a kind of lemur, curls up in a tree in Madagascar. When resting, it often coils its tail.

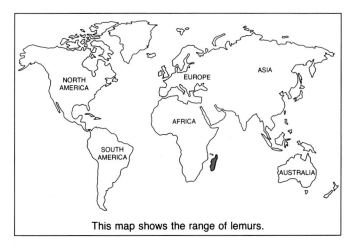

This map shows the range of lemurs.

THROUGHOUT THE FORESTS of Madagascar live large-eyed animals called lemurs. Lemurs are found only on this large island off the southeastern coast of Africa and on the small neighboring Comoro Islands. Lemurs, like apes, monkeys, and humans, belong to the primate order.

Some scientists think that Madagascar was once part of the continent of Africa. Gradually, the island

Sifaka (below) soars gracefully through the air. Long hind legs help it spring from one branch to another. At right, sifakas rest in the branches of a tree. On the ground, they sometimes run in an upright position.

Sifaka: 18 in (46 cm) long; tail, 22 in (56 cm)

318

Black lemur: 10 in (25 cm) long; tail, 15 in (38 cm)

△ *Eyes shining, black lemurs peer from a perch in the trees. Despite their name, only males have black fur. Females have coats of rusty brown.*

◁ *Among the smallest of all primates, a mouse lemur clings to a limb. The animal looks for food at night. It sleeps all day curled in a hollow tree or in a leafy nest.*

leaping and climbing. They use their hands and feet to grip the branches.

There are many species, or kinds, of lemurs, and they vary greatly in size. The mouse lemur, one of the smallest of the primates, measures only 5 inches (13 cm) long, not including its tail. The indri (IN-dree) is the largest lemur. Its body measures more than 2 feet (61 cm) long.

Mouse and dwarf lemurs usually feed alone and scurry along tree branches at night. Their big ears help them search for food and hear such enemies as catlike fossas. All lemurs eat plants, but mouse and dwarf lemurs also feed on insects.

Both the fat-tailed dwarf lemur and the mouse lemur have tails that are sometimes padded with fat.

Mouse lemur: 5 in (13 cm) long; tail, 6 in (15 cm)

separated from the continent. Because of their isolation, lemurs have little competition for their food and only a few enemies. They are well suited to their environment. Today lemurs remain relatively unchanged from their ancestors.

Many lemurs have slender bodies and narrow, pointed snouts. Lemurs move about in the trees by

Brown lemur: 15 in (38 cm) long; tail, 20 in (51 cm)

△ *Brown lemur travels on all fours along the stiff, broad leaf of a coconut palm. The animal's long tail helps it balance. Brown lemurs feed on insects and fruit during the day and at night.*

Mongoose lemur: 14 in (36 cm) long; tail, 19 in (48 cm)

△ *Downy light fur covers the chest of a mongoose lemur. Strong, flexible hands help it grip branches.*

Tail held high, a ruffed lemur strides across a field. ▷ *Usually ruffed lemurs stay in the trees. The white fur under its chin gives the animal its name.*

Ruffed lemur: 22 in (56 cm) long; tail, 24 in (61 cm)

Troop of ring-tailed lemurs feasts on leaves. These lemurs spend much of the time on the ground.

Lemur

When food becomes scarce, these animals begin to absorb the fat stored in their tails.

Typical lemurs are larger than dwarf and mouse lemurs. They usually grow as big as house cats. Nearly all typical lemurs live in groups. Some kinds, such as the mongoose lemur and the ruffed lemur, stay together in small families. Others, such as the ring-tailed lemur and the black lemur, live in larger groups called troops.

When moving through the trees, typical lemurs walk along the branches on all fours. Often they make long jumps from branch to branch. The ring-tailed lemur, however, spends more time traveling on the ground than do other lemurs.

The indri, the avahi (uh-VAH-hee), and the sifaka (suh-FAHK-uh) make up the indri family. Unlike other lemurs, members of this family occasionally stand upright when walking or running. At rest, they sit up and cling to branches. Sifakas often make spectacular leaps. Their long back legs give them a powerful take-off. With arms and legs outstretched, they may leap 20 feet (6 m) or more.

During the day, the black, hairless snouts and light-colored fur of many sifakas are easy to see. The woolly avahi, however, curls up in trees and sleeps in the daytime. Little is known about the animal in the wild because it is rarely seen by people.

Lemur pregnancies range from two to nearly five months, depending on the kind of lemur. A female may give birth to one, two, or three young. Ruffed lemurs, mouse lemurs, and dwarf lemurs build nests for their offspring. A female ruffed lemur often parks her offspring on a branch while she looks for food. Other lemurs take their young with them. The newborn cling tightly to their mother's fur as she moves among the branches. Young lemurs begin to play as soon as they can walk. At about two years of age, they are independent.

LEMUR   🐾 21 of 30 species

LENGTH OF HEAD AND BODY: 5-28 in (13-71 cm); tail, 5-26 in (13-66 cm)

WEIGHT: 2 oz-13 lb (57 g-6 kg)

HABITAT AND RANGE: forests of Madagascar and the Comoro Islands

FOOD: fruit, flowers, leaves, bark, insects, and tree gum

LIFE SPAN: up to 40 years in captivity

REPRODUCTION: usually 1 to 3 young after a pregnancy of about 2 to 4½ months, depending on species

ORDER: primates

Leopard

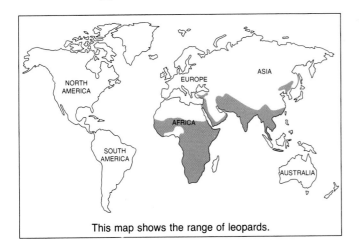

This map shows the range of leopards.

STARING INTENTLY, the leopard pauses quietly in tall grass. It flicks its tail. Then the big cat rushes toward its prey—an antelope. Seizing its victim with its claws, the leopard pulls the animal to the ground. It kills the antelope by biting into the neck or the throat. Instead of eating its meal on the spot, the leopard usually drags it away. It finds a place safe from hyenas, vultures, and lions.

A leopard may weigh only 100 pounds (45 kg). But the muscular cat is so strong that it can carry an animal its own weight up a tree. There it wedges its prey among the branches. The leopard feeds in the tree. Any meat that is left will be used for later meals. Leopards also hunt small animals such as rodents, birds, monkeys, and even fish. They will eat almost anything they can catch.

The leopard hunts mostly at night. Except at mating time, it avoids other leopards. If it sees another leopard, it will usually turn away. Like all cats, it uses many signals to alert other leopards to its presence. Rubbing its cheek against a tree, a leopard leaves a scent on the bark. The leopard may claw the tree trunk, or it may spray the tree with urine.

Leopards also let other leopards know where they are by making sounds. All big cats—jaguars, leopards, lions, and tigers—roar. But a leopard's roar does not sound (Continued on page 326)

Slinking through the grass, a leopard stalks prey in Sri Lanka. Leopards are smaller than lions and tigers and slimmer than jaguars. They live in more climates and habitats than these other big cats do.

Leopard

Body molded to the branches, a leopard lounges in a tree. Its paws and tail dangle. Leopards in

Africa often hide food high among the branches where hyenas, lions, and vultures cannot reach it.

Female leopard carries her month-old cub in her mouth. She gently grasps the loose skin at its neck in her teeth. Leopards sometimes move their cubs from one spot to another. They try to keep them hidden in a safe place such as the base of a hollow tree.

at all like a lion's. The leopard has a call that sounds like a deep, rasping cough.

Leopards live in many parts of Africa and Asia. They survive in forests and on grasslands, in warm and cold climates, but eight subspecies in North Africa and Asia are now endangered. Wherever leopards live, their yellowish fur with dark spots called rosettes helps hide them. A few leopards appear to be solid black because they have black rosettes on black backgrounds. People call these leopards black panthers.

Leopard cubs are born with dull gray fur. Their spots are barely visible. Females usually give birth to two cubs. At first, a female leopard hides her cubs in a quiet spot—in a cave or a hollow tree. Later, she may

move the cubs from place to place. When the cubs are older, the mother will lead them to a kill. The young play by stalking and pouncing. The games help prepare them to hunt on their own. After about two years, when they are almost fully grown, the cubs go off to live by themselves.

Read about snow leopards and other cats beginning on page 126. Find out about jaguars, lions, and tigers in their own entries.

LEOPARD 🐾 1 of 1 species

LENGTH OF HEAD AND BODY: 41-67 in (104-170 cm); tail, 26-38 in (66-97 cm)

WEIGHT: 66-176 lb (30-80 kg)

HABITAT AND RANGE: forests, open woodlands, scrublands, plains, and mountains in parts of Africa, the Middle East, and Asia

FOOD: antelopes, deer, rodents, birds, monkeys, and fish

LIFE SPAN: as long as 23 years in captivity

REPRODUCTION: 1 to 4 young after a pregnancy of about 3½ months

ORDER: carnivores

△ Almost hidden, a leopard waits in tall grass in Africa. The animal's spotted coat blends with its surroundings. The leopard creeps very close to such prey as antelopes, deer, and wild pigs. Then it rushes out, pulls its victim to the ground, and kills it with a bite.

Two young female leopards plunge into a river in India (left). In the shallow water, they tussle and play (above). Strong swimmers, leopards often find food in or near water. They eat fish, crabs, and other water animals.

Linsang

WITH ITS SHARP, CURVED CLAWS, the linsang of Asia and Africa can climb almost anywhere. The animal is a skillful hunter. It looks like a cat, and it can retract its sharp claws. But the linsang is a kind of civet. Read about other civets on page 154.

Dark spots, like the shadows of leaves on a tree limb, mark the linsang's short, light-colored fur. Dark rings circle its long tail. The linsang usually becomes active after dark. It moves silently among the trees.

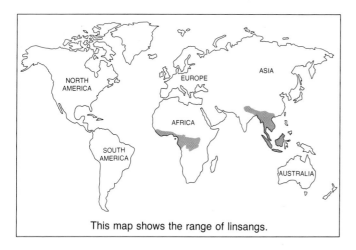

This map shows the range of linsangs.

LINSANG

LENGTH OF HEAD AND BODY: 13-18 in (33-46 cm); tail, 12-15 in (30-38 cm)

WEIGHT: 21-28 oz (595-794 g)

HABITAT AND RANGE: dense forests of western and central Africa and parts of southern and southeastern Asia

FOOD: rodents, insects, reptiles, birds, and fruit

LIFE SPAN: up to 11 years in captivity

REPRODUCTION: 2 or 3 offspring after a pregnancy of unknown length

ORDER: carnivores

A bird, a rat, or a lizard may not hear the linsang until it is too late.

The African linsang not only hunts in trees, but it lives there as well. Not much is known about the animal. Scientists think that these linsangs build nests of leaves and vines among the branches. The animals sleep there during the day. A linsang may have several nests in its home range.

There are two kinds of Asian linsangs. They live in parts of southern and southeastern Asia. Asian linsangs, like their African relatives, usually live alone. They hunt in forests and near fields. They sleep in hollow trees or among tangled roots.

A female linsang gives birth to two or three offspring each year.

Bold pattern marks the soft fur of a banded linsang of Asia. The spots help hide the animal, a kind of civet, in shadowy forests.

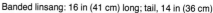
Banded linsang: 16 in (41 cm) long; tail, 14 in (36 cm)

Lion

DUSK SETTLES on the grassy plains of Africa. A pride, or group, of lions begins to stir. The golden cats, each about 6 feet (183 cm) long, rub against one another in greeting. Stretching, they groom themselves. A male shakes his mane, the ruff of hair on his head and neck. Then the lions hear a distant roar—the call of a member of the pride or that of a stranger. The lions respond with more roars.

The roaring is a signal. To pride members it means "Here I am." To other lions it is a warning to stay away. Lions in the same pride keep in touch with a variety of other sounds as well—grunts, meows, growls, and moans.

Lions are the only cats that live in permanent groups. A pride may include as many as six adult males and even more lionesses and cubs—perhaps

Wide yawn reveals the long, sharp teeth of a meat eater. Only an adult male lion has a mane, a ruff of long, thick hair. The bigger the mane, the more impressive a lion looks to other males.

25 animals in all. The lionesses in the pride are all related. Female cubs usually stay with the pride. Male cubs, however, leave when they reach three years of age. Brothers often wander together. Later, they may take over prides from other males.

Other wild cats usually live alone in wooded areas and hunt relatively small prey. Lions, however, live on grassy plains and in open woodlands where herds of large animals roam widely. There, by hunting together, lions can bring down such prey as a wildebeest or a zebra. The kill provides food for many animals. But a hungry lion will hunt whenever it finds prey—even if the lion is alone.

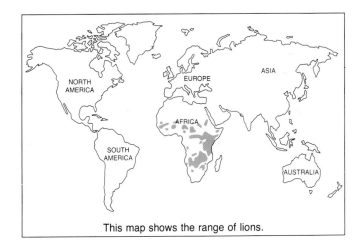

This map shows the range of lions.

The home area of a pride may cover about 100 square miles (259 sq km). Within this area, males mark certain places with urine. This lets other lions know that the area is taken. The animals also roar to announce their presence. Within their area, lionesses know the best places to hide cubs and to catch prey. When a strange lion enters another's range, it is chased from the area.

Female lions do most of the hunting for a pride. Because lionesses have no manes, they can stalk their prey unseen more easily than males can.

A pride may rest all day near a herd of antelopes or zebras. At night, the lions begin to stalk the herd. They fan out and circle their prey, drawing as close as possible. When they are within a few feet, one or two of the lionesses may rush at the herd. They may catch a victim themselves, or they may drive it within reach of

◁ *Keeping their distance, thirsty zebras wait until a resting lion has left a water hole. Already well fed, the big cat shows no interest in hunting.*

other lions. Sometimes they may kill more than one of the herd.

Prey is often difficult to catch. Most animals can outrun lions. In some parts of Africa, zebras and wildebeests move away from the plains during the dry months. Lions then must hunt the scattered animals that remain on the plains and in the woodlands. The lions sometimes steal the kills of wild dogs and hyenas. When there is much food, lions gorge themselves. Members of the pride often fight over a kill. Each lion tries to take as much food as possible. When prey is plentiful, cubs get a share. When there is little prey, the cubs may starve.

Newborn lion cubs are covered with spotted, woolly fur. Their eyes usually open after a few days. At first, the cubs are helpless. For the first weeks of their lives, they stay hidden in the grass. Although they usually nurse for about seven months, they may start eating meat at three months of age.

Cubs join the pride when they can move well enough to keep up—after about three months. At that

▽ *Adult lions feed on a wildebeest on a plain in Tanzania. Cubs watch and wait their turn.*

Lion

time, several lionesses bring together their litters—born within a few weeks of each other. A lioness will nurse or guard any cub, not just her own.

The young animals play games with other cubs, learning to be members of a pride. Play strengthens ties between the lions. It also gives cubs practice in hunting. They will not actually take part in a kill for about a year. In the meantime, the cubs wrestle. They stalk their mothers' tails, pouncing and swatting. One cub may rub against an adult male. Another may sit on its mother's outstretched forelegs.

Lions once roamed most of Africa as well as parts of Europe and Asia. Today scattered groups of lions live in Africa, but only south of the Sahara. In the Gir Forest in India, about 250 lions struggle to survive in an ever shrinking habitat.

▽ *Pride, or group, of lions stretches out lazily under an acacia tree. Lions may rest for twenty hours a day.*

Curled up in tall grass, a lioness in Africa seeks ▷ *shelter from the midday sun. The animal's yellowish coat blends well with her habitat.*

◁ *Female lion and her six-month-old cubs sit panting in the morning heat after feasting on a zebra.*

▽ *Two-month-old lion cub peers over a rock. The dark spots on a newborn's coat fade gradually as it grows.*

Lion

▽ *Four male lions cross a grassland in Africa while a jackal prowls nearby. A group like this one can win a pride and hold a territory longer than a single male lion can. Males may be driven out by other lions, but females in the pride are closely related and stay in the same area for generations.*

△ *Hunting alone, a lioness dashes from her hiding place to attack a group*

of warthogs. After the kill, members of the pride fight over the meat. Each tries to get as much as it can.

LION   🐾 I of I species

LENGTH OF HEAD AND BODY: 60-72 in (152-183 cm); tail, 24-34 in (61-86 cm)

WEIGHT: 265-420 lb (120-191 kg)

HABITAT AND RANGE: grassy plains and open woodlands in parts of Africa and in the Gir Forest in western India

FOOD: antelopes, zebras, buffaloes, and smaller animals

LIFE SPAN: up to 30 years in captivity

REPRODUCTION: 1 to 6 young after a pregnancy of 3$\frac{1}{2}$ months

ORDER: carnivores

▽ *Swishing her tail, an Asian lioness prowls a forest in search of food. In India, only about 250 of these rare animals survive in the wild. Lions once roamed parts of Europe and Asia and most of Africa.*

Llama
(LAHM-uh)

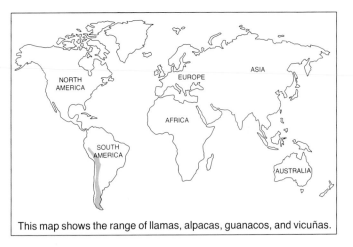

◁ *Ears perked, a woolly young llama—a South American relative of the camel—waits in a dusty field.*

This map shows the range of llamas, alpacas, guanacos, and vicuñas.

Llama: 45 in (114 cm) tall at the shoulder when fully grown

△ *Colorful ear tassels dangling, llamas travel a high mountain trail in Peru. The tassels indicate the animals' owners. Llamas provide transportation, food, and fuel for the Indians of South America.*

A PACKTRAIN of llamas winds slowly along a rugged mountain trail, carrying goods to a market town. The strong, surefooted animals look like small camels without humps. And they are! Llamas and their close relatives are members of the camel family. They all live on the slopes of the high Andes of western South America. Llamas and alpacas (al-PAK-uhs) are now domestic, or tame, animals. Guanacos (gwuh-NAHK-ohs or wuh-NAHK-ohs) and vicuñas (vi-KOON-yuhs) live in the wild.

During the day, the animals feed mainly on grasses. They chew their food for only a little while before they swallow it. After eating, they bring up a wad of the partly digested food, called a cud, and then they chew it completely. They swallow it again and digest it.

For centuries, Indians of the Andes have used male llamas as pack animals. Female llamas are kept to bear young. The llamas have provided their owners with meat, hides for leather, and wool for ropes, rugs, and other useful objects. Their droppings are burned as fuel.

A llama usually carries a load of 50 to 75 pounds (23-34 kg) strapped on its back. If a pack is too heavy, though, the animal may lie down and refuse to move. Even the shouts and prods of its annoyed owner may not move the stubborn animal. A packtrain may contain several hundred llamas. It can travel as many as 20 miles (32 km) a day.

Alpaca: 39 in (99 cm) tall at the shoulder when fully grown

Blanket of thick, soft wool covers a young alpaca—to the feathery tips of its ears.

LLAMA, ALPACA, GUANACO, VICUÑA 🐾 1 of 4 species

HEIGHT: 28-49 in (71-124 cm) at the shoulder

WEIGHT: 100-290 lb (45-132 kg)

HABITAT AND RANGE: mainly dry areas in the Andes and in plains of southern South America

FOOD: grasses, herbs, and other plants

LIFE SPAN: as long as 28 years in captivity

REPRODUCTION: 1 young after a pregnancy of about 11 months

ORDER: artiodactyls

Alpacas look like shaggy, long-haired llamas. Some alpacas' coats grow so long that their woolly hair drags along the ground! South American Indians raise the animals for their soft, thick wool. The Indians shear the wool and sometimes dye it. Then they weave it into a warm, lightweight fabric that sheds rain and snow. This fabric is called alpaca.

Guanacos—the most widespread members of the South American camel family—range from the coast to the mountains. The vicuña is found only in a few areas high in the Andes. Because people hunted these wild animals for their wool, their numbers decreased sharply. Today laws help protect the animals.

△ *Only a few days old but already surefooted, a young alpaca stands near its mother. If left unsheared, the coats of some alpacas may drag along the ground.*
▽ *Alpacas in Peru stroll past a lake dotted with flamingos. Alpacas graze on high plains during the day. At night, they return to the corrals of their owners.*

Vicuña: 36 in (91 cm) tall at the shoulder

◁ *Alert male vicuña stands guard over his territory. He shares this area with several females and their young. Vicuñas live only in a few areas high in the Andes.*

▽ *Vicuña family kicks up a cloud of dust as it gallops across a dry lake bed in Peru.*

Guanaco: 42 in (107 cm) tall at the shoulder

△ *Family group of guanacos races across a plain in Argentina. If chased by such enemies as mountain lions, the guanacos can run nearly 35 miles (56 km) an hour. The male usually stays in the rear, allowing females and young to escape first.*

Vicuña wool is among the finest in the world. Centuries ago, only Indian royalty could wear clothing made from this wool.

Guanacos and vicuñas sometimes graze near herds of domestic alpacas and llamas. The wild animals live in family groups or in bachelor herds. Young males without territories wander in herds of as many as 150 animals.

The family groups include a male, about six females, and their young. They roam together in a territory, or area, defended by the male. He mates with the females in the group. The animals often feed in the valleys. They sleep on the ridges and slopes. If attacked by such enemies as mountain lions, male vicuñas and guanacos sound a warning. They usually bring up the rear as the group runs away.

About 11 months after mating, female llamas, alpacas, guanacos, and vicuñas each bear a single young. When young vicuñas and guanacos are about one year old, they are chased away from the group by the male. A young male will join a bachelor herd. A female will wander off in search of a new group. Because llamas and alpacas are domestic animals, they remain in their owners' herds.

Loris

Slow loris: 15 in (38 cm) long; tail, about 1 in (3 cm)

Clutching a branch, a slow loris rests in a mountain forest in India. Large, round eyes help the loris find food at night. With a quick, powerful motion, it easily grabs such prey as lizards and large insects.

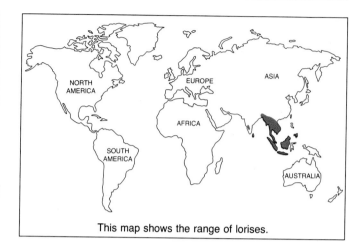

This map shows the range of lorises.

CREEPING AMONG THE TREES after prey, the loris moves along slowly. At each step, it grasps a branch tightly with its broad, muscular feet and hands. The loris inches forward first with one hand and then with the opposite foot. It seems to be traveling in slow motion. This animal moves so carefully that even the tree leaves do not rustle as it passes by. The loris can easily sneak up on a lizard or a grasshopper—then quickly grab its prey. Enemies such as leopards and civets usually do not notice the grayish brown loris climbing in the trees.

Lorises are found deep in the tropical forests of Asia. They rarely come down to the ground. These squirrel-size animals belong to the primate order, which also includes monkeys, apes, and humans. The loris is a relative of the potto, which lives in Africa. Read about the potto on page 453.

Lorises have pointed snouts and small, triangular faces. Their eyes are large and round, and small ears are hidden away in thick, coarse fur. Their tails are too short to see.

Lorises usually live alone. Occasionally, however, they roam in pairs or in small family groups. The animals hunt after dark and sleep during the day, rolled up in hollow trunks or in forks of trees. A sleeping loris looks like a ball of fur. It tucks its head and arms between its legs and curls up.

The loris can grip tightly with its hands and its feet, even when it sleeps. It can dangle from a tree limb by its feet and use its hands to hold fruit or plants to nibble on. Sometimes lorises hang from branches to stretch, to cool off in hot weather, or to play with each other. When a loris wants to take a drink, it sometimes finds a leaf covered with raindrops or dew. The animal touches the wet leaf and sucks the moisture from its fingers.

Some lorises have long arms and legs and very thin bodies. They are called slender lorises, and they live in the forests of India and Sri Lanka. Slender lorises measure about 10 inches (25 cm) long. The slow loris—a larger, stockier animal—also lives in India and as far east as Indonesia. It may grow as long as 15 inches (38 cm).

After a pregnancy of about six months, a female loris gives birth to a single offspring or sometimes to twins. The young are born with their eyes open, and they are covered with a thin layer of fine fur.

A young loris clings to fur on its mother's belly as she sleeps during the day. At night, a female loris parks her offspring on a tree branch while she searches for food. She cares for her young for about a year, until it is grown. Then the young goes off into the forest alone.

LORIS 🐾 **2 of 3 species**

LENGTH OF HEAD AND BODY: 7-15 in (18-38 cm); tail, about 1 in (3 cm)

WEIGHT: 10 oz-4 lb (284 g-2 kg)

HABITAT AND RANGE: tropical forests in southern and southeastern Asia

FOOD: lizards, insects, fruit, and tender shoots

LIFE SPAN: as long as 26 years in captivity

REPRODUCTION: usually 1 young after a pregnancy of about 6 months

ORDER: primates

Slender loris: 10 in (25 cm) long; tail, about 1 in (3 cm)

△ *Slender loris creeps carefully along a tree branch. The animal moves one hand or foot at a time. Slender lorises live in southern India and in Sri Lanka.*

◁ *Young slow loris hangs on tightly with hands and feet and climbs down a tree headfirst. As it descends, the animal makes a high-pitched, chattering sound.*

Lynx

DURING WINTER, thick fur protects the lynx in its home throughout much of the Northern Hemisphere. Even the bottoms of a lynx's large paws are covered with fur. The furry toes spread and make it easier for the animal to walk in deep snow.

The lynx's fur varies greatly in color. It can be light brown, gray, or a shade in between. Sometimes the fur is marked with spots of dark brown. Because of the richness and beauty of the fur, people have hunted the lynx for hundreds of years. As a result of hunting and of destruction of the lynx's habitat, the animals now remain only in scattered areas in Europe. They also live in Asia, in Canada, and in Alaska. The kind of lynx in Europe and Asia is usually much larger than the kind in North America.

Lynxes are short-tailed cats like their close relatives, bobcats. But the lynx has longer legs, larger paws, and bigger tufts of hair on its ears. The lynx also has much longer side-whiskers on its face than the bobcat does. Read about the bobcat on page 104.

Like most wild cats, the lynx lives alone in a home range. Though it thrives in forests, it easily adapts to dry scrubland and rocky hillsides. It lives in

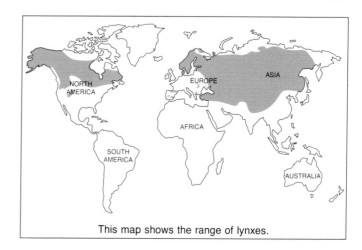

This map shows the range of lynxes.

areas undisturbed by people—wherever it can find prey. In North America, lynxes feed on mice, squirrels, birds, and especially on snowshoe hares. In Europe, where lynxes are about twice as heavy, they hunt deer as well as smaller prey.

About every ten years, the number of snowshoe hares in North America declines. The number of lynxes then also decreases. Because of lack of food, lynxes give birth to fewer young. The offspring that are born often starve. Normally, a female lynx bears one to six young in the spring.

LYNX 🐾 **I of 3 species**

LENGTH OF HEAD AND BODY: 31-51 in (79-130 cm); tail, 4-9 in (10-23 cm)

WEIGHT: 13-66 lb (6-30 kg)

HABITAT AND RANGE: forests, scrublands, and rocky hillsides in Europe, Asia, and northern North America

FOOD: hares, rabbits, rodents, deer, and birds

LIFE SPAN: up to 20 years in the wild

REPRODUCTION: I to 6 young after a pregnancy of about 2 months

ORDER: carnivores

Canada lynx: 34 in (86 cm) long; tail, 4 in (10 cm)

◁ *Tracks lead to a Canada lynx in a clearing. In winter, the broad, furry paws of the animal serve as snowshoes and help keep it from sinking in deep snow.*

Soft coat of spotted light brown fur covers the body ▷ of a Eurasian lynx. These animals—prized for their coats by hunters—once lived in much of Europe.

Eurasian lynx: 46 in (117 cm) long; tail, 7 in (18 cm)

Macaque The macaque is a kind of monkey. Read about monkeys on page 370.

Manatee

(MAN-uh-tee)

In the clear waters of Florida's Crystal River, a West ▷
Indian manatee moves away from two divers. In places
where divers often swim, some manatees seek attention
from people. Most avoid people, however. In past years,
manatees were hunted for food, for hides, for oil, and
for bones. Today laws protect them.

West Indian manatee: 13 ft (4 m) long

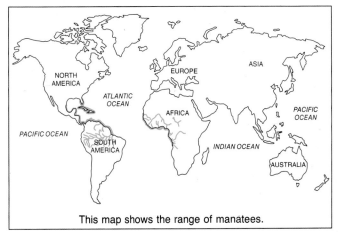

This map shows the range of manatees.

IT'S HARD TO BELIEVE that sailors once mistook manatees for mermaids. These sea mammals look more
like small blimps than beautiful women. Manatees
grow much larger than people. Some reach 13 feet
(4 m) in length and weigh as much as 1,300 pounds
(600 kg). Manatees are harmless. They rarely fight
each other, and they have no natural enemies. Manatees are as calm as cows grazing in a meadow. Sometimes they are called sea cows.

There are three kinds of manatees, but all of
them look and behave much the same. They all stay in
warm waters. One kind ranges from Florida to the
coastal areas of Brazil. Another inhabits the Amazon

◁ Graceful in its watery world, a West Indian manatee
rises to the surface to breathe. Although it spends all its
life in the water, a manatee comes up for air every few
minutes while swimming. A resting manatee can stay
underwater for as long as 15 minutes.

347

River. The third kind is found along the western coast of Africa.

Though the manatee is about as long and as heavy as a subcompact car, it is a graceful and agile swimmer. Manatees swim alone, in pairs, or in small groups of three to six animals. Usually they move in slow motion. They cruise, or swim at a steady pace, at 5 miles (8 km) an hour. But they can cover short distances at 15 miles (24 km) an hour.

When a manatee cruises through the water, it keeps its flippers by its sides. Its strong tail strokes up and down, pushing the animal forward. A manatee's flippers are flexible and useful. They help it steer. In shallow water, manatees use their flippers to walk on the bottom. As they move, they slowly place one flipper in front of the other.

Boaters on the water usually see only the nose of a swimming manatee. When the animal rises to take a

Manatees surface to breathe at a warm spring in Florida. In the fall, when their river home becomes chilly, about 25 manatees migrate to these warmer waters. They will stay there until March.

breath, most of its body stays underwater. Cruising manatees breathe noisily every three or four minutes. When they are not active, they can stay submerged for as long as 15 minutes.

Manatee calves are born underwater. Each calf must come up immediately to breathe air. The mother helps her newborn reach the surface for the first time. Usually the calf can swim alone within one hour after birth. A manatee weighs from 25 to 80 pounds (11-36 kg) at birth.

After a few months, a calf begins to graze, though it still drinks milk from its mother. The two stay close together for as long as two years—cruising, resting,

and coming to the surface to breathe. Calves often play with other manatees. They squeak, squeal, and scream. They nuzzle, nibble, and nudge one another. They even embrace with their flippers. Manatees probably recognize each other by the sounds they make and by touch. Their skin is thick and wrinkled but very sensitive.

Manatees feed on plants that grow in the water

▽ *Adult manatee feeds on stringy water plants. Manatees eat huge amounts of food—about a tenth of their weight every 24 hours. The animals help clear clogged waterways by eating plants that grow there.*

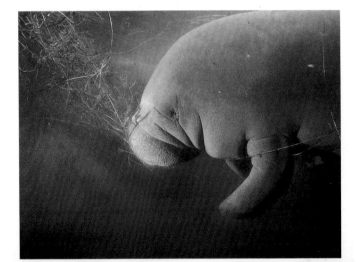

MANATEE 🐾 **3 of 3 species**

LENGTH OF HEAD AND BODY: 8-13 ft (244 cm-4 m)

WEIGHT: 440-1,300 lb (200-600 kg)

HABITAT AND RANGE: rivers, bays, and coastal areas from the southeastern United States to central South America, including the Caribbean Sea, and western tropical Africa

FOOD: water plants, sea grasses, and algae

LIFE SPAN: 40 years in the wild

REPRODUCTION: usually 1 young after a pregnancy of as long as 13 months

ORDER: sirenians

▽ *Lying on its back, flippers folded on its chest, eyes closed, a manatee naps upside down. These animals spend about one-third of the day resting.*

Breathing with its nostrils just above the surface, a manatee hangs ▷ *suspended in the water. Bristles on its upper lip help the animal eat. With these whiskers, it pushes food toward its mouth.*

and at the water's edge: water weeds, sea grasses, and algae. Every 24 hours, a manatee consumes as much as 1 pound (½ kg) of food for every 10 pounds (5 kg) of its body weight. A human child weighing 80 pounds (36 kg) would have to eat 8 pounds (4 kg) of salad a day to keep up with a manatee!

People have hunted manatees for food and for their hides, oil, and bones. In the past century, the number of manatees has steadily decreased. As a result, laws have been passed to help protect the animals. But manatees are often harmed by motorboats that travel through the waters where they live. Many of the slow-moving animals have scars on their bodies caused by propeller blades.

The manatee is related to another sea mammal, the dugong. The animals look and behave much alike. But they inhabit completely different parts of the world. Read about the dugong on page 186.

Mara

(muh-RAH or MAH-ruh)

Sitting up, a female mara nurses her young. In this position, she can watch for enemies such as foxes. A mara's long ears help pick up distant sounds.

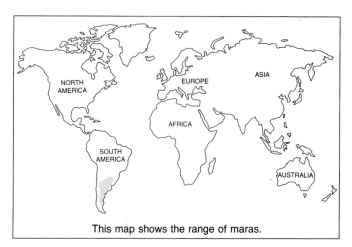

This map shows the range of maras.

BOUNCING ACROSS THE DRY PLAINS of South America, the long-legged mara looks almost like an antelope—but a very small one! It measures only about 30 inches (76 cm) from nose to stubby tail. The mara is actually a large rodent—a relative of the guinea pig. It lives in Patagonia, a dry, windy area in the southern part of South America.

Because of its long ears, some people call the mara the Patagonian hare. Maras are not related to hares, however.

When a mara rests, it sometimes lies with its long front legs tucked under its chest. It grooms itself carefully, wiping its face with a foreleg. As it sits in the sun, the mara flicks its ears. It stays alert to every sound, ready to escape if an enemy such as a fox threatens. Maras can run quickly. As they dash away, patches of white hair on their rumps may serve as danger signals to other maras.

Maras can run across the pebbly ground of Patagonia without being hurt. The bottoms of their feet are protected by hair and thick pads.

The rodents are well adapted, or suited, to their rugged homeland in other ways, too. Maras rarely drink water. They get most of the moisture they need from plants. Their thick coats of brown-and-gray hair blend with the colors of their habitat.

During the day, maras feed on grass and on the scrubby plants of the Patagonian plains. By gnawing and chewing, the animals keep their teeth from growing too long. Like the front teeth of all rodents, a mara's front teeth never stop growing.

Maras dig burrows in which to raise young. A female bears one to three offspring. The young have hair and teeth at birth, and their eyes are open. A female mara nurses her young sitting up. In this position, she can watch for danger.

Young maras follow their mother across the dry ▷
plains of Patagonia in South America. Born with hair
and open eyes, offspring can walk soon after birth.

▽ *Five small maras run into their burrow for shelter.*
A sixth has already dashed underground. Several adult
females may leave their offspring in one burrow and go
off to feed. They come back to nurse the young.

MARA

LENGTH OF HEAD AND BODY: 24-29 in (61-74 cm); tail, as long as 2 in (5 cm)

WEIGHT: 20-35 lb (9-16 kg)

HABITAT AND RANGE: dry grasslands and scrubby plains in parts of southern South America

FOOD: grass and other plants

LIFE SPAN: about 14 years in captivity

REPRODUCTION: 1 to 3 young after a pregnancy of 3 months

ORDER: rodents

Marmoset
The marmoset is a kind of monkey. Read about monkeys on page 370.

Marmot
(MAR-mut)

BY THE END OF SUMMER, marmots usually are very fat animals. For several months, they have stuffed themselves with food. They have eaten grasses, leaves, flowers, fruit, and—once in a while—a grasshopper or a bird's egg.

By early fall, these large rodents—about 2 feet (61 cm) long including their tails—have begun to waddle when they walk. Their furry bellies often drag the ground. When a marmot sits up on its hind legs, it looks like a chubby little man.

When the weather turns cold, marmots retreat into burrows. They sleep for six months or more. The body temperatures drop, and the heart rates slow down. This kind of sleep is called hibernation (hye-bur-NAY-shun). While they hibernate, marmots live on the fat in their bodies.

Marmots are found in parts of Europe, Asia, and North America. They make their homes near fields, in woods, in high valleys, on grassy mountain slopes, and among rocks.

Most species, or kinds, of marmots live in groups called colonies. They eat and sleep in a large underground burrow that they share.

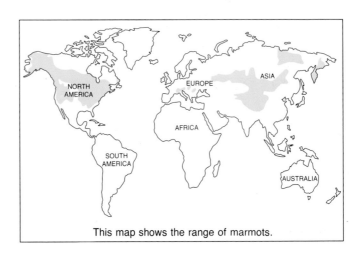
This map shows the range of marmots.

The woodchuck, a North American marmot, behaves differently. This animal—often called a groundhog—lives alone most of the year. It stays with other woodchucks for only a few months, when there are young. The woodchuck usually digs its burrow in a wooded area or in a field. A burrow may extend more than 40 feet (12 m).

Other marmots, such as the hoary marmot and

▽ *Its mouth full of grass, a hoary marmot in Alaska heads for its burrow. Marmots make grassy nests inside their burrows. There they hibernate, or sleep deeply, during the winter—for six months or more.*

△ *Young hoary marmot greets an adult by nuzzling it. Marmots often live in large family groups called colonies. They play and sun together.*

◁ *Hoary marmot picks its way along rocks in Montana. The rodent always remains alert to danger.*

Hoary marmot: 19 in (48 cm) long; tail, 8 in (20 cm)

Marmot

the yellow-bellied marmot, often dig their burrows under boulders on mountainsides. There they are safe from most animals. The yellow-bellied marmot is often called the rockchuck because it lives in rocky parts of western North America.

Marmots mate in the spring. Females usually bear two to six young a few weeks later. The young begin to wander outside the burrow after about a month. But they usually stay with their parents and hibernate with them during their first winter.

Young marmots play together much of the time. They roll and tumble while one family member keeps

watch. Their play helps the marmots learn to live in the colony. Marmots are friendly with each other. A young animal often greets an adult by nuzzling it and touching it with its paws.

Marmots have good eyesight, and they hear well. At the sight or sound of a bear, a fox, or an eagle, a marmot usually gives a high-pitched alarm call. All the marmots then run for cover.

Marmots are the largest members of the squirrel family. Read about their relatives—chipmunks, prairie dogs, and squirrels—in their own entries.

MARMOT 🐾 **2 of 14 species**

LENGTH OF HEAD AND BODY: 12-24 in (30-61 cm); tail, 4-10 in (10-25 cm)

WEIGHT: 7-17 lb (3-8 kg)

HABITAT AND RANGE: fields, valleys, mountains, plains, and wooded areas in parts of North America, Europe, and Asia

FOOD: grasses, leaves, flowers, fruit, and sometimes insects and birds' eggs

LIFE SPAN: as long as 20 years in captivity

REPRODUCTION: 2 to 6 young after a pregnancy of about 1 month

ORDER: rodents

△ *Hoary marmot licks sap that oozes from a willow branch in early spring. Marmots eat mainly plants, including leaves and grasses.*

◁ *Hoary marmot (above, left) basks in the sun on a rock in Alaska. Hoary marmots often dig their burrows on rocky slopes of mountains. There they can lie on boulders and keep watch for danger. Below left, another hoary marmot peers cautiously from its burrow.*

Woodchuck in North Carolina ▷ sits up to eat a tomato. Like other marmots, woodchucks often hold their food in their forepaws. These animals, also called groundhogs, give their name to Groundhog Day, on February 2. According to tradition, if a groundhog sees its shadow on that day, there will be six more weeks of winter.

Woodchuck: 17 in (43 cm) long; tail, 5 in (13 cm)

September sunshine bathes an Alpine marmot sitting on a mountain ▷ slope in Switzerland. Soon it will go underground and hibernate. Its breathing will slow down, and its heart rate will drop. For energy, the plump animal will use the fat stored in its body.

Alpine marmot: 22 in (56 cm) long; tail, 6 in (15 cm)

Marsupial mouse

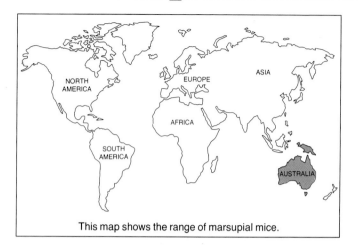

This map shows the range of marsupial mice.

Narrow-footed marsupial mouse: 4 in (10 cm) long; tail, 3 in (8 cm)

△ On the lookout, a narrow-footed marsupial mouse watches for prey in a forest in Australia.
◁ Jerboa marsupial mouse balances on a rock. Like the jerboa, a rodent found in parts of Asia and Africa, the marsupial mouse can bound across the ground. Though the animals look alike, they are not related.

Jerboa marsupial mouse: 4 in (10 cm) long; tail, 5 in (13 cm)

WITH THEIR BIG EARS, pointed noses, and long tails, marsupial mice certainly look like field mice. The animals are not related, however. Field mice are rodents. Marsupial mice are members of the same group as kangaroos, koalas, and opossums.

Marsupials give birth to tiny, underdeveloped young. The offspring usually crawl into a pouch on their mother's belly soon after birth. They stay there for several weeks, nursing and growing larger and stronger. The narrow-footed marsupial mouse has a front-opening pouch that is well developed. The jerboa marsupial mouse has a rear-opening pouch. Other kinds of marsupial mice may have no pouch at all—or they may have just a small flap of skin around the nipples. In some species, the males all die after their first mating season.

Unlike field mice, which eat mostly plants, marsupial mice eat small animals, including insects. There are about fifty kinds of marsupial mice. They live in all kinds of habitats in Australia, New Guinea, and on nearby islands.

MARSUPIAL MOUSE 🐾 **12 of 54 species**

LENGTH OF HEAD AND BODY: 2-9 in (5-23 cm); tail, 2-9 in (5-23 cm)

WEIGHT: $1/5$ oz-6 oz (6-170 g)

HABITAT AND RANGE: all kinds of habitats throughout Australia, New Guinea, and neighboring islands

FOOD: insects, rodents, and other small animals

LIFE SPAN: about 4 years in captivity

REPRODUCTION: 3 to 12 young after a pregnancy of about 3 to 7 weeks, depending on species

ORDER: marsupials

356

Marten

American marten: 16 in (41 cm) long; tail, 8 in (20 cm)

American marten peers from a branch in the Adirondack Mountains of New York.

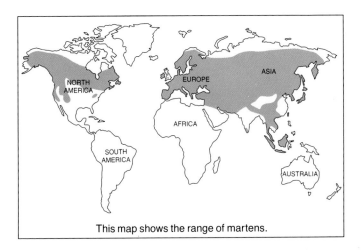

This map shows the range of martens.

LIKE A TIGHTROPE WALKER in an evergreen forest, an American marten scurries along a high branch after a red squirrel. Martens, members of the weasel family, seem to be always on the move. The animals bound across the snow in winter. They dash through hollow logs or scamper through brush. Martens hunt alone. They sniff the air for scents and listen for the rustling noises of small animals. When they spot their prey, they pounce.

Two kinds of martens—fishers and American martens—live in Canada and the northern United States. Beech martens and pine martens live in Europe and Asia. The sable, another kind of marten, lives in Asia.

Martens are about 2 feet (61 cm) long from nose to tip of tail. They grow thick coats in winter. For centuries, people have hunted the animals for their fur. Some of the most expensive fur coats are made of the skins of martens, especially sables and fishers.

In North America, the marten is at home on the ground or in the trees. It may mark its territory, or area, by leaving traces of a strong-smelling substance produced by glands in its body.

American martens and fishers hunt hares, birds, and rodents. They may kill more than they can eat. They hide the food and return to eat it later. Martens may also eat insects and fruit.

From late morning to late afternoon, American martens, sometimes called pine martens, rest. They

357

Fisher: 22 in (56 cm) long; tail, 14 in (36 cm)

△ *In the woods of northern Minnesota, a fisher, a kind of marten, tests a branch. Larger and faster than American martens, fishers usually hunt larger prey. They can even kill porcupines, despite the sharp quills.*

◁ *Light snow clings to the fur of an American marten in Wyoming. Skillful climbers, martens live in parts of North America, Europe, and Asia.*

Young beech martens, sometimes called stone ▷ *martens, play near a tree in Germany.*

become active in the evening and at night. The fisher hunts by day as well as by night. It is larger than the American marten and usually goes after larger prey. The fisher is one of the few animals that can kill and eat a porcupine. It attacks a porcupine from the front, biting the animal's face again and again. Finally, the fisher flips the porcupine onto its back. It bites into its underbelly, where there are no quills.

American martens and fishers often bear their young in holes in trees. The American marten may sometimes use a hollow log. A female gives birth to

Beech marten: 18 in (46 cm) long; tail, 9 in (23 cm) when fully grown

Marten

her young—usually three kits—in the spring. By about four months of age, the kits have begun to learn to hunt. In the fall, they are able to leave home.

Beech martens, sometimes called stone martens, rarely go into the trees, though they are good climbers. Most of the time, these animals scamper along the rocky ground looking for rodents, young hares, birds, and berries. Beech martens may live near people—in parks and gardens, in cities and villages. They sometimes go into farmyards to catch rabbits and chickens. Usually brownish in color, beech martens have lighter underfur that shows through their longer, darker outer fur.

The sable has a coat of thick, silky fur that ranges from the color of straw to nearly black. Sables live in forests and feed on small rodents, nuts, and berries. Though they stay mostly on the ground, sables may climb trees to escape enemies or to look for food. Sables mate in summer and give birth the following spring. The kits are blind and covered with fur that has a light color. After a month, their eyes open. By July, they are ready to go off on their own.

MARTEN   🐾 **3 of 8 species**

LENGTH OF HEAD AND BODY: 15-28 in (38-71 cm); tail, 5-15 in (13-38 cm)

WEIGHT: less than 2-12 lb (1-5 kg)

HABITAT AND RANGE: forests and rocky areas in North America, Europe, and Asia

FOOD: small mammals, birds, fruit, berries, insects, eggs, and the remains of dead animals

LIFE SPAN: 9 to 17 years in captivity, depending on species

REPRODUCTION: 1 to 6 young after a pregnancy of 8 to 12 months, depending on species

ORDER: carnivores

Red persimmons make a tasty meal for a Japanese marten on a nighttime search for food.

Japanese marten: 25 in (64 cm) long; tail, 8 in (20 cm)

Meerkat

Meerkat is another name for the suricate. Read about the suricate on page 526.

Mink

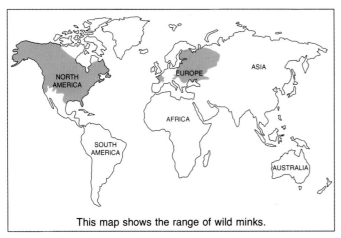

This map shows the range of wild minks.

MINK 🐾 1 of 2 species

LENGTH OF HEAD AND BODY: 13-22 in (33-56 cm); tail, 6-7 in (15-18 cm)

WEIGHT: as much as 3 lb (1 kg)

HABITAT AND RANGE: streams, lakes, rivers, marshes, and swamps in parts of North America, Europe, and western Asia

FOOD: small mammals, frogs, shellfish, fish, eggs, insects, and water birds

LIFE SPAN: 8 to 10 years in captivity

REPRODUCTION: 2 to 6 young after a pregnancy of about 2 months

ORDER: carnivores

American mink: 18 in (46 cm) long; tail, 6 in (15 cm)

On an ice-covered stream, an American mink pauses while looking for food. Besides hunting, minks find places to nest among roots and logs at the water's edge.

SLENDER, SHORT-LEGGED members of the weasel family, minks make their homes along the edges of lakes and streams. There they find food and shelter in thickets, in rock crevices, and among tree roots. These animals—known for their thick, shiny fur—live from Florida into the Arctic in North America. Some are found in Europe and western Asia.

With their partly webbed feet, minks are good swimmers and divers. They slip into and out of the water, looking for fish, crayfish, and frogs to eat. Their prey includes muskrats, hares, and mice. Minks also eat insects and water birds. They may kill more than they can eat at one time. They store what is left and return to it later.

A mink hunts alone, and it seems to be constantly on the prowl. The animal marks its territory, or area, with a strong-smelling substance that is produced in glands under its tail. These scent marks warn other minks to hunt somewhere else. Minks defend themselves fiercely. When a large owl or a bobcat threatens, a mink quickly fluffs up its fur, hisses, and rushes at its enemy.

Minks mate in late winter or early spring. About two months later, the female makes a nest in a hollow log. Or she may burrow into a riverbank. She bears two to six kits. The young nurse until they are about five weeks old. They play, tumble, and chase each other. After a few months, they begin to hunt with their mother. In the fall, the young minks go off and seek their own territories.

For hundreds of years, people have trapped minks and used their skins for clothing. Today the animals are raised on farms called ranches. Wild minks usually have coats in a shade of brown. But a mink bred on a ranch may have one of many colors of fur—from pure white to jet black.

Mole

IN THE DARKNESS of its burrow, the mole eats, sleeps, mates, and raises its young. This nearly sightless, chipmunk-size animal spends most of its life underground. About forty kinds of moles live in woodlands and fields and along riverbanks in parts of Europe, Asia, and North America. Distant relatives of moles called golden moles live in Africa. There are about twenty kinds of golden moles.

To make its burrow, a mole tunnels through the

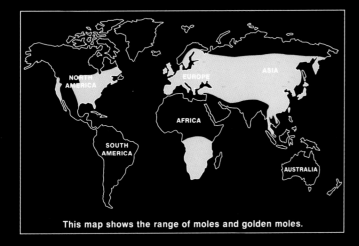

This map shows the range of moles and golden moles.

European mole: 5 in (13 cm) long; tail, 1 in (3 cm)

Dirt clinging to its head and body, a European mole (below) surfaces from underground. The shovel-like front feet of this common mole seem to stick straight out from its shoulders. Even when a mole leaves its dark burrow (above), it still cannot see. It has tiny, weak eyes hidden by fur.

ground. For its nest, it digs out a small room. There the mole sleeps on a bed of grass. In passages that lead from the nest, the mole hunts for food.

A mole's body is well adapted, or suited, for digging. Its powerful front feet are big. They seem to grow right out of the animal's shoulders. At the end of each foot are thick claws. As a mole digs, it looks as if it is swimming. First one foot and then the other moves into the earth, pushing back the soil. The mole twists its body forward and presses loose dirt into the walls of the tunnel. Occasionally, it digs up through the surface of the ground. It pushes extra dirt out of this opening, forming a molehill on the surface.

A mole can scurry through its dark burrow backward as well as forward. Its body is tapered at both ends. Its ears are simply fur-covered holes in its head. Thick, velvety fur on its body lies flat, whichever way it is brushed by the walls of a tunnel.

Most kinds of moles depend mainly on their sense of touch. The whiskers on a mole's face and the hairs on its tail and feet help it find its way in the dark. The tip of its long, narrow snout is covered with many tiny bumps. Each one is extremely sensitive. One kind of mole—the star-nosed mole—has a snout with 22 finger-like feelers that help the mole find food.

△ *Still hairless three weeks after birth, young European moles fill a grassy nest. A female European mole gives birth to three or four young each year.*

◁ *Webbed feet and a long, powerful tail make a desman an excellent swimmer. This Russian mole uses its long, flexible snout to hunt for food underwater. Largest of all moles, the desman pokes its snout above water when it needs to breathe.*

MOLE 21 of 61 species

LENGTH OF HEAD AND BODY: 2-9 in (5-23 cm); tail, 1-9 in (3-23 cm)

WEIGHT: $1/3$ oz-6 oz (9-170 g)

HABITAT AND RANGE: fields, woodlands, riverbanks, and deserts in parts of Europe, Asia, North America, and Africa

FOOD: insects, earthworms, mice, fish, and other small animals

LIFE SPAN: about 3 years in the wild

REPRODUCTION: 1 to 7 young after a pregnancy of about 1 month, depending on species

ORDER: insectivores

Mole

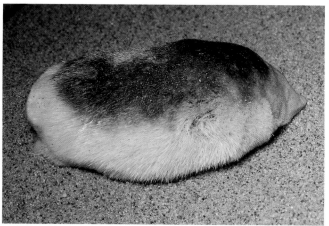

Desert golden mole: 6 in (15 cm) long

△ *Desert golden mole, distant relative of the mole, scurries across sand in southern Africa.*

Star-nosed mole: 4 in (10 cm) long; tail, 3 in (8 cm)

△ *Waving the feelers on its snout, a star-nosed mole emerges from a snowbank in northern Minnesota.*

A mole's body burns energy quickly, and the animal eats its weight in food each day. Every three or four hours, a mole searches for food. Besides worms and insect larvae, it gobbles spiders, lizards, and mice. Some moles dig out passages that end under-water in ponds or streams. There moles can catch insects, fish, shellfish, and frogs.

Moles usually live alone. They meet only during the mating season. Four to six weeks after mating, females bear as many as seven offspring.

Mole rat

Like a wrinkled sausage with teeth, a naked mole rat rests in a scientist's hand. This small rodent lives in underground colonies in parts of eastern Africa.

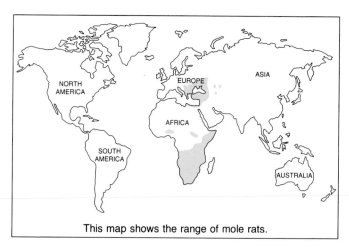

This map shows the range of mole rats.

BURROWING THROUGH THE GROUND, the mole rat chisels with its large front teeth. It packs the walls of its tunnel by pushing with its snout. Its legs swiftly kick dirt toward the entrance.

There are about thirty kinds of mole rats. They

364

live in parts of Europe, Africa, and Asia. Though these animals live underground like moles, they are really rodents. Their front teeth keep growing, like the front teeth of all rodents. Mole rats gnaw on roots and bulbs and wear down their teeth.

Most mole rats have stocky bodies with gray, black, or brown hair. Their ears are very small, and their tails are short. The lesser mole rat and the greater mole rat seem to have no eyes at all. Actually, their eyes are hidden under the skin. They feel their way with the sensitive hairs on their heads.

The naked mole rat has only a few hairs on its body. Unlike most mole rats, which live alone or in small family groups, naked mole rats live in large colonies. They use teamwork to dig and repair tunnels, to gather food, and to take care of their young. Apparently, only one female naked mole rat in a colony gives birth. Like a queen bee, she bears all the young—as many as 12 in a litter.

MOLE RAT   🐾 **7 of 29 species**

LENGTH OF HEAD AND BODY: 3-13 in (8-33 cm); tail, as long as 3 in (8 cm)

WEIGHT: 1-53 oz (28-1,503 g)

HABITAT AND RANGE: plains, forests, deserts, and some mountainous areas in parts of Europe, Africa, and Asia

FOOD: mainly roots and bulbs

LIFE SPAN: more than 16 years in captivity

REPRODUCTION: 1 to 12 young after a pregnancy of 1 to 2½ months

ORDER: rodents

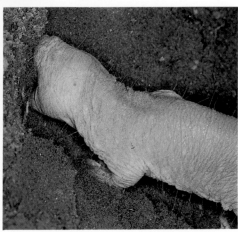

◁ *Flying dirt and a mound of earth give away the presence of a naked mole rat digging a burrow.*
▽ *Naked mole rat sniffs the ground (below, left). Another tunnels through dirt with its large front teeth. Naked mole rats often cooperate when they dig. One mole rat digs and kicks dirt to animals in a line behind it. Each mole rat in turn receives its load of dirt and kicks it backward to the opening. It returns for another load by scampering over the other mole rats.*

Naked mole rat: 3 in (8 cm) long; tail, 1 in (3 cm)

Mongoose

(MONG-goose)

◁ *Stretching its sleek body, a small Indian mongoose watches for eagles and hawks. It uses its pinkish tongue to clean its face after eating.*

▽ *Gray mongoose bites the twisting body of a snake. A group of mongooses sometimes attacks a large snake. Then they fight among themselves for the food.*

Gray mongoose: 16 in (41 cm) long; tail, 13 in (33 cm)

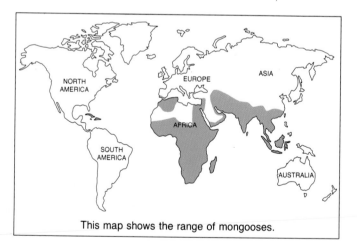

This map shows the range of mongooses.

HAIR BRISTLING on its graceful, slender body, a mongoose circles a cobra. The animal lunges at the poisonous snake. The cobra strikes back. The mongoose dodges and tempts the snake again. With each strike, the snake tires a little more. Finally, the mongoose pounces on the weary cobra. It grabs the snake in its teeth and holds on. Then the mongoose kills the cobra by biting it on the head.

Small Indian mongoose: 12 in (30 cm) long; tail, 9 in (23 cm)

Slender mongoose pauses watchfully on a log in ▷
Africa. These animals run easily along branches. They
usually live alone in scrublands or in open woodlands.

Such battles usually are staged for entertainment
on streets in India. In the wild, however, snakes make
up only a small part of a mongoose's diet. Most often,
mongooses eat whatever food happens to be nearby.
Some eat mostly insects. Other mongooses hunt larger prey such as rodents and birds. Many eat fruit and
other plants.

Just as mongooses eat many kinds of foods, they
live in many places—Asia, Africa, and parts of southern Europe. People have taken mongooses to Hawaii
and to the West Indies where they have thrived. Some
mongooses make their homes on open, grassy plains
or in dense forests. Some are found in swampy areas
or in dry scrublands. There are about 38 species, or
kinds, of mongooses. Read about one species, the suricate, on page 526.

Slender mongoose: 12 in (30 cm) long; tail, 10 in (25 cm)

▽ *Nipping and tumbling, two young dwarf mongooses play together. Dwarf mongooses cooperate*
when they care for young. One or two pack members stay with the offspring while others hunt.

Dwarf mongoose: 8 in (20 cm) long; tail, 6 in (15 cm) when fully grown

Mongooses rest during the heat of the day. They sleep in termite mounds, in piles of rocks, among tangled tree roots, or in burrows.

MONGOOSE 🐾 **7 of 37 species**

LENGTH OF HEAD AND BODY: 8-25 in (20-64 cm); tail, 6-21 in (15-53 cm)

WEIGHT: 12 oz-11 lb (340 g-5 kg)

HABITAT AND RANGE: forests, open woodlands, grasslands, marshes, and scrublands throughout most of Africa, and parts of Europe, Asia, the Middle East, Madagascar, some Caribbean islands, and Hawaii

FOOD: small animals as well as fruit, nuts, and seeds

LIFE SPAN: up to 20 years in captivity

REPRODUCTION: 1 to 6 young after a pregnancy of 1½ to 3 months, depending on species

ORDER: carnivores

Some mongooses hunt during the morning and afternoon. Others move around at night.

To find food, a mongoose pokes its pointed nose into a hole, overturns rocks with its paws, or scratches in the dirt with sharp claws. Some find food by reaching underwater with their nimble fingers. If a marsh mongoose catches a hard-shelled animal such as a crab, it stands on its hind legs and hurls the crab to the ground to break it open and get at the meat. To crack an egg, the banded mongoose stands with its back to a large rock. It picks up the egg in its front paws and tosses it backward between its legs. The egg breaks against the rock.

A mongoose uses scent to communicate. The animal has several glands in its body that produce an

Mongoose

Banded mongoose: 15 in (38 cm) long; tail, 10 in (25 cm)

◁ *Banded mongoose crosses a round termite mound on a plain near a lake in Uganda. Banded mongooses often roam in packs of 15 or more animals. During the day, they look for such insects as beetles. At night, the packs return to their dens, often in termite mounds.*

▽ *Tail held high, a ring-tailed mongoose looks for lizards. These rare mongooses live on Madagascar, an island off the southeastern coast of Africa.*

Ring-tailed mongoose: 14 in (36 cm) long; tail, 9 in (23 cm)

oily substance. As a mongoose roams its home range, it sometimes leaves scent marks on certain objects along its trail. Dwarf mongooses and banded mongooses even mark one another. The scents help them recognize members of their group.

Some kinds of mongooses can have several litters a year. Each litter may include six offspring. Banded mongooses and dwarf mongooses cooperate among themselves in caring for young. One or two members of the pack clean, feed, and protect the offspring while the other adults hunt.

Yellow mongoose rests in the sun in South Africa. ▷
These animals live in family groups. They often share their burrows with other mongooses called suricates.

Yellow mongoose: 14 in (36 cm) long; tail, 10 in (25 cm)

369

Monkey

Japanese macaque: 21 in (53 cm) long; tail, 4 in (10 cm)

Snow dusts the thick fur of a female Japanese macaque and her young, huddled against the cold.

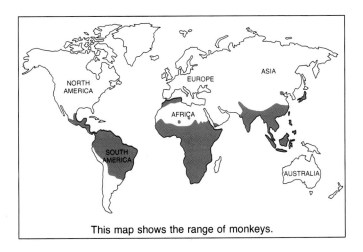

This map shows the range of monkeys.

Red spider monkey: 20 in (51 cm) long; tail, 27 in (69 cm)

△ *Young red spider monkey gets a ride through a rain forest in Central America. To swing from branch to branch, its mother uses her tail like an extra arm.*

▽ *Three young chacma baboons, escorted by an adult, cross an open grassland in Africa. Baboons spend most of their waking hours on the ground. For safety, they sleep high in trees or on rocky cliffs.*

WHAT'S MORE FUN than a barrel of monkeys? A whole forest full of them! Many of the world's forests are filled with monkeys—the familiar, intelligent animals that sometimes look and act like humans. That may be one reason why we find them so interesting. People usually think of monkeys as lively and playful. We say that children playing pranks are up to monkey business. If someone teases us, we often say, "Don't monkey around."

Chacma baboon: 32 in (81 cm) long; tail, 23 in (58 cm)

Monkey

Monkeys, along with apes and human beings, belong to the primate order. Apes, though they look somewhat like monkeys, have no tails. They are usually larger than monkeys. Chimpanzees, gibbons, gorillas, and orangutans are all apes. Read about them under their own headings.

There are about 180 species, or kinds, of monkeys in the world. People usually imagine monkeys swinging through trees in tropical forests. Many monkeys of South America and southern North America do behave that way. But monkeys also live in other habitats and climates. In Africa, monkeys live on open grasslands, as well as in forests. They are found in the mountains of Japan and on the treeless plains high in the Himalaya of Asia. One kind of monkey even makes its home on the Rock of Gibraltar in extreme southern Europe.

Scientists place monkeys in two groups. North and South American monkeys are called New World monkeys. Those found in Africa, Asia, and Europe are called Old World monkeys.

Both groups of monkeys look and act much alike. They eat many of the same foods—fruit, nuts, seeds, leaves, flowers, insects, birds' eggs, spiders,

Pygmy marmoset bites into a grasshopper in a dense ▷
Amazon rain forest. The animals—smallest of all
monkeys—have speckled brown-and-yellow coats.

▽ *Among the green leaves of an acacia tree in Kenya, a troop of olive baboons finds shelter.*

Olive baboon: 27 in (69 cm) long; tail, 20 in (51 cm)

Pygmy marmoset: 5 in (13 cm) long; tail, 8 in (20 cm)

Red howler monkey: 22 in (56 cm) long; tail, 25 in (64 cm)

△ *Loud cries fill a forest in Venezuela as two male red howler monkeys announce their presence. Before they set out each morning to find food, they arouse animals in the forest with their calls. By howling, they warn other howler monkeys, "This is our territory. Keep out!"*

373

NEW WORLD MONKEYS—identified by their round, wide-set nostrils—make their homes in North and South America. Some New World monkeys have prehensile, or grasping, tails. Above, a red spider monkey uses its long tail to dangle from a tree.

▽ *In Peru, a dusky titi gazes skyward. These small, red-bearded monkeys eat fruit, leaves, and insects.*

and sometimes small mammals. But the bodies of monkeys in each group differ in certain ways. The nostrils of most of the New World monkeys are round and set far apart on short snouts. The nostrils of many of the Old World monkeys are curved and set close together on their snouts. Old World monkeys have pads of tough skin on their rumps. The pads cushion them while they sit to eat or to sleep. The New World

Dusky titi: 15 in (38 cm) long; tail, 16 in (41 cm)

◁ *Upside-down weeper capuchin quenches its thirst at a river in Venezuela. These monkeys sometimes climb onto branches hanging just inches above water. They lean down to drink.*
Weeper capuchin: 17 in (43 cm) long; tail, 17 in (43 cm)

▽ *Softly furred night monkey, or douroucouli, grips a tree in an Amazon rain forest. Sometimes called owl monkeys because of their large, round eyes, these South American primates sleep during the day. At night, they look for insects, leaves, and flowers to eat.*

Night monkey: 13 in (33 cm) long; tail, 13 in (33 cm)

White-faced saki: 19 in (48 cm) long; tail, 16 in (41 cm)

△ *Vivid mask of light fur on its face identifies a white-faced saki as a male. Female sakis have only narrow, light-colored bands streaking their dark faces. Sakis live in the rain forests of South America.*

monkeys do not have this kind of built-in pillow.

Some Old World monkeys have pouches in their cheeks. These pouches allow them to store an extra supply of food to eat later. No New World monkeys have cheek pouches. But some do have a useful characteristic that no Old World monkey has: a prehensile (pree-HEN-sul) tail. This tail can grasp objects and support the animal's weight. Wrapping the tail firmly around a branch, a monkey can dangle upside down while eating. And it can use its tail to help it swing from limb to limb.

Some monkeys have hands like those of humans. These hands help the animals grasp while they are feeding and while they are traveling about. Although a few kinds of monkeys have no thumbs at all, many others have thumbs that help them hold on to objects.

Monkey _____

Like a guided missile, a squirrel monkey makes a ▷ spectacular leap from tree to tree. Its outstretched tail helps this South American monkey keep its balance.

▽ *Bareback riders, young squirrel monkeys travel through a forest in Colombia with two older females. A female relative often cares for another's young.*

Squirrel monkey: 12 in (30 cm) long; tail, 16 in (41 cm)

The guenons (guh-NOHNS) of Africa and the capuchins (kuh-PYOO-shunz) of Central and South America can move their thumbs around to touch some of their other fingers. They can pick up bits of food with their thumbs and fingertips. And their thumbs help them grip branches as they climb. Some New World monkeys cannot use their thumbs in this way. These monkeys must hold objects by pressing them between their fingers and the palms of their hands.

A few kinds of monkeys, such as baboons and some macaques (muh-KACKS), spend much of the time on the ground. But most monkeys live in trees. Their slender, light bodies are well suited to climbing, swinging, and leaping. With their long, muscular arms and legs, they can move easily among the trees.

Black-mantle tamarin: 9 in (23 cm) long; tail, 13 in (33 cm)

Cotton-top tamarin: 9 in (23 cm) long; tail, 15 in (38 cm)

△ *White patch around its mouth looks like a broad smile on a black-mantle tamarin. To climb, tamarins and their close relatives, marmosets, use their long claws.*
◁ *Long mustache lends a dignified air to an emperor tamarin in Peru. This small monkey feeds on fruit and insects.*

Black-and-white tassel-ear marmoset: 8 in (20 cm) long; tail, 13 in (33 cm)

△ *Bushy white fur on its head gives the cotton-top tamarin its name.*
◁ *Forked tree provides a perch for a black-and-white tassel-ear marmoset. Silky tufts of fur hide the ears of this small monkey with the long name.*

Emperor tamarin: 9 in (23 cm) long; tail, 14 in (36 cm)

377

Woolly monkey: 20 in (51 cm) long; tail, 25 in (64 cm)

△ *Young woolly monkey in Brazil reaches for a leaf. People often capture these monkeys to sell as pets.*
◁ *Gripping with toes, tail, and fingers, a red howler monkey plays acrobat in a rain forest in Colombia. Huge trees there provide howlers with a plentiful supply of a favorite food—fresh green leaves.*

The star acrobat among monkeys is the spider monkey of Central and South America. It is named for its long, thin, spiderlike limbs and prehensile tail. The monkey uses its limbs and tail to climb nimbly among the tallest trees in the forest. It makes its home in the topmost branches. There, as high as 100 feet (30 m) above the ground, it eats, sleeps, and raises its young. The spider monkey descends to the lower branches to feed on fruit and nuts.

Most monkeys are active during the day. As these animals climb, swing, and jump, they chatter, shriek, and scold one another. Only the night monkey, or douroucouli (dur-uh-COO-lee), of South America moves around after dark. These monkeys usually travel in pairs.

MONKEY 🐾 89 of 187 species
LENGTH OF HEAD AND BODY: 5-40 in (13-102 cm); tail, as long as 36 in (91 cm)
WEIGHT: 4 oz-100 lb (113 g-45 kg)
HABITAT AND RANGE: forests, grasslands, and mountains in Africa, Asia, and North and South America
FOOD: leaves, fruit, insects, nuts, seeds, grasses, roots, birds' eggs, spiders, and small mammals
LIFE SPAN: as long as 45 years in captivity, depending on species
REPRODUCTION: 1 or 2 young after a pregnancy of about 4½ to 7½ months, depending on species
ORDER: primates

Probably the loudest voices belong to male howler monkeys, the largest of the New World monkeys. Each morning, their cries echo through the forest. They roar to let other monkeys know where they are. By their roars, howlers remind other howlers to keep out of their territories, or areas.

High in the trees of dense rain forests in South America, monkeys have few enemies other than eagles and hawks. The monkeys' most dangerous enemies are people who hunt them for food.

One monkey that has been hunted often in South America is the uakari (wah-KAR-ee). When alarmed, the rare red uakari fluffs up its shaggy fur, and its face turns bright red.

Like humans, most monkeys usually have only one offspring at a time. The helpless newborn depends on its mother for warmth, food, and transportation. During the first days or weeks of its life, it clings

▽ *Red uakari, known by its scarlet face and bald head, pauses as it climbs up a slender tree trunk. Unlike most other monkeys, the rare uakari has a short tail.*

Red uakari: 18 in (46 cm) long; tail, 7 in (18 cm)

Monkey

OLD WORLD MONKEYS, found mostly in Africa and Asia, generally grow larger than their New World relatives. Curved and close-set nostrils and hard pads on their rumps help identify them. No Old World monkey has a prehensile tail.

Barbary macaque: 23 in (58 cm) long

△ *Barbary macaques rest in the sun. The two on the right groom each other near a mother and her offspring. The monkeys are often called Barbary apes because, like apes, they have no tails. Barbary macaques live in North Africa and on Gibraltar, a British territory at the southern tip of Spain.*

Bright white band on its upper lip gives a mustached guenon its name. Tropical ▷ *forests of Africa provide homes for these fruit and leaf eaters. The animals sometimes sniff the ground looking for plants to eat. In cheek pouches they store food to carry back to the trees.*

Mustached guenon: 19 in (48 cm) long; tail, 30 in (76 cm)

to the fur on its mother's belly as she moves about looking for food. Later the young monkey becomes more daring and playful. It rides on its mother's back or scampers about on its own. Sometimes it climbs onto the backs of other members of the monkey group. The adults are usually very patient with the young monkey.

Among some kinds of monkeys, the care of their young is shared by several family members. For example, male marmosets (MAR-muh-sets) and tamarins (TAM-uh-rins) of South America carry their young, usually twins, on their backs. They may hand the offspring to the mothers only at feeding time.

Monkeys are social animals—that means they live in groups. While resting, they spend a great deal of time grooming other members of their group. One monkey combs through another's hair, picking out dirt and insects. Such careful grooming helps keep relations friendly among monkeys.

Groups of monkeys may vary in number. Some

Rhesus monkey: 22 in (56 cm) long; tail, 10 in (25 cm)

△ *Rhesus monkey and her offspring eat yellow blossoms on the grounds of a Hindu temple in Nepal.*
◁ *Two hanuman langurs in India use bamboo stalks as stools. Like rhesus monkeys, they run free in villages and temples in Asia. But some are losing their habitat.*
▽ *Pig-tailed macaque pauses in a field in Indonesia. These large monkeys often raid crops for food.*

Pig-tailed macaque: 21 in (53 cm) long; tail, 8 in (20 cm)

Hanuman langur: 24 in (61 cm) long; tail, 31 in (79 cm)

381

Monkey

Lion-tailed macaque: 21 in (53 cm) long; tail, 13 in (33 cm)

Proboscis monkey: 25 in (64 cm) long;
tail, 26 in (66 cm)

△ *How was the proboscis monkey of Borneo named? Proboscis means long, flexible snout. A male proboscis monkey's snout serves as a loudspeaker when he calls out to other monkeys in his group.*

◁ *Face framed by a shaggy mane, a lion-tailed macaque feeds on plants in India.*

Black-and-white colobus monkey: 22 in (56 cm) long; tail, 32 in (81 cm)

Female black-and-white colobus monkeys in Kenya gather round as a mother (second from left) cradles her offspring. The tiny newborn still wears a coat of white. Adult monkeys often groom another's young.

monkeys live in pairs. They may stay with their mates for life, raising one offspring after another. Others live in larger troops, groups made up of adult males and females with young. Some troops contain one male and many females. In certain troops, a strong male acts as leader and protects the others.

Baboons, the largest of all monkeys, live and travel in tightly organized troops. Sometimes baboon troops number several hundred members. The hamadryas (ham-uh-DRY-uhs) baboons of eastern Africa live in smaller groups. One male usually leads several females and their offspring.

Baboons are ground dwellers. These primates may roam as many as 12 miles (19 km) a day to look for food. They search for plants, roots, insects, and small mammals in the rocky, open countryside of Africa. Because baboons spend most of their time on the ground, they are in danger from leopards, cheetahs, wild dogs, and other hunters. If a baboon spies an enemy, it may try to run away. Or it may bark loudly and bare its sharp teeth. If necessary, it will fight to defend the troop. A male baboon, which may measure more than 3 feet (91 cm) long and weigh about 100 pounds (45 kg), is a fierce foe!

Monkeys range in size from the large baboon to the tiny pygmy marmoset of South America—the smallest monkey in the world. Its body is only 5 inches (13 cm) long—shorter than a toothbrush.

Monkeys differ in appearance and special abilities as much as they do in size. The short-haired woolly monkey of South America has a big potbelly. In fact, the Portuguese name for this large monkey, *barrigudo,* means "big belly." These animals eat huge quantities of fruit and leaves.

The Barbary macaque, also known as the Barbary ape, has no tail. But it too is a monkey. Barbary macaques live on the Barbary Coast of North Africa and on Gibraltar, a British territory at the southern tip of Spain. They are the only primates in Europe living outside of zoos. According to a long-held tradition, as long as the Barbary macaques remain on Gibraltar, the British will keep control of the area.

Many other kinds of macaques live in Asia. The

Young vervet clings to its mother in a forest in ▷
southern Africa. A vervet's tail may measure as long as
3 feet (91 cm), almost twice the length of its body.

Vervet: 21 in (53 cm) long; tail, 36 in (91 cm)

Monkey

△ *Two male olive baboons challenge each other on a grassland in Kenya. Fights like this sometimes occur among members of baboon troops. Such contests end quickly*

◁ *Baring long, sharp teeth, a male olive baboon threatens an unwelcome visitor. By this gesture, known as a threat-yawn, it signals intruders to stay away.*

Japanese macaque, called the snow monkey, lives farther north than any other monkey. Its long, shaggy hair protects it from the cold. The rhesus (REE-suss) monkey of India is also a macaque. It has been used in many experiments in medical research and in the exploration of space.

A large macaque, the pig-tailed macaque of Malaysia, helps out when inhabitants harvest coconuts there. Malaysians teach intelligent young animals to climb coconut palms and pick the ripe fruit. The monkeys drop the coconuts down to their owners who are waiting below.

Crab-eating macaques that live along riverbanks in southeastern Asia are very good swimmers. These long-tailed monkeys usually look for fish and shellfish at the water's edge. They add these to their diet of fruit and insects.

The small, easily trained capuchins are among the best-known monkeys in the world. In the past, street musicians called organ-grinders dressed the capuchins in costumes. As an organ-grinder played an instrument called a hand organ, his monkey performed stunts and collected money from onlookers.

In contrast to the playful capuchins, some monkeys may seem idle. Leaf eaters like the Asian langur (LAHNG-gur) and the African colobus (KAHL-uh-bus) monkeys spend many hours each day just sitting and digesting their food. But when they do move, these monkeys can leap amazing distances. Colobus monkeys have been seen jumping as far as 30 feet (9 m) from one tree to another.

In some parts of the world, monkeys are considered sacred. In India, langurs live on the grounds of Hindu temples. They often roam unharmed in towns and villages. People bring them offerings of food—bits of pumpkin or handfuls of rice. Langurs are familiar sights in open-air markets, where they help themselves to fruits and vegetables.

Hindus in India consider all monkeys to be holy. One kind of langur—the hanuman (HUN-uh-mahn) langur—is named for the Hindu monkey god, Hanuman. According to Indian mythology, Hanuman bravely came to the aid of a prince. So, to Hindus, monkeys are a symbol of devotion.

when one male gives in to the other. The strong males in a troop usually help each other protect the rest of the baboons from enemies.

△ Up on her hind legs, a young female olive baboon stretches to pick an acacia pod. Baboons also eat fruit, grasses, and small animals. They roam several miles a day in search of food.

▽ Members of a hamadryas baboon troop gather on a sunny rock. The leader, a large light-colored male, has a long cape of fur and full side-whiskers. While resting, baboons often groom one another's fur.

Hamadryas baboon: 27 in (69 cm) long; tail, 19 in (48 cm)

Moose

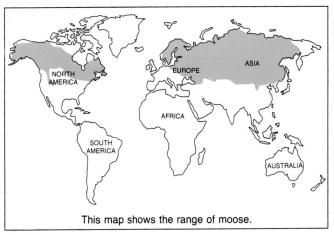

This map shows the range of moose.

MOOSE

HEIGHT: 5½-7 ft (168-213 cm) at the shoulder

WEIGHT: 500-1,800 lb (227-816 kg)

HABITAT AND RANGE: forests in northern North America, Europe, and Asia

FOOD: bark, leaves, twigs, shrubs, herbs, and underwater plants

LIFE SPAN: 15 to 20 years in the wild

REPRODUCTION: 1 or 2 young after a pregnancy of about 8 months

ORDER: artiodactyls

LAKES, STREAMS, AND MARSHES provide feeding grounds for moose in forests in North America, Europe, and Asia. The moose is the largest member of the deer family. But it does not look much like its smaller, more delicate relatives. The moose has a long face and a muzzle that hangs loosely over its chin. A large fold of skin, called a bell, dangles at the animal's throat. Its thick neck is topped with a heavy mane that stands up when the moose becomes angry or alarmed.

The bull, or male, moose of Alaska is the biggest moose of all. It measures 7 feet (213 cm) tall at the shoulder and may weigh as much as 1,800 pounds (816 kg). Its coat, dark brown in summer, turns a lighter gray-brown in winter.

The moose's legs are too long for easy grazing. The animal must kneel to reach the ground. Or, like a

Antlers of two bull moose of Alaska stand out against a background of blazing fall colors in the foothills of Mount McKinley. Largest member of the deer family, the moose feeds on leaves and shrubs.

387

giraffe, it must spread its forelegs wide apart and bend its head down. More often, the moose browses, feeding on shrubs, tree bark, and the leaves and twigs of higher branches.

A moose chews a mouthful only a few times before swallowing. Then it quickly takes another bite. After eating, the animal brings up a wad of partly digested food, called a cud. It chews the cud thoroughly, swallows, and completely digests it.

In summer, a moose often feeds in water. Wading chest-deep, the animal nibbles water lilies and other water plants. It often dips its head beneath the surface. With its sensitive lips, it feels for plants and tears them from the bottom.

Occasionally, this large animal feeds in deep water. Diving as far down as 18 feet (5 m), it can stay under the surface for half a minute at a time.

A moose walks easily over marshy ground on its large, split hooves. Broad feet help support the moose and keep it from sinking in the soft earth. In winter, a moose can move without difficulty through snowdrifts as deep as 3 feet (91 cm).

A moose has keen senses of smell and hearing. Its long ears turn to catch the faintest rustle. At the sound or scent of an enemy—usually a wolf or a bear—a moose stands motionless. If the enemy comes close, the moose races off.

Over a long distance, a moose is able to trot at about 20 miles (32 km) an hour. When threatened, the animal can run 35 miles (56 km) an hour in a

Moose

◁ Long-legged twins explore a forest clearing while their mother feeds on a leafy shrub. Moose calves lack the spotted coats that help hide their deer relatives. But a cow moose fiercely protects her young.

△ Dripping wet, a cow moose pulls up a mouthful of food. With nostrils closed, a moose dips its head underwater to feed. Sensitive lips pluck plants from the bottom.

◁ Leaving a trail of spray, a young moose dashes through a lake in Alaska. When only five days old, a calf can outrun a person.

389

sprint. Sometimes a moose tries to lose its pursuer by diving into a river or a lake. The moose is a strong swimmer. Paddling with its hooves, a moose can swim for several miles without stopping. The hollow hairs of its coat are filled with air. They help keep the animal afloat.

Except during the mating season, adult moose live separately. Bulls usually travel alone. Females, or cows, feed by themselves or with their calves.

One or two reddish brown calves are born to each cow in spring. Calves lack the spotted coats of some other newborn in the deer family. Moose young do not rely on their coloring to hide them from enemies. Their mother fiercely guards them.

At first, calves drink their mother's milk. Soon they begin to eat plants as well. Weighing about 30 pounds (14 kg) at birth, each calf doubles its weight within a few weeks. For the first year, the young moose follow their mother. Then, shortly before she

△ Antlers fully grown and hardened in early fall, a bull moose thrashes the bony growths against branches. Velvet that nourished the antlers peels off painlessly.

gives birth again, she drives the year-old calves away. They learn to live on their own.

At the end of a male calf's first summer, two bony bumps begin to rise on his forehead. The next spring, a set of short spike antlers will form. Adult males grow new antlers in spring. They shed their old sets from December to February.

Strong and solid, moose antlers are flat at the center like the palm of a person's hand. Their sharp edges may have more than forty points. The largest antlers belong to moose in Alaska. They may measure more than 6 feet (183 cm) from tip to tip.

While growing, a bull's antlers are protected by a covering of soft skin and fine hairs called velvet. Blood vessels in the velvet nourish the bony growths. Tender and rubbery during spring and summer, the antlers are fully grown and hardened by early fall. The bull rubs his head against shrubs and trees, peeling the velvet off in strips. Shedding the velvet looks bloody, but the process does not hurt the moose. A bull keeps his antlers for just a few months. He uses them only during the mating season, in September and October.

At that time, bulls have contests to find out which is the stronger. Frequently, two males clash head-on. The powerful animals brace their antlers and push and shove. Usually the weaker one turns away. But sometimes the moose fight to the death. The stronger bull mates with a cow and stays with her for several days. Then he finds another mate.

When the mating season ends, the bulls leave the cows. Adult males and females may not meet again for a year. But where food is plentiful, moose may gather to feed in the same area. Even when many moose are close together, cows and bulls pay no attention to each other.

Read about other members of the deer family—caribou, deer, and elk—in their own entries.

Searching for a mate, a bull moose (above) sniffs the air and listens. Cows call to a bull with a moaning cry. Bulls answer with grunts. Cautious bulls (left) confront each other nose to nose. The older bull shows his larger antlers to the younger one. If the younger bull does not retreat, the two will battle by furiously pushing each other with their antlers. The winner will mate with a cow moose.

Mouflon

The mouflon is a kind of wild sheep. Read about sheep on page 500.

Mouse

CITIES AND FARMS, deserts and mountains, meadows and forests—mice live in all kinds of habitats almost everywhere in the world. These small rodents make their homes wherever they can find food and shelter. Because of their size—usually less than 6 inches (15 cm) long, not counting their tails—they can hide in small spaces.

Mice resemble their close relatives, rats, except that mice are generally smaller. Mice usually have pointed noses, rounded ears, and skinny tails. Most have soft gray or brown fur, but some mice have special coats or markings. Stiff, sharp hairs cover the backs of spiny mice of Africa and Asia. The striped

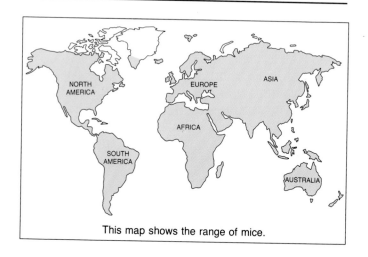

This map shows the range of mice.

grass mouse of Africa has stripes on its back that help the animal hide in grassy surroundings.

Most mice scurry along the ground. They use their long whiskers to feel the way. Some kinds of mice, though, move by hopping on powerful hind legs. The woodland jumping mouse of North America is able to escape its enemies by bounding quickly away. It may jump as far as 7 feet (213 cm), using its long tail for balance.

Other mice scamper up and down tree trunks and along twigs and slender branches. The African

◁ *Golden mouse in Florida uses its forepaws to clean its whiskers. These mice usually live in trees and bushes. They can grasp branches and vines with their tails.*
▽ *Holding a hazelnut in its forepaws, a wood mouse feeds in front of its deep burrow. Wood mice live in parts of Europe, Asia, and Africa.*

Wood mouse: 4 in (10 cm) long; tail, 3 in (8 cm)

Golden mouse: 3 in (8 cm) long; tail, 3 in (8 cm)

House mouse: 3 in (8 cm) long; tail, 3 in (8 cm)

△ *Female house mouse nurses her blind, hairless young. Every year, she may have five or more litters with as many as twelve young in each.*
◁ *Like a tiny singer, a southern grasshopper mouse in Mexico tilts back its head and squeaks to the sky. Its calls probably warn other mice to stay away.*

MOUSE 🐾 **83 of about 500 species**

LENGTH OF HEAD AND BODY: 2-6 in (5-15 cm); tail, 1-8 in (3-20 cm)

WEIGHT: ¹/₄ oz-2 oz (7-57 g)

HABITAT AND RANGE: almost every type of habitat worldwide

FOOD: plants and some small animals

LIFE SPAN: up to 8 years in captivity

REPRODUCTION: 1 to 12 young after a pregnancy of about 1 month

ORDER: rodents

Southern grasshopper mouse: 4 in (10 cm) long; tail, 2 in (5 cm)

Mouse

Some activities in the daily lives of European harvest mice: Below, two harvest mice greet each other in a wheat field in England. At right, a harvest mouse perches among stalks of wheat. It holds its tail in its tiny paws and grooms it.

climbing mouse often winds its long tail loosely around a twig to help it climb.

One species, or kind, of mouse is called the house mouse because it often lives in houses and other buildings. House mice like the food and warmth they find where people live. House mice make their nests in walls of houses, in cupboards, in boxes in attics, and even in pockets of coats hanging in closets. Mice have been found living in cold-storage rooms, burrowed in frozen meat.

Most other kinds of mice—and many house mice, too—build their nests away from people. The pencil-tailed tree mouse of Asia often lives inside a bamboo stalk. The Florida mouse may build its nest in a burrow made by a turtle. In the fall, the European harvest mouse weaves blades of tall grass together to form a ball-shaped nest.

The Australian field mouse usually digs a burrow on a sandy plain. It hides the entrances to its burrow by piling twigs and plants around the holes. The white-footed mouse of North America sometimes nests in a hole in a dead tree or moves into an unused bird's nest.

Mice not only live almost anywhere in the world, but they also eat almost anything—including glue, leather, and soap. In the wild, these little animals nibble grain, roots, fruit, leaves, seeds, stems, and grasses. The pocket mouse of western North America carries seeds in fur-lined pouches on the sides of its face. When a pocket mouse is ready to empty these pouches, it pushes the food out by flicking its forepaws against its cheeks. A pocket mouse usually takes its food to a chamber in its burrow. There it stores the food for later use.

Some kinds of mice also eat meat. The grasshopper mouse, which lives in dry regions in western North America, feeds on grasshoppers, other insects, scorpions, worms—and even other grasshopper mice! This fierce little mouse sometimes stands on its hind legs, tosses back its head, and lets out a loud squeak—probably to warn other grasshopper mice to stay away.

When they do not live in houses, house mice may stay together in large family groups. All the mice in a group share a burrow. They recognize each other by scent. The mice take turns grooming one another.

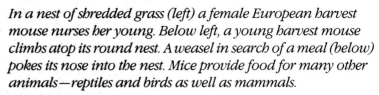

In a nest of shredded grass (left) a female European harvest mouse nurses her young. Below left, a young harvest mouse climbs atop its round nest. A weasel in search of a meal (below) pokes its nose into the nest. Mice provide food for many other animals—reptiles and birds as well as mammals.

If any mice from other groups try to come into the burrow, they are attacked and driven out.

In each group of house mice, one strong male is always the leader. But this mouse may be challenged by another male. The two mice bite and claw each other until one scurries away. If a burrow becomes too crowded, younger mice will leave and dig their own burrow.

Female mice have several litters of young every year. There may be as many as 12 tiny, helpless young in each litter. Most newborn mice weigh much less than 1 ounce (28 g). They may nurse for a month, but they begin eating solid food about two weeks after birth. Then they begin to follow their mother on short trips outside the burrow.

Almost all meat-eating animals, from weasels

▽ Black eyes shining, a harvest mouse eats a grain of wheat cradled in its forepaws. Harvest mice spend much of the day looking for seeds, grasses, and insects.

and cats to hawks and owls, prey on mice. Only one or two young in a litter will grow up to become adults. Some mice live only two or three months in the wild. But because they have young so often, many kinds of mice are plentiful.

Mice are also killed by people because a few of the many species of mice can be pests. Those mice eat or spoil millions of dollars' worth of grain and other foods every year. Some carry diseases. They can do damage just by gnawing on wood and clothing.

Like all rodents, mice have front teeth that grow throughout their lives. They must gnaw to keep these teeth worn down.

Mice can sometimes be helpful in the fight against disease. Scientists use mice in experiments that may lead to cures for illnesses. Mice also play an important role in nature. They form one link in a food chain from plants to meat-eating animals. Mice feed mainly on plants. They themselves provide food for other animals—birds, reptiles, and mammals.

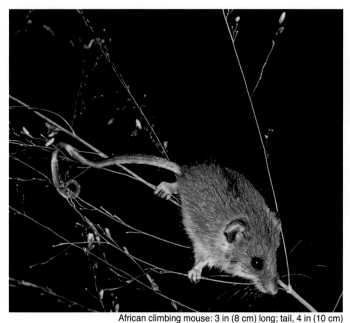

African climbing mouse: 3 in (8 cm) long; tail, 4 in (10 cm)

△ *Holding on to a stem with its tail, an African climbing mouse in Tanzania works its way toward the ground. These mice look for food in trees and on vines.*

Deer mouse: 3 in (8 cm) long; tail, 3 in (8 cm)

Tasmanian mouse: 4 in (10 cm) long; tail, 4 in (10 cm)

Australian hopping mouse: 4 in (10 cm) long; tail, 5 in (13 cm)

Mice can move their tails into many positions. A deer mouse (top) curls its tail under its body as it sits near its nest in a fallen tree. A Tasmanian mouse (above) wraps its tail over a branch as it rests while searching for food. For balance, an Australian hopping mouse (left) holds its tail out behind as it moves across the ground.

Long, coarse coat of a male musk-ox sweeps the ground as he travels over ice-crusted snow.

Musk-ox

(MUSK-ox)

FOR THOUSANDS OF YEARS, shaggy, humped musk-oxen have lived in cold, rocky areas of the arctic region. Musk-oxen are well equipped for life on the tundra, a harsh, treeless land. They have thick coats that protect them during the cold winters. An outer layer of long hairs, called guard hairs, covers a shorter undercoat. The outer coat hangs down nearly to the

ground. When warmer weather comes in spring, the soft, woolly undercoat begins to fall out through the long guard hairs.

A musk-ox's curved hooves help the animal travel easily across the rugged arctic plain. Its hooves have sharp rims and soft pads. They allow the musk-ox to paw through the snow for food and to clamber over rocky slopes.

Musk-oxen travel in herds during the entire year. A female, called a cow, sometimes leads the herd. The animals spend the warmer months feeding near

This map shows the range of musk-oxen.

MUSK-OX

HEIGHT: 4-5 ft (122-152 cm) at the shoulder

WEIGHT: 500-800 lb (227-363 kg)

HABITAT AND RANGE: tundra in Alaska, Canada, and Greenland; brought by people to Norway and Siberia

FOOD: grasses, willows, and some arctic flowers

LIFE SPAN: 12 to 20 years in the wild

REPRODUCTION: 1 young after a pregnancy of about 8 months

ORDER: artiodactyls

Musk-ox

streams and lakes. There they eat grasses, willows, and some flowers.

Traveling in a herd offers protection against enemies. When a wolf approaches, musk-oxen defend themselves by forming a line. If the wolf comes even closer, the adults take turns driving it away.

When threatened, both male and female musk-oxen are fierce fighters. Their sharp horns look like huge, hard bows. They curve down beside the animals' faces, then turn up at the ends. The horns of a male, called a bull, form a bony shield across his forehead. A musk-ox charges with its head lowered. It tries to gore its enemy with the tips of its horns.

When the summer mating season comes, bulls may begin to fight among themselves for females. The stronger bulls try to drive the weaker ones away by charging at them. Again and again, the bulls crash together, horn to horn, until one bull gives up.

Calves are born after a pregnancy of about eight months. A newborn can keep up with its mother only

a few hours after birth. It grows quickly. By the time it is five or six years old, a musk-ox has reached its full size. A bull may weigh as much as 800 pounds (363 kg) and may measure almost 5 feet (152 cm) tall at the shoulder. Cows are smaller and lighter.

For many years, musk-oxen were hunted for their hides and meat. So many were killed that only a small number remained. Today there are laws to protect musk-oxen. Herds have been put on special preserves in Alaska, Norway, and Siberia.

△ *Ready for attackers, a herd of musk-oxen (above) forms a line for defense. When surrounded, the animals often make a protective circle. Horns frame the face of an old male musk-ox (top). Patches of fur under his eye show bits of his winter coat. As the weather becomes warmer, he sheds this woolly undercoat.*

◁ *Small herd of shaggy, brown musk-oxen pounds across the beach of Nunivak Island, off the coast of western Alaska. Herds live there on a preserve.*

Muskrat nibbles on a bulrush in shallow water in Montana. Muskrats feed on plants and shellfish.

Muskrat

(MUSK-rat)

LIKE THE BEAVER, the muskrat often builds a dome-shaped home in the water. This rodent piles up water plants in a marsh until a mound is formed. Mud helps hold the muskrat's mound together. The animal then dives to the base of the mound. It gnaws out tunnels as well as a living space inside, above the water level. There the muskrat is safe from enemies such as turtles and alligators.

Other muskrats make their homes in burrows that they dig in the banks of streams or on the shores of lakes. These muskrats dig tunnels that open underwater. Then muskrats can swim and hunt for food even when ice covers the surface.

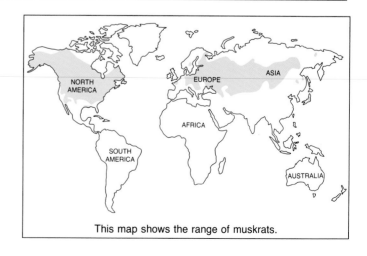

This map shows the range of muskrats.

400

Muskrats live in parts of North America. People have also taken them to Europe and Asia, where they now live in the wild. Muskrats are excellent swimmers and divers. They paddle with their partly webbed hind feet, and they steer with their scaly tails. Muskrats eat mainly water plants, but sometimes they feed on shellfish.

A female muskrat usually bears five to seven blind, hairless young twice a year. The young begin to swim within their first three weeks.

On land, muskrats move awkwardly. There they are hunted by foxes and raccoons. Trappers also take muskrats for their thick brown fur. The animals have scent glands that produce a strong-smelling substance. Its musky odor helps explain how the animal got its name.

On the frozen surface of a lake in Wyoming, a ▷
muskrat looks for food in early winter.
▽ *Muskrat house rises in a marsh in North Dakota. Muskrats pile up grasses to form mounds. By cutting down these plants, they sometimes create moats around their homes.*

MUSKRAT

LENGTH OF HEAD AND BODY: 10-14 in (25-36 cm); tail, 8-11 in (20-28 cm)

WEIGHT: 2-4 lb (1-2 kg)

HABITAT AND RANGE: marshes, lakes, streams, and ponds in North America; brought by people to Europe and Asia

FOOD: mainly water plants and shellfish

LIFE SPAN: about 4 years in the wild

REPRODUCTION: usually 5 to 7 young after a pregnancy of about 1 month

ORDER: rodents

N

Narwhal The narwhal is a kind of porpoise. Find out about porpoises on page 446.

Numbat

(NUM-bat)

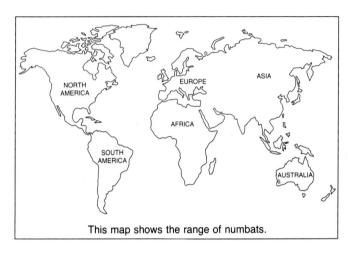

This map shows the range of numbats.

FROM SUNRISE TO SUNSET, the nimble numbat hunts for termites, its favorite food. It climbs dead trees, searching for the wood-eating insects. It scampers over old stumps and fallen limbs. Sharp senses of sight and smell help this animal find its prey. A numbat can eat 20,000 termites a day! It also eats ants that invade termite nests.

To get at the insects, a numbat uses its sharp front claws. It scratches the ground or rips open rotten logs. Then its long, thin tongue darts out and laps up termites and ants.

At sunset, the numbat returns to its den in a shallow hole or a hollow log. There it sleeps in a nest of dry leaves and grass. Except during the mating season, numbats live alone.

Most numbats live in the eucalyptus forests of southwestern Australia. Their grayish brown coats blend well with the dead trees and dried leaves of the forest floor. Some numbats live on the plains just east of the forests. They have brick-red fur. All the animals have bushy tails and bold white bands across their backs. These markings give the numbat another name: banded anteater.

Once a year, a female numbat gives birth to as many as four tiny offspring. Each newborn climbs onto its mother's belly and attaches itself to a nipple. It will stay there for four months as it grows.

The numbat is a marsupial (mar-SOO-pea-ul). Most marsupials have pouches for their young. But numbats have no pouches. Long fur on the female numbat's belly protects her offspring. Many other Australian mammals are marsupials. Read about bandicoots, kangaroos, phalangers, and wombats under their own headings.

Bushy tail held high, a numbat follows its sensitive ▷ nose to prey. With sharp claws, the animal rips open rotten wood where termites live. The numbat uses its quick, darting tongue to lap up the insects. Unlike many marsupials, numbats move about in the daytime.

Nutria Nutria is another name for the coypu. Read about the coypu on page 166.

Nyala The nyala is a kind of antelope. Learn about antelopes on page 52.

O

Ocelot The ocelot is a kind of cat. Read about cats on page 126.

Okapi

(oh-COP-ee)

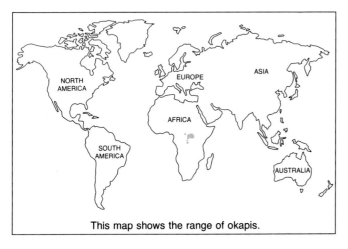

This map shows the range of okapis.

Dazzling leg stripes mark the chocolate-colored coat of an okapi in Africa. Scientists began to learn about this shy forest dweller about a century ago.

UNTIL A CENTURY AGO, scientists did not know that the okapi even existed. In the 1890s, European explorers obtained skins of the animal from tribesmen who hunted it deep in the rain forests of central Africa. News reports of this shy, dark-coated mammal—a relative of the giraffe—made newspaper headlines all over the world.

Okapis have brown bodies with creamy-white stripes on their legs and hindquarters. The stripes help hide the horse-size animals in the forest. Both males and females have long, muscular necks. Males, like giraffes, have short, skin-covered knobs on their foreheads. Okapis greet each other with a sound like "chuff" when they meet.

Okapis eat leaves, which they pick with their long, gray tongues. The animal's tongue is so long that

it can reach up and lick the corners of its eyes as it washes its face.

Little is known about the behavior of okapis in the wild because only a few scientists have observed them there. Several animals may live in the same area, but they do not travel together in herds. Except for mothers with young, each adult roams alone, following paths worn smooth by other okapis.

A female okapi gives birth to a single young. Only half an hour after its birth, the infant can stand. It begins eating leaves after a few weeks.

OKAPI

HEIGHT: 59-67 in (150-170 cm) at the shoulder

WEIGHT: 440-550 lb (200-249 kg)

HABITAT AND RANGE: rain forests of central Africa

FOOD: buds and leaves of shrubs and trees

LIFE SPAN: up to 33 years in captivity

REPRODUCTION: usually 1 young after a pregnancy of about 15 months

ORDER: artiodactyls

Opossum

(uh-PAHS-um)

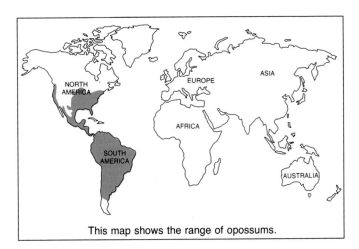

This map shows the range of opossums.

HAVE YOU EVER "PLAYED POSSUM"? Have you kept still and pretended to be asleep when you really weren't? This trick gets its name from the way an opossum sometimes acts. Playing possum can save its life. When an opossum is attacked by an enemy such as a fox or a dog, it lies so still that it seems to be dead. The opossum's eyes close, or the animal stares without blinking. Its tongue hangs out. The attacker may shake the opossum or toss it about. Even then the victim doesn't move.

Most attackers soon lose interest in what seems

Hanging on with all four feet, a young Virginia ▷ *opossum looks down from a branch of a wild cherry tree. Foxes and dogs cannot reach it there.*

Virginia opossum: 17 in (43 cm) long; tail, 13 in (33 cm)

to be a dead animal. They leave to look for livelier prey. Cautiously, the opossum lifts its head and looks about. If the danger is gone, it scurries off.

There are more than 65 kinds of opossums. They live in wooded areas in many parts of North and South

◁ *Hollow tree in New Jersey makes a cozy den for a Virginia opossum. Opossums in North America also make homes in the empty dens of such large rodents as marmots. The opossums line their nests with leaves.*

▽ *Nearly too big to ride piggyback, three-month-old Virginia opossums still scramble aboard their mother. Soon they will go off to live and hunt by themselves. Within a year, they may have offspring of their own.*

Coiled around a twig, the long tail of a mouse ▷ opossum helps the animal keep its balance. This kind of opossum has no pouch. As many as 15 tiny offspring simply hang on to the nipples on their mother's belly.

Mouse opossum: 3 in (8 cm) long; tail, 4 in (10 cm)

Gray four-eyed opossum: 13 in (33 cm) long; tail, 11 in (28 cm)

America. But only one kind plays possum—the Virginia, or common, opossum of North America. This opossum is the largest of all—about 2½ feet (76 cm) from nose to end of tail. It is also the only kind found in the United States.

At one time, opossums probably lived only as far north as southern North America. Gradually, they spread farther. They were in Virginia by the time the first Europeans arrived. Today the animals are also found in Canada.

Opossums are marsupials (mar-SOO-pea-ulz), or pouched mammals. They give birth to tiny, underdeveloped young. Just after birth, the young crawl into their mother's pouch, where they feed and continue to grow. Opossums are the only marsupials that live in North America. Most marsupials, like kangaroos and koalas, live in Australia and on its neighboring islands. Read about kangaroos on page 304 and koalas on page 312.

Virginia opossums have one or two litters a year. As many as twenty young are born at one time. But usually no more than eight offspring survive. Newborn opossums are blind and hairless. No bigger than bees, they have tiny claws that help them crawl into the pouch.

The young stay in the pouch for about two months. Then they begin to go in and out. They nurse for another month. When their mother hunts for food, they cling to the fur on her back.

Newborn mouse opossums ride with their mother even though she has no pouch. At first, the young dangle from her nipples. They are protected only by her fur. If a tiny opossum falls off, it makes a high-pitched sound. Human beings cannot hear its call, but its mother can. She goes back to find it. After a month, young mouse opossums crawl onto their mother's back and ride there. Mouse opossums are among the smallest opossums. They are found from Mexico south into Argentina.

When opossums reach full size, they leave their mother and go off to live alone. Some kinds have no regular shelters. They may sleep in a new place every

△ Gray four-eyed opossum of South America sniffs for food on a tree limb. The animal has only two eyes. It gets its name because of the white spots on its forehead.

day. Virginia opossums sometimes use old marmot burrows. Or they may make their dens in hollow trees. The opossum lines its den with leaves. It hooks its tail around a bunch of leaves and carries them back to its den.

The opossums that live in tropical forests— woolly opossums, four-eyed opossums, and mouse opossums—spend most of their time in the trees. There they often build nests of twigs and leaves.

Opossum _____

◁ *Hanging upside down, a woolly opossum licks nectar from night-blooming flowers in Panama. Woolly opossums have thick fur and tails longer than their bodies. Their tails help them hold on to branches.*

Sometimes a mouse opossum simply moves into an empty bird's nest.

Climbing trees is easy for an opossum. Its sharp claws hook into the bark. Its rear paws help it hold on to small branches. Its long tail can also grip branches, as if it were an extra hand. This helps an opossum keep its balance as it travels about.

Opossums sleep and rest most of the day. At night, they search for food such as grasses, fruit, nuts, insects, worms, and even snakes. They eat mice and birds if they can catch them. They also eat dead animals. Opossums will eat almost anything they can find. Those that live near people—on farms, in suburbs, and even in city parks—will go after chickens or search for garbage.

If an opossum has been prowling around a house, its tracks are easy to spot. An opossum's tail leaves a wavy mark in the dirt. On either side of this mark are paw prints. Because an opossum's big toes are far apart from the other toes on its hind feet, its tracks look like little human handprints.

Other marsupials called possums live in Australia. They are members of the phalanger family. Read about them on page 430.

◁ *With big brown eyes open wide, a woolly opossum peers into the shadows of a tropical forest in Peru. A stripe runs between the animal's eyes, from the top of its head almost to the tip of its nose. This nimble climber hunts for fruit and insects in trees. It moves around in the dark and rarely comes down to the ground.*

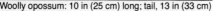

Woolly opossum: 10 in (25 cm) long; tail, 13 in (33 cm)

OPOSSUM 🐾 **21 of 66 species**

LENGTH OF HEAD AND BODY: 3-20 in (8-51 cm); tail, 4-21 in (10-53 cm)

WEIGHT: $\frac{1}{2}$ oz-12 lb (14 g-5 kg)

HABITAT AND RANGE: wooded areas in parts of North and South America

FOOD: grasses, fruit, nuts, insects, reptiles, and other small animals

LIFE SPAN: about 3 years in the wild

REPRODUCTION: usually about 20 young after a pregnancy of about 2 weeks

ORDER: marsupials

Orangutan

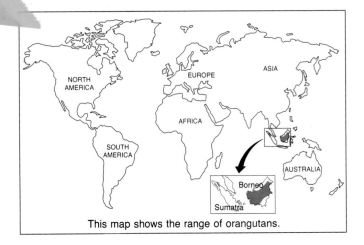

This map shows the range of orangutans.

ORANGUTAN 🐾 1 of 1 species

STANDING HEIGHT: 44-54 in (112-137 cm)

WEIGHT: 73-180 lb (33-82 kg)

HABITAT AND RANGE: tropical rain forests in parts of Sumatra and Borneo

FOOD: mostly fruit and leaves and some flowers, bark, and insects

LIFE SPAN: more than 50 years in captivity

REPRODUCTION: usually 1 young after a pregnancy of about 8½ months

ORDER: primates

"PERSON OF THE FOREST"—that's the meaning of the word *orangutan* in the Malay language of Southeast Asia. These long-haired orange apes live in tropical rain forests in parts of Sumatra and Borneo. Like the other apes—chimpanzees, gorillas, and gibbons—orangutans belong to the primate order, which also includes human beings.

For the size of an orangutan's body, its arms are extremely long. Stretched out to the sides, the arms of a full-grown male may measure 7 feet (213 cm) from fingertip to fingertip. When the animal stands upright, its hands reach almost to the ground. An orangutan uses its strong arms to climb and to move among the trees, where it spends much of the time.

The adult males may grow to be about 4½ feet (137 cm) tall. They weigh about 155 pounds (70 kg). Females weigh about half that much. As they become older, male orangutans develop big cheek pads on their faces and pouches on their throats. The females seem to prefer bigger males as mates.

The orangutan is a less social animal than other apes. Most of the time, an adult male travels alone

Stretching out its lower lip, a young orangutan uses a leaf to get a drink. The animal dips the leaf into a puddle and lets the water run into its mouth. These apes live only on the islands of Sumatra and Borneo.

through the forest. He lets other orangutans know of his presence by giving a "long call"—a series of grumbling and burbling sounds ending in a bellow. This warns other males to stay away—but females may be attracted by the call.

Orangutan

When males and females mate, they stay together for several days. About eight and a half months after mating, a female orangutan gives birth, usually to only one young. The newborn animal is almost entirely helpless. Although the infant can hold on to its mother soon after it is born, its mother usually cradles it in her arms.

A young orangutan depends on its mother for warmth, food, and transportation for a long period.

◁ *Covering its forehead with its hands, an orangutan takes a rest. Orangutans begin searching for food early in the morning. At midday, they nap.*

Using long, powerful arms to pull herself up, a ▷ female orangutan scales a tall tree on Borneo. Orangutans spend more time in the trees than do their African relatives—chimpanzees and gorillas. As people cut down more of the forests, orangutans have fewer places to roam and to find food.

▽ *Hefty adult male orangutan huddles in a nest in the trees. The animal bends leafy branches down to make a safe place to sleep. Every night, he builds a new nest.*

Orangutan

Natural rain bonnet protects a young orangutan ▷
from wet weather on Sumatra. During downpours,
orangutans often take shelter under leafy covers.

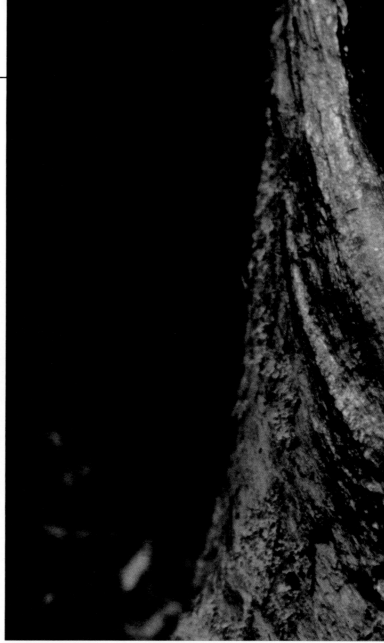

△ *Twisting and*
stretching, a young
female orangutan
practices the climbing
skills she needs for life
in the rain forest.
Still clinging to its ▷
mother after two years,
an orangutan rides on
the adult's back. Mothers
and young usually stay
together for six or seven
years, until the offspring
can take care of itself.

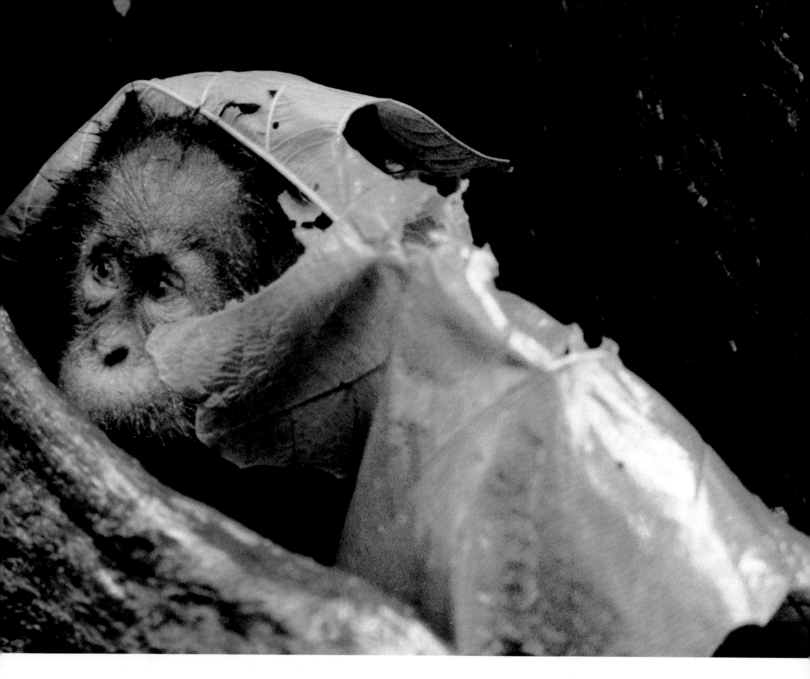

Even at the age of four years, a young orangutan does not stray far from its mother. It is just beginning to climb and to search for its own food. An orangutan will not become independent until it is six or seven years old.

Orangutans eat mostly fruit and leaves. They also feed on flowers, bark, and occasionally on insects. They rise early in the morning and spend the day looking for food. They may travel as far as 1 mile (2 km) a day to reach trees that have fruit.

Before dark, orangutans make sleeping nests by bending down branches in the trees. Orangutans often build day nests for naps. These animals sometimes put together an overhead cover of leaves for shelter during heavy rainstorms. Scientists have even seen orangutans hold leafy branches over their heads to protect themselves during downpours—just as people use umbrellas.

Orangutans live for a relatively long time. In captivity, some have reached more than fifty years of age. These apes have few enemies. The greatest danger they face comes from humans. People capture young orangutans to sell as pets. And as loggers and farmers cut down the forests where orangutans live, their numbers become smaller. Laws have been enacted and reserves have been set aside to help protect the animals. But orangutans are still among the most endangered of all primates.

Oryx

The oryx is a kind of antelope. Read about antelopes on page 52.

Otter

(OTT-er)

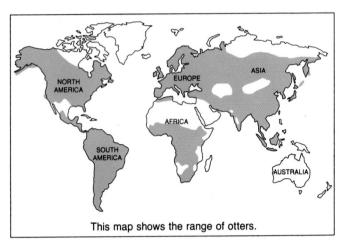

This map shows the range of otters.

OTTERS HARDLY EVER REMAIN STILL. These sleek, streamlined members of the weasel family are full of energy. They are constantly on the move. They look for food in water or on land. And they often seem to be playing in rivers, lakes, or oceans. They push sticks and leaves along the surface, chase one another underwater, and dive for pebbles. A river otter may tease a beaver by giving its flat tail a playful tug.

There are many kinds of otters. They live nearly everywhere in the world—in all kinds of terrain, except for polar regions and deserts.

The sea otter, which is found along the Pacific

▽ *No sleds are needed as river otters glide along a snow-covered hill. Otters bound for a short distance, and then they slide. A muddy slope or a snowbank near water becomes a playground for an otter family.*

Pausing as it hunts for fish, a ▷ river otter in Yellowstone National Park pokes its head out of an icy lake. When the water is frozen, otters use holes in the ice so that they can come to the surface to breathe.

▽ Falling snow does not prevent a female river otter and her three large pups from looking for food on the shore of a pond. Otters usually make their dens at the edge of a lake or a stream. Often one tunnel leads directly into the water.

River otter: 28 in (71 cm) long; tail, 14 in (36 cm)

coasts of North America and Asia, lives mainly in the ocean. In some areas, it may come ashore to sleep. The river otter spends most of the time in streams, rivers, lakes, and marshes. But, as it looks for food or for a mate, it may travel long distances between bodies of water. River otters are found in Europe, Asia, Africa, and North and South America.

With their webbed feet, short legs, and long bodies, otters are well adapted, or suited, to life in the water. They swim easily, flexing their bodies up and down and paddling with their hind feet. Sometimes they also use their front feet. The animals move their powerful tapered tails as they swim.

An otter's flexible body makes it an underwater

Otter

Anchored by strands of kelp, a kind of large seaweed, a sea otter in California (above) rests easily on its back. The kelp keeps the animal from drifting while it naps. Otters often sleep this way in groups (below) along the rocky coasts of the northern Pacific Ocean. When awake, the otters dive for shellfish and fish.

△ Underwater, a sea otter holds a sea urchin with its front paws. The otter will make a meal of the sea urchin despite its spines.

acrobat. Floating lazily in the water, an otter will suddenly twist and dive down. It glides under the surface. Otters turn somersaults in the water. They swim on their backs or on their sides. Sometimes an otter's sleek, dark head pops out of the water as the animal takes a look around.

Like all mammals, otters breathe air, so they must come to the surface often. When they swim underwater, their nostrils and ears close tightly. This helps keep the water out.

Otters can move quickly on land, but they do not look as graceful as they do in water. When they run, they bound along with their backs arched. Whenever possible, they slide in mud or snow.

416

OTTER 🐾 5 of 13 species

LENGTH OF HEAD AND BODY: 16-47 in (41-119 cm); tail, 10-28 in (25-71 cm)

WEIGHT: 6-82 lb (3-37 kg)

HABITAT AND RANGE: bodies of water in North America, South America, Africa, Europe, and Asia. Sea otter: coastal areas of western North America and northeast Asia

FOOD: fish, shellfish, small mammals, water birds, eggs, frogs, earthworms, and plants

LIFE SPAN: as long as 25 years in captivity

REPRODUCTION: 1 to 6 young after a pregnancy of 2 to 12 months, depending on species

ORDER: carnivores

Some otters live in groups, but they usually search for food on their own. Otters can hunt by day or night. In areas where there are people, otters prefer the night. During the day, river otters may sun themselves on rocks.

River otters eat almost anything they can find. They feed on fish, shellfish, and frogs in shallow water and on birds, eggs, small mammals, and plants on land. Otters eat small fish in the water. Large ones are carried ashore.

Sea otters eat many different sea animals—sea urchins, crabs, clams, mussels, squid, octopuses, fish, and abalone. When a sea otter finds a clam, it has a special way to get at the food inside. The otter brings up a rock from underwater. Then it floats on its back with the rock on its chest. Again and again, the otter bangs the clam against the rock until the shellfish breaks open.

After a sea otter has finished eating a mussel or an abalone, it rolls over in the water to wash the bits of shell and food off its fur. It also grooms its fur by nibbling at its coat with its teeth and by pressing its fur with its paws. Such grooming helps the sea otter's fur stay waterproof. As long as the fur is clean, a layer of dense underfur traps air and insulates the otter against the cold.

For almost 200 years, people hunted sea otters for their soft, thick fur until few of the animals were left. Today they are protected by law.

Another otter sought by hunters is the giant otter of South America. The longest member of the otter family, the giant otter grows as long as 6 feet (183 cm)

△ *After a successful fishing expedition, an African clawless otter drags its catch ashore.*

◁ *Once on land, the otter bites off the fish's head with its sharp front teeth. It often uses its long, sensitive fingers to probe under rocks and in mud for such prey as crabs and crayfish.*

▽ *African clawless otter rolls on a riverbank and removes the water from its coat. The animal may nibble at its fur and use its fingers to groom itself.*

Otter

and weighs about 75 pounds (34 kg). Giant otters live in family groups.

Most otters come ashore to give birth. Females bear one to six young in underground dens sometimes lined with dry grasses and leaves. The newborn are blind, and they are carefully guarded by their mother. A mother teaches her offspring to survive in the water. When young river otters are about two months old, their mother pushes them in. She watches over them until they learn to swim.

Only the sea otter gives birth in the water, usually to a single pup. The mother lies on her back and holds her pup on her chest. She nurses it, plays with it, and teaches it to dive for its food.

In Venezuela, giant otters (right) poke their heads high above the surface of a river. These sleek animals weigh about 75 pounds (34 kg) and grow as long as 6 feet (183 cm). They live in family groups. At left, a young giant otter pauses on land. Its webbed feet help the animal move easily through the water.

▽ *South American otter glides through the water searching for fish. When it dives for prey, its nostrils and ears close tightly to keep water out.*

South American otter: 26 in (66 cm) long; tail, 20 in (51 cm)

Giant otter: 41 in (104 cm) long; tail, 22 in (56 cm)

Paca

Common paca: 28 in (71 cm) long; tail, about 1 in (3 cm)

White dots mark the coat of a common paca in Venezuela. The pattern helps hide the animal as it searches for food along wooded riverbanks.

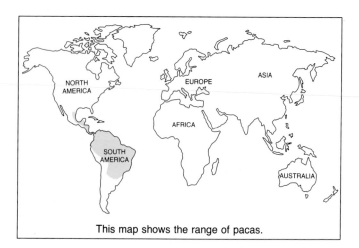

This map shows the range of pacas.

PACA

LENGTH OF HEAD AND BODY: 24-32 in (61-81 cm); tail, about 1 in (3 cm)

WEIGHT: 14-22 lb (6-10 kg)

HABITAT AND RANGE: wooded areas near water from Mexico into South America

FOOD: stalks, leaves, roots, crops, and fallen fruit

LIFE SPAN: about 16 years in captivity

REPRODUCTION: usually 1 young after a pregnancy of about 4 months

ORDER: rodents

LIKE DOTTED LINES, rows of white patches of hair mark the dark coat of the paca. This stocky rodent measures more than 2 feet (61 cm) long. It is one of the largest rodents in the world. It lives in forests from Mexico into Brazil. There its spotted coat helps it hide among forest shadows.

Pacas live alone. During the day, they sleep in burrows. In the evening, they come out to look for leaves, stalks, roots, and fallen fruit.

Pacas frequently make their burrows in riverbanks. With their claws and sharp teeth, they dig burrows that may reach 5 feet (152 cm) in depth. Pacas usually have several openings into their burrows. That way, they have more than one escape route from an enemy, such as a jaguar or an ocelot. The animals swim well. Often a paca will leap into the water to avoid danger. At other times, a paca will snap at an enemy with its teeth. It gives a low, coughing growl if it is angry or alarmed.

Like its close relative the agouti, the paca is especially fond of avocados and mangoes. Read about the agouti on page 47. Near towns and farms, pacas sometimes eat sugarcane, yams, and other crops. People in Mexico and Central and South America sometimes kill pacas for meat and because the animals damage their crops.

Another kind of paca, the mountain paca, lives high in the Andes. Smaller than the common paca, this animal has thicker hair marked with spots.

Both common pacas and mountain pacas usually bear only one young at a time. A female may give birth twice a year.

Panda

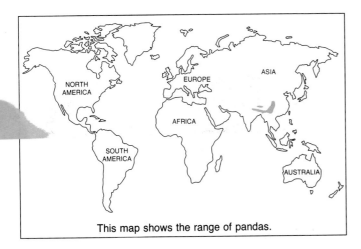

This map shows the range of pandas.

Giant panda: 5 ft (152 cm) long; tail, 5 in (13 cm)

TURNING SOMERSAULTS and standing on their heads, giant pandas are crowd pleasers. Visitors flock to zoos to see the black-and-white animals—among the best-loved in the world.

Though the giant panda's bearlike appearance is familiar to most people, its behavior in the wild is still largely a mystery. Much of what scientists know about pandas has been learned from those in captivity. About a hundred pandas live in zoos.

Pandas are difficult to study in their natural surroundings. They live only in remote mountain areas of the central People's Republic of China. There the climate stays cool and wet all year. Snow remains on the ground from fall until late spring. At other times, heavy rains soak the dense bamboo forests where the pandas make their homes. The animals may live as high as 13,000 feet (3,962 m). In the summer, the animals stay on the higher slopes. In the winter, they move down to the valleys.

Though pandas sometimes eat birds and small rodents, their main food is bamboo. A panda consumes huge amounts of the plant. Munching for hours at a time, it may eat about 28 pounds (12½ kg) of bamboo every day.

With its paw, a panda clutches the tender shoots and leaves of bamboo plants. The animal's long wristbones serve almost as thumbs and help it grasp even thin pieces of food.

When eating, a panda sits down and stretches out its hind legs. Sometimes it rolls backward until its legs stick up in the air. The animal mashes food with its powerful jaws and strong back teeth. As the panda

Bending a bamboo stalk to its mouth, a giant panda in a zoo in Europe firmly clutches its favorite food. A long wristbone serves almost as a thumb. It allows the panda to grip its food. The panda may eat as much as 28 pounds (12½ kg) of bamboo a day. The tough, stringy plant does no damage going down. A thick lining in the panda's throat protects it from splinters. Giant pandas occasionally feed on birds and small rodents.

421

Panda

swallows, the thick lining of its throat protects it from bamboo splinters.

Occasionally, there are shortages of bamboo. The plants flower rarely, but when they do, the stalks soon die. For several years, the new seedlings are too small for pandas to eat. Because pandas eat little else, some of the animals may starve when food is scarce. There are thought to be about a thousand pandas in the wild today.

Pandas usually live alone. They meet at mating time in the spring. About five months later, a female may give birth to one or two cubs in a cave or other sheltered spot. With its coat of thin, white fur, a panda cub looks like a tiny kitten. By the time it is a month old, it has an adult panda's black-and-white markings. Born with its eyes closed, the offspring cannot see until it is about two months old. It crawls at three months of age.

Until the cub is about four months old, it drinks only its mother's milk. Then the young panda begins to nibble bamboo leaves and tender shoots. Although it weighs only about 5 ounces (142 g) at birth, the cub gains weight rapidly. When fully grown, a female weighs about 250 pounds (113 kg). A male may grow to 300 pounds (136 kg). Both measure about 5 feet (152 cm) long.

Many years before the giant panda became known to scientists outside of China, another panda had been discovered. Until the mid-1800s, the red panda was thought to be the only kind of panda in the world. Named for the fiery color of its coat, the red panda is the size of a large house cat. This animal weighs about 12 pounds (5 kg) and measures about 2 feet (61 cm) long. Its bushy, ringed tail adds another 18 inches (46 cm).

The red panda lives in the same kind of habitat as its larger relative. Its range, though, is much wider—from Nepal to northern Burma and into the central part of China.

The red panda spends much of its life in trees. When asleep, this panda curls up on a branch and wraps its tail around its body. In warm weather, it

Big and barrel-shaped, a giant panda lumbers slowly along the ground. The animal swims well, however, and climbs trees with ease. Though a popular sight in zoos, the panda remains a mystery in the wild.

Red panda: 26 in (66 cm) long; tail, 18 in (46 cm)

Striped face of a red panda peers from behind a tree. Some scientists group red pandas and giant pandas together in their own family. Other experts place the smaller red panda in the raccoon family.

stretches out on a limb, legs dangling on either side.

The red panda has a wristbone much like that of the giant panda. Like its larger relative, the red panda eats bamboo. It feeds on fruit, acorns, roots, and perhaps on small animals as well. It grasps the food and carries pieces to its mouth.

Red pandas are shy animals, and they usually live alone. The adults meet only in the mating season. About four months later, the female panda usually bears one to three young. Their eyes open within three weeks.

◁ *Hsing-Hsing—a gift from China to the United States in 1972—feeds among bamboo stalks. His companion, Ling-Ling, died in 1992, leaving him alone at the National Zoological Park, in Washington, D. C.*

Some scientists put the red panda in the raccoon family and the giant panda in the bear family. Other scientists group the two kinds of pandas together in their own family.

PANDA 🐾 **2 of 2 species**

LENGTH OF HEAD AND BODY: 5-6 ft (152-183 cm); tail, 5 in (13 cm). Red panda: 20-26 in (51-66 cm); tail, 11-20 in (28-51 cm)

WEIGHT: 165-300 lb (75-136 kg). Red panda: 7-13 lb (3-6 kg)

HABITAT AND RANGE: mountain forests in the central People's Republic of China. Red panda: mountain forests from Nepal to northern Burma and into central China

FOOD: bamboo, grasses, roots, acorns, fruit, and small animals

LIFE SPAN: giant panda 34 years; red panda 17 years, in captivity

REPRODUCTION: 1 to 3 young after a pregnancy of 4 to 5½ months

ORDER: carnivores

Pangolin

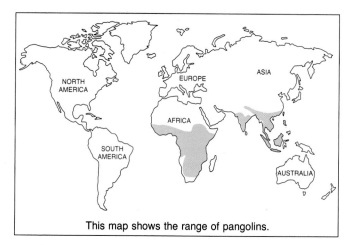

This map shows the range of pangolins.

PANGOLIN

LENGTH OF HEAD AND BODY: 12-31 in (30-79 cm); tail, 12-31 in (30-79 cm)

WEIGHT: 10-60 lb (5-27 kg)

HABITAT AND RANGE: grasslands and forests of Africa and southern and southeastern Asia

FOOD: mainly ants and termites

LIFE SPAN: up to 20 years in captivity

REPRODUCTION: usually 1 young after a pregnancy of 2 to 4 months

ORDER: pholidotes

THE PANGOLIN LOOKS like a pinecone with legs. Tough, overlapping scales cover most of the animal's stocky body. As it moves through the darkness, it walks on all fours, dragging its tail. From time to time, it sniffs the air for food or danger.

Because of their scales, pangolins often are called scaly anteaters. But the animals are not related to other anteaters. Scientists place pangolins in an order, or group, of their own.

Pangolins are born with scales that are small and soft at first. They become harder and larger as the pangolin grows. An adult can measure 5 feet (152 cm) long, including its tail.

Pangolins live on grasslands and in forests in Africa and in Asia. There are seven kinds. The larger ones stay mostly on the ground and live in burrows. Smaller pangolins make their homes in trees. Tree pangolins use their strong tails to grip branches as they move about. Sometimes they even hang upside down, holding on only with their tails. Pangolins usually live alone.

Chinese pangolin: 21 in (53 cm) long; tail, 14 in (36 cm)

Cape pangolin: 19 in (48 cm) long; tail, 13 in (33 cm); diameter rolled up, 10 in (25 cm)

△ *Chinese pangolin (top) searches for food as it climbs a tree limb. Tough scales cover most of the animal's body. Some pangolins live in trees. Enemies like lions or tigers cannot reach them there. Other pangolins stay on the ground. They curl up into hard, scaly balls when enemies come near. Two young lions poke at a curled-up Cape pangolin (above) in Africa. Usually only a lion, a tiger, or a person can unroll the armored ball.*

Pangolins search for food mostly at night. When one finds a nest of ants or termites, it claws it open. Then it uses its long tongue to gather the insects from inside the nest. The pangolin has no teeth, so the insects are swallowed whole.

A pangolin usually sleeps all day, curled up in a ball. The hard scales on its back protect its soft, hairy belly. A mother shields her soft-scaled young by curling herself around her offspring. A female pangolin usually has one young a year.

Indian pangolin feeds at a termite mound. To get at the food, the animal tears holes in the nest with its thick front claws. Then it pushes its snout inside and extends its long, wet tongue. As a protection against the bites of termites, the pangolin can close its nostrils, ears, and thick-lidded eyes.

Indian pangolin: 24 in (61 cm) long; tail, 18 in (46 cm)

Pangolins also curl up when threatened. Only a strong or a skillful hunter—a lion, a tiger, or a person—can unroll it. Even when a pangolin is not curled up, it has other defenses: Larger kinds use their muscular tails to swat attackers. Other pangolins spray enemies with strong-smelling urine.

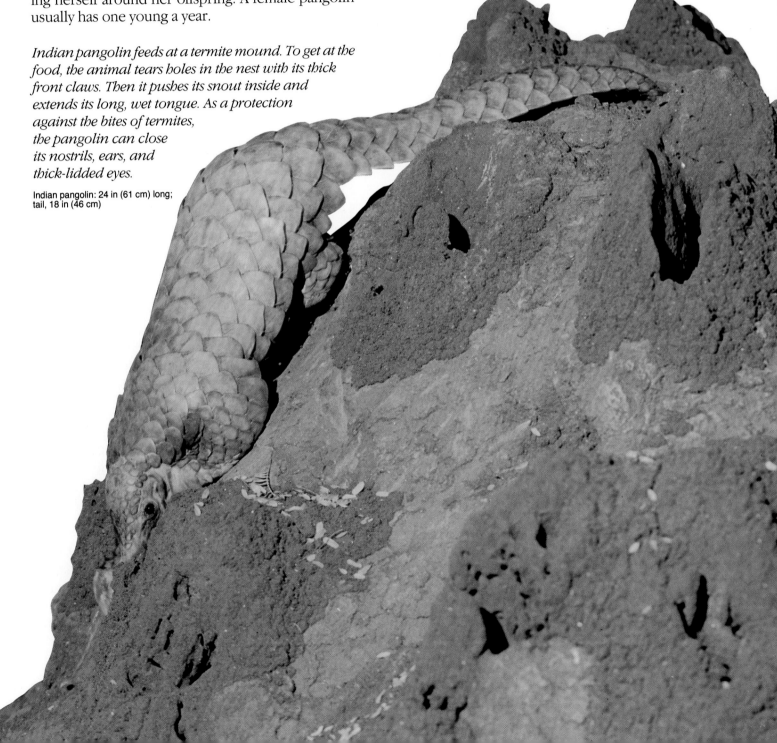

Panther

Panther is another name for the leopard. Read about the leopard on page 323.

Peccary

(PECK-uh-ree)

Collared peccary: 22 in (56 cm) tall at the shoulder

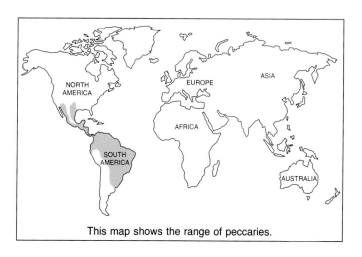

This map shows the range of peccaries.

△ *Sniffing and touching snouts, a young collared peccary and an adult greet each other. Newborn peccaries can travel with the herd only one day after birth. Young animals usually stay very close to adults.*

△ *Collared peccary bites into a prickly poppy flower in Texas. Peccaries use their razorlike teeth for fighting off coyotes, wild dogs, and bobcats. Because of their long, sharp teeth, peccaries are sometimes called javelinas, from a Spanish word meaning "spear."*

A HERD OF PIGLIKE ANIMALS steps out of the shade where the group has rested during the midday heat. A dozen peccaries—old and young, male and female—are looking for food in a Texas desert.

Some of the peccaries sniff the ground. They can detect plant bulbs under as much as 6 inches (15 cm) of soil. The peccaries dig out the bulbs with their rubbery snouts. Other peccaries munch cactuses—spines and all. They also eat mushrooms, berries, fruit, acorns, and new shoots of grass.

Peccaries drink from streams or ponds. Unlike some animals that live in deserts, peccaries cannot get all the moisture they need from plants. Their small hoofprints mark the trails that lead to water.

Peccaries are found from the southwestern United States into South America. When resting or feeding, the animals usually keep out of sight among cactuses, small shrubs, or rocks. But the noises they make give them away. The animals snort and grunt softly as they move about. They bark sharply when they fight over food.

Peccaries look and sound much like their distant relatives, wild pigs. They are about the size of small pigs, and they have piglike snouts. Their chunky, short-legged bodies are covered with coarse, salt-and-pepper-colored bristles.

The stiff hairs on the peccary's rump hide a scent gland that produces an oily, strong-smelling

428

Small herd of collared peccaries—young and old, male and female—trots across a grassy field in Texas.

substance. When a peccary rubs its back against a rock, it leaves a scent mark. Other peccaries in the herd recognize the smell because they often rub their faces against one another's backs. Members of a herd keep track of each other by the scent. People can smell the mild skunklike odor from as far as 300 feet (91 m) away.

When an enemy is near, or when a peccary is angry, it raises the bristles along its back. Then it woofs loudly. Alerted, the other peccaries in the herd scoot quickly into the underbrush.

Peccaries are timid and will run away from danger if they can. If attacked, however, they defend themselves fiercely. They bite and slash with razor-sharp teeth. Fighting as a group, the members of a herd can overcome a wild dog, a coyote, or a bobcat. They may even be able to drive away a jaguar.

Once a year, a female peccary may give birth. She bears her young—usually twins—in a sheltered place. The next day she returns to the herd with her offspring. The young peccaries will be protected by all the members of the herd.

Only the smallest peccary—the collared peccary—lives in the United States. It gets its name from a band of light-colored bristles around its neck. Collared peccaries live in deserts in the Southwest and in dry woodlands and dense rain forests in Central and South America.

The white-lipped peccary lives only in tropical rain forests in Central and South America. It may roam in herds of a hundred animals. The largest peccary, the tagua (TAHG-wah), lives on dry grasslands and in forests in central South America.

PECCARY   🐾 **1 of 3 species**

HEIGHT: 20-30 in (51-76 cm) at the shoulder

WEIGHT: 30-66 lb (14-30 kg)

HABITAT AND RANGE: deserts, woodlands, and rain forests in parts of North and South America

FOOD: cactuses, grass shoots, bulbs, nuts, berries, flowers, mushrooms, and fruit

LIFE SPAN: about 25 years in captivity

REPRODUCTION: usually 2 young after a pregnancy of about 5 months

ORDER: artiodactyls

Phalanger

Greater glider: 15 in (38 cm) long; tail, 20 in (51 cm)

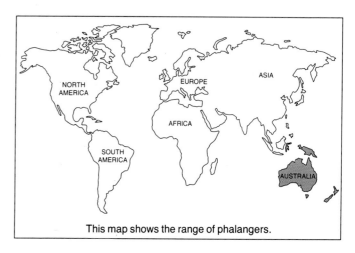

This map shows the range of phalangers.

PHALANGER 🐾 **9 of 37 species**

LENGTH OF HEAD AND BODY: 3-32 in (8-81 cm); tail, as long as 25 in (64 cm)

WEIGHT: 1 oz-20 lb (28 g-9 kg)

HABITAT AND RANGE: forests of Australia, New Guinea, New Zealand, and neighboring islands

FOOD: leaves, fruit, flowers, nectar, sap, and small animals

LIFE SPAN: 3 to 20 years, depending on species

REPRODUCTION: 1 to 6 young after a pregnancy of 2 to 5 weeks, depending on species; length of pregnancy unknown for some

ORDER: marsupials

Brush-tailed possum: 18 in (46 cm) long; tail, 12 in (30 cm)

△ *Largest of the gliding phalangers, a greater glider balances on a branch. It soars from tree to tree by extending flaps of skin that connect wrists and ankles.*

Young brush-tailed possum in Australia looks to its ▷ mother at mealtime. Like other marsupials, phalangers carry their young in pouches while they develop. Brush-tailed possum offspring stay in the pouch for about five months and nurse for several months more.

Wait for me! Tiny feather-tailed glider hurries after its mother as she searches for insects to eat.
Smallest of the gliders, this kind of phalanger uses its fringed tail to steer as it glides from tree to tree.

WHEN ENGLISH EXPLORER James Cook first visited Australia in 1770, his men captured a cat-size woolly animal. It had a partially naked tail and a pouch on its belly. It reminded the Englishmen of the American mammal called the opossum. So they gave the same name to the Australian animal. Over the years, the name was shortened to possum to distinguish it from the American opossum.

Scientists have learned that possums and opossums are not closely related. Both animals belong to the group of pouched mammals called marsupials (mar-SOO-pea-ulz). But each animal is a member of a separate group. Australian possums are in the same group as the phalangers. That name comes from a Greek word that means "bone of a finger or toe." The flexible fingers and toes of phalangers help these animals climb. Other animals related to the phalangers include the cuscus and the koala. Read about them under their own headings.

Phalangers live in the forests of Australia, New Guinea, New Zealand, and neighboring islands. Some are as small as *(Continued on page 434)*

431

Phalanger

Fluffy glider dines on the sap of a eucalyptus tree. ▷
*These phalangers are long-distance gliders. They
can sail as far as 300 feet (91 m). Because of the
color of the fur on their bellies, some people call
them yellow-bellied gliders.*

▽ *Standing on three paws,
a green ring-tailed possum
feeds on a leaf. This animal's
name comes from the greenish
color of its fur and the way its
tail curls up. Ring-tailed
possums usually travel in
pairs. In the trees, they build
ball-shaped nests of branches
and leaves.*

Fluffy glider: 10 in (25 cm) long; tail, 15 in (38 cm)

Green ring-tailed possum: 12 in (30 cm) long; tail, 11 in (28 cm)

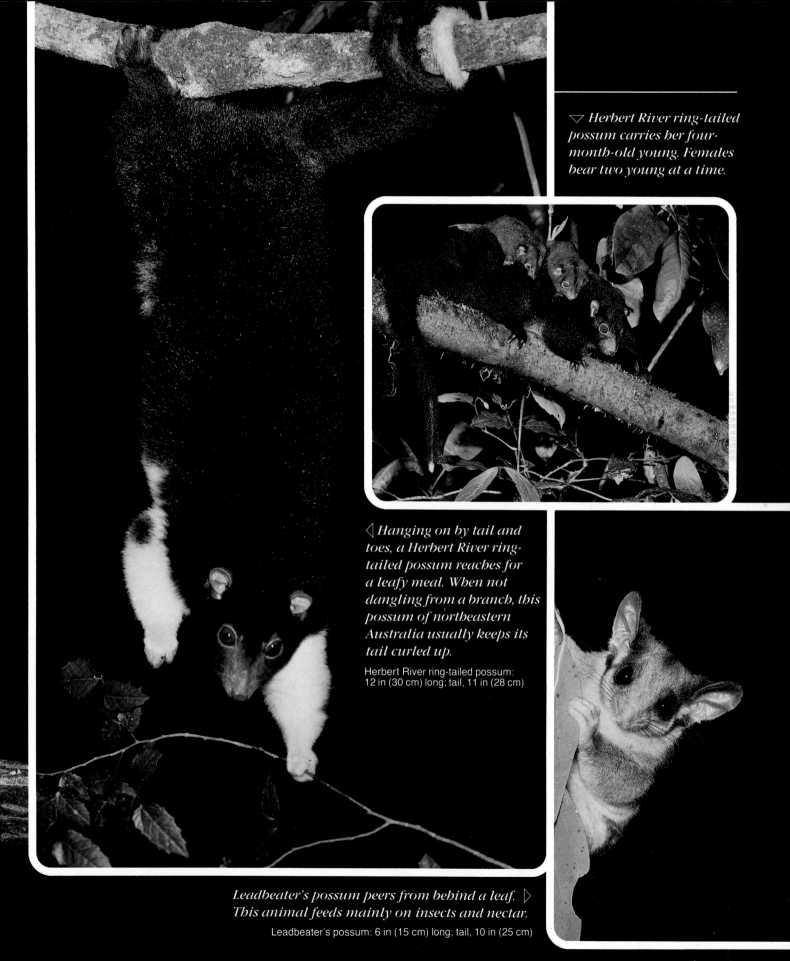

▽ *Herbert River ring-tailed possum carries her four-month-old young. Females bear two young at a time.*

◁ *Hanging on by tail and toes, a Herbert River ring-tailed possum reaches for a leafy meal. When not dangling from a branch, this possum of northeastern Australia usually keeps its tail curled up.*

Herbert River ring-tailed possum: 12 in (30 cm) long; tail, 11 in (28 cm)

Leadbeater's possum peers from behind a leaf. ▷ *This animal feeds mainly on insects and nectar.*

Leadbeater's possum: 6 in (15 cm) long; tail, 10 in (25 cm)

field mice. Others are about the size of house cats. Most phalangers are skillful climbers. Their sharp claws dig into tree branches, and their toes spread apart for a firm grip. Most have soft, thick fur and long tails. A phalanger may use its tail like an extra hand when it climbs. The animal's tail can curl tightly

▽ *On the prowl, a striped possum searches for insect larvae. With strong teeth and a long claw on each front foot, a "stripey" can dig out larvae beneath tree bark.*

Striped possum: 10 in (25 cm) long; tail, 12 in (30 cm)

Honey possum: 3 in (8 cm) long; tail, 3 in (8 cm)

△ *Honey possum feeds from a flower. A long snout and a bristle-tipped tongue help this animal gather nectar and pollen from blossoms.*

around a tree limb, supporting it until its paws have a grip on the next branch.

Other phalangers have another way of moving through the trees. They glide in swooping dives. These animals are called gliders. They leap into the air and spread out their arms and legs. Flaps of skin extend from their wrists to their ankles. The animals float gently down to another tree. Some of the larger gliders make glides as long as 300 feet (91 m)—the length of a football field.

Phalangers usually bear one to six offspring after a pregnancy of a few weeks. The tiny, hairless newborn crawl into their mother's pouch. There they continue to grow and develop. Within a few months, the young are covered with fur. Then they are able to go into and out of the pouch. Sometimes the mother carries them on her back.

When they are fully grown, many kinds of phalangers go off on their own. Some phalangers, such as honey possums, travel about in pairs. Others, like the gliders, often live in family groups.

Phalangers rest during the day. For shelter, some phalangers build nests of leaves, twigs, and branches. Others sleep curled up in hollow limbs or tree trunks. Some just stretch out along branches, hidden among leafy shadows.

At night, phalangers wake up and move about in the trees. They search for such food as leaves, fruit, flowers, nectar, sap, and pollen. One of the gliding phalangers is called the sugar glider because of its fondness for sweet food. Read about this animal on page 524. Some phalangers also eat insects and other small animals.

Phalangers have few enemies. They include snakes, monitor lizards, and large owls. The scratching noise of a lizard climbing a tree makes a phalanger scream in alarm. Some phalangers, like the brush-tailed possum, will fight fiercely. Gliders will leap to another tree. But others, like the slow-moving ringtailed possum, stay perfectly still. If the enemy does not leave, the possum tries to creep away quietly. It often gets caught.

Climbing upward, a squirrel glider stretches from ▷ *one bare branch to another. On the way down to another tree, the animal may make a daredevil dive. It can glide more than 100 feet (30 m) at a time.*

Squirrel glider: 8 in (20 cm) long; tail, 9 in (23 cm)

Pig
Pig is another name for the hog. Read about hogs on page 264.

Pika
(PEA-kuh or PIE-kuh)

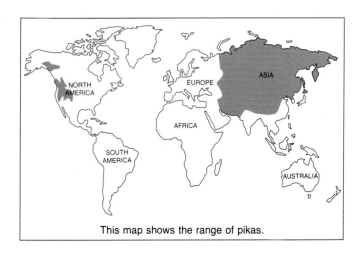

This map shows the range of pikas.

SCURRYING OVER ROCKS on a mountain slope in late summer, the pika carries a mouthful of plants. Soon the small, grayish brown animal reaches the haystack it is building. It climbs to the top and adds the plants it has gathered. In time, the sun-dried heap—the pika's winter food supply—may be several feet high and equally as wide.

Some kinds of pikas live on the rocky slopes of mountains in Asia, southern Russia, and western North America. Other kinds make their homes on grassy plains and in some deserts of Asia. From spring until late fall, there are plenty of plants for the animals to eat. The hardworking pikas begin in midsummer to

Perched on top of its haystack, a pika in Wyoming guards its winter food supply. If another pika tries to steal a leaf or a blade of grass, the pika will promptly chase away the intruder.

Pika: 8 in (20 cm) long

pile up grasses, herbs, and twigs. When cold weather sets in and plants become scarce, the haystacks provide food. Pikas stay active in winter. Covered with thick, soft fur, they travel about in tunnels they dig under the snow.

Many pikas live in colonies, or families. Those that live on plains and in deserts make their homes in underground burrows. On mountain slopes, pikas seek shelter among rocks. The animals find high places to use as lookouts. There they watch for danger. If they spot an enemy—a hawk, an eagle, or a weasel—the pikas call out a warning and scamper into rock crevices to hide.

Smaller than their relatives, hares and rabbits, pikas measure about 8 inches (20 cm) long. Read about hares on page 250 and rabbits on page 466.

Although hares and rabbits are usually silent, most pikas make sounds. Pikas that live in some areas have calls that may sound like sharp barks. And pikas in other areas make sounds that resemble the bleats of lambs.

A pika litter usually includes two to six young. When eight days old, the offspring can crawl and make peeping noises. Less than two months after birth, the young pikas reach full size. By then, their mother may have a new litter to care for.

△ *On guard duty, a pika in Montana barks an alert. Its rocky lookout provides a view of the slope below. After sounding a warning, the pika will dash for cover.*

PIKA 🐾 **9 of 26 species**

LENGTH OF HEAD AND BODY: 6-10 in (15-25 cm)

WEIGHT: 6-14 oz (170-397 g)

HABITAT AND RANGE: rocky slopes of mountains, grassy plains, and some deserts in western North America, southeastern Europe, and parts of Asia

FOOD: grasses, herbs, and twigs

LIFE SPAN: up to 7 years in captivity

REPRODUCTION: 2 to 6 young after a pregnancy of about 1 month, depending on species

ORDER: lagomorphs

▽ *Large leaf makes a snack for a collared pika in Alaska. Pikas feed on many kinds of plants. In the spring and early summer, they spend much of their time eating. Then pikas begin to pile up food for winter.*

▽ *Rubbing its cheek against a rock, a pika leaves a substance made by a gland in its face. The pika marks rocks with this scent or with urine to claim an area as its own. Scent marks may also help pikas find mates.*

Collared pika: 8 in (20 cm) long

Platypus

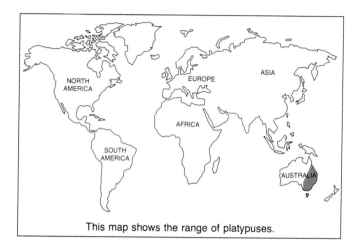

This map shows the range of platypuses.

PLATYPUS

LENGTH OF HEAD AND BODY: about 15 in (38 cm); tail, 5 in (13 cm)

WEIGHT: about 3 lb (1 kg)

HABITAT AND RANGE: near lakes and streams in eastern Australia

FOOD: worms, young shellfish, insects, and insect larvae

LIFE SPAN: up to 21 years in captivity

REPRODUCTION: usually 1 or 2 young hatched from eggs after an incubation period of about 10 days

ORDER: monotremes

WHEN SCIENTISTS IN BRITAIN first saw a platypus almost 200 years ago, they doubted that it was a real animal. This strange creature does exist in Australia, however. Its forefeet are webbed like those of a duck. Its muzzle looks like a duck's bill. Its tail resembles that of a beaver. And its fur looks like an otter's fur. The animal measures less than 2 feet (61 cm) long from its muzzle to the tip of its tail.

The platypus is a monotreme (MON-uh-treem). Besides the echidna, it is the only mammal that bears its young by laying eggs. Read about the echidna on page 188.

On land, the platypus shuffles along. In the water, it moves much more gracefully. The animal dives for food at dawn and at dusk. As the platypus submerges, folds of skin close over its ears and eyes. It also can close off its nostrils.

The platypus can stay beneath the surface for a minute or two at a time. Using its sensitive, skin-covered muzzle, the platypus probes the bottoms of lakes and streams for food. The animal scoops up worms, young shellfish, insects, and insect larvae, along with some mud and gravel. It stores this mixture in its cheek pouches.

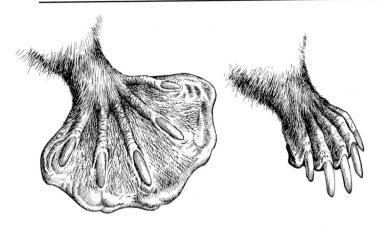

△ *Webbing of the forefoot of a platypus extends beyond its nails and forms a fan-shaped paddle (above, left). The paddle helps push the animal through the water. When the platypus moves on land, the webbing folds back (above, right). Then the platypus can walk or run more easily. It also uses its nails for digging.*

▽ *Sleek and streamlined when submerged, an adult platypus swims along a gravelly bottom. It paddles with its front feet and steers with its tail and hind feet. Folds of skin cover its eyes and ears when it is underwater. Its nostrils also can close. The platypus gets food by sifting through mud and gravel with its sensitive muzzle.*

When its pouches are full, the platypus rises to the surface to chew its food. The adult platypus has grinding pads instead of teeth. The mud and gravel in the animal's mouth help crush the food between these pads.

The male platypus has sharp spurs on the heels of its hind feet. To defend itself, it can jab enemies with these spurs and discharge a strong poison.

The platypus lives in a burrow that it digs at the edge of a lake or a stream, just above the water's surface. Using its thick nails and muzzle, it loosens dirt and then packs it to form the walls of its burrow.

A female platypus digs a nesting burrow where she lays her eggs. This winding tunnel usually is about 25 feet (8 m) long. At the end of the tunnel, the female lines a small chamber with grass and leaves. She seals herself into the chamber with a plug of dirt and lays one or two sticky, leathery eggs. She keeps the eggs warm between her body and her tail.

The eggs hatch in about ten days. The hairless newborn platypuses are only about the size of jelly beans. The young suck milk that flows from pores on their mother's belly. After several months, they begin to swim and to dive on their own.

Pocket gopher

Botta's pocket gopher: 6 in (15 cm) long; tail, 3 in (8 cm)

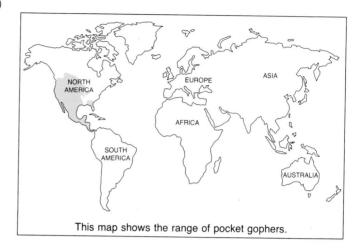

This map shows the range of pocket gophers.

△ *Botta's pocket gopher pops out of its burrow in Arizona for a quick look around.*
▽ *Plains pocket gopher in Minnesota carries food in its bulging cheek pouches. A pocket gopher gets its name from the fur-lined pouches on the sides of its face.*

Plains pocket gopher: 8 in (20 cm) long; tail, 4 in (10 cm)

POCKET GOPHER   🐾 **10 of 40 species**

LENGTH OF HEAD AND BODY: 4-14 in (10-36 cm); tail, 2-5 in (5-13 cm)

WEIGHT: 3-32 oz (85-907 g)

HABITAT AND RANGE: deserts, open forests, grasslands, valleys, and mountain slopes in parts of North America

FOOD: mainly roots and bulbs

LIFE SPAN: about 2 years in the wild

REPRODUCTION: 1 to 8 young after a pregnancy of 3 or 4 weeks

ORDER: rodents

HURRYING THROUGH ITS BURROW, the pocket gopher patrols its underground home. It looks for food and for intruders—weasels, snakes, and other pocket gophers. About forty species, or kinds, of pocket gophers live in parts of North America. Most of the time, these stocky rodents, sometimes simply called gophers, live alone in their burrows. If two gophers happen to meet, they may fight to the death.

A pocket gopher, though usually less than 1 foot (30 cm) long, can move an amazing amount of dirt for an animal its size. One gopher's burrow may extend for hundreds of feet. Loosening dirt and stones with its large teeth and claws, the animal digs separate chambers for sleeping, for storing food, and for waste. It seldom ventures above ground to browse.

Some burrows lie just below the surface of the ground. There the gopher finds roots and bulbs to eat. When it nibbles on the root of a plant, it may pull the stalk underground, too. People have watched entire plants disappear, yanked down by a gopher.

The gopher usually does not eat all its food at once. It cuts up plants with its large front teeth. Then it uses its paws to stuff the food into fur-lined pouches on the sides of its face. The gopher carries the food to its underground storeroom. There it empties its pouches. Like pockets, these pouches can be turned inside out for cleaning.

The only time gophers live together and socialize is when they have young. A female usually gives birth once or twice a year. A litter may include as many as eight offspring. The young stay with their mother for only about two months.

Stripes and spots of brown, white, and yellow color the fur of a marbled polecat, a relative of the weasel.

Polecat

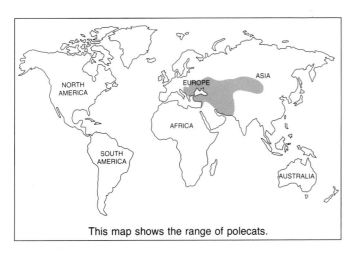

This map shows the range of polecats.

POLECAT 🐾 1 of 1 species

LENGTH OF HEAD AND BODY: 11-14 in (28-36 cm); tail, 5-7 in (13-18 cm)

WEIGHT: about 2 lb (1 kg)

HABITAT AND RANGE: dry, grassy plains and brushy areas in parts of Europe and Asia

FOOD: small mammals, birds, reptiles, and frogs

LIFE SPAN: more than 9 years in captivity

REPRODUCTION: 4 to 8 young after a pregnancy of 2 months

ORDER: carnivores

ON WINDSWEPT PLAINS in parts of Europe and Asia, the marbled polecat seeks its prey. This relative of the weasel hunts in the morning and evening. It usually feeds on mice, young hares, ground squirrels, birds, frogs, and lizards.

Like some of its relatives—weasels, ferrets, and grisons—the long, slender marbled polecat can slither through narrow openings into underground burrows after prey. The polecat may kill more food than it can eat. It hides what is left over in a burrow and returns to eat it later.

Marbled polecats live and hunt alone, except during the mating season. In an underground nest, a female polecat bears four to eight young in the springtime. The young polecats stay with their mother until the summer.

When attacked by enemies such as dogs or foxes, the polecat fluffs its marbled fur and curves its tail over its back. It bares its teeth and growls. Then the polecat may turn around and squirt a smelly liquid, produced by glands under its tail, at its enemy. The polecat's vivid markings may serve as a warning signal for other animals to stay away.

Porcupine

Sharp point of a quill of a North American porcupine (far right) can easily pierce an attacker's body. Overlapping scales, or barbs (right), cover the quill's tip. Like barbs on a fishhook, they catch in skin and are difficult to pull out.

◁ *North American porcupine pauses while nibbling twigs with its orange front teeth. Like other rodents, the porcupine wears down the teeth by gnawing on stems and other hard foods.*

▽ *Gripping a branch with its strong, curved claws, a North American porcupine rests in a birch tree in Alaska. Pads on its hind feet help it hold on. These animals spend much of their time in trees.*

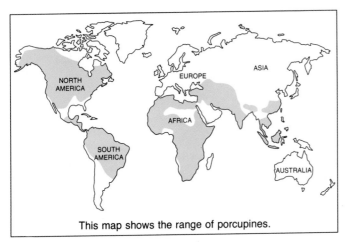

This map shows the range of porcupines.

WHEN ALARMED, a porcupine may stamp its feet, click its teeth, and growl or hiss. But a prickly coat of needle-sharp quills is the animal's best defense. The pointed quills are stiff, thick spines banded with black, brown, pale yellow, or white. The quills usually cover the porcupine's back, sides, and tail. They are mixed in with the animal's softer hairs.

Usually a porcupine's quills lie flat against its body. But if an enemy such as a bobcat, a hyena, or a fisher comes too close, a porcupine raises and spreads its quills. Contrary to a popular belief, the animal cannot shoot them at an attacker. But the quills

◁ *Turning its back, a North American porcupine warns an attacker to stay away. A halo of guard hairs surrounds its quills. When the porcupine brushes against an enemy, the quills may lodge in the enemy's flesh.*

North American porcupine: 29 in (74 cm) long; tail, 8 in (20 cm)

Crested porcupine: 26 in (66 cm) long; tail, 5 in (13 cm)

Ground dwellers, a pair of crested porcupines looks for shelter in a termite mound in Kenya.

are loosely attached. They may come off when a porcupine slaps its tail or brushes against an enemy. New quills grow in to replace lost ones.

The word *porcupine* means "quill pig" in Latin. Porcupines, however, are not pigs. They are large rodents. They live in deserts, forests, and grasslands. There are two groups of porcupines. One group lives in North and South America. These animals differ in looks and habits from porcupines that are found in Europe, Africa, and Asia. They all shuffle along the ground. But the porcupines in North and South America also climb trees. Some can even use their tails to grasp branches.

The only porcupine found in the United States and Canada is the North American porcupine. In winter, the animal feeds on bark and evergreen needles. In spring and summer, it eats leaves, buds, stems, and fruit. In campgrounds, porcupines may gnaw on ax handles or canoe paddles.

A female porcupine bears one to four young after a pregnancy of two to seven months, depending on the species. The newborn can see at birth. Hair and soft quills cover most of their bodies. Within a few days, their quills harden. When the offspring are about two months old, they leave their mother and go off on their own.

444

Prehensile-tailed porcupine: 18 in (46 cm) long; tail, 16 in (41 cm)

PORCUPINE 🐾 **2 of 23 species**

LENGTH OF HEAD AND BODY: 12-34 in (30-86 cm); tail, 2-18 in (5-46 cm)

WEIGHT: 2-60 lb (1-27 kg)

HABITAT AND RANGE: forests, deserts, and grasslands in parts of **North** and **South America, Europe, Africa,** and **Asia**

FOOD: bark, leaves, buds, stems, fruit, and sometimes crops

LIFE SPAN: as long as 20 years in captivity

REPRODUCTION: 1 to 4 young after a pregnancy of 2 to 7 months, depending on species

ORDER: rodents

◁ *Prehensile-tailed porcupine skillfully climbs along a tree branch in Bolivia. Its grasping tail coils around another branch.*

▽ *Two bristly bodyguards protect a young crested porcupine in Tanzania. By raising their quills—which may be 1 foot (30 cm) long—they may frighten away an attacker.*

Porpoise  (POR-pus)

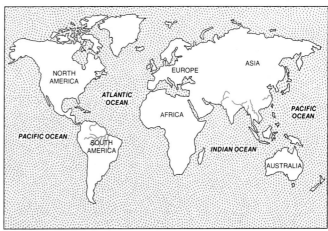

This map shows the range of porpoises and dolphins.

PORPOISE AND DOLPHIN 🐾 **9 of 45 species**

***LENGTH OF HEAD AND BODY:* 5-31 ft (152 cm-9 m)**

***WEIGHT:* 75 lb-9 t (34-8,165 kg)**

***HABITAT AND RANGE:* all oceans and some freshwater rivers**

***FOOD:* fish, squid, shrimps, birds, and mammals**

***LIFE SPAN:* up to 60 years in the wild**

***REPRODUCTION:* 1 young after a pregnancy of 10 to 16 months, depending on species**

***ORDER:* cetaceans**

SHOOTING OUT OF THE WATER like a rocket, a porpoise moves through the air in a graceful arc and splashes back into the sea. Another porpoise leaps, and then another. Soon a whole school, or group, of porpoises is taking part in a playful water ballet.

Porpoises live in all the oceans of the world and in several freshwater rivers. Though they may look a little like fish, porpoises are actually mammals. They are small, toothed whales. You can find out about larger whales on page 562. Some porpoises are called dolphins (DOLL-fins). People often use both words to refer to the same animal.

There are about fifty species, or kinds, of porpoises. These mammals vary greatly in size and shape. The harbor porpoise weighs 75 pounds (34 kg) and measures 5 feet (152 cm) long. The largest porpoise, the huge orca (OR-kuh), may weigh as much as 9 tons

◁ *Porpoise with a grin, a bottlenose dolphin glides through waters off Hawaii. These porpoises frequently perform in oceanariums. People often use the words* dolphin *and* porpoise *to refer to the same animal.*

Bottlenose dolphin: 9 ft (274 cm) long

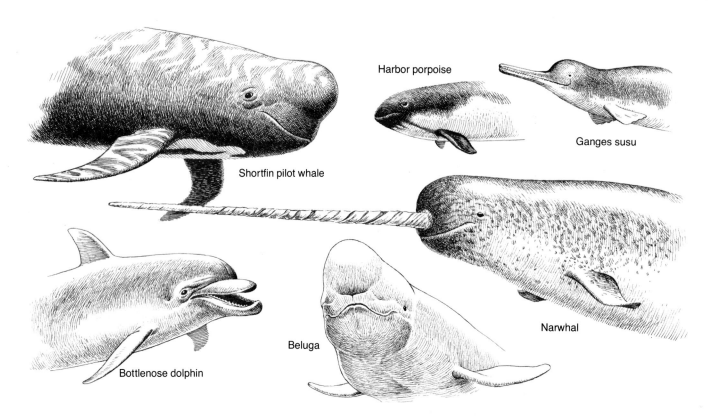

Harbor porpoise

Ganges susu

Shortfin pilot whale

Narwhal

Beluga

Bottlenose dolphin

△ *About fifty kinds of porpoises live around the world. They swim in several freshwater rivers and in all the oceans. Clockwise, from lower left: The bottlenose dolphin uses its beaklike snout to catch fish in coastal areas. The shortfin pilot whale feeds mostly on squid. A harbor porpoise has a cone-shaped head. It eats herring and cod. The long beak of a Ganges susu helps it probe muddy river bottoms for food. The male narwhal has a long tusk, but scientists do not know what it is used for. The beluga lives in cold, northern waters. To breathe, it may ram holes in newly formed ice with its back.*

Largest of all porpoises, a mighty orca, or killer ▷ *whale, hurls itself into the air. The crashing sound it makes as it splashes down may scare fish into coves and bays. There the orca can hunt them for food.*

(8,165 kg). The orca is sometimes called the killer whale, and an average adult animal measures about 25 feet (8 m) in length.

Some porpoises have round heads. Others have long, beaklike snouts. The male narwhal (NAR-whahl) has an ivory tusk—a long tooth—growing from the tip of its snout. The tusk may measure 8 feet (244 cm) long. There are different ideas about its purpose. Some scientists think that males use the tusk to battle one another to win mates.

The porpoise must surface from time to time to

Orca: 25 ft (8 m) long

get a breath. The animal has a single nostril, called a blowhole, on the top of its head. Right below this opening is a valve like a plug. When the porpoise surfaces, it contracts a muscle and opens the valve. The animal exhales a breath and inhales another. As the porpoise dives back under the water, it closes the valve again.

Most porpoises come up to breathe about every four minutes. Even when they are sleeping, the animals move to the surface to get a breath. Some, like the bottlenose dolphin, breathe about every twenty seconds. Other kinds of porpoises can hold their breath for as long as thirty minutes.

Porpoises are well suited to their environment. A thick layer of blubber, or fat, protects them from cold temperatures. Their torpedo-shaped bodies are streamlined for swift, easy movement. Flippers on their sides help them balance and steer. Tail fins,

△ *Attack! Hungry orcas speed toward a seal. They will knock it off the ice and into the waters off Antarctica. Orcas often prey on other marine mammals.*

called flukes, move up and down. They push the porpoises forward. These fast swimmers often speed through the water. Some kinds can travel more than 25 miles (40 km) an hour.

Porpoises that live in coastal areas have good eyesight. Some that live in rivers, such as the Ganges susu of India, are nearly blind. They depend mainly on their keen sense of hearing to find their way.

Most porpoises navigate by using echolocation (ek-oh-low-KAY-shun). They also use echolocation to find such food as fish and other sea animals. As a porpoise swims, it makes a series of clicking sounds that travel through the water. When the sounds hit an object, echoes bounce back to the porpoise. By listening to the echoes, a porpoise can tell the size, shape, and location of the object. And it can tell if the object is moving. Using echolocation, porpoises can stay out of the way of enemies. They also can avoid obstacles such as icebergs or boats. Bats also use echolocation to find food and to avoid obstacles. Read about bats beginning on page 77.

Porpoises also may avoid attackers because of their coloring. Most porpoises have dark backs. From above, they are hard to spot in the murky depths. Seen

Dusky dolphin: 8 ft (244 cm) long

◁ *Dusky dolphin sails through the air off the coast of Argentina. Its companions speed alongside. Duskies swim in schools of as many as a hundred animals.*
▽ *Shortfin pilot whale in the Pacific Ocean leaps straight out of the water. These big porpoises get their name from their habit of following a leader, or pilot— usually the largest animal in the group.*

Shortfin pilot whale: 22 ft (7 m) long

from below, their light bellies blend with the brighter water near the surface.

Swimming together in large numbers helps give porpoises additional protection against danger. Schools may range in size from a few animals to perhaps 10,000. While swimming in schools, porpoises communicate with each other. They whistle, squeak, growl, and moan. When in trouble, porpoises sometimes cry out for help.

Porpoises have been known to go to the rescue of a sick or injured porpoise. Often the distressed animal has difficulty swimming to the surface to breathe.

451

Beluga: 15 ft (5 m) long

△ *Belugas, or white whales, cruise the Arctic Ocean near Somerset Island off Canada. In these clear, shallow waters, more than a thousand belugas come together to give birth.*

Porpoise

The others may support it with their flippers and swim with it to the surface. Porpoises help one another in other ways, too. When a female porpoise gives birth, nearby females may assist her.

About a year after mating, a pregnant female gives birth to one young, usually in early spring. If the newborn does not rise immediately for its first breath of air, it may drown. The mother and the other females gently push it to the surface.

The mother nurses her young for about ten months. Special muscles allow her to squirt her milk into its mouth.

Intelligent and curious, porpoises have been taught to do many tricks. They often perform at oceanariums. There they jump through hoops, play catch, and snatch fish from a person's hand. Scientists are teaching these animals many things. Someday, they hope, porpoises may learn a language made up of signs and symbols. If so, they will be able to communicate with humans.

Air bubbles rise from a beluga's blowhole as it ▷ *sounds off underwater. All porpoises make whistling noises, but belugas also growl, roar, squeal, and trill.*

Potto

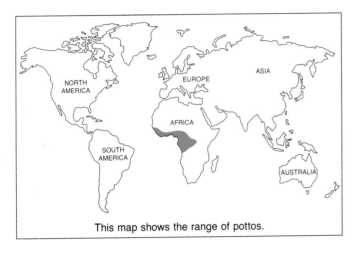

This map shows the range of pottos.

POTTO

LENGTH OF HEAD AND BODY: 12-16 in (30-41 cm); tail, 2-3 in (5-8 cm)

WEIGHT: about 2 lb (1 kg)

HABITAT AND RANGE: forests in central and western Africa

FOOD: fruit, tree gum, insects, and snails

LIFE SPAN: up to 26 years in captivity

REPRODUCTION: 1 young after a pregnancy of about 6 months

ORDER: primates

▽ *Long-fingered and stubby-tailed, a potto clings to a branch with a powerful grip. It uses the claws on its hind feet to groom its fur. These small primates climb slowly through the trees of central and western Africa.*

NOISELESSLY, the potto climbs through the forests of central and western Africa at night. The squirrel-size animal usually moves very slowly and carefully. It lets go with one foot only after the other three have firmly gripped a branch. The loris, an Asian relative of the potto, moves in a similar way. Read more about lorises on page 342.

Pottos, like monkeys, apes, and humans, are members of the primate order. Their thumbs resemble those of other primates, and pottos can use their thumbs and fingers to grip strongly.

Clinging to branches, pottos sleep the day away. Their bodies are curled into tight woolly balls. When they wake up at dusk, pottos begin to feed on fruit, tree gum, and insects. Their keen noses and eyes help them find food in the dark.

Under the sensitive skin on the back of the potto's neck are several long spine bones. Scientists are not sure what the bones are for. Some think that they may help the animal defend itself. When alarmed, a potto may tuck its head between its front legs and butt against its enemy. If necessary, it can defend itself by biting with its sharp teeth. But the potto's best defense is remaining unnoticed.

A potto has one young each year. The offspring nurses for about two months. Then it begins to feed on fruit. When it is grown, it will go off on its own.

Prairie dog

△ Black-tailed prairie dog remains on the lookout as it feeds. The small rodent eats grasses, seeds, and roots.
◁ Head thrown back, a black-tailed prairie dog calls a signal to other members of its town. Bison and prairie dogs often share an area. Sometimes the huge bison roll in the dirt on prairie dog mounds.

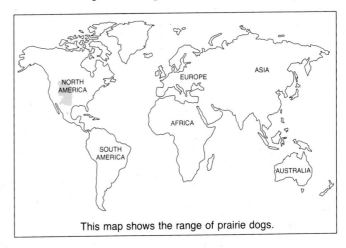

This map shows the range of prairie dogs.

Black-tailed prairie dog: 14 in (36 cm) long; tail, 3 in (8 cm)

455

ACROSS THE PRAIRIES of North America, people sometimes see mounds of firmly packed dirt. The mounds mark the bustling towns of black-tailed prairie dogs. Among the mounds, a hundred plump, rabbit-size rodents may scurry about. Some search for grasses, roots, and seeds. Others busily shape the entrance mounds to their underground burrows. A few may sun themselves. As they move around, the prairie dogs stay alert to danger.

The enemies of prairie dogs can often spot their prey on the flat, open prairies. But the prairie dogs have an alarm system to protect themselves. When one of the small rodents senses danger, it may sit up and cry a warning that can be heard throughout the town. Hearing the alarm call, other prairie dogs quickly dash for safety and vanish inside their underground homes.

After a few minutes, several prairie dogs will cautiously peer from their burrows. If the danger has passed, they may give an all-clear signal. They come out of their burrows, rear on their hind legs, and call out loudly. Gradually, more of the animals emerge. They scamper about the prairie and carry on their daily activities.

Inside a prairie dog burrow are one or more long tunnels a few feet below the ground. Several chambers, or rooms, lie along each tunnel. One of the chambers may serve as a nursery where prairie dog young nestle in a bed of dry grasses. Another chamber is a listening post. From that room, prairie dogs can hear what is happening above ground.

The entrance mound of the burrow provides a

△ *Young prairie dog peeks over the entrance mound to its burrow after hearing an all-clear signal. Black-tailed prairie dogs also have calls that warn of danger, help them claim territory, and express contentment.*

lookout station for prairie dogs. It also keeps water from flooding the burrow. Prairie dogs form the mound with loose dirt. They spend a great deal of time keeping it in good shape. They kick dirt onto the mound and then pack the soil with their noses and foreheads. Around some mounds, there is actually a pattern of noseprints.

Some people who live on the Great Plains think prairie dogs are a nuisance. The rodents dig holes in fields and in pastures. So people sometimes kill prairie dogs. Some black-tailed prairie dogs remain on

Rebuilding after a storm, a prairie dog shapes an entrance mound. First it kicks loose dirt onto the mound (above, left). Then it rams its nose against the soil (above, center) to pack it down. Covered with dirt, the animal sits in front of its ring of earth (right) and looks around the prairie dog town.

456

the Great Plains, however. The resourceful rodents continue to dig their burrows.

Black-tailed prairie dogs live in towns that include many small groups of animals. Each group is usually made up of an adult male, several females, and young born that year. Every group has its own territory, or area. If a strange prairie dog approaches, the residents try to chase the intruder away. Members of the group share food, play together, and groom one another. When they meet, they kiss or nuzzle each other. In these ways, the animals can identify members of their group.

A prairie dog town may be home to hundreds of other animals. Snakes and burrowing owls may take shelter in the burrows. Coyotes, eagles, and other enemies hunt the prairie dogs in the towns.

A few black-footed ferrets may also live there.

Enemy of black-tailed prairie dogs, a coyote prowls ▷ through the grass. If the coyote comes too near, the prairie dogs will duck into their burrows.

Underground homes, prairie dog burrows provide places to sleep, to raise young, and to find shelter. Too quick for a coyote, a prairie dog quickly disappears into a hole. In a nursery chamber (below, right), a mother huddles with her pups. Nearby is a sleeping chamber with a nest. Along the tunnel (from right to left), the prairie dogs also have built a toilet chamber and a higher, dry chamber that rarely floods. Another prairie dog stations itself at a listening post close to the mound entrance. There it can hear when the coyote leaves.

△ *Relaxing in a field of wild flowers in South Dakota, a prairie dog family basks in the June sun. The mother stands watch while one of her pups nurses.*

◁ *Prairie dog carries a mouthful of grass to line its nursery chamber. This nest inside the burrow will provide a warm, safe place to sleep and to raise young.*

During the 20th century, people killed off about 98 percent of prairie dogs—the ferrets' prey. With so few prairie dogs around, the black-footed ferret suffered from lack of food. Today only a very few of the animals may still roam the prairie. You can read about ferrets on page 202.

Less numerous than black-tailed prairie dogs are their white-tailed relatives. White-tailed prairie dogs make their homes on high mountain plains farther to the west than the towns of black-tailed prairie dogs. The white-tailed animals live in smaller groups. Instead of building large towns, the animals may dig widely scattered burrows with only a few other prairie dogs nearby. White-tailed prairie dogs make fewer calls than their relatives do.

During the winter months, both white- and black-tailed prairie dogs usually stay underground. They live mostly on the fat stored inside their bodies.

PRAIRIE DOG 🐾 1 of 5 species

LENGTH OF HEAD AND BODY: 12-15 in (30-38 cm); tail, 3-4 in (8-10 cm)

WEIGHT: 2-4 lb (1-2 kg)

HABITAT AND RANGE: prairies and mountain plains in parts of the western United States and Mexico

FOOD: grasses, seeds, roots, and leafy plants

LIFE SPAN: about 8 years in captivity

REPRODUCTION: 3 to 5 young after a pregnancy of 1 month

ORDER: rodents

△ *Do I know you? Prairie dog pups nuzzle each other. Small groups of black-tailed prairie dogs live together and share a territory. By touching and sniffing, the animals identify members of their own group.*

White-tailed prairie dogs hibernate (HYE-bur-nate), or sleep, for as long as six months. Their body temperatures drop, and their heart rates slow down. Black-tailed prairie dogs may wake up on warmer days and look for food outside.

In late winter or early spring, female prairie dogs may give birth to tiny offspring. A litter usually includes three to five young, called pups. Until the pups are about six weeks old, their mother nurses them. Then they leave the safety of the burrow and begin to eat grasses and leafy plants. Soon they are frisking playfully with other young prairie dogs.

△ *In a friendly romp, two young prairie dogs take a tumble. Pups may play together when they meet. Adults often stop to kiss and to groom one another.*

Pronghorn

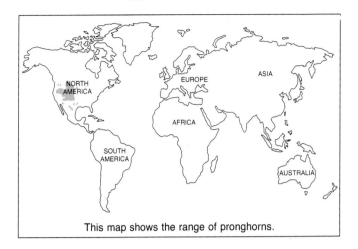
This map shows the range of pronghorns.

◁ *Dark-eyed pronghorn doe alertly watches a prairie in northern Mexico. Large eyes and ears alert her to distant movements and sounds. The creamy-white bands on her throat, mouth, and cheeks contrast with the brownish color of her coat.*

▽ *Pair of pronghorns trots across a rolling grassland in the Black Hills region of South Dakota. The male, or buck, wears the pronged horns that give these animals their name. The female, or doe, has only bony knobs on her forehead.*

FASTEST MAMMAL IN NORTH AMERICA, the pronghorn can sprint more than 50 miles (80 km) an hour. At half that speed, this graceful, deer-size animal can run for several miles. Pronghorns move about in small bands or large herds. Though still numerous in parts of western North America, two subspecies face extinction in the United States and Mexico because of illegal hunting and loss of habitat.

Males, or bucks, have two horns, pronged and curved at the tips. Females, or does, have smaller horns without prongs. Some does have no horns at all. Each fall, the outer covers of the horns drop off, leaving only skin-covered, bony cores. By summer, the coverings have grown back—even larger.

On older animals, the pronged horns may measure more than 1 foot (30 cm) long. Because of the horns, some people believe that pronghorns are related to antelopes. Scientists disagree about this.

Pronghorns eat mostly sagebrush and other shrubs that grow in the dry areas where they live. Where water is scarce, pronghorns can survive for a long time on moisture they get from plants.

Pronghorns swallow their food without chewing it thoroughly. After eating, the animals bring up a wad

Pronghorn _____

Newborn pronghorn lies hidden in prairie grass in ▷ South Dakota. Its mother is probably grazing a short distance away. She stays close to her offspring that way, but she does not reveal its hiding place.

▽ Sniffing the air for the scent of a coyote or a bobcat, a pronghorn buck in Montana snorts an alarm. The hairs of his white rump patch stand on end and serve as a warning signal to pronghorns farther away.

of partly digested food, called a cud. They chew the cud, swallow it, and digest it completely.

Pronghorns are always alert to such enemies as coyotes or bobcats. Pronghorns have keen eyesight. Because their eyes are on the sides of their heads, they can keep watch in most directions.

When the pronghorn is alarmed, hairs on its neck and rump stand on end. The flash of white hair on its rump acts as a signal to other pronghorns. As the pronghorns speed away, glands near their tails produce a strong-smelling liquid. The scent of this liquid also helps warn of danger.

The pronghorn has a brownish coat with white markings. The hairs in its coat are coarse and about 2 inches (5 cm) long. During cold weather, these hairs lie flat. They hold body heat next to the pronghorn's skin, helping to keep the animal warm. In hot weather, the pronghorn flexes certain muscles, and the hairs in its coat stand up. Air flows among the hairs and cools the animal.

A buck has a dark mane on his neck and black

PRONGHORN 🐾 I of I species

HEIGHT: about 3 ft (91 cm) at the shoulder

WEIGHT: 90-150 lb (41-68 kg)

HABITAT AND RANGE: grasslands and shrubby areas of western North America

FOOD: shrubs and grasses

LIFE SPAN: up to 12 years in captivity

REPRODUCTION: usually 2 young after a pregnancy of about 8 months

ORDER: artiodactyls

masklike markings on his head. In the mating season in September, he marks his territory with a liquid from a gland in his face. A buck then selects several does. Herding the females together—and chasing other bucks away—keeps him busy. Rival bucks snort and fight. Sometimes the animals injure each other with their horns.

In the spring, the does go off by themselves to give birth, usually to twins. A mother hides her offspring among tall grass. After four days, the young pronghorns can run faster than a human. They will be fully grown after a year and a half.

▽ *Surrounded by sagebrush, a favorite food, pronghorns move from one grazing area to another. Pronghorns feed on the low shrubs and grasses that grow in the dry, open areas where they live.*

Puma Puma is another name for the mountain lion. Read about it and other cats on page 126.

Quokka

IN THE COOL EVENING, quokkas leave the shallow, grassy resting places where they have slept most of the day. They move along well-traveled pathways through swamps and thickets in southwestern Australia and on two nearby islands. The animals stop often to nibble tender shoots. If frightened, they quickly hop away. With their short hind legs, quokkas spring through the underbrush.

Quokkas are small members of the kangaroo family—only about 3 feet (91 cm) long from head to tail. They are marsupials (mar-soo-pea-ulz), or pouched mammals, like many other mammals in Australia. Read about kangaroos on page 304.

Short, coarse, grayish brown hair covers the quokka's stocky body. Its thin tail is nearly hairless and not very long. Its ears are small and rounded.

Each quokka usually stays within a home range that may overlap those of other quokkas. Sometimes a group of more than a hundred quokkas lives in a large area made up of many overlapping home ranges. Members of one group of quokkas rarely enter another group's area.

Quokkas can go for a long time without drinking water. They get most of the moisture they need from the plants they eat. Even so, many of the animals do not survive during very hot, dry summers.

Mating occurs during the winter. One tiny, underdeveloped offspring is born about a month later. It crawls into its mother's pouch, where it grows larger and stronger. About five months after birth, the young quokka begins to leave the pouch. At six months of age, the animal goes off on its own. But it remains in the same area as its mother.

Quokkas are also known as wallabies. Read about other wallabies on page 548.

◁ *Paws drawn toward her chest, a bright-eyed female quokka rests standing up. Thick, coarse hair covers her body and hides the opening to her pouch.*

Hungry quokkas nibble seeds scattered over sandy ▷ *soil. When feeding, quokkas move slowly about on all fours. But if frightened, they quickly hop away.*

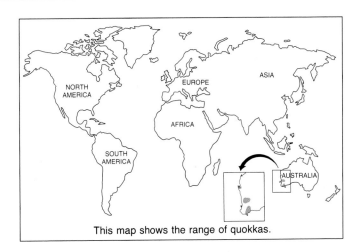

This map shows the range of quokkas.

QUOKKA   🐾 1 of 1 species

LENGTH OF HEAD AND BODY: 19-23 in (48-58 cm); tail, 10-14 in (25-36 cm)

WEIGHT: about 7 lb (3 kg)

HABITAT AND RANGE: brushy areas of southwestern Australia and nearby islands

FOOD: grasses and other plants

LIFE SPAN: up to 10 years in the wild

REPRODUCTION: 1 offspring after a pregnancy of about 1 month

ORDER: marsupials

R

Rabbit

EVEN IF YOU LIVE IN A CITY, you may have spotted the white flash of a rabbit's tail as the small mammal raced for cover. If you are sharp-eyed, you may have spied a rabbit as it crouched—absolutely still.

Rabbits are among the most familiar mammals in the world. There are nearly 25 species, or kinds, of rabbits. They live on all continents of the world except Antarctica. They inhabit swamps, marshes, deserts, woodlands, grasslands, prairies, and volcanic slopes. Some rabbits are found near people in cities and suburbs.

European rabbits live together in a complex burrow system called a warren. Using their forepaws and powerful hind feet, the rabbits dig out several openings and a network of tunnels and chambers. In North America, most rabbits spend the day resting in shallow dens called forms. But when danger threatens, these rabbits may seek shelter in the abandoned burrows of other animals.

The rabbit looks very much like its close relative the hare. But rabbits are usually smaller than hares—

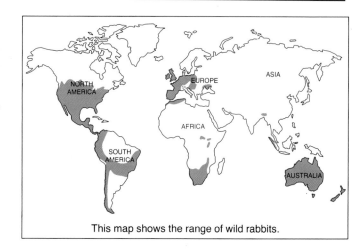

This map shows the range of wild rabbits.

Ears alert, a Nuttall's cottontail remains still as it ▷ *watches for enemies in a snowy field in South Dakota. Winter or summer, Nuttall's cottontails are most active in the morning and the evening.*
▽ *Desert cottontail in southern Arizona samples a bright yellow flower on a brittlebush plant. Found in many kinds of habitats in southwestern North America, this kind of rabbit feeds mainly on grasses and herbs.*

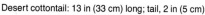
Desert cottontail: 13 in (33 cm) long; tail, 2 in (5 cm)

Nuttall's cottontail: 12 in (30 cm) long; tail, 2 in (5 cm)

Rabbit

only about 16 inches (41 cm) long and 2 pounds (1 kg) in weight. Rabbits also have shorter ears and shorter hind legs than hares do. Newborn rabbits start life helpless, without hair on their bodies, and with their eyes closed. Young hares, on the other hand, can leap about almost as soon as they are born. They have fur, and their eyes are open. Read more about hares on page 250.

Like hares, rabbits eat many kinds of plants. They nibble on grasses and herbs. When grass is scarce in winter, the animals gnaw on twigs or bark. Rabbits that live near people sometimes eat vegetables and other crops.

In fields, rabbits usually can find plenty of grasses and herbs to eat. But open areas can be dangerous places for rabbits. The list of the rabbit's enemies is long. Foxes, dogs, bobcats, coyotes, lynxes, weasels, raccoons, hawks, and eagles are some of the animals that prey on rabbits. And people hunt them for sport, for food, and for fur. Rabbits usually defend themselves by running away swiftly. Sometimes they may freeze, or sit very still, trying not to be seen. European rabbits may race into the safety of their warren. Some rabbits may swim to escape danger. Others, like the desert cottontail and the brush rabbit, may even climb trees. In spite of all these defenses, life is very difficult for rabbits that live in the wild. Most live for only about a year. If rabbits did not have so many young every year, the small mammals might have become extinct long ago.

Different kinds of rabbits mate at different times throughout the year. During courtship, male rabbits, called bucks, become rivals for the females, called does. European bucks may fight by boxing with their forepaws. They also strike at each other with their powerful hind feet. At mating time, males and females seem to be very affectionate. They may lick each other's ears and heads.

About a month after mating, a doe digs a shallow den and lines it with fur and grasses. There she bears two to seven tiny offspring, often called kittens. Each kitten weighs less than 2 ounces (57 g). It looks more like a little hairless guinea pig than like a rabbit. The doe covers the nest with grass to protect the young from heat and cold. The grass also helps to hide the

---

RABBIT 🐾 **9 of 23 species**

LENGTH OF HEAD AND BODY: 11-23 in (28-58 cm); tail, 1-5 in (3-13 cm)

WEIGHT: 1-16 lb (454 g-7 kg)

HABITAT AND RANGE: all kinds of habitats on all continents except Antarctica; brought by people to Australia; domestic rabbits live all over the world

FOOD: grasses, herbs, twigs, and bark

LIFE SPAN: up to 9 years in captivity

REPRODUCTION: 2 to 7 young after a pregnancy of about 1 month

ORDER: lagomorphs

European rabbit: 16 in (41 cm) long; tail, 2 in (5 cm)

Newborn European rabbits (far left) lie naked and helpless in a nest lined with fur and grasses in England. By four days of age (left, center) the young rabbits—called kittens—are much larger and have fine, thin fur. They still spend most of the time curled up asleep. After about 14 days, the bright-eyed kittens have become more active. Like the kitten at left, they begin to groom their own fur. By the time the kittens are about a month old, they may begin to explore outside. Below, an adult peers from the entrance to its warren. If it spots danger, the rabbit will disappear down the hole.

kittens during the daytime, when their mother is away from the nest. Each night, the mother rabbit returns to the nest and nurses her young. The kittens gain weight quickly, doubling their size in the first ten days after birth.

Within a week, the young rabbits have grown coats of short, soft fur. By the time they are a month old, they have begun to play outside the nest and can find their own food. The offspring are ready to breed in less than a year. By then, their mother may have had other litters. A female may bear as many as thirty young a year, in about four litters. People often make pets of rabbits. There are more than fifty breeds of domestic, or tame, rabbits and hundreds of varieties. They range in size from the Netherland Dwarf rabbit, at about 2 pounds (1 kg), to the Flemish Giant rabbit, at about 16 pounds (7 kg). Domestic rabbits may have short, plush fur like that of the Rex rabbit or long, woolly fur like that of the Angora (ang-GORE-uh) rabbit. All of the domestic rabbits are descendants of the wild European rabbit. These animals belong to a single species.

Domestic rabbit: 11 in (28 cm) long; tail, 1 in (3 cm)

Marsh rabbit: 16 in (41 cm) long; tail, 1 in (3 cm)

△ *Marsh rabbit nibbles on a leaf in Everglades National Park, in Florida. These rabbits live near the water's edge. There they walk through the soft mud, instead of hopping as other rabbits do. They swim well.*

◁ *Small domestic rabbit sits in a meadow in Germany. Domestic, or tame, rabbits come in many sizes and colors. This one weighs about 2 pounds (1 kg). The largest domestic rabbit may weigh eight times as much.*

Raccoon

(rack-KOON)

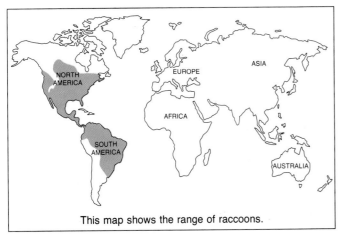

This map shows the range of raccoons.

RACCOON   🐾 **4 of 7 species**

LENGTH OF HEAD AND BODY: **18-26 in (46-66 cm); tail, 9-12 in (23-30 cm)**

WEIGHT: **7-26 lb (3-12 kg)**

HABITAT AND RANGE: **forests, marshes, prairies, and urban areas in many parts of North and South America and on a few tropical islands; also brought by people to Europe**

FOOD: **small animals, including frogs, shellfish, crayfish, worms, mice, and insects, as well as fruit, nuts, and vegetables**

LIFE SPAN: **up to 20 years in captivity**

REPRODUCTION: **1 to 7 young after a pregnancy of 2 months**

ORDER: **carnivores**

MANY ANIMALS AVOID PEOPLE and the places they live—but not the raccoon. Its masked face and bushy, ringed tail are familiar to city dwellers as well as to campers in the wilderness. The raccoon is often found in forests near water. It also makes itself at home in marshes, prairies, cities, and suburbs in many areas of North and South America.

Raccoons thrive because they are adaptable—they are able to change their behavior to suit their situation. They will eat almost anything. With their nimble front paws—and a great deal of curiosity—raccoons can find whatever food is available, according to the season. Raccoons have a keen sense of touch. They are always poking their fingers into crevices, searching for small animals, such as mice and insects, to eat. They can even open garbage cans and live

Masked faces peer from a hollow tree as a female North American raccoon and her cub poke their heads out from their den. Raccoons make dens in many sheltered spots—from hollow logs to the attics of houses.

Young North American raccoons explore a hole in a ▷ sycamore tree in Ohio. A litter of cubs—as many as seven—stays with its mother for several months.

well on the contents. Near farms, they help themselves to fruit, vegetables, and grain.

Raccoons find much of their food in the water. They feel under rocks and in the mud for crayfish and frogs. A captive raccoon may carry food to its water dish. It seems to lose the food in the water and then to find it again by feeling in the dish with its paws. For a long time, people thought that raccoons were washing their food when they did this. The scientific name of the raccoon even means "the washer." Now most scientists think that captive raccoons are really acting the way they would in the wild by "finding" food in the water.

Raccoons sleep anywhere that seems safe. A hollow tree or the attic of a building may be used as a den. Often a raccoon has several resting spots within its home range, the area it roams and knows well. The raccoon stays in this area as it searches for food at night. Usually raccoons try to avoid one another. In places where there are many raccoons and plenty to eat, however, several animals may feed together. But they keep their distance from one another.

In early spring, raccoons find mates. About two months later, a female gives birth to one to seven young, called cubs, in a den—often a hole in a tree. Newborn raccoons do not have dark masks on their faces or rings on their tails. These markings appear within a few days.

As the weeks pass, the cubs become more active and the nest becomes crowded. After about two months, the cubs are ready to start exploring their surroundings. Their mother moves them from a den high in a tree to one on the ground. That way, if the cubs take a tumble, they won't be hurt. Soon the cubs

With long, nimble fingers, a young North American ▷ raccoon pulls persimmons to its mouth. The animal can skillfully use its paws to investigate an object.

◁ *Dwarfed by their tree-trunk home, two raccoon cubs in the state of Washington watch their mother return from hunting for food. Like their relatives—coatis and ringtails—raccoons have ringed tails.*

North American raccoon: 24 in (61 cm) long; tail, 10 in (25 cm)

go everywhere with their mother. The family stays in touch by using many sounds—purrs, churrs, twitters, and growls.

During the summer, the cubs become more independent. They often spend several days away from their mother and each other. Raccoons that live in the north eat as much food as they can find during the autumn. Both cubs and adults gain a great deal of weight. By winter, the young rejoin their mother for a few months. The family spends most of that time asleep together in a den. Only on mild winter nights do the animals emerge to look for food. The rest of the time they live on fat stored in their bodies.

A long, freezing winter is hard on young raccoons. Many starve because they do not have as much fat stored up as their parents do. In the spring, a raccoon may weigh only about half as much as it did in the fall. By summer, the year-old cubs have found their own home ranges. In warmer areas, raccoon cubs leave their mothers at any time of the year. When food is plentiful and available all year long, cubs reach their full size earlier. Then they can go off on their own sooner.

There are seven species, or kinds, of raccoons. Five of them live on tropical islands. The raccoon that is most familiar roams throughout North America. It can weigh as much as 26 pounds (12 kg). The crab-eating raccoon lives in Central and South America, usually near water. With its sturdy teeth, it can eat hard food such as crabs and other shellfish.

Raccoon in Texas (above) searches for food in a stream. Another animal in Florida (right) licks its paws dry after eating. Raccoons eat almost anything they can find—fish, berries, nuts, mice, eggs, and garbage.

◁ *Lazily draped among branches, a raccoon (top, left) takes a nap. Adaptable animals, raccoons make homes in forests, marshes, prairies, cities, and suburbs. In Arizona, a mother raccoon (left) carries her month-old cub to her den among the rocks.*

Raccoon dog

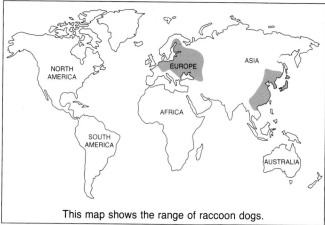

This map shows the range of raccoon dogs.

RACCOON DOG

LENGTH OF HEAD AND BODY: 19-31 in (48-79 cm); tail, 6-10 in (15-25 cm)

WEIGHT: 9-22 lb (4-10 kg)

HABITAT AND RANGE: forests and river valleys in parts of Asia and Europe

FOOD: small mammals, fish, birds, frogs, insects, fruit, nuts, and grain

LIFE SPAN: 10 years in captivity

REPRODUCTION: 5 to 7 young after a pregnancy of about 2 months

ORDER: carnivores

Behind raccoonlike masks, two raccoon dogs prowl a grassy area in Japan. These small wild dogs usually search at night for mice, fish, insects, and other food.

DARK SPOTS AROUND THE EYES give this small wild dog a raccoonlike mask—and its name. Slim in summer, the raccoon dog fattens up for the icy winter by eating large amounts of food. As cold weather sets in, the animal's brownish fur gets longer and thicker. Bundled up in this heavy coat, the raccoon dog looks fat and roly-poly.

Raccoon dogs once were found only in the Far East. There they were prized for their winter fur. During the last century, some were released in western Russia. As the animals bred in the wild, some were trapped for their fur. Wild raccoon dogs have since spread into other parts of Europe.

Nose to the ground, a raccoon dog hunts for food at night. It eats mice, fish, birds, frogs, and insects. It also gobbles berries, nuts, and grain.

In some places, raccoon dogs may sleep through the coldest weather. A pair may curl up together in a moss-lined burrow. Young, usually five to seven pups, are born in early summer.

Rat

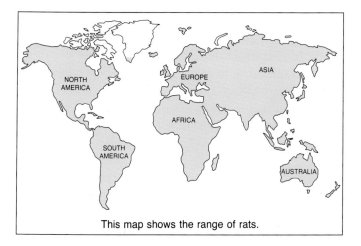

This map shows the range of rats.

RAT 🐾 **12 of about 500 species**

LENGTH OF HEAD AND BODY: 6-23 in (15-58 cm); tail, 3-18 in (8-46 cm)

WEIGHT: 5 oz-15 lb (142 g-7 kg)

HABITAT AND RANGE: most kinds of habitats around the world

FOOD: seeds, nuts, grains, vegetables, fruit, eggs, fish, insects, birds, and other meat

LIFE SPAN: usually less than 1 year in the wild

REPRODUCTION: 1 to 12 young after a pregnancy of 3 weeks to 2½ months, depending on species

ORDER: rodents

FEELING THE WAY with its long whiskers, the rat scurries about, searching for something to eat. With its pointed nose, rounded ears, and long tail, it is a familiar sight. Like its close relative the mouse, the rat is one of the world's most numerous mammals. Read about the mouse on page 392.

There are hundreds of species, or kinds, of rats. Most rats are bigger than mice. Some kinds of rats may measure as long as 23 inches (58 cm), not counting their tails. These animals may weigh as much as 15 pounds (7 kg). Most rats have scaly tails. But those of the bushy-tailed wood rats of western North America are hairy.

Most rats have short brown, black, or gray hair with light-colored bellies. Their coats may be soft or coarse. But a few rats have special coats. Some kinds of spiny rats in Central and South America have stiff, sharp-pointed hair. The bushy-tailed cloud rat of the Philippines has long hair on its body and tail.

Like mice, rats live in all kinds of habitats—forests, mountains, deserts, and grasslands. Rats live in cities and in the country. Some rats, like the Australian water rat, can swim like a beaver. Others, like the

▽ *Black-footed tree rat perches on a stump in Australia and flicks its white-tasseled tail. Active at night, these rats usually spend the day in hollow trees.*

Brown rat: 9 in (23 cm) long; tail, 7 in (18 cm)

△ *On a farm in England, a brown rat nibbles stalks of wheat stored after a harvest. One brown rat can eat about 25 pounds (11 kg) of grain in a year.*

Black-footed tree rat: 12 in (30 cm) long; tail, 13 in (33 cm)

Rat

black rat, can climb trees and jump with ease. Rats make their nests between rocks and in houses, trees, bushes, and burrows.

Some rats build their own homes. Wood rats of North America sometimes pile sticks, twigs, or parts of cactuses against a rock or a bush. Inside, the rats dig out several passageways and chambers. The stick-nest rat of Australia piles sticks together. This animal sometimes places stones on top to keep the nest from being blown away by strong winds. Inside the nest, the rat is safe from its enemies. A stick-nest rat's home may measure about 4 feet (122 cm) across and 3 feet (91 cm) high.

The two most common rats—the black rat and

Karroo rat: 6 in (15 cm) long; tail, 4 in (10 cm)

◁ *Emerging from its burrow, a karroo rat watches for enemies. This shy animal rarely travels far from its home. At a hint of danger, it dashes underground. The karroo rat, also known as the whistling rat, lives in open sandy and grassy regions in southern Africa.*

▽ *Using a wet log as a dining table, an Australian water rat sniffs at its meal—a fish. These rats live near rivers, lakes, and marshes. Their broad, partly webbed feet help them swim after their prey.*

Australian water rat: 11 in (28 cm) long; tail, 11 in (28 cm)

Desert wood rat: 6 in (15 cm) long; tail, 5 in (13 cm)

◁ Leaving the safety of its rocky home, a desert wood rat in California goes in search of material for its nest. Other wood rats live in nests in trees or on the ground. Wood rats collect all kinds of objects—especially shiny ones—for their nests. Sometimes an animal will drop one object to pick up another. Because of these habits, the wood rat has other names: pack rat and trade rat. People have found glass, cans, silverware, and even mousetraps in the nests of wood rats.

the brown rat—often live near people. The black rat is also known as the roof rat. It nests in upper stories of buildings as well as in trees. The brown rat, also known as the Norway rat, lives in lower parts of buildings. It is found under floors, in cellars, and in sewers. Although it often lives in filthy surroundings, the brown rat is actually a clean animal. The rat grooms its fur carefully.

When it lives away from cities, the brown rat digs burrows that include separate living and eating areas. Tunnels connect these chambers and lead to the surface. In their burrows, brown rats live together in family groups called colonies. Usually there are about fifty rats in a colony. But as many as two hundred may stay together. The members of a colony of brown rats recognize one another by their scent. If a strange rat tries to enter the burrow, the intruder is usually chased away.

Most brown rats are born in nests made of soft, shredded material. Young rats generally nurse for about three weeks. Then they begin to leave the nest to search for food. At about three months of age, they are ready to have their own young.

Some female brown rats produce seven litters in

On a grassland in Australia, two paler field rats ▷ huddle as they look for food. Unlike black rats and brown rats, which often live in towns and cities, paler field rats usually live away from people.

one year, with as many as 12 young in each litter. Very few rats live longer than a year. But a female brown rat can have many offspring. Therefore a colony can grow and remain large.

At night, a brown rat usually leaves its burrow to search for food. Brown rats will eat almost anything, including meat. They sometimes kill such animals as chickens, mice, and fish. Or they will eat meat that people have stored.

Other kinds of rats also eat meat. The cotton rat of North and South America sometimes eats eggs and young birds. The Australian water rat feeds on fish, frogs, water birds, and shellfish. The rat can crush

Paler field rat: 6 in (15 cm) long; tail, 4 in (10 cm)

White-faced spiny rat: 8 in (20 cm) long; tail, 7 in (18 cm)

White-faced spiny rat slips over a log in South America. The tails of spiny rats break off easily. Scientists believe this helps the animal escape if an enemy grabs it by the tail.

some mussels in its jaws. It must place others in the sun. The mussel dies in the heat, and the shell opens. Then the rat can eat its meal.

Many rats eat grain and other plants. Every year, a few species eat or spoil much of the grain grown in the world. Some kinds of rats are very harmful. The brown rat and the black rat cause millions of dollars in crop and property damage in the United States and in other parts of the world. The lesser bandicoot rat destroys many crops in fields and storerooms in India and in neighboring countries. The Polynesian rat also is a pest in parts of Southeast Asia and on some islands in the Pacific Ocean.

Rats do further damage by gnawing. Like all rodents, they have front teeth that grow throughout their lives. They must gnaw to keep their teeth from growing too long. Besides chewing plants, rats sometimes gnaw and damage books, furniture, metal pipes, and electrical wires.

Rats carry many diseases, including typhus and rabies. But rats sometimes are helpful as people search for cures for sicknesses. Scientists often use the animals in medical experiments in laboratories.

Most kinds of rats avoid people and do very little damage to crops. Karroo (kuh-ROO) rats live together in burrows that they dig in plains in southern Africa. During the day, they leave their burrows to feed on nearby plants. The shy animals rarely travel far from their homes. When an intruder comes too close, karroo rats quickly return underground.

Wood rats build their nests far from cities—in trees, on the ground, or in rock crevices. These rats are often called pack rats because they carry off shiny objects such as nails, silverware, glass, and cans. Wood rats use their finds to build their nests. A wood rat often may be carrying one object when it sees something it likes better. It will put the first object down and take the second one, as if it were making a trade. Because of that habit, the wood rat is also called the trade rat.

Another rat that collects objects is the giant pouched rat of Africa. It picks up pens, earrings, keys, or other small things it finds. It takes them to a storeroom in its burrow by carrying them in its teeth or in pouches in its cheeks.

Rats of all kinds are the prey of many other animals, including snakes, owls, weasels, cats, dogs, coyotes, hawks, and foxes.

Ratel

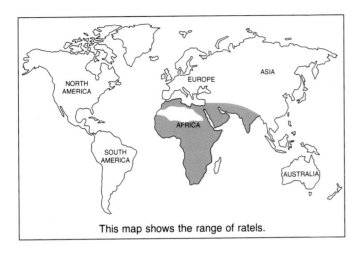

This map shows the range of ratels.

RATEL

LENGTH OF HEAD AND BODY: 24-30 in (61-76 cm); tail, 6-12 in (15-30 cm)

WEIGHT: 15-29 lb (7-13 kg)

HABITAT AND RANGE: many kinds of habitats in parts of Africa and Asia

FOOD: honey, fruit, and large and small animals, including insects

LIFE SPAN: 26 years in captivity

REPRODUCTION: 1 to 4 young after a pregnancy of 6 months

ORDER: carnivores

SNIFFING AT A HOLLOW TREE, a ratel grunts and growls. Soon the black-and-gray relative of the badger finds its goal—a nest of bees. Because it eats honey, the ratel is often called the honey badger.

When hunting for its favorite food, the ratel of Africa may have a helper. A small bird called a honey guide sometimes leads the ratel to a bees' nest. Then the bird waits for the ratel to claw open the nest. After the larger animal has eaten its fill of honey and bee larvae, the honey guide swoops in for the larvae and wax that are left. The ratel's thick skin helps protect it from bee stings.

Besides honey, the ratel feeds on snakes and small mammals as well as on insects and birds. Sometimes a ratel will kill the young of larger animals, such as wildebeests or African buffaloes.

Ratels are found in parts of Asia as well as in Africa. The animals have scent glands that produce a strong-smelling substance. Ratels travel alone, in pairs, or in small groups. They often curl up in rock crevices or in burrows that they have dug with their sharp front claws. There the animals give birth to young. A female ratel probably bears one to four offspring each year.

With its sharp claws, a ratel pokes into a crack in a dead tree. It searches for ants and termites to eat.

Reedbuck

The reedbuck is a kind of antelope. Read about antelopes on page 52.

Rhinoceros

(rye-NOSS-uh-russ)

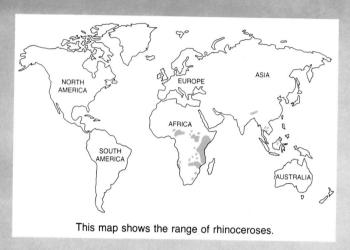

This map shows the range of rhinoceroses.

▽ *Tufted tail raised, a black rhinoceros bull splashes through a shallow lake in Tanzania. Except for females with young, black rhinos live alone—in the mountains and on the dry plains of Africa.*

WITH A SPEAR ON ITS NOSE and thick gray hide covering its body, the rhinoceros looks as tough and protected as an army tank. By the time it is fully grown, this huge plant eater has few enemies except people. People have killed most of the world's rhinoceroses to get their horns to use for carving and making medical potions.

Rhinoceros means "nose horn." Some kinds of rhinos have one large horn curving upward from their snouts. Other kinds have two. The hard horn, made of a hairlike substance, grows from the rhino's skin. Like hair, the rhino's horn keeps growing—as much as 3 inches (8 cm) a year. The longest known rhino horn measured more than 5 feet (152 cm). If a horn is broken off, a new one will grow.

In Africa, female rhinoceroses use their horns to

defend their young. The rhinos fight off attackers by hooking and butting with their horns.

There are five species, or kinds, of rhinoceroses. Two kinds live in Africa: the black rhino and the white rhino. Despite their names, both of these two-horned animals are gray.

The white rhinoceros may reach $6\frac{1}{2}$ feet (198 cm) at the shoulder. It weighs about 5,000 pounds (2,268 kg) and lives on grassy plains in temporary groups of up to a dozen animals. White rhinos carry their square muzzles close to the ground. Their heads nod as they walk and graze. Closing the hard edges of their lips tightly, they nip off the grass.

Black rhinos are smaller than white rhinos. Adults live alone in many parts of Africa—in dry inland areas, along the coast, and in the mountains. Instead of grazing, the animals browse on trees and bushes. Wrapping their pointed upper lips around twigs, leaves, thorns, and occasionally fruit, they pull the food into their mouths.

Black rhino: 5 ft (152 cm) tall at the shoulder

Both white and black rhinos feed at dawn, at dusk, and at night. When the noonday sun beats down, the animals lie in the shade or roll in the dust of dry riverbeds. When water holes are nearby, they cool off by wallowing in mud. The coating of mud or dust on their skin helps keep off insects and protects the large animals from the sun.

The Indian rhino lives in Nepal and northern India. The thick skin of this one-horned animal looks

---

RHINOCEROS ♟ **5 of 5 species**

HEIGHT: $3\frac{1}{2}$-$6\frac{1}{2}$ ft (107-198 cm) at the shoulder

WEIGHT: 2,240-5,000 lb (1,016-2,268 kg)

HABITAT AND RANGE: grasslands, shrubby areas, and dense forests of Africa and southern and southeastern Asia

FOOD: shrubs, leafy twigs, and grasses

LIFE SPAN: about 47 years in captivity

REPRODUCTION: 1 young after a pregnancy of 8 to 16 months, depending on species

ORDER: perissodactyls

◁ *Cattle egret perched on its armored back, a black rhino looks like a rock in the darkness. Sighing and rumbling, the sleeping giant frequently shifts position in the tall grass. The bird catches insects that the rhino disturbs.*

▽ *Close to its mother's side, a white rhino calf stays safe from lions and hyenas. A rhino mother defends her young furiously. If an enemy approaches, a female white rhino charges and tries to toss it into the air with her horn.*

◁ *Heavy heads nod as white rhinos cross a grassy plain in Africa. Among the largest land animals in the world, these calm giants feed in groups of as many as a dozen animals. They clear paths to their grazing grounds by walking through high grass or dense brush.*

like a suit of armor. Between stiff sections of hide are folds of thinner, more flexible skin. The folds allow the animal's body to move.

On its way to grazing grounds, the Indian rhino travels tunnel-like paths through grass that grows 25 feet (8 m) high. To feed, it curls its pointed upper lip around tall grass stems. It bends the stems over and bites them off. The Indian rhino has large, sharp teeth. A female defends her young by swinging her head and slashing with the teeth in her lower jaw.

In Indonesia, on the western tip of the island of Java, lives another one-horned rhinoceros. It once ranged over much of southeastern Asia. But today only about fifty animals remain in an isolated preserve on the island.

Another kind of rhino lives on the island of Sumatra and in other parts of southeastern Asia. The Sumatran rhino has two horns. The smallest of all rhinos, it measures about 4 feet (122 cm) high at the shoulder and weighs about 2,240 pounds (1,016 kg). The Sumatran rhino has bristlelike hairs on its body. In captivity, the rhino may grow a shaggy coat. Other

White rhino: 6 ft (183 cm) tall at the shoulder

rhinos are nearly hairless, except for tufts at the tips of their ears and at the ends of their tails.

Rhinoceroses look awkward, but they are surprisingly nimble and quick. The Indian rhino may charge at 30 miles (48 km) an hour. Rhinos can jump, twist, and turn quickly. Thick, spongy pads cushion

Rhinoceros

△ One-horned Indian rhino feeds on tall elephant grass. The animal grasps the food with its pointed upper lip. Then it bends the stem over and bites it off.

In the rainy dawn, Indian rhinos wade in a forest ▷ pond. Mud covers their armored hides. When dry, the mud forms a crust that helps protect the animals from sun and insects. Indian rhinos feed during the coolest parts of the day. To escape the midday heat, they wallow chin-deep in water (lower right).

the animals' feet as they move. Rhinos depend on their keen senses of hearing and smell. Often one rhino finds another by sniffing along its trail.

The huge animals communicate with many sounds. They snort, snarl threateningly, and roar. Fighting rhinos grunt and scream. Males and females court with whistling noises.

Every three or four years, a female rhino, called a cow, bears a single calf. On the calf's nose is a smooth, flat plate where its horn will grow. Two-horned rhino calves have two plates. The playful newborn frisks and runs. A rhino cow comforts her young with soft mewing noises. She fiercely defends it from such enemies as lions, hyenas, and crocodiles. The young rhino goes off on its own shortly before its mother bears another calf.

Indian rhino: 5¹/₂ ft (168 cm) tall at the shoulder

Ringtail

DURING THE GOLD RUSH in the American West, prospectors often kept ringtails in their camps to catch rats and mice. The animal's slender body, long whiskers, and big appetite for small rodents earned it other names: miner's cat and coon cat.

This expert ratcatcher is not a cat at all. The dark rings on its bushy tail mark it as a member of the raccoon family. The animal's most striking feature has led to its common name, ringtail. The tail—measuring as long as 17 inches (43 cm)—may be longer than the ringtail's head and body.

Active at night, the ringtail roams forests, deserts, and canyons in parts of the western United States and Mexico. It feeds on small animals, fruit, and plants. This skilled climber easily darts up and down trees. Its hind feet turn backward, and the animal can grasp a tree's bark with its sharp claws when it goes down a trunk headfirst.

During the day, the ringtail rests in a sheltered spot. It lives alone, except during the mating season. As many as four young are born in the spring.

The cacomistle (KACK-uh-miss-ul) is a slightly larger relative. It spends most of its time in trees in tropical regions in Mexico and Central America.

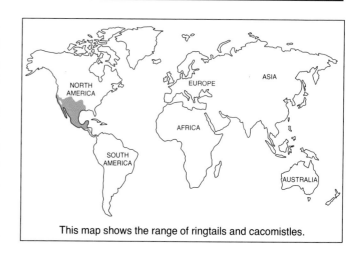

This map shows the range of ringtails and cacomistles.

RINGTAIL AND CACOMISTLE

LENGTH OF HEAD AND BODY: 12-20 in (30-51 cm); tail, 13-20 in (33-51 cm)

WEIGHT: 24 oz-3 lb (680 g-1 kg)

HABITAT AND RANGE: deserts, canyons, and forests from Oregon to Panama

FOOD: rodents, insects, birds, fruit, and plants

LIFE SPAN: 23 years in captivity

REPRODUCTION: 1 to 4 young after a pregnancy of about 2 months

ORDER: carnivores

Bushy, banded tail ▷ dangles as a ringtail rests on a narrow limb in Arizona. An expert climber, the ringtail uses its sharp claws for gripping and its tail for balancing. The tail may be longer than its head and body.

◁ Bright-eyed ringtail pokes its head out of a hollow log. Inside, it has lined a den with grass, leaves, and moss. The opening is just large enough for the ringtail to squeeze through. Ringtails often sleep in crowded spaces in small caves or between rocks.

Ringtail: 12 in (30 cm) long; tail, 17 in (43 cm)

Saki
The saki is a kind of monkey.
Read about monkeys on page 370.

Seal and Sea lion

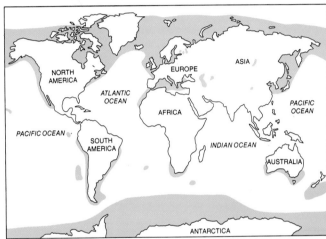

This map shows the range of seals and sea lions.

AMONG THE STAR PERFORMERS at many circuses are trained California sea lions. These sleek, playful seals balance balls on their noses, bark on command, and jump through hoops. In the wild, California sea lions live in the Pacific Ocean off the rocky coast of western North America and around the Galapagos Islands off South America. The sea lion is one of more than thirty kinds, or species, of seals that inhabit seacoasts throughout much of the world. The largest seal—the southern elephant seal—weighs as much as 8,000 pounds (3,629 kg). An adult ringed seal may weigh as little as 107 pounds (49 kg).

Seals feed on fish, squid, seabirds, and other sea animals called krill that they catch with their pointed teeth. They have keen eyesight and excellent hearing. Not all seals have ears that can be seen, however. Some have only tiny holes in the sides of their heads.

Crabeater seals stretch out on an iceberg. By moving their front flippers in a circle and twisting their bodies, these seals can skim the ice at 15 miles (24 km) an hour!

Crabeater seal: 8½ ft (259 cm) long

Seal and Sea lion

Nose to nose, a female ▷
harp seal and her pup sniff
each other. This young white-
coated seal will begin to shed
its baby fur soon after birth.
Gradually, its light coat will
turn dark.

▽ *Young harbor seal swims*
with its mother off the coast of
California. Pups are born
on the shore. They can swim
immediately, and sometimes
they must. The next tide may
cover their birthplace.

Harp seal: 6½ ft (198 cm) long

Harbor seal: 6 ft (183 cm) long

These animals are called earless seals or hair seals. Other seals—called eared seals or sea lions and fur seals—have small ears.

Many kinds of seals live in cold, icy water. A thick layer of fat, called blubber, lines their skins and protects them from low temperatures. Like all marine mammals, seals must swim to the surface to breathe. Weddell seals keep holes open in the ice by gnawing with their sharp teeth.

A few kinds of seals live in warmer waters. Rare monk seals, for example, are found near the Hawaiian Islands and in the Mediterranean Sea.

Seals spend most of the time in the water. Many kinds may not come ashore for weeks at a time. Seals are natural and graceful swimmers. A harbor seal swims by holding its front flippers flat against its body and moving its back flippers from side to side. Sea lions, however, paddle with their front flippers. They use their back flippers only to steer.

When on land, sea lions and fur seals move by lifting themselves up and walking on all four flippers. Hair seals, such as crabeater seals, can only wriggle along on their stomachs. Surprisingly, the crabeater is the fastest seal on land. It can slide along the ice as fast as 15 miles (24 km) an hour.

For most of the year, fur seals swim alone or in small groups. But during the breeding season they come ashore in great numbers. On the islands off the coast of Alaska, older males, called bulls, stake out territories, or areas. There as many as forty females may crowd together. The bulls bark and growl as each fights to control his territory. Younger males without territories gather elsewhere.

During this time, a female fur seal, or cow, bears a single pup. A few days later, the cow mates with a bull. The next year, *(Continued on page 497)*

In shallow waters, a Hawaiian monk seal swims past ▷
a coral reef. Only about 600 monk seals remain in
Hawaii. Laws now protect these endangered animals.

Hawaiian monk seal: 7½ ft (229 cm) long

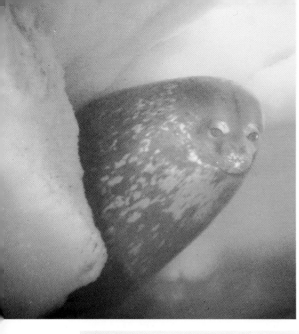

Seal and Sea lion _____

◁ *Snug beneath the ice, a Weddell seal finds shelter in antarctic waters. Closing its nostrils to keep water out, a Weddell seal can dive as deep as 1,900 feet (579 m). It can hold its breath for as long as an hour.*
Weddell seal: 11 ft (3 m) long

Leopard seal clutches a penguin with its teeth. Skillful hunters, leopard ▷ *seals prey on seabirds, grabbing them from below as they rest on the water.*

▽ *Southern elephant seals crowd together among clumps of grass on an island off South America. Largest of the seals, male elephant seals may grow more than 20 feet (6 m) long and weigh 8,000 pounds (3,629 kg). They get their name not because of their size but because of their trunklike snouts.*

△ *Young northern elephant seals play in waters off Mexico. Their snouts may grow 15 inches (38 cm) long.*

SEAL AND SEA LION 🐾 **12 of 33 species**

LENGTH OF HEAD AND BODY: **4-20 ft (122 cm-6 m)**

WEIGHT: **107-8,000 lb (49-3,629 kg)**

HABITAT AND RANGE: **coastal waters throughout much of the world, especially in the polar regions, and some freshwater lakes in Asia**

FOOD: **fish, krill, squid, octopuses, shellfish, and seabirds**

LIFE SPAN: **17 to 46 years in the wild, depending on species**

REPRODUCTION: **I young after a pregnancy of 7 to 12 months, depending on species**

ORDER: **pinnipeds**

she will return to give birth again. She nurses her young for four months.

Most newborn hair seals nurse for two to six weeks. A hair seal cow does not take care of her pup for very long. The offspring must survive on its own after only a few weeks.

Polar bears, sharks, and large porpoises called orcas all prey on seals, especially the young. When attacked, a seal may try to defend itself by biting. Or it may quickly dive deep or hide in a hard-to-reach place between rocks or under ice.

People kill seals for their fur or for their blubber. For centuries, some kinds of seals, such as the monk seals and the northern fur seals, were hunted until they were almost extinct. Today laws help to protect these animals.

◁ *South African fur seals gather along a beach in Namibia at the beginning of the mating season. The animals communicate by making a wide variety of noises: honks, bleats, growls, and roars.*
▽ *Underwater acrobats, Australian sea lions glide gracefully through the Indian Ocean. These playful marine mammals have flexible, streamlined bodies.*

▽ *Female northern sea lion barks a threat at a male nearly three times her size. The male, called a bull, controls a small area of land on the rocky coast of Alaska. Within this territory lives a harem of as many as thirty females, or cows. The bull will mate with them, and the cows will each bear a pup the following year.*

Northern sea lion: 10 ft (305 cm) long

South African fur seal: 7¹/₂ ft (229 cm) long

Australian sea lion: 6¹/₂ ft (198 cm) long

Serow

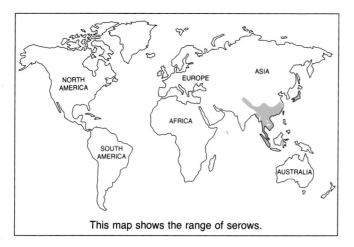

This map shows the range of serows.

SEROW 🐾 2 of 3 species

HEIGHT: 22-39 in (56-99 cm) at the shoulder

WEIGHT: 110-309 lb (50-140 kg)

HABITAT AND RANGE: wooded mountainous areas in parts of Asia

FOOD: grasses, herbs, leaves, shoots, and twigs

LIFE SPAN: up to 19 years in captivity

REPRODUCTION: usually 1 young after a pregnancy of about 7 months

ORDER: artiodactyls

IN THE RUGGED MOUNTAINS in parts of Asia, the serow picks its way across steep, thickly wooded slopes. Like its close relative the chamois, the serow rarely loses its footing. Short, pointed horns grow from the heads of both males and females, and rough coats cover the animals' goat-size bodies. An adult serow's hair may range from black to red. Some kinds of serows have manes and beards.

Serows may rest much of the day among rocks, in caves, or in dense underbrush. They feed on grasses, herbs, leaves, shoots, and twigs.

Adult serows often live alone in a territory, or area. Each animal marks out its territory by rubbing rocks and branches with a sticky substance produced by glands under its eyes.

Serows mate in the fall. About seven months later, the female gives birth, usually to one young, called a kid. A male serow may stay with the female and kid for a few months. At about a year old, the kid may go off on its own.

Japanese serow: 22 in (56 cm) tall at the shoulder

◁ *Chest-deep in snow, a Japanese serow and her kid find dry leaves to eat. A female serow usually gives birth to one kid. The young stays with its mother for about a year.*

Thick woods line a steep ▷ gorge, home of a Japanese serow and her kid. Serows— surefooted relatives of chamois—live in many Asian countries. They clamber easily along well-worn paths on mountain slopes. They often rest among rocks, in caves, or in dense underbrush.

Serval
The serval is a kind of cat. Read about cats on page 126.

Sheep

HIGH ON A RIDGE, two Rocky Mountain bighorn sheep prepare to battle. Both are males, called rams. They show off their large, curved horns. They growl and kick at each other. Then the rams walk away, turn to face one another, and rise on their hind legs. Suddenly, they lunge, charging at 20 miles (32 km) an hour. Their horns clash, making a loud bang. The sound can be heard a mile away. The rams' stocky, grayish brown bodies actually compress as they come together. After standing still for a moment, the rams repeat the display and clash again.

The battle may continue for hours. But often a fight ends after four or five charges. One ram finally turns away. By giving up, he recognizes the winner as a stronger ram.

Bighorn sheep live in the Rocky Mountains from New Mexico into Canada. Their close relatives, desert

Rocky Mountain bighorn sheep: 40 in (102 cm) tall at the shoulder

bighorns, are found from the southwestern United States into Mexico. Smaller and thinner than Rocky Mountain sheep, desert bighorns roam where few large animals can survive.

Two other kinds of wild sheep inhabit North

From a ridge in Montana, Rocky Mountain bighorn sheep watch for coyotes and mountain lions. Male sheep, called rams, roam together in herds. Rams usually stay with females only during mating season.

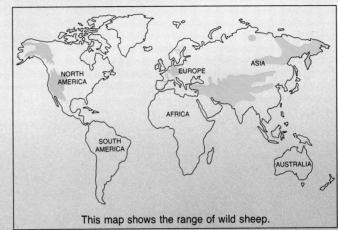

This map shows the range of wild sheep.

America. White Dall's sheep and grayish black Stone's sheep live in the mountains of Alaska and western Canada. Both have slender, widely curving horns that are lighter than those of bighorn sheep. People sometimes call them thinhorns. Other kinds of wild sheep are found in Europe and in Asia.

Wild sheep are relatives of wild goats, and the animals somewhat resemble each other. Like goats, many sheep can move quickly and easily on uneven ground. Their hooves spread out to help them keep their footing. The rough bottoms and hard outer edges usually do not slip as the animals leap from rock to rock. Read about goats on page 232.

All wild rams—and most females, called ewes—have horns. Unlike a deer's antlers, which drop off

△ *In a snowstorm, young Rocky Mountain bighorn rams fight to determine which is stronger. They rise on their hind*

each winter, a sheep's horns grow longer every year. Most of the growth takes place in spring and summer, when the sheep can find plenty to eat. The deep grooves across a ram's horns show where they stopped growing each fall. By counting the grooves, it is possible to find out a ram's age.

A ram's curving horns can show other details of the animal's life. Broken and splintered tips are the results of fights with other rams. Horns that form a complete circle show that the ram is old. A bighorn ram's horns may weigh 30 pounds (14 kg)—perhaps more than all the bones in his body. The horns of a ewe are smaller than those of a ram.

Like other wild sheep, male and female bighorns and thinhorns live apart for most of the year. Rams

◁ *In Yellowstone National Park, a Rocky Mountain bighorn lamb nibbles tiny plants called lichens from a rock.*

Sheep

roam in herds with other rams. Ewes remain with their lambs and other ewes. In the fall, bighorn rams begin to gather in larger groups. At that time of the year, the number of fights increases. The older rams with larger, heavier horns generally win.

Usually only the strongest rams mate with the ewes when the males and females meet in November and December. After the mating season, the male and female herds separate. When the snow falls, the animals descend to lower mountain slopes.

Older rams lead the male group to the feeding grounds, which may be 25 miles (40 km) away. The

Bighorn ram in Montana munches seeds. Bighorns ▷
usually feed on grass, but they also eat other plants.

legs (above, left) and lunge straight at each other (above, center). The rams try to crash head-on. But the horns slip sideways (above, right) and hit the shoulders. In contrast to older rams, the horns of these animals are still small.

females sometimes travel, but usually for shorter distances. At their feeding grounds, the sheep nibble plants that poke through the snow. Or they may paw through deep, soft drifts to reach the grasses underneath. They may also look for places where the wind has swept the ground clear.

While eating, the sheep must be alert to such enemies as wolves, bears, coyotes, and mountain lions. Bighorns feed mainly on grasses. They swallow the grass after chewing it only a little. The food is stored in the bighorn's stomach. After eating, the animal brings up a wad of the partly digested food—called a cud. It chews it thoroughly. Then it swallows the cud, so that it can be digested further.

Late in May, many bighorn ewes pick their way along rocky cliffs to high ledges where enemies can't reach them. There the lambs are born. A ewe and her lamb remain by themselves for about a week. Then

they join the other females and young. Bighorn lambs play often. They butt heads, paw the ground, and jump into the air. As the lamb grows, it spends less time with its mother. The ewe pays little attention to her offspring, except to nurse it. She may defend her young, though, especially against golden eagles, which swoop down from the sky.

SHEEP　🐾 **6 of 7 species**

HEIGHT: 22-51 in (56-130 cm) at the shoulder

WEIGHT: 40-450 lb (18-204 kg)

HABITAT AND RANGE: mountains, forests, and rocky regions in North America, Europe, and Asia; domestic sheep are found in many parts of the world

FOOD: grasses, herbs, leaves, shoots, and twigs

LIFE SPAN: as long as 25 years in the wild

REPRODUCTION: 1 to 4 young after a pregnancy of about 5 or 6 months, depending on species

ORDER: artiodactyls

Sheep

Bighorns and other wild sheep look very different from the domestic, or tame, sheep raised by people in many parts of the world. Scientists believe that domestic sheep are descended from a wild relative called the mouflon (MOO-flun).

Mouflons are among the smallest wild sheep. In Europe, they once lived only on rocky islands near Italy. By the mid-1800s, the mouflon had nearly died out there because of hunting. But people took some of the animals into forested mountains in France, Austria, and Germany. Though they are still rare in their island homes, thousands of mouflons live in other parts of Europe. Like other wild sheep, mouflons may have summer and winter ranges. But mouflons do not live very high in the mountains. They often stay on lower, forested slopes.

Mouflons and the closely related urial (OOR-ee-ul) also live in Asia. The urial is usually larger than the mouflon. All male urials have neck ruffs of long hair. Asian sheep live mainly in rolling country and on high plains, rather than in steep, craggy areas. Most Asian sheep are thinner and have longer legs than the bighorns of North America.

The largest of all the wild sheep also lives in the wilderness areas of Asia. The argali (ARE-guh-lee) of Siberia and Mongolia may measure more than 4 feet (122 cm) tall at the shoulder. It can weigh as much as

▽ *Dall's sheep graze on a mountain slope in Alaska. Because of their slender, widely curved horns, people sometimes call the animals thinhorns.*

White coats dot a grassy ridge as Dall's sheep ▷ *graze in front of Alaska's Mount McKinley, the highest peak in North America.*
▽ *Come on, get up! A Dall's lamb paws its mother's back. It may want to play.*

△ Surefooted Dall's ewe leads her lamb across the rocky face of a mountain.

△ Crowned with curving horns, a Dall's ram grazes in Alaska. A sheep's horns grow throughout the animal's life. On older rams, the horns may form more than a complete circle.

Dall's sheep: 36 in (91 cm) tall at the shoulder

505

German Heath sheep: 27 in (69 cm) tall at the shoulder

△ Shepherd and his sheep dog herd a flock of Romney ewes through a rolling pasture in New Zealand. Domestic, or tame, sheep like the Romney look very different from their wild relatives. Romney sheep lack horns. People raise the sheep for meat and for their long wool.

△ Long coat of grayish white wool covers an adult German Heath sheep, a centuries-old breed. The black wool of a newborn will change color as the offspring grows older. People raise these sheep for milk, meat, and wool.

◁ Mouflon ram chews his cud in a forest clearing in France. There he finds shelter from winter winds. European mouflons had nearly died out about a hundred years ago. Today they live in many places. Scientists think all breeds of domestic sheep developed from the closely related Asian mouflon.

Mouflon: 27 in (69 cm) tall at the shoulder

450 pounds (204 kg). Slightly smaller is the Marco Polo sheep, a kind of argali named for the explorer who traveled from Italy to Asia in the 1200s. Marco Polo sheep are famous for the size of their horns. A horn may measure 6 feet (183 cm) along the curl!

Scientists think sheep were first tamed at least 10,000 years ago. People probably used the animals for meat, hides, and milk. The first domestic sheep had coarse outer coats of straight hair with soft, fine undercoats. Over the centuries, people have developed breeds with coats of fleecy wool. The wool is sheared off, spun into yarn, and woven to make cloth. Sheep are not hurt by the shearing. Their wool grows back in a few months.

Some sheep, like the Merino (muh-REE-no) sheep, a breed that was developed in Spain, are known for their very fine wool. These animals were once so valuable that it was a crime to take a Merino sheep out of Spain. Long-wooled Romney sheep were first developed in England for meat, called lamb or mutton, as well as for wool. Shropshire sheep from England have been bred mainly for meat.

Thin grooves on the deeply ridged horns of a Punjab urial in Pakistan show where the horns stopped growing each fall. This five-and-a-half-year-old ram has a neck ruff of long hair that will fall out after the mating season. Urial ewes have no ruffs. Their horns do not grow as large as the males' horns. Like goats, urials have pointed ears.

Punjab urial: 31 in (79 cm) tall at the shoulder

Shrew

SHREW 🐾 **113 of 322 species**

LENGTH OF HEAD AND BODY: 1-12 in (3-30 cm); tail, 1-10 in (3-25 cm)

WEIGHT: less than $1/15$ oz-19 oz (2-539 g)

HABITAT AND RANGE: almost every kind of habitat throughout most of Asia, Africa, Europe, North America, and northern parts of South America

FOOD: insects, worms, snails, and other small animals

LIFE SPAN: 1 to 4 years in the wild

REPRODUCTION: 1 to 10 young after a pregnancy of about 2 to 8 weeks, depending on species

ORDER: insectivores

Golden-rumped elephant shrew: 12 in (30 cm) long; tail, 10 in (25 cm)

△ *With its long, pointed snout, a golden-rumped elephant shrew probes for insects in a forest in Kenya. Elephant shrews—unrelated to other shrews—spend the day looking for food on the forest floor.*

▽ *Plump and furry, a short-tailed shrew seems harmless. For its weight, however, the shrew is one of the world's fiercest animals. A short-tailed shrew can quickly kill small prey with its poisonous bite.*

Short-tailed shrew: 3 in (8 cm) long; tail, 1 in (3 cm)

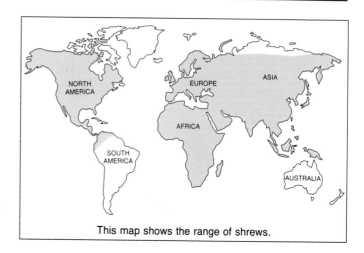

This map shows the range of shrews.

FEROCIOUS AND OFTEN HUNGRY, the shrew is quick to attack small animals, including other shrews. For its size—just inches long—it is one of the fiercest animals in the world. It keeps its active body supplied with energy by feeding almost constantly. Many shrews eat their weight in food every day. A 50-pound (23-kg) child would have to eat about 200 hamburgers to do the same thing!

Sniffing about, a shrew searches for such foods as insects, worms, snails, and other small animals. One kind of shrew, the short-tailed shrew, has poison in its saliva that kills small prey. The animal will even attack and eat a large mouse.

The short-tailed shrew is only one of more than thirty species, or kinds, of shrews found in the United States. In all, more than 300 species of shrews live in many parts of the world.

Most shrews look like sharp-nosed gray or brown mice. But shrews are not rodents. They are relatives of moles. Shrews have soft, dense fur that is darker on their backs than on their bellies. Although a few kinds of shrews have bodies 12 inches (30 cm) long, most of the animals are much smaller. The tiniest shrew—the Etruscan pygmy shrew—is one of the smallest mammals on earth. Shorter than 3 inches (8 cm) from its nose to the tip of its tail, it weighs less than a dime.

Shrews have keen hearing. Some kinds make

Northern water shrew rests on a log before taking a ▷ dip in a lake in Colorado. A good swimmer, the animal spends most of its life in or near streams and lakes.

Northern water shrew: 3 in (8 cm) long; tail, 3 in (8 cm)

Shrew

Common shrew: 3 in (8 cm) long; tail, 2 in (5 cm)

◁ *Exploring a bed of moss and grass, a common shrew searches for worms and insects in an English woodland. A sensitive snout leads the animal to its prey.*

Shrews seek shelter in piles of leaves, between rocks, or in underground burrows. Many sleep during the day and come out at night. Others scurry about during both the day and the night, taking short rests from time to time.

Many shrews live alone in areas called territories. Some kinds of elephant shrews—named for their long, flexible snouts—have scent glands at the bases of their tails. They mark their territories with an oily substance from these glands. If one elephant shrew comes into another's territory, the intruder is quickly chased away. Other kinds of shrews claw and bite unwelcome visitors. Usually they do not fight to the death. Instead, the loser surrenders by lying on its back and squealing.

Some kinds of shrews give birth to young about two weeks after mating. These shrews may have several pregnancies a year. Females bear from one to ten offspring at a time, depending on the species.

high-pitched, clicking sounds that human beings cannot hear. When the sounds hit an object, echoes bounce back. From the echoes, shrews can locate food—or obstacles. This process is called echolocation (ek-oh-low-KAY-shun). Bats and porpoises also use echolocation to hunt and to find their way. You can read about them under their own headings.

Follow the leader! A chain of bicolor white-toothed shrews moves like a snake through the woods. Young shrews fall into line behind their mother. Each bites onto the fur of the animal in front of it.

Siamang The siamang is a kind of gibbon. Read about gibbons on page 222.

Sifaka The sifaka is a kind of lemur. Read about lemurs on page 318.

Skunk

Stretching for food, a striped skunk in Minnesota licks insects from a stump.

BUSHY TAIL WAVING and front feet stamping, the skunk tries to scare an attacker away. If it does not succeed, it turns around, looks back, and sprays a bitter-smelling mist. Some skunks can spray an area as far as 10 feet (305 cm) away.

The spray—an oily, yellow liquid—is produced by two glands under the skunk's tail. The smell is very strong and can linger for days. The spray may produce a burning feeling in the eyes of the victim. But it causes no permanent damage.

Because of its scent, the small black-and-white skunk has little to fear. It trots boldly through open woodlands and across fields in North America. The

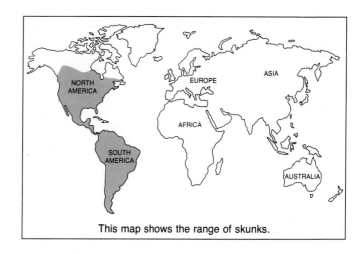

This map shows the range of skunks.

511

Hog-nosed skunk: 16 in (41 cm) long; tail, 9 in (23 cm)

△ *Tail in the air, a hog-nosed skunk in Chile looks for small prey to eat. Its broad, bare snout gives the animal its name. The blunt shape of the nose allows the skunk to root easily in the dirt for insects and larvae. It also feeds on rodents.*

Spotted skunk waves its ▷ bushy, white-tipped tail in a canyon in Arizona. Although most skunks are marked by broad bands of white fur, this animal's coat has spots and streaks.

Spotted skunk: 11 in (28 cm) long; tail, 7 in (18 cm)

Skunk _____

Claws gripping the bark, a pygmy spotted skunk ▷
pauses on a log. These rare Mexican skunks move more
nimbly than most of their larger relatives.

hog-nosed skunk also roams South America. Though
most skunks are small animals, large meat eaters often avoid them. Foxes, bobcats, coyotes, and owls may
attack skunks if there is little other food. But after they
have been sprayed once, they probably will have
learned their lesson and will stay away. Some scientists think that the skunk's markings serve as a warning signal to other animals.

There are several kinds of skunks. All have black-
and-white fur. But the patterns of their coats vary. The
striped skunk can be easily recognized by the two
white stripes along its back. The hog-nosed skunk often has a white back and tail. The spotted skunk has
streaks and spots of white on its body. Its tail is tipped
with white.

Skunks take shelter in burrows that were built by
other animals. There they may make a dry, leaf-lined
nest. They also live in piles of rocks or in hollow logs.

▽ *Spotted skunk takes its warning position. To spray*
an attacker, it returns to all fours. Before they stand on
their forefeet, skunks usually try to frighten enemies
away by stamping their feet and waving their tails.

Pygmy spotted skunk: 8 in (20 cm) long; tail, 5 in (13 cm)

Sometimes they build their nests in old buildings.

When the weather is cold, striped skunks often
sleep for a few weeks at a time. Several of them may
huddle in the same den. At other times of the year,
skunks usually rest most of the day. At night, they
prowl and sniff among leaves and underbrush. They
search for insects and larvae, earthworms, eggs, reptiles, and small mammals.

A female skunk bears from two to ten young
once a year. Though the newborn are hairless, they already have light and dark markings in their skins.
Young skunks may leave their mother after four
months. But some sleep in her den all winter.

SKUNK

LENGTH OF HEAD AND BODY: 8-19 in (20-48 cm); tail, 5-15 in
(13-38 cm)

WEIGHT: 7 oz-14 lb (198 g-6 kg)

HABITAT AND RANGE: open woodlands, brushy areas, fields,
prairies, and deserts in North and South America

FOOD: insects and larvae, earthworms, eggs, reptiles, small
mammals, fish, fruit, and plants

LIFE SPAN: up to 13 years in captivity

REPRODUCTION: 2 to 10 young after a pregnancy of at least
2 months, depending on species

ORDER: carnivores

Sloth

(SLAWTH)

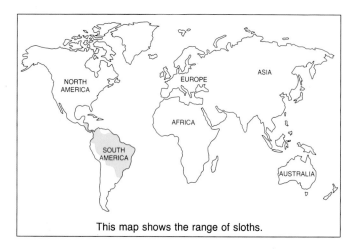

This map shows the range of sloths.

MOTIONLESS FOR HOURS, a sleeping sloth hangs upside down from a branch or curls up in the fork of a tree. The fur of this shaggy animal blends well with the trees of dense forests in Central and South America. Because the climate where it lives is moist and warm, tiny plants called algae often grow on the animal's fur. The plants give a green shimmer to the sloth's grayish brown coat.

This protective coloring makes the sloth difficult to see in the trees and helps hide it from enemies. The

Three-toed sloth: 22 in (56 cm) long; tail, 2 in (5 cm)

△ *Young three-toed sloth hugs its mother, clinging tightly to her long fur. A sloth offspring rides with its mother until it reaches the age of nine months.*

Under a roof of broad leaves, a shaggy ▷ three-toed sloth hangs on and stretches out an arm. The number of claws on each front foot makes it easy to distinguish the animal from its two-toed relative.

◁ *Arm over arm, a three-toed sloth swims in a river in Colombia. By accident, a sloth sometimes tumbles from a tree into the water. This good swimmer may travel a long way before getting out and climbing another tree. On the ground, however, a sloth is the slowest mammal on earth. Its belly rubs the ground as it pulls itself along with its front claws. The animal's weak hind legs and long claws make walking impossible.*

Two-toed sloth: 24 in (61 cm) long

△ *Two-toed sloth makes its way along a tree branch upside down. When it rains, water runs off the sloth's long, coarse fur. Unlike the coats of other animals, a sloth's fur grows from its belly toward its back.*

◁ *From any direction, juicy leaves look good to a two-toed sloth. Because the animal has no front teeth, it must pull the food off with its lips. It chews with side teeth. The leafy diet contains almost all the water a sloth needs.*

sloth, about 2 feet (61 cm) long, is the slowest mammal in the world. It cannot outrun the jungle cats that prey on it. It cannot run at all!

When cornered, a sloth tries to defend itself by clawing and nipping. Its heavy, coarse fur and thick skin give it some protection.

Unlike its relatives, the anteater and the armadillo, the sloth is almost helpless on the ground. The sloth's curved claws—useful for climbing—make it hard for the animal to stand. The sloth's legs are too weak to support its weight. To move on the ground, it must lie on its stomach and reach ahead for a claw hold. Then it slowly drags its body forward. In the water, though, the sloth is a good swimmer.

Sloths spend almost all of their lives in the trees. Sloths sleep, eat, and mate high above the ground. Females give birth to young while they hang from tree limbs by their hooklike claws. Sloths have such firm

grips that, even when they die, they sometimes remain attached to branches!

The word *sloth* means "laziness." The animal lives up to its name. A sloth sleeps about 15 hours each day. At night, it travels through the trees in slow motion, feeding on leaves, shoots, and fruit. It rarely drinks water. The sloth gets most of the moisture it needs by eating leaves and licking dew.

The sloth does not hear well. But it has keen senses of smell and touch, which it depends on to find food. The sloth also has very good eyesight. And it can turn its flexible neck far to each side so that it can see in almost every direction.

All of these animals have three toes on each hind foot. But the number of toes on their front feet varies. Scientists divide sloths into groups by the number of toes the animals have on each front foot: two-toed sloths and three-toed sloths. A three-toed sloth is also called an ai (EYE) because of its long, drawn-out call: "ah-eee."

Sloths live alone or occasionally in pairs. A female sloth gives birth to one offspring a year. The newborn sloth has tiny claws, which it uses to climb onto its mother's belly soon after birth. For about a month, it clings to her long hair. Then it begins to move about by itself. When the young sloth is about nine months old, the mother forces it to go off on its own. She nips her offspring whenever it tries to catch a ride with her.

SLOTH 🐾 I of 5 species

LENGTH OF HEAD AND BODY: 20-25 in (51-64 cm); tail, as long as 3 in (8 cm)

WEIGHT: 9-20 lb (4-9 kg)

HABITAT AND RANGE: forests in parts of Central and South America

FOOD: leaves, shoots, and fruit

LIFE SPAN: as long as 30 years in captivity

REPRODUCTION: I young after a pregnancy of 3 to II months

ORDER: xenarthrans

Solenodon

(so-LEAN-uh-don)

SOLENODON 🐾 2 of 2 species

LENGTH OF HEAD AND BODY: about 12 in (30 cm); tail, about 9 in (23 cm)

WEIGHT: about 2 lb (I kg)

HABITAT AND RANGE: remote forests and rocky, shrubby areas in parts of the West Indies

FOOD: insects, worms, and small reptiles

LIFE SPAN: about 10 years in captivity

REPRODUCTION: I to 3 young after a pregnancy of unknown length

ORDER: insectivores

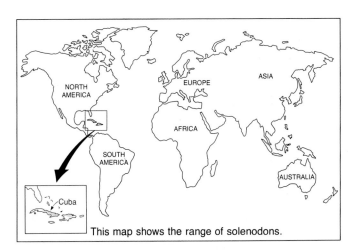

This map shows the range of solenodons.

WITH ITS POINTED SNOUT and long, hairless tail, the solenodon looks like a member of the rat family. But it is not. This animal's relatives include the shrew and the mole. A rare animal, the solenodon lives only in a few remote parts of the West Indies.

As the solenodon moves about, it makes clicking noises in its throat. Echoes that are caused when the sounds hit objects may help the solenodon find its way. It digs into hollow logs with its sharp front claws, looking for insects, worms, and small reptiles. Glands in the solenodon's mouth produce a deadly liquid. The animal's bite poisons its prey.

A female solenodon bears one to three young.

Snout up, a Haitian solenodon sniffs the night air for the scent of prey—insects and other small animals.

Haitian solenodon: 12 in (30 cm) long; tail, 9 in (23 cm)

Springbok

The springbok is a kind of antelope. Read about antelopes on page 52.

Squirrel

(SKWURL)

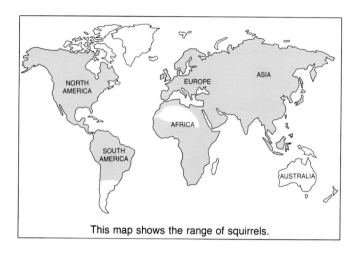

This map shows the range of squirrels.

BRIGHT-EYED AND BUSHY-TAILED, a tree squirrel scampers headfirst down a tree. The furry rodent searches for food on the ground. Suddenly rising on its hind feet, the squirrel looks around. It senses danger and leaps onto a nearby tree, disappearing behind the trunk. Back on a limb near its nest, it flicks its tail, noisily chattering the entire time.

Squirrels live almost everywhere on earth. There are more than 200 species, or kinds. They are found in forests, deserts, mountains, and grasslands. They range in size from the African pygmy squirrel, only about 5 inches (13 cm) long including its tail, to the Indian giant squirrel, about 3 feet (91 cm) long.

Harris's antelope ground squirrel: 6 in (15 cm) long; tail, 3 in (8 cm)

△ *White fur rings the eye of a red squirrel eating a plant in Alaska. These small, noisy tree squirrels of North America often chatter loudly in trees.*

Though most squirrels have coats of gray or brown, some may be red, black, or white. The Indian giant squirrel has a brightly colored coat of red, black, and pale yellow. The thirteen-lined ground squirrel has stripes and spots.

Despite their differences, all squirrels have front teeth—two upper and two lower—that continue to grow all their lives. Like all rodents, squirrels must gnaw to keep these teeth worn down.

There are three main groups of squirrels: ground squirrels, tree squirrels, and flying squirrels. Ground squirrels rarely climb trees. Some kinds live alone in burrows that they dig. Others, like the California ground squirrel, live together. Their tunnel systems may have several openings and may extend hundreds of feet.

During the day, ground squirrels eat low-growing plants and other food that they find on the

△ *Nose to cheek, two arctic ground squirrels nuzzle each other. These large squirrels hibernate in their burrows for seven months or more during cold winters in parts of northern North America.*

◁ *Harris's antelope ground squirrel in Arizona perches carefully on the spines of a barrel cactus. It eats the fruit at the center. This kind of squirrel also feeds on other desert plants, seeds, and insects.*

519

Squirrel

ground—seeds, roots, bulbs, nuts, and leaves. They also eat insects. To catch a grasshopper, a ground squirrel will chase it and pounce. It pins the insect to the ground with its front paws and then bites off its head. A squirrel kills a caterpillar by striking it with the claws on its front feet. All ground squirrels have pouches in their cheeks. They use these to carry food to storerooms in their burrows.

Some kinds of ground squirrels in cold regions spend most of the winter sleeping in their burrows. This sleep is called hibernation (hye-bur-NAY-shun). When a ground squirrel hibernates, it rolls up in a ball. Its tail curls over its head, and its nose touches its belly. The squirrel lies very still. Its breathing and heart rate slow down, and its temperature drops. It eats little during the cold months, waking up only a few times. It usually lives on fat it has stored in its

In the Rocky Mountains of Wyoming, a golden- ▷ mantled ground squirrel carries grass for its nest.

Golden-mantled ground squirrel: 7 in (18 cm) long; tail, 4 in (10 cm)

Kaibab squirrel: 11 in (28 cm) long; tail, 8 in (20 cm)

△ With food in its paws, a white-tailed Kaibab squirrel in Arizona sits up for a snack. This kind of tree squirrel has tufts on its ears. It lives only in a small area north of the Grand Canyon.

▽ Stripes and spots mark the coat of a thirteen-lined ground squirrel in North Dakota. These animals inhabit the plains and prairies of North America.

Thirteen-lined ground squirrel: 5 in (13 cm) long; tail, 4 in (10 cm)

▽ From a boulder in a meadow in California, a Belding ground squirrel calls out a warning. A fox or a weasel may have come close. At the sound, other ground squirrels will run for cover.

Belding ground squirrel: 8 in (20 cm) long; tail, 3 in (8 cm)

△ *Northern flying squirrel glides above a snowy slope in the Rocky Mountains. Flying squirrels do not really fly. They can glide, however—as far as 150 feet (46 m)!*
▽ *Spreading front and hind legs, a flying squirrel stretches flaps of skin along the sides of its body. Its flat, furry tail helps the animal steer. When it nears a tree, the squirrel will raise its body and its tail. The skin flaps will act as brakes, slowing the animal as it lands. It will grip the trunk with all four feet.*

body. About six months later, when spring comes, the ground squirrel pops out of its burrow. It is much thinner than it was in the fall.

Some ground squirrels that live in dry areas sleep in summer, too. In deserts of Asia, ground squirrels called large-toothed susliks (SUH-slicks) go into their burrows in the summer when food is scarce. This summer sleep is called aestivation (es-tuh-VAY-shun). The antelope ground squirrel, which also lives in deserts, has other ways of surviving high temperatures. If the animal gets too hot, it will stretch out on the ground in a shady spot or go underground where it is cooler.

Like most rodents, ground squirrels have many enemies. Meat eaters such as hawks, foxes, coyotes, and weasels often prey on them. Some ground squirrels may stand on their hind legs to watch for these predators (PRED-ut-erz), or hunters. If they spot danger, the squirrels give an alarm whistle before running for their underground homes.

Tree squirrels escape from these same kinds of enemies by moving quickly among the trees. Tree

521

Squirrel _____

Dining upside down, a gray squirrel in Minnesota ▷
hangs from a tree trunk by its hind claws. This position
leaves the animal's forepaws free to hold food.

squirrels are the animals that people often see scurrying through woods and city parks. With their powerful hind legs, tree squirrels jump easily from branch
to branch. Long, bushy tails help them balance as they
run along tree limbs.

Sometimes a tree squirrel will run headfirst
down a tree. It races jerkily from one side to the other.
Sharp, hooklike claws help it cling to the trunk.

Tree squirrels spend most of the time in the
trees. But they come to the ground to look for nuts,
berries, seeds, and mushrooms to eat. Sometimes a
tree squirrel will bury nuts and return to dig them up
later. It may not find all of them. Trees often sprout
from a squirrel's uneaten meals.

There are many kinds of tree squirrels. North
American red squirrels, fox squirrels, chickarees, and
Kaibab squirrels live in parts of North America. Anoth-
er kind of red squirrel lives in Europe and Asia. The

▽ *Tail laid along its back, a Cape ground squirrel*
nibbles on food in Namibia, in Africa. White stripes
along its sides mark the animal's coarse, brownish hair.

Cape ground squirrel: 9 in (23 cm) long; tail, 8 in (20 cm)

Gray squirrel: 9 in (23 cm) long; tail, 9 in (23 cm)

Fox squirrel: 12 in (30 cm) long; tail, 10 in (25 cm)

△ *Fox squirrel in Nebraska gnaws an ear of corn.*
This large North American tree squirrel often lives in
city parks as well as in woodlands.

SQUIRREL   🐾 **35 of 228 species**

**LENGTH OF HEAD AND BODY: 3-18 in (8-46 cm); tail, 2-18 in
(5-46 cm)**

WEIGHT: $\frac{1}{2}$ **oz-4 lb (14 g-2 kg)**

HABITAT AND RANGE: many kinds of habitat worldwide

**FOOD: plants, especially nuts and seeds, and some insects,
small birds, and birds' eggs**

LIFE SPAN: more than 20 years in captivity

**REPRODUCTION: usually 2 to 8 young after a pregnancy
of 3 to 6 weeks, depending on species**

ORDER: rodents

Eurasian red squirrel: 10 in (25 cm) long; tail, 8 in (20 cm)

△ *Eurasian red squirrel feeds as it perches on a branch of a maple tree in Germany.*

gray squirrel, native to North America, was brought by people to Europe and Africa.

Flying squirrels spend most of the time among branches, too. They make their homes in hollow trees, in holes made by woodpeckers, and in birds' nests. Flying squirrels usually look for food at night. Their big, bulging eyes help them find the food they eat—nuts, fruit, insects, and even baby birds.

Flying squirrels do not really fly. They glide through the air. To move from one tree to another, a flying squirrel first studies the distance, turning its head from side to side. Pushing off from a limb, the animal stretches out its arms and legs. Flaps of skin extend along the sides of its body and connect its limbs. The animal pushes off and glides to another tree. It steers by moving its legs and tail.

Before it lands, a flying squirrel raises its body and its tail. The skin flaps slow the animal down. The animal's claws grip the surface as it brings all four feet to the tree. A glide can take a flying squirrel 150 feet (46 m) through the air!

Female flying squirrels and tree squirrels give birth in nests made of bark, twigs, leaves, and moss. Ground squirrels make their nests in their burrows.

523

Squirrel

Indian giant squirrel uses its bushy tail to balance as ▷ *it munches fruit. Unlike many other squirrels, these brightly colored rodents do not sit up while eating.*

A squirrel usually bears two to eight blind, hairless young once or twice a year. The offspring stay in the nest one or two months while their mother nurses them. Then they begin to move around outside and to hunt for food.

Squirrels are in the same family as marmots, chipmunks, and prairie dogs. Read about these other animals under their own headings.

Indian giant squirrel: 18 in (46 cm) long; tail, 18 in (46 cm)

Stoat

Stoat is another name for a kind of weasel. Read about weasels on page 558.

Sugar glider

(SHOOG-er GLY-der)

FRUIT, NECTAR, SAP, AND FLOWERS make up most of the sugar glider's diet. This furry, grayish, squirrel-like animal feeds mostly on sweet food. Occasionally, it eats insects. Sugar gliders grunt, chirp, and gurgle as

▽ *Without a magic carpet, a sugar glider in Australia sails through the air. These marsupials extend flaps of skin that connect their limbs. They move from tree to tree, often traveling 150 feet (46 m) in one glide.*

they eat. They also make noise as they move among tree branches in the forests of Australia and New Guinea. Sugar gliders have few enemies, so they don't have to be quiet.

The sugar glider gets to its food by sailing through the air. It extends thin flaps of skin along the sides of its body that connect its wrists and ankles. The sugar glider leaps into the air and then glides from one tree to another. It steers by moving its fluffy tail. The animal can travel as far as 150 feet (46 m) in a single glide.

Sugar gliders are related to the phalanger family.

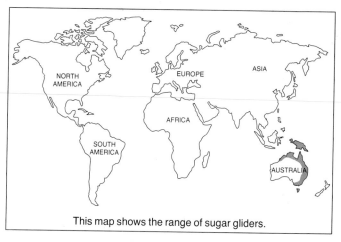

This map shows the range of sugar gliders.

Striped face close to a blossom, a sugar glider licks sweet nectar from flowers of a eucalyptus tree.

Like their relatives, sugar gliders are active at night. For this reason, people rarely see the bushy-tailed animals. During the day, groups of sugar gliders curl up in nests of leaves and twigs that are hidden in holes in trees.

Each nest may shelter two gliders or a family group of a dozen or more animals. Several generations of gliders may share the same nest.

Sugar gliders are marsupials (mar-SOO-pea-ulz), or pouched mammals. A female bears one to three tiny, underdeveloped young. The hairless offspring stay in their mother's pouch for several weeks, nursing and growing. Then they begin to climb in and out of the pouch. They go almost everywhere with their mother for a few weeks more, riding on her back.

Read about the sugar glider's phalanger relatives on page 430.

SUGAR GLIDER

LENGTH OF HEAD AND BODY: 5-7 in (13-18 cm); tail, 6-8 in (15-20 cm)

WEIGHT: 3-5 oz (85-142 g)

HABITAT AND RANGE: forests in parts of Australia and New Guinea

FOOD: fruit, nectar, sap, flowers, and insects

LIFE SPAN: about 10 years in captivity

REPRODUCTION: 1 to 3 young after a pregnancy of about 16 days

ORDER: marsupials

Suni

The suni is a kind of antelope. Read about antelopes on page 52.

Suricate

(SOOR-uh-kate)

Motionless suricates stand in the sun at the entrance of their burrow in southern Africa.

ON BRIGHT, CLEAR MORNINGS, groups of suricates bask in the sun outside their burrows. As many as 25 of these slender, squirrel-size animals live together in burrows on the plains of southern Africa.

While some of the suricates sit on the ground, others stand on their hind legs and watch the sky for such enemies as eagles and hawks. If a suricate spots danger, it gives a shrill cry of alarm. The others dash for the safety of their burrows.

As they search for food, suricates move slowly with their noses to the ground. They scratch in the dirt for insects and larvae. Sometimes they catch mice and lizards. While suricates hunt, they make purring sounds to stay in contact with each other.

◁ *Female suricate stands up to nurse her offspring. Male suricates also care for the young by guarding them, grooming them, and playing with them.*

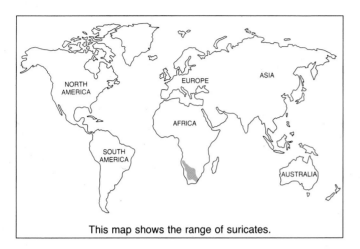

This map shows the range of suricates.

A group of suricates has several burrows within its range. It moves from one to another in search of food. The animals may dig new burrows with their sharp claws. Or they may move into burrows dug by ground squirrels. The suricate—often called the meerkat (MEER-cat)—is a kind of mongoose. Yellow mongooses, close relatives of suricates, often share the same burrows. Read about other mongooses on page 366.

Suricates give birth in their burrows and raise young there. Wild female suricates usually have one litter of two to four young every year. Suricates are born blind and nearly hairless. They do not leave the burrow until they are about a month old.

The young play much of the time. They wrestle and nip each other. Older brothers and sisters as well as parents groom, guard, and play with the young. They are fully grown within a year.

Suricate keeps watch on a rock, alert for hawks and ▷ *eagles. At first, any flying object—even an airplane— will send a young suricate to cover. After several months, it learns which birds mean danger.*

SURICATE

LENGTH OF HEAD AND BODY: 10-14 in (25-36 cm); tail, 7-10 in (18-25 cm)

WEIGHT: about 2 lb (1 kg)

HABITAT AND RANGE: dry plains in southern Africa

FOOD: insects and other small animals and some plants

LIFE SPAN: up to 13 years in captivity

REPRODUCTION: 2 to 4 young after a pregnancy of about 2½ months

ORDER: carnivores

T

Tahr

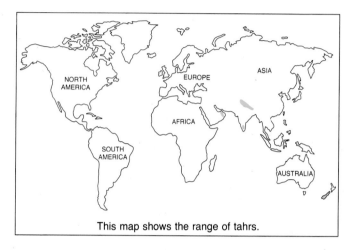

This map shows the range of tahrs.

TAHR 🐾 **3 of 3 species**
HEIGHT: 24-42 in (61-107 cm) at the shoulder
WEIGHT: 50-240 lb (23-109 kg)
HABITAT AND RANGE: mountainous and hilly regions in parts of Asia and New Zealand
FOOD: grasses, herbs, leaves, shoots, and twigs of shrubs and trees
LIFE SPAN: as long as 21 years in captivity
REPRODUCTION: usually 1 young after a pregnancy of about 8 months
ORDER: artiodactyls

LEAPING NIMBLY among cliffs, tahrs look much like beardless goats. These stocky animals with thick, curving horns are close relatives of wild goats. Read more about goats on page 232.

Rare Nilgiri (NIL-guh-ree) tahrs are found in the hills and mountains of southern India. Largest of the tahrs, male Nilgiris measure about 40 inches (102 cm) tall at the shoulder. Except during the mating season, adult males often travel alone or in small groups. The females and young live in herds of five to fifty animals. About six months after mating, a female tahr usually bears one young.

Tahrs eat grasses, herbs, leaves, shoots, and twigs. While the animals rest or feed, they may watch for such enemies as leopards and human hunters. If the tahrs sense danger, they may whistle an alarm and dash to the safety of the cliffs.

There are two other kinds of tahrs. Small Arabian tahrs live only in one dry mountainous area on the Arabian Peninsula. Himalayan tahrs have dark red or brownish black coats and live mainly in the southern parts of the Himalaya. People took them to New Zealand in the early 1900s.

Himalayan tahr: 38 in (97 cm) tall at the shoulder

◁ Long, shaggy mane hangs from the neck of a male Himalayan tahr in Nepal. Several females with shorter coats graze below him. The goatlike animals spend each day feeding on the steep slopes and narrow ledges of mountains. They watch for enemies like snow leopards.

Pointed ears alert, three ▷ Nilgiri tahrs peer watchfully down a steep hillside. The rare animals survive mainly in protected areas of southern India.

Tamandua

The tamandua is a kind of anteater. Read about anteaters on page 48.

Tamarin

The tamarin is a kind of monkey. Read about monkeys on page 370.

Tapir

(TAY-per)

Brazilian tapir: 36 in (91 cm) tall at the shoulder when fully grown

▽ Wading through a peaceful, marshy pool, a young Brazilian tapir takes an early morning drink after feeding on bushes along the water's edge. Brazilian tapirs spend much of their time in water or mud. Wallowing cools the animals off and rids them of pests—especially ticks. To reach the water, tapirs may slide down wooded hillsides near a pond or a river.

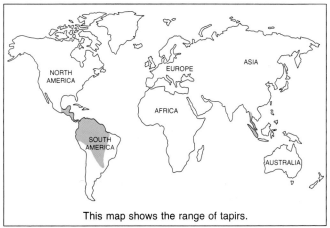

This map shows the range of tapirs.

STANDING MOTIONLESS at the edge of a rain forest, a Brazilian tapir raises its short trunk. The animal sniffs the evening air for the scent of a dangerous enemy— the jaguar. The tapir's white-rimmed ears rotate as it listens for danger. All seems safe. So it steps into a clearing to feed. It nibbles fallen fruit. Using its trunk, it strips leaves and buds from bushes and brings them to its mouth.

Each morning and evening, tapirs visit their feeding and watering places. Although many tapirs may live in the same area, the animals travel alone or in pairs. They trot along tunnel-like paths they have worn through the dense undergrowth during years of use. The tunnels may extend for miles.

Three kinds of tapirs are found in the Western Hemisphere. Both the Brazilian tapir and the Baird's

▽ Nose and upper lip of a Brazilian tapir form a small trunk. Like all tapirs, it can stretch its trunk to grasp a branch and bring the leaves to its mouth.

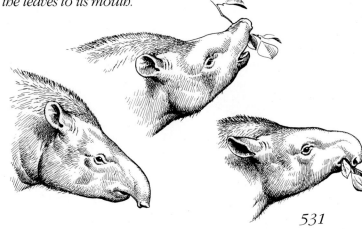

531

△ *Sitting next to an adult, a weeks-old tapir looks like a brown watermelon with legs. The patterned coat of the offspring will darken with age.*
▽ *Brazilian tapir sniffs the forest floor near the Amazon River in Peru. The animal searches for shoots and fallen fruit.*

Malay tapir: 42 in (107 cm) tall at the shoulder

◁ Short, stiff mane bristling, a Brazilian tapir swims easily through the water. It opens its mouth to catch its breath. Or it may be snarling at a pursuer. Now and then, the animal dives to the bottom. There it roots, or digs, for swamp grass and other water plants to eat.

Boldly marked Malay tapir has ▷ coloring that helps hide it in the shady forest. The broad white belt around the Malay tapir's middle looks like a blanket. For this reason, people sometimes call the animal the blanket tapir. A tough hide may protect the tapir from the sharp fangs of its enemy, the tiger.

tapir make their homes in forests, thickets, and grasslands of South America. The Baird's tapir is also found as far north as Mexico. Near the snow line of the high Andes lives the smallest tapir—the woolly, or mountain, tapir. Its long, wavy coat—much denser than that of other tapirs—protects the animal from chilly temperatures where it lives.

The largest and strongest tapir is the Malay tapir, which weighs as much as 800 pounds (363 kg). It measures about 42 inches (107 cm) tall at the shoulder. This shy animal roams swamps and forests in southeastern Asia. A large patch of light hair makes this kind of tapir look like a black animal with a white blanket tossed over its back. So the animal is sometimes called the blanket tapir.

Scientists think that tapirs have probably lived on earth for about 35 million years. During that time, the animals have changed very little. Once tapirs roamed Europe and North America, but they died out there long ago.

Plump and short-legged, the tapir looks like a large pig. But it is related to the horse and the rhinoceros. Like those animals, the tapir can run quickly, even through tangled vines and thorny bushes.

Tapirs are expert swimmers. To get to the water, they may slide down steep hillsides in dense forests.

They also wear down paths on the riverbanks above their swimming holes.

At midday, the animals often wade or wallow in mud. Wallowing helps tapirs rid themselves of ticks. Sometimes tapirs rub their bodies against rocks and tree trunks to scrape off the pests. Or, like dogs, they sit and scratch their chests and front legs with their hind feet.

A female tapir may bear a single offspring at any time of the year. The young tapir has a dark coat patterned with yellow and white stripes and spots. Because of the markings, the offspring is hard to see in the leafy shadows. It keeps its protective coloring for about six months. Within a year, the young tapir is ready to leave its mother and go off on its own.

TAPIR 🐾 **3 of 4 species**

HEIGHT: 29-42 in (74-107 cm) at the shoulder

WEIGHT: 500-800 lb (227-363 kg)

HABITAT AND RANGE: woodlands, grasslands, and rain forests of southern Mexico, Central and South America, and southeastern Asia

FOOD: water plants, leaves, buds, twigs, and fruit

LIFE SPAN: about 35 years in captivity

REPRODUCTION: usually 1 young after a pregnancy of about 12 or 13 months

ORDER: perissodactyls

Tarsier

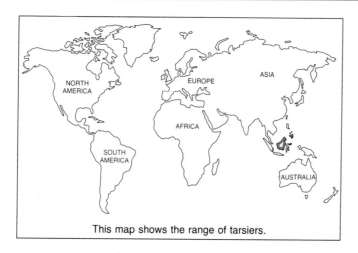

This map shows the range of tarsiers.

HIDDEN BY THE LEAVES of a rain forest, tarsiers move quietly through the darkness. These tiny animals of Indonesia and the Philippines—relatives of apes, monkeys, and human beings—are among the smallest primates in the world.

A tarsier grows only about as large as a chipmunk. But its tail may be twice as long as its body. When it clings to a tree trunk, the animal uses its tail for extra support. The tail also helps a tarsier balance

▽ *Large eyes shining, a western tarsier climbs a tree in a rain forest on Borneo. At night, tarsiers hunt for lizards and insects to eat. They sleep during the day, clinging to trees. Sometimes they hide in hollow trees.*

and steer as it jumps long distances among the trees. The animal can spring almost 2 feet (61 cm) into the air and cover a distance of about 4 feet (122 cm) in a single leap.

Like a frog, a tarsier jumps using its long, powerful back legs. As it leaps, a tarsier jumps backward and twists its body around. It tightly tucks in its arms and legs. It uses its tail to help balance in midair. The tarsier lands feetfirst on a tree trunk with its tail pointed straight up. Flat pads on the ends of its fingers and toes help the animal get firm footing. The tarsier hugs the trunk with all fours.

Tarsiers wake up at sunset and begin to hunt for food. They seek insects, lizards, and other small animals in their homes in the trees. As they move through the forest, tarsiers mark the branches with their urine. By these scent marks, one tarsier announces its presence to others.

Large eyes help the little primate spot its prey in the darkness. The tarsier can turn its head so far around that it can almost see behind itself. Like a bush baby, another small primate, the tarsier can turn each ear in the direction of a sound. It moves its ears almost constantly. The animal's sensitive hearing can detect faint noises in the forest. Read about the bush baby on page 112.

A female tarsier gives birth to a single young. The offspring, born with fur, clings to its mother's belly immediately after birth. Soon the young animal can climb and leap about in the trees.

Long, powerful back legs of a western tarsier help ▷
the animal climb the trunk of a tree. Flat pads on its
fingertips and toes give the small primate a sure grip.
The gray-brown coat helps camouflage, or hide, it
in the forest. Huge eyes help it spot prey in dim light.

TARSIER

LENGTH OF HEAD AND BODY: 3-6 in (8-15 cm); tail, 5-11 in (13-28 cm)

WEIGHT: 4-5 oz (113-142 g)

HABITAT AND RANGE: rain forests in Indonesia and the Philippines

FOOD: insects, lizards, small bats, snakes, and small birds

LIFE SPAN: at least 13 years in captivity

REPRODUCTION: 1 young after a pregnancy of about 6 months

ORDER: primates

Western tarsier: 5 in (13 cm) long; tail, 10 in (25 cm)

Tasmanian devil

(taz-MAY-nee-un DEV-ul)

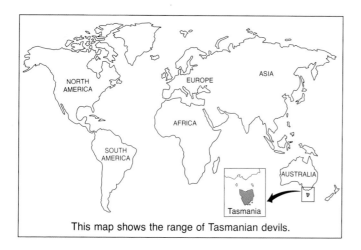

This map shows the range of Tasmanian devils.

TASMANIAN DEVIL

LENGTH OF HEAD AND BODY: 20-31 in (51-79 cm); tail, 9-12 in (23-30 cm)

WEIGHT: 10-20 lb (5-9 kg)

HABITAT AND RANGE: brushy areas on Tasmania

FOOD: small mammals, birds, reptiles, and dead animals

LIFE SPAN: about 8 years in the wild

REPRODUCTION: 3 or 4 young after a pregnancy of about 1 month

ORDER: marsupials

WITH ITS MUSCULAR JAWS and large teeth, the Tasmanian devil snaps up anything it can catch. This meat-eating marsupial (mar-soo-pea-ul), or pouched mammal, even eats poisonous snakes. It also feeds on dead animals that it finds.

Because of its heavy head and stocky body, a Tasmanian devil looks a little like a black bear cub. But a Tasmanian devil has a hairy tail about 10 inches (25 cm) long. The animal lives only on the island of Tasmania, a part of Australia.

Tasmanian devils hunt at night. With their tails off the ground, they run awkwardly through thick underbrush. During the day, the animals sleep in caves, in hollow logs, or among rocks.

Except during the mating season, Tasmanian devils live alone. If two meet, they scream, snort, spit, and snarl at each other. But the animals rarely attack one another. One of them usually runs away.

Like other marsupials, female Tasmanian devils give birth to three or four tiny, underdeveloped young. Immediately after birth, the raisin-size offspring crawl into the pouch on their mother's belly. They remain there for about four months, nursing and growing larger.

Tasmanian devil's ears turn red with alarm as it stands ready to defend its home among tall grasses. Once found in other parts of Australia, these pouched mammals now live only on the island of Tasmania.

Tenrec

Sniffing the ground, a tailless tenrec hunts in the ▷ daylight. Usually tenrecs sleep all day in burrows.
▽ Short, stiff spines stand up on the back of a streaked tenrec. A crest of longer spines grows on its head.

Streaked tenrec: 7 in (18 cm) long

Tailless tenrec: 12 in (30 cm) long

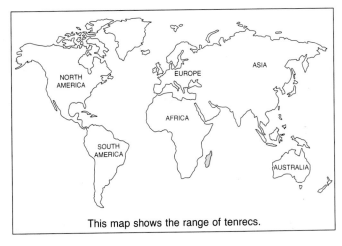

Madagascar hedgehog tenrec: 6 in (15 cm) long

FOR MANY MILLIONS OF YEARS, scientists think, tenrecs have lived on Madagascar, an island off the east coast of Africa. There these relatives of hedgehogs have developed in many ways. Some tenrecs look like hedgehogs. Others resemble shrews or moles. The tailless tenrec, the largest of the tenrecs, grows as big as a rabbit. The small streaked tenrec fits easily in a person's hand.

During the day, tenrecs rest in burrows. At night, the animals scurry across grasslands and through forests. There they look for insects, earthworms, mice, small reptiles, and roots to eat.

Most female tenrecs bear more than ten tiny offspring two months after mating. But a tailless tenrec may bear more than 25 young in a litter—more young at one time than any other mammal!

△ *Thick coat of spines covers the head and body of a Madagascar hedgehog tenrec. Like its relative the hedgehog, this tenrec rolls into a prickly ball when threatened. Tenrecs live only on Madagascar and nearby islands. They eat mainly insects and worms.*

TENREC 🐾 **7 of 22 species**

LENGTH OF HEAD AND BODY: 3-15 in (8-38 cm); tail, as long as 6 in (15 cm)

WEIGHT: 1 oz-5 lb (28 g-2 kg)

HABITAT AND RANGE: grasslands and forests of Madagascar and nearby islands

FOOD: insects, earthworms, mice, small reptiles, and roots

LIFE SPAN: about 4 years in captivity

REPRODUCTION: 1 to 25 young after a pregnancy of about 2 months, depending on species

ORDER: insectivores

This map shows the range of tenrecs.

Tiger

(TIE-ger)

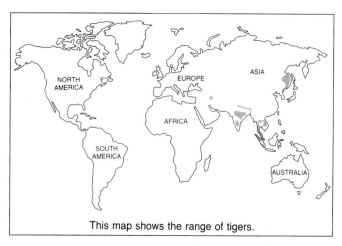

This map shows the range of tigers.

TIGER 🐾 1 of 1 species

LENGTH OF HEAD AND BODY: 5-6 ft (152-183 cm); tail, 2-3 ft (61-91 cm)

WEIGHT: 240-500 lb (109-227 kg)

HABITAT AND RANGE: forests, wooded hillsides, and swamps in parts of Asia

FOOD: deer, wild cattle, antelopes, and smaller animals

LIFE SPAN: as long as 26 years in captivity

REPRODUCTION: 1 to 6 young after a pregnancy of about 3½ months

ORDER: carnivores

BEAUTY, MYSTERY, AND STRENGTH are all qualities for which the tiger has been admired and feared. In some Asian myths, the tiger—with its striking pattern of stripes—is the king of beasts. But in most stories, the tiger is a demon. Because of the animal's reputation as a dangerous foe, those who hunted the tiger often were respected for their bravery. Tiger hunting became a popular sport.

A century ago, thousands of tigers roamed much of Asia. Tigers lived wherever water, prey, and places to hide were plentiful. They prowled rain forests, wooded hillsides, and swamps in many parts of Asia. Today they survive only in a few parts of that range. On the islands of Java and Bali, the tiger is probably extinct. In the forested areas of India, perhaps 3,000 animals remain. The tiger is now protected by law. But it is still being hunted, and its habitats are being gradually destroyed.

Partly hidden by tall grass and shadows, a Bengal tiger looks across a field in India. No two tigers have the same pattern of stripes on their coats.

538

Tiger

The tiger is the largest member of the cat family, and the Siberian tiger is the biggest tiger of all. It usually measures about 9 feet (274 cm) long from its nose to the tip of its tail. In winter, its light orange coat is long and thick. Tigers that live farther to the south are smaller. Some are dark in color with heavy black stripes on a reddish orange background. A few tigers are white with brown stripes, but there is no record of any black tigers.

During the day, the tiger rests in the shade. It may lie in a quiet pool of water to escape the heat. At dusk, the tiger begins to hunt for food. Tigers usually prey on deer, wild cattle called gaur, and wild pigs. But if the tiger is hungry and cannot find large prey, it will

Indian tiger rubs its head against a tree, leaving ▷ its scent. Tigers live and hunt alone. They communicate by scent marks and sounds as well as by spraying urine. ▽ At the edge of a stream, a tiger rests with its hindquarters in the water and its front legs stretched out in the grass. Tigers, the largest of all the cats, spend time in the water to cool off in the daytime heat.

eat any kind of meat. A few tigers have become man-eaters. Man-eaters are sometimes sick or wounded animals that cannot hunt their normal prey. Generally, tigers avoid people.

As it hunts, a tiger uses its keen eyesight and hearing. A tiger cannot run great distances. Instead, it stalks until it is close to its prey. Then it rushes and pulls the prey to the ground with its teeth and claws. It strangles a larger animal by biting the throat, and it breaks the necks of smaller ones.

A tiger may camp near its kill for several days, until it has eaten all the meat and most of the bones. It feeds for a while, grooms itself, takes a drink of water, rests, and then feeds some more. The cat usually eats

◁ *Three ten-month-old cubs crowd close to their mother as she rests in a pool. Two of the cubs prepare to greet each other by rubbing their heads together. Offspring usually stay with their mother for about two years.*

▽ *Male tiger charges through a pond in India. Strong swimmers, tigers may cross a large river to find prey.*

Tiger

about 12 pounds (5 kg) at a time, but it may eat as much as 60 pounds (27 kg) in one night.

Tigers usually live and hunt alone. But when food is plentiful, several animals may gather at a kill. They often stay together for short periods. Tigers keep in touch by scents and sounds. They spray

Widely varying climates provide homes for the tiger. A male and a female Sumatran tiger (right) peer through dense bushes. In Sumatra, tigers often live in swamps. On a mountain slope, two Siberian tigers (below) pause in the snow. The big cats are hunted for their striking fur and for other body parts that some people believe can serve as medicine. In 1920, there were about 100,000 wild tigers. Today as few as 5,000 survive in the wild.

bushes and trees with urine. They roar, moan, and grunt. If two tigers meet, they may greet each other by rubbing heads and making a puffing sound.

A female tiger usually gives birth every two or three years, about three and a half months after mating. Her litter may include two to four cubs the size of large kittens. Cubs nurse for about six months. But their mother begins to take them to a kill when they are only two months old. Gradually, the cubs spend more time on their own. Males usually can hunt by themselves earlier than females. The cubs become independent within two years.

Read about other wild cats in the entries on bobcat, cat, cheetah, jaguar, leopard, lion, and lynx.

Topi

The topi is a kind of antelope. Read about antelopes on page 52.

Tuco-tuco

(TOO-koh-TOO-koh)

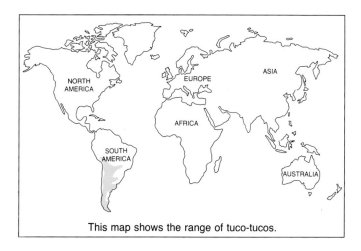

This map shows the range of tuco-tucos.

LIKE THE STRIKING OF A HAMMER, the calls of a tuco-tuco ring out from the animal's underground home. The sounds it makes give this rodent its name. The noises may warn of danger or help the animal claim its territory.

Tuco-tucos look somewhat like pocket gophers. They live in forests and on grasslands and plains in parts of South America. The rodents spend most of the time in burrows they have dug with their claws and large front teeth.

A tuco-tuco may peer out of its burrow to look for enemies. And if a fox, skunk, wild cat, or hawk approaches, the animal darts back in. The tuco-tuco rarely leaves its home, even to find food. From inside the burrow, it can pull down plants by the roots. In her burrow, a female bears from one to six young each year.

△ *Tuco-tuco grasps a blade of grass. Usually these stocky rodents of South America stay underground. There they can pull down their food by the roots.*

TUCO-TUCO

LENGTH OF HEAD AND BODY: 6-10 in (15-25 cm); tail, 2-4 in (5-10 cm)

WEIGHT: 4-24 oz (113-680 g)

HABITAT AND RANGE: forests, grasslands, and plains in parts of South America

FOOD: roots, bulbs, stems, and grasses

LIFE SPAN: probably less than 3 years in the wild

REPRODUCTION: 1 to 6 young after a pregnancy of about 3 months

ORDER: rodents

543

U

Uakari
The uakari is a kind of monkey. Read about monkeys on page 370.

V

Vervet
The vervet is a kind of monkey. Find out about monkeys on page 370.

Vicuña
The vicuña is a relative of the llama. Read about both animals on page 336.

Vizcacha

(vis-KOTCH-uh)

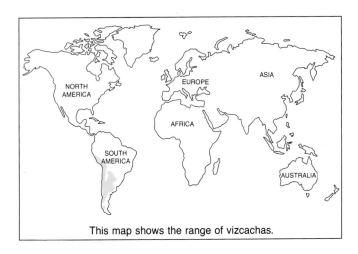

This map shows the range of vizcachas.

VIZCACHA
LENGTH OF HEAD AND BODY: 12-26 in (30-66 cm); tail, 6-15 in (15-38 cm)
WEIGHT: 2-18 lb (1-8 kg)
HABITAT AND RANGE: rocky, mountainous regions and grassy plains in parts of South America
FOOD: plants such as grasses and mosses
LIFE SPAN: as long as 19 years in captivity
REPRODUCTION: 1 or 2 young after a pregnancy of 4 or 5 months, depending on species
ORDER: rodents

TWO RODENTS OF SOUTH AMERICA share the same common name, though they differ in many ways. High in the Andes, the mountain vizcacha leaps gracefully among rocks. The plains vizcacha runs across the grasslands of southern South America.

The mountain vizcacha's body measures about 13 inches (33 cm) long. Its gray or brown fur is thick, soft, and short. A black stripe often runs down its back. The animal has long ears and a tail tipped with black or reddish brown hairs.

During the day, groups of mountain vizcachas feed on grasses and other plants. They also perch on rocks, basking in the sun or grooming their fur.

Mountain vizcachas live in colonies that number as many as several hundred animals. When alarmed, they signal to one another with whistling calls. Then they dash for shelter among the rocks.

The mountain vizcacha's larger relative, the plains vizcacha, has a stockier body that usually measures about 24 inches (61 cm) long. The rodent has black whiskers and black-and-white stripes on its face. Its coarse coat ranges from gray to light brown, and the animal has a white belly.

Plains vizcachas dig networks of burrows with many entrances. Usually about 15 to 30 plains vizcachas share a burrow. But the animals often have guests. Lizards, snakes, toads, foxes, and burrowing owls also may live in the underground homes.

At dawn and at dusk, plains vizcachas look for grasses, roots, stems, and seeds to eat. They also pick up unusual objects and carry them home. On top of

544

Mountain vizcacha: 13 in (33 cm) long; tail, 11 in (28 cm)

Plains vizcacha: 24 in (61 cm) long; tail, 7 in (18 cm)

△ Rabbitlike rodent—except for its tail—a mountain vizcacha basks in sunshine near its home in the Andes of Peru. Agile jumpers, mountain vizcachas live in rock crevices, but they feed in open grassy areas. These vizcachas live in colonies that may number several hundred animals.

◁ Plains vizcacha stops for a snack on an open grassland. Larger than its mountain relative, the plains vizcacha has a black-and-white striped face. A junk collector, it picks up bones, stones, and other objects that it finds. Then it piles them on top of its burrow.

their burrows, these junk collectors heap bones, stones, branches, lumps of earth—even jewelry that people have lost nearby. The pile on a single burrow is often enough to fill a wheelbarrow! Why the animals collect these objects remains unknown.

Vizcachas, like all rodents, have front teeth that grow throughout their lives. The animals must gnaw to keep their teeth from growing too long.

Female vizcachas give birth once or twice a year, four or five months after mating. A female mountain vizcacha usually bears a single young. A plains vizcacha has a set of twins.

545

Vole

Bank vole: 4 in (10 cm) long; tail, 2 in (5 cm)

AMONG THE MOST NUMEROUS mammals on earth, voles live in parts of North America, Europe, Asia, and Africa. The stocky, grayish brown vole looks much like its relative the mouse. Voles have shorter tails and ears than mice do, however. There are about 120 species, or kinds, of voles.

Voles live in many habitats—forests, grasslands, marshes, and mountains, as well as in orchards and in gardens. Voles eat whatever plants they can find. They nibble on stems, leaves, roots, flowers, seeds, grasses,

◁ *Moving through grass and clover, a bank vole in Germany watches cautiously for such enemies as snakes, hawks, owls, cats, dogs, and weasels.*

▽ *Water vole nibbles a willow leaf at the edge of a small stream in England. Like muskrats, their relatives, water voles swim well, both on the surface and underwater.*

Water vole: 8 in (20 cm) long; tail, 4 in (10 cm)

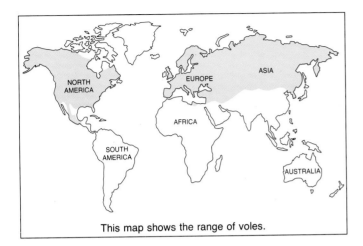

This map shows the range of voles.

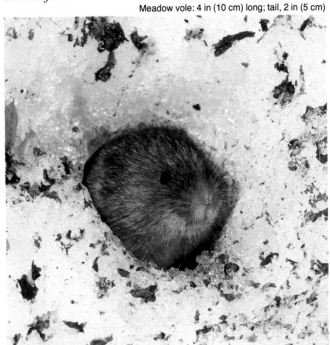

▽ *Meadow vole in Michigan (below) peeks out of a tunnel in the snow. Voles often build runways, or paths, from their nests to their feeding grounds. In summer, they keep the runways clear by running back and forth. At bottom, a short-tailed vole stretches to nibble a blade of wet grass in a field in England. A vole sometimes carries food back to a storeroom in its burrow.*

Meadow vole: 4 in (10 cm) long; tail, 2 in (5 cm)

and bark. Some voles, such as the meadow vole, can eat almost their own weight in food in a day—nearly 3 ounces (85 g).

Many voles live in nests of shredded plants under logs or rocks or in trees. Other voles dig burrows. The rodents usually connect their nests to feeding grounds with runways, or networks of paths, through the grass. They keep the paths clear by running back and forth and by nibbling on the plants that are in their way. In the winter, some voles make their runways under snow.

Voles reproduce often. A female vole can bear several litters a year with as many as eight young in each litter. Blind and helpless, newborn voles weigh less than a quarter of an ounce (7 g). They usually stay in the nest less than one month.

Sometimes the vole population grows too large. The small rodents can destroy entire fields as they try to find enough to eat. Usually, however, the natural enemies of voles keep them from becoming too numerous. Snakes, owls, hawks, cats, dogs, weasels, and many other animals prey on voles.

VOLE 🐾 11 of 121 species

LENGTH OF HEAD AND BODY: 3-8 in (8-20 cm); tail, as long as 4 in (10 cm)

WEIGHT: $^1/_2$ oz-7 oz (14-198 g)

HABITAT AND RANGE: many kinds of habitats in parts of North America, Europe, Asia, and a small area in Africa

FOOD: plants, especially grasses

LIFE SPAN: up to almost 3 years in the wild

REPRODUCTION: 1 to 8 young after a pregnancy of 3 or 4 weeks

ORDER: rodents

Short-tailed vole: 5 in (13 cm) long; tail, about 1 in (3 cm)

W

Wallaby

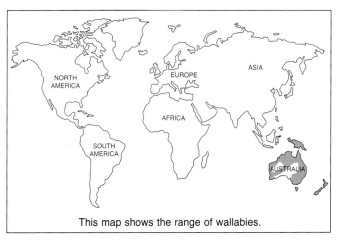

This map shows the range of wallabies.

Red-necked wallaby and her young, called a joey, ▷
share a meal. They carefully strip a branch of its leaves.
▽ *Miniature marsupial, an unadorned rock wallaby*
grips the surface of a rock with its rough, thickly padded
hind feet. These surefooted jumpers can leap as far as
12 feet (4 m) to get from one rock to another.

Unadorned rock wallaby: 24 in (61 cm) long; tail, 20 in (51 cm)

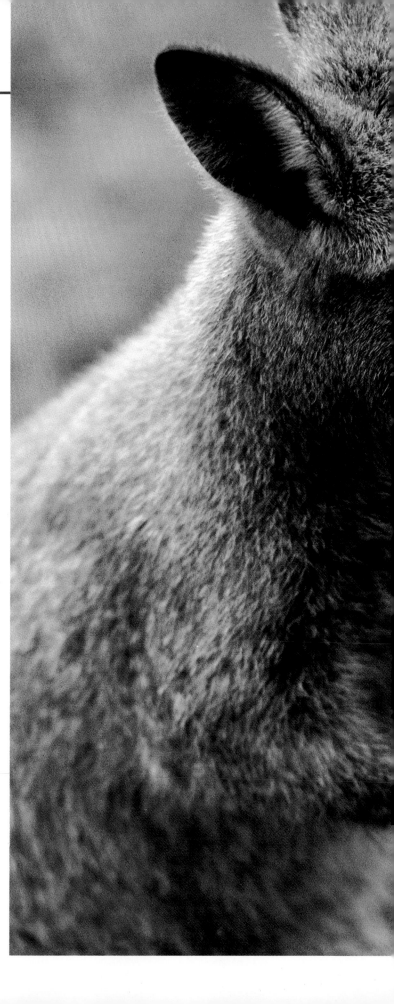

Red-necked wallaby: 35 in (89 cm) long; tail, 29 in (74 cm)

NOT ALL KANGAROOS are called wallabies, but many are. Wallabies are small and medium-size members of the kangaroo family. More than thirty kinds of wallabies live in parts of Australia, New Guinea, and nearby islands. People also took them to New Zealand in the 1800s.

The largest wallaby is almost 6 feet (183 cm) long from its nose to the tip of its tail. The smallest wallaby is about the size of a rabbit. Read about kangaroos on page 304. Find out about the quokka, a small wallaby, on page 464.

The coats of wallabies come in a wide range of colors. Their fur may be gray, brown, red, or nearly black. Some wallabies have patches of bright yellow or orange fur. A light orange ring encircles each eye of the spectacled hare wallaby. The tail of the ringtailed rock wallaby is ringed with bands of white, brown, and pale yellow.

Red-legged pademelon: 25 in (64 cm) long; tail, 16 in (41 cm)

△ *Red-legged pademelon, a kind of scrub wallaby, searches the forest floor for leaves and grasses to eat. When feeding, the animal moves at a leisurely pace on all fours. If startled, however, it hops away on its hind legs. The pademelon always follows the same paths, or runways, through the woods.*

Sightseeing from a safe spot, a joey peeks through ▷ tall grass from its mother's pouch. The young sandy wallaby may leave the pouch to graze. But it returns at the slightest hint of danger.

Wallabies are usually found in shrubby areas or in rocky regions. The smaller shrub wallabies are often called scrub wallabies or pademelons (PAD-ee-mel-unz). These animals seek cover among the tangled plants of swamps, thickets, and forests. Larger wallabies are often called brush wallabies. They live among high grasses and tall shrubs.

Rock wallabies inhabit regions that are rocky and hilly. They find shelter in caves or between rocks during the day. There they are shielded from the hot sun. They also are hidden from such enemies as the wild dogs called dingoes.

In the cooler temperatures of evening, wallabies leave their shelters and begin to look for food. These animals feed mainly on plants. They do not need to drink much water. When water is scarce, they get most of the moisture they need from food they eat. One kind of wallaby, the tammar (TAM-ur), will even drink salt water when fresh water is not available to it.

When grazing, wallabies move slowly about on all fours. If startled, however, they hop swiftly away on their strong hind legs. Hare wallabies, named for their harelike size and movements, can jump higher than a person's head. If discovered by an enemy, a hare wallaby escapes with twists and turns. Leaping away, it leaves its attacker behind.

Surefooted rock wallabies hop nimbly about Australia's steep, rocky hills. Thick pads of rough skin on the animals' hind feet give them a good grip on the uneven terrain.

Wallabies use their tails for balance as they leap. Most have strong tails that support them when they sit. The most unusual tail among wallabies belongs to the nail-tailed wallaby. This animal has a horny spike at the tip of its long tail.

Wallabies, like all kangaroos and many other Australian animals, are marsupials (mar-SOO-pea-ulz), or pouched mammals. A few weeks after mating, a female wallaby gives birth to one tiny, underdeveloped offspring, called a joey. Blind and helpless, the newborn immediately crawls into its mother's pouch. There it remains, nursing for several months, until it is big enough to digest solid food.

Even when it begins to leave the pouch to graze, the joey stays close to its mother. She continues to nurse and to protect the young wallaby, though, until it can take care of itself.

WALLABY 🐾 10 of 44 species

LENGTH OF HEAD AND BODY: 12-41 in (30-104 cm); tail, 10-29 in (25-74 cm)

WEIGHT: 4-53 lb (2-24 kg)

HABITAT AND RANGE: shrubby, rocky areas of Australia, New Guinea, neighboring islands, and New Zealand

FOOD: mostly grasses and other plants

LIFE SPAN: as long as 15 years in captivity

REPRODUCTION: usually 1 young after a pregnancy of about 1 month

ORDER: marsupials

△ *Heads pulled back, two male sandy wallabies challenge one another (above, left) for a female. With the claws of the front paws, each slashes at the other's body (above, center). One wallaby aims a kick at his opponent's belly (above, right). Such contests rarely end in serious injury.*

Walrus

A BRISTLY MUSTACHE and long ivory tusks make the walrus look like a storybook creature. The animal is real, however. Walruses are relatives of seals and sea lions. Like these animals, walruses live mostly in the water. They are found in the Far North—in the Arctic Ocean and nearby waters. Those that live off Greenland and eastern Canada are usually smaller than the others. In the northern oceans, the water is cold, and huge chunks of ice float on the surface. The floating ice provides walruses with places to bear young and to rest.

◁ *Under the sharply peaked mountains of an island off Alaska, thousands of Pacific walruses bask in the sun. These older males spend the summer in this area. Females and young males head farther north.*

A walrus's tusks are important for survival. Both male and female walruses have tusks. These long teeth keep growing throughout a walrus's life. Some may reach a length of 30 inches (76 cm).

Male walruses—called bulls—often fight with their tusks to determine which of the animals is stronger and more important. At first, the male walruses raise their heads and show off their tusks. Sometimes that is enough to make a walrus with smaller tusks move out of the way. If two walruses do fight, however, they usually just poke and jab. They rarely hurt one another very badly. The skin of a walrus is thick, and the animal's neck is covered with tough lumps. Usually the largest bull—which often has the longest tusks—wins. During the mating season, injuries are more common. Bulls fight each other in earnest.

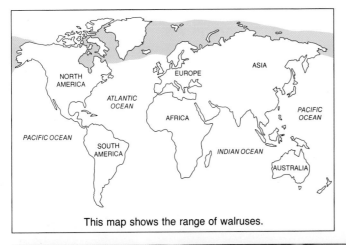

This map shows the range of walruses.

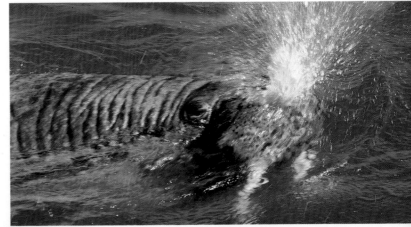

△ *Blast away! A Pacific walrus clears its nose of water. Like all sea mammals, walruses must come to the surface to breathe. They can dive as deep as 260 feet (79 m) and remain underwater for up to ten minutes.*

◁ *Long ivory tusks cast shadows on the thick hides of two Pacific walruses. Both males and females grow tusks, which may reach 30 inches (76 cm) long. With these teeth, the animals can get a hold on pack ice and pull their bulky bodies out of the water.*

Pacific walrus: 12 ft (4 m) long

Walrus

Sometimes their tusks break off during battles.
 The animals also poke each other to keep the best spots on a beach or on a piece of ice. Occasionally, walruses fight off such enemies as polar bears with their tusks. Walruses also use their tusks to help pull their bulky bodies out of the water. A walrus sticks its head up and hooks its tusks on a chunk of ice. Then it hauls itself up.

A walrus uses its mustache when it roots, or digs, for food. The animal dives to the ocean floor and feels in the sandy bottom with its stiff, sensitive whiskers. When the walrus finds snails or clams, it scoops up the shellfish with its tongue and lips. Then it sucks out the meat and leaves the shells on the bottom. Walruses also eat worms, crabs, and shrimps—as much as 176 pounds (80 kg) of food a day. That adds up to about

▽ *Jammed together for warmth, walruses huddle on a rocky beach. Sometimes one walrus will poke another with its tusks. This signal means "move over and make room."*

◁ *Pale walruses come ashore after a swim. In cold water, a walrus's blood circulates to the tissues within its body. This helps the walrus stay warm. On land, the blood flows back to its skin, which returns to its reddish brown color.*

▽ *Resting walrus shades its face with one of its flippers. Its tusk may have broken off with heavy use.*

800 large clams or as many as 10,000 smaller ones!

A thick layer of fat—called blubber—helps protect walruses from the cold. Blubber makes up about one-third of a walrus's total weight. In the winter, when its layer of fat is as thick as 6 inches (15 cm), a walrus may weigh 2 tons (1,814 kg). Despite its weight, the walrus is graceful in the water. To propel itself, it moves its rear flippers from side to side. It usually swims about 5 miles (8 km) an hour.

On land, the walrus walks awkwardly. Like many seals, it can use its flippers as legs out of the water. It turns its rear flippers forward and walks along on all fours. The rough bottoms of its flippers prevent it from slipping.

Reddish brown is the usual color of a walrus's hide. But when the animal comes out of the water after a cold swim, it often appears pinkish white. That's because its blood has moved away from the skin surface to the tissues inside its body. This helps the walrus keep its body heat up. When the animal comes

Walrus

ashore, the blood moves back to the skin. This cools the animal. After a few minutes, a walrus's skin returns to its reddish brown color.

Walruses live in herds of as many as several thousand animals. They hunt and rest together. When they come out of the water, they may remain on land or on ice for nearly two days at a stretch. The animals sleep most of the time. They sprawl out, warming themselves in the sun and making deep grunting noises. Polar bears sometimes charge at resting herds. They try to catch calves or slower walruses before they can escape into the water.

As the seasons change, walruses move to other feeding grounds. In the spring, large herds of walruses move north. Some older bull walruses do not make the trip, however. They stay in the same area year

△ *Sunlight reaches into the water, streaking two walruses. A walrus moves through the water by sweeping its rear flippers from side to side.*

△ *Surrounded by blue sea, a walrus herd crowds onto huge chunks of ice in the Arctic Ocean. In the small picture, a female walrus nuzzles her months-old calf.*

round. When the northern waters begin to freeze in the fall, the walruses that did migrate, or travel, swim south again. Walruses are strong swimmers. They can remain in the water for several days at a time, although they sometimes catch rides on drifting chunks of ice.

Walruses even sleep in the water. Males and females may doze beneath the surface, or they may hold their heads above the water so they can breathe. An adult male walrus has two pouches in his throat. He can fill the pouches with air until they are as big as beach balls. The pouches help the animal stay afloat. Females do not have these pouches. Male walruses also use their pouches to make deep, ringing sounds. These noises may help them attract females during the mating season.

Walruses mate in the water, and the female usually bears a single calf in May. Like seals and sea lions, walruses come onto land or ice to give birth. The newborn calves weigh as little as 85 pounds (39 kg). Short, grayish brown hair covers their wrinkled skin. At first, the newborn walruses stay out of the water,

---

WALRUS
LENGTH OF HEAD AND BODY: 6½-12 ft (198 cm-4 m)
WEIGHT: 1,650 lb-2 t (748-1,814 kg)
HABITAT AND RANGE: Arctic Ocean and nearby waters
FOOD: clams, snails, crabs, and worms
LIFE SPAN: 40 years in the wild
REPRODUCTION: 1 young after a pregnancy of 15 months
ORDER: pinnipeds

557

but they can swim to escape such enemies as polar bears. At about three months of age, their tusks begin to grow.

A mother walrus watches over her calf carefully. She protects it from icy winds with her body. Later, she may carry it in the water between her flippers. Or it may perch on her back when she swims near the surface. The offspring remains with its mother for about two years. Occasionally, a male calf may stay as

long as four years. Then it leaves to join a herd of other young males.

The Eskimo have hunted walruses for hundreds of years. Harpoon heads and other tools were made from walrus bones and tusks. The walrus's stiff whiskers were used for toothpicks. In some places today, oil made from the blubber is still burned for heat and light. And the Eskimo eat walrus meat and cover their boats with walrus hide.

Waterbuck
The waterbuck is a kind of antelope. Read about antelopes on page 52.

Weasel

TIRELESS HUNTERS, weasels bound and zigzag across brushy ground after rodents and small birds. They even dart into burrows after ground squirrels. With its slender body and short legs, a weasel can easily squeeze into underground dens where it can kill its prey. Larger weasels sometimes hunt rabbits. A weasel may kill more food than it needs. The animal

stores the food in a safe place and returns to it later.

Weasels live in meadows, forests, and grasslands in many parts of the world. They take shelter in burrows and rock crevices or among tree roots. Of about ten kinds of weasels, only the long-tailed weasel, the short-tailed weasel, and the least weasel are found in North America.

The weasel has glands that produce a strong-smelling substance. Scientists think that the animal leaves this and its waste in its hunting area. The scent tells other weasels to hunt elsewhere.

Long-tailed weasel: 12 in (30 cm) long; tail, 5 in (13 cm)

◁ *Standing beside a ground squirrel's burrow, a long-tailed weasel in Nebraska listens for prey. The animal keeps its brownish coloring all summer.*

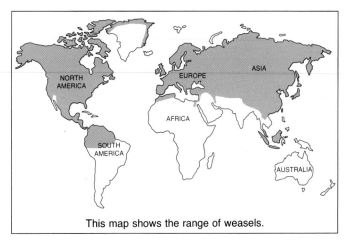

This map shows the range of weasels.

Long-tailed weasel in Canada climbs among branches. The coats of many weasels change color with the season. In fall, new, lighter hair gradually grows in. By winter, the weasel's coat is white.

Weasel

WEASEL 🐾 **3 of 11 species**

LENGTH OF HEAD AND BODY: 5-16 in (13-41 cm); tail, as long as 7 in (18 cm)

WEIGHT: less than 2-11 oz (57-312 g)

HABITAT AND RANGE: meadows, forests, and grasslands in many parts of the world

FOOD: small mammals, birds, berries, and insects

LIFE SPAN: about 10 years in captivity

REPRODUCTION: 3 to 13 young after a pregnancy of 1 to 12 months, depending on species

ORDER: carnivores

Short-tailed weasel: 10 in (25 cm) long; tail, 3 in (8 cm)

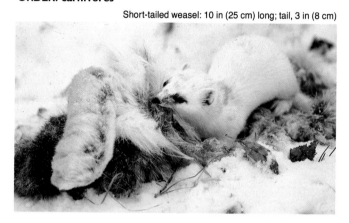

Most weasels have brownish fur with lighter underfur. In northern parts of North America, Europe, and Asia, however, many weasels grow a white coat by winter. They are hard to see in snowy country. The tail tips of some weasels stay black. Enemies such as owls and hawks sometimes swoop at the black spot of tail fur and miss the weasel's body.

The short-tailed weasel is called an ermine when it has its winter fur. In Europe, it is called a stoat when it has its brown summer coat. The white fur of other weasels is also known as ermine.

A female weasel bears from 3 to 13 young once or twice a year. After about four months, the offspring begin to look for their own hunting areas.

◁ *Feeding on the leg of a snowshoe hare, a short-tailed weasel finishes the remains of a lynx's kill.*

▽ *Protective winter coloring almost hides a short-tailed weasel bounding across a snowy mountainside in Switzerland. Hawks or owls may swoop at the black tip of a weasel's tail—and miss the body of their prey!*

△ *Eyes bright, a short-tailed weasel in Alaska pops out of an arctic ground squirrel's burrow. Weasels hunt whenever they are hungry. They may mark their hunting areas with scent.*

561

Whale

WHAT WEIGHS more than thirty elephants and lives in the sea? The female blue whale—the largest animal in the world! It weighs 200 tons (181 t) or more and grows as long as 100 feet (30 m). Even a baby blue whale is big. Two tons (1,814 kg) at birth, a blue whale calf gains 200 pounds (91 kg) a day until it stops nursing at about one year of age.

People once thought that whales were fish. Whales look somewhat like fish. And they live in water—in all the oceans of the world. But whales actually are large sea mammals. The largest whales are often called great whales. Smaller relatives of toothed whales are called porpoises or dolphins. Find out about them on page 446.

Accompanied by her calf, a female humpback whale (above, left) swims in breeding grounds off Hawaii. Mothers and young often seem to show affection by patting each other with their flippers. A female nurses her young by squirting milk into its mouth. The calf stays close to her for nearly a year, drinking her milk and growing larger. The calf will not reach its full size—about 45 feet (14 m) long—for some ten years.

◁ Air bubbles stream from the blowhole of a humpback whale. The animal may be making sounds—grunts, moans, bellows, or whistles. Humpbacks also sing. Again and again they repeat an eerie melody.

Humpback mother and calf perform a graceful ▷ water ballet as they swim. They swing their broad flukes, or tail fins, up and down to push themselves forward. To steer, they use long, winglike flippers.

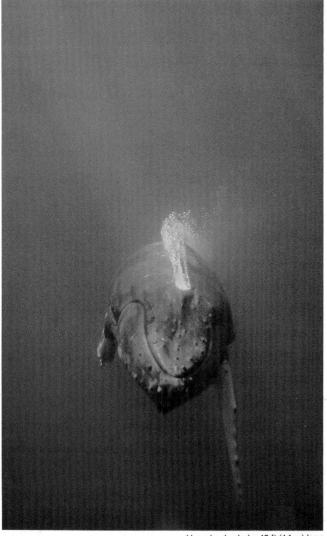

Humpback whale: 45 ft (14 m) long

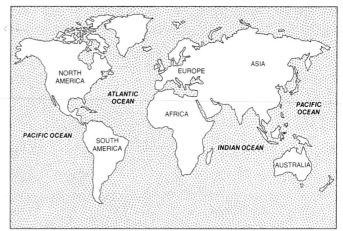

This map shows the range of whales.

Enormous acrobat, a humpback whale leaps skyward. It hurls its body into the air and splashes back into the sea with a thunderous smack. This behavior, called breaching, occurs often among whales.

Whale

Gliding through the water, a whale looks as graceful as a dancer. The water supports its huge body. Despite its size, a whale can swim as if it were almost weightless. The animal can turn, twirl, and swim upside down. It uses the flippers on the sides of its body to steer. By swinging its tail fins—called flukes—up and down, the whale pushes itself through its watery world.

A whale is well equipped for life in the water. Its body is smooth and torpedo-shaped for easy movement. A thick layer of fat, called blubber, covers the animal's body and protects it from the cold temperatures of the ocean depths.

One kind of whale, the sei (SAY) whale, has an especially sleek and streamlined body. With its pointed snout, the animal cuts through the water. Perhaps the fastest of all the whales, the sei whale can swim 31 miles (50 km) an hour in short spurts.

The champion deep diver among whales is the sperm whale. The sperm whale can dive a mile or more in search of food. It can stay underwater for longer than fifty minutes. Then, like all whales, it must surface to breathe.

The whale breathes air through a blowhole, a kind of nostril, which is located on top of its head. As a whale breaks the surface of the ocean, spray shoots into the air. This spray, or spout, appears as the whale exhales. The whale's warm breath gushes out of its blowhole, hits the cooler air, and forms a cloud of mist. Different kinds of whales blow spouts in different shapes and directions.

After spouting, a whale inhales. Then by relaxing a muscle, it closes its blowhole. That way, water stays out of its nostril as the animal dives underwater again. Most great whales come up for air every 5 to 15 minutes. Since whales must come to the surface often, they cannot sleep for very long. Instead, they doze lightly near the surface. They sometimes continue to swim as they sleep.

Scientists divide whales into two groups, toothed whales and baleen (buh-LEAN) whales, depending on how the animals feed. Toothed whales catch their prey with peglike teeth. The largest kind of toothed whale is the sperm whale. A male grows 55 feet (17 m) long and weighs 53 tons (48 t). The sperm whale lives in all the ice-free oceans of the world. Like

---

WHALE   🐾 **8 of 33 species**

LENGTH OF HEAD AND BODY: 7-100 ft (213 cm-30 m)

WEIGHT: 75 lb-200 t (34 kg-181 t)

HABITAT AND RANGE: all the oceans of the world

FOOD: krill, squid, fish

LIFE SPAN: 8 to more than 100 years in the wild, depending on species

REPRODUCTION: 1 young after a pregnancy of 10 to 16 months, depending on species

ORDER: cetaceans

But scientists can only guess why whales act this way. Breaching may help whales communicate or show their strength. It may help to clean their skins of pests. Whales may also leap and splash for fun.

all toothed whales, it uses echolocation (ek-oh-low-KAY-shun) to find its food.

As it swims, a toothed whale sends out pulses of high-pitched clicking sounds. When the sounds hit an object in the water—a fish or a giant squid—echoes bounce back. By listening to the echoes, a sperm whale can tell where an object is and if it is moving. In this way, it can find a meal or avoid an obstacle in its path. Porpoises use echolocation. So do bats. Read how bats use echolocation beginning on page 77. When the sperm whale locates a squid, it grabs the animal in its teeth and swallows it whole.

Scientists think that baleen whales may not use echolocation. Baleen whales such as the humpback whale and the minke (MINK-ee) whale have no teeth. Instead, they have comblike plates called baleen in their upper jaws. The baleen serves as a huge strainer. As a whale moves through the ocean, it takes in mouthfuls of water filled with small fish or shrimplike animals called krill. The whale presses its tongue against the baleen and pushes the water out of its mouth. The food is trapped by the baleen, and the whale can swallow it.

With a flick of its tail, a humpback whale dives deep. ▷
Great whales usually stay underwater for only 5 to 15 minutes at a time. Then they must surface again to breathe. A whale breathes through a blowhole, a kind of nostril, on the top of its head. As the warm breath hits the air, it turns into a moist spray, called a spout.

Whale

Gray whale: 49 ft (15 m) long

△ *Showing a mouthful of baleen, a gray whale surfaces near California. Like all baleen whales, it feeds by using the comblike bristles in its upper jaw as a strainer. Most baleen whales feed near the surface on shrimplike animals called krill. But gray whales eat tiny animals from the sea bottom.*

Baleen, sometimes called whalebone, is made of a hard, flexible material similar to that of fingernails. The size and shape of the baleen differs from one kind of whale to another. The gray whale has baleen that measures about 18 inches (46 cm) long. But the bowhead whale grows plates of baleen as long as 14 feet (4 m)!

During the summer, most baleen whales feed in the cold waters of the polar regions. There krill and other small animals often fill the sea like a soup. An adult blue whale may feast on as much as 8 tons (7,258 kg) of krill a day.

After adult baleen whales feed for four or five months—and gain as much as 40 tons (36 t)—most migrate, or travel, to warmer waters for the winter. Some gray whales of the northern Pacific swim 5,000 miles (8,047 km) from their feeding grounds near Alaska to their winter homes off the coast of Mexico.

Scientists do not know how they find their way to the same place year after year. But they follow the same path in fall and in spring. During the months away from their feeding grounds, baleen whales eat little. They feed whenever they can. But if they cannot find food, they live off their blubber.

Some toothed whales also migrate long distances when the seasons change. In their winter homes, or breeding grounds, both toothed whales and baleen whales mate and bear young. About a year after mating, a female whale gives birth to a single calf. The calf must surface immediately to breathe. Otherwise it may drown.

As a young whale nuzzles up to its mother, she squirts milk into its mouth. A calf nurses for as long as a year, growing quickly. During that time a mother and calf stay close to each other. They show affection by touching each other with their flippers.

After swimming through an underwater forest of giant kelp (below), a gray whale surfaces with a mouthful of seaweed (right). Experts think that whales play with seaweed rather than eat it. Gray whales live in the coastal waters of the northern Pacific. They take their name from the grayish color of their skin. Many people watch gray whales pass the coast of California as they migrate, or travel, with the change of seasons. The animals seek warmer waters in winter and return to colder ones in spring. Though people once hunted them extensively, laws now protect the whales.

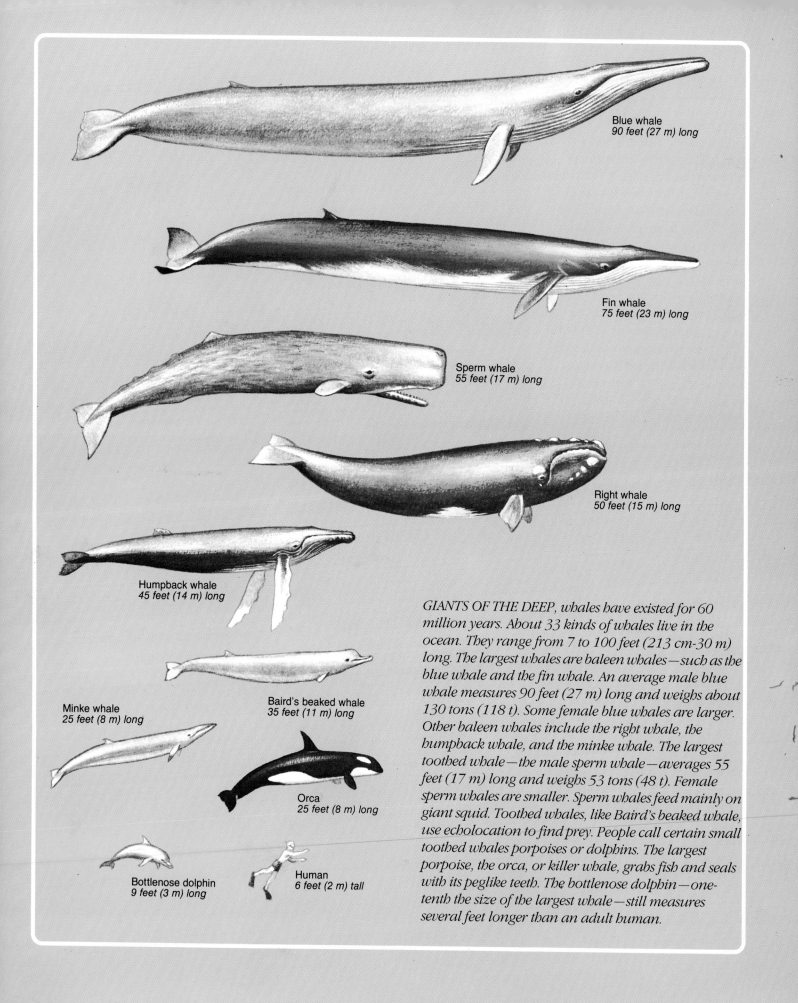

Blue whale
90 feet (27 m) long

Fin whale
75 feet (23 m) long

Sperm whale
55 feet (17 m) long

Right whale
50 feet (15 m) long

Humpback whale
45 feet (14 m) long

Baird's beaked whale
35 feet (11 m) long

Minke whale
25 feet (8 m) long

Orca
25 feet (8 m) long

Bottlenose dolphin
9 feet (3 m) long

Human
6 feet (2 m) tall

GIANTS OF THE DEEP, whales have existed for 60 million years. About 33 kinds of whales live in the ocean. They range from 7 to 100 feet (213 cm-30 m) long. The largest whales are baleen whales—such as the blue whale and the fin whale. An average male blue whale measures 90 feet (27 m) long and weighs about 130 tons (118 t). Some female blue whales are larger. Other baleen whales include the right whale, the humpback whale, and the minke whale. The largest toothed whale—the male sperm whale—averages 55 feet (17 m) long and weighs 53 tons (48 t). Female sperm whales are smaller. Sperm whales feed mainly on giant squid. Toothed whales, like Baird's beaked whale, use echolocation to find prey. People call certain small toothed whales porpoises or dolphins. The largest porpoise, the orca, or killer whale, grabs fish and seals with its peglike teeth. The bottlenose dolphin—one-tenth the size of the largest whale—still measures several feet longer than an adult human.

Southern right whale: 50 ft (15 m) long when fully grown

△ *Young southern right whale dwarfs a photographer as it cruises off Australia's coast. At about 25 feet (8 m) in length, the whale has reached only half its adult size. When fully grown, it will weigh about 40 tons (36 t). Unlike other right whales, which have mostly dark skin, this whale is a rare whitish color.*

Most kinds of whales travel together in groups that are called pods. But female sperm whales and their young live together most of the year. They are only joined by a few males during the mating season. Some males swim alone, while others may travel together in pods.

Whales often communicate with one another. They make many different kinds of noises, from high-pitched squeaks to low, rumbling groans. Humpbacks sing. They repeat the same song, with slight differences from whale to whale. Over and over again, they sing their eerie combination of wails, moans, and shrieks. No one knows why.

Other kinds of whale behavior also puzzle the experts who study these huge animals. Whales often slap the water with their flippers and flukes. They leap out of the water and splash down on their backs. This activity is called breaching.

Scientists do not know why whales breach. It may be a form of communication or a way of playing. Or it may be that breaching whales are trying to shake off annoying parasites—small animals that cling to their bodies.

Parasites can be harmful to whales. But there are bigger dangers that lurk in the ocean: sharks and large porpoises known as orcas. Both of these animals prey on whales, particularly on the young ones. Orcas—also known as killer whales—hunt together in packs.

Aggressive and fast, they can attack and kill an adult blue whale many times their size.

The whale's most dangerous enemies, though, are people. For centuries, human hunters have killed whales—for meat, for oil, and for baleen. Sperm whales are valued for a waxy substance called ambergris (AM-ber-griss), located in the intestines. It is used in making some perfumes.

Until about a hundred years ago, whaling was a major industry in the United States. Whalers would set out on long voyages in pursuit of the animals. When the men on deck sighted a whale's spout, they sang out loudly, "Thar she blows!" Then, in smaller boats, they followed the whale until they were close enough to throw their harpoons at it, kill the animal, and pull it in.

After several years at sea, the whaling ships would return to port loaded with baleen and oil melted down from blubber. The oil was made into soap, or it was used to keep lamps burning. Stiff and springy, the baleen was formed into umbrella ribs and horsewhips. It also was used in undergarments for women.

Later, more deadly methods of hunting whales were developed. Whalers went to sea in large factory ships and fast boats with harpoon guns. In the animal's feeding grounds, whalers killed huge numbers of the gigantic sea mammals.

Over the centuries, whalers hunted some kinds of whales more than others. The right whale got its name because it was considered the "right" whale to hunt. It swam slowly, floated when dead, and supplied large quantities of oil. Sperm whales, gray whales, humpback whales, and other kinds were also hunted extensively. So many were killed that some species were in danger of extinction.

Today the great whales are protected by international treaties. However, a few countries still hunt some of them.

▽ *Surfacing through a hole in the ice near Antarctica, a minke whale shoots a cloud of mist into the air. The waters around it have frozen almost completely. Baleen whales such as minkes travel to polar seas in summer. They retreat to warmer waters in winter.*

Minke whale: 25 ft (8 m) long

Western white-bearded wildebeest: 53 in (135 cm) tall at the shoulder

Kicking up dust, western white-bearded wildebeest bulls gallop through a clearing in Tanzania.

Wildebeest

(WILL-duh-beast)

QUIETLY GRAZING, a male wildebeest, called a bull, stands on a vast grassland in Africa. Suddenly the big, bearded animal tosses his head. He snorts, paws the ground, rolls in the dust, digs his horns in the earth, and thrashes his tail. To an observer, the wildebeest might seem to be clowning or frisking. But such a display is a way in which the animal shows that he controls a territory, or area.

The wildebeest—also known as the gnu (NYOO)—is a large antelope. It looks like a combination of different animals. The wildebeest has a broad head and thick horns somewhat like those of a bison, a flowing tail like that of a horse, and long, thin legs like an antelope's. A mane grows on its neck and shoulders, and a coat of short hair covers its hide. The bull's deep grunts sound like a giant croaking frog. Because of its unusual appearance and spirited behavior, Dutch settlers in South Africa named the animal *wildebeest*, which means "wild beast."

A male wildebeest may weigh as much as 550

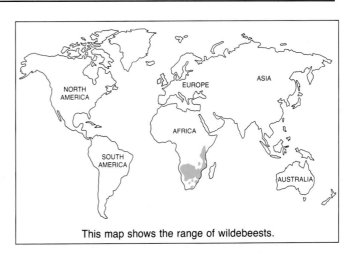

This map shows the range of wildebeests.

pounds (249 kg) and may measure more than 4 feet (122 cm) tall at the shoulder. Like the male, a female, called a cow, has horns. But she is smaller.

Two species, or kinds, of wildebeests make their homes in Africa: the blue wildebeest and the black wildebeest. The grayish blue color of its coat gives the

571

△ *Still wobbly, a western white-bearded wildebeest calf rises to its feet minutes after birth. The mother cleans the newborn by licking it.*

blue wildebeest its name. Dark bands streak the animal's neck, shoulders, and sides. Some of the blue wildebeests have fringes of light-colored chin and neck hair. And these animals are known as white-bearded wildebeests.

The black wildebeest has no stripes. Most of its body is dark. But its long, silky tail, sweeping almost to the ground, is a whitish color. Sometimes the animal is known as the white-tailed wildebeest.

The blue wildebeest ranges from southern to eastern Africa. The black wildebeest, which once roamed the grasslands of South Africa, nearly died out in the last century. Several thousand black wildebeests now live protected on private farms and on wildlife preserves, mostly in small herds.

Wildebeests feed mainly on grasses. They look for tender green blades. Those that live on East Africa's Serengeti Plain have no trouble finding food during the rainy season. But when the dry season begins,

▽ *With zebras nearby, western white-bearded wildebeest cows graze with their young in Tanzania. Most wildebeest calves are born during a three-week period in the rainy season.*

the animals there are forced to leave the parched area. They migrate, or travel, more than 800 miles (1,287 km). Always on the move, they search for green grass and water.

The migration from the plains often is heaviest in May. Then more than a million wildebeests—joined by zebras, gazelles, and other animals—wind across the Serengeti like a slow-moving train. The animals head westward and northward into open woodlands. There they can find food and water until November.

As soon as the rains change the dry plains back to a green grassland, the animals return to the Serengeti. Where food and water are available all year, wildebeests usually do not migrate.

The strong bulls in every wildebeest group defend territories that they have marked with their waste. They also mark the areas with substances produced by glands on their faces and hooves. When wildebeests migrate, the bulls establish territories wherever they stop. Bulls that remain in one area may

Two Egyptian geese move away as blue wildebeests approach a water hole in Namibia. At certain times of the year, wildebeests often travel miles across parched plains to find food and water.

Blue wildebeest: 53 in (135 cm) tall at the shoulder

keep the same territories year after year. Usually, a bull must have a territory to attract females during the mating season.

When a bull claims a territory, he may be challenged by a neighboring male that trespasses. No two challenges are exactly alike. Often, the bull turns his side to the intruder and blocks his path. The two then circle each other. If the invader refuses to take part in the challenge, the first wildebeest may begin bucking, spinning, and kicking.

The two may start to graze, cautiously eyeing each other. Suddenly both drop to their knees. Thrusting their horns into the ground, they raise a

shower of dust. Sometimes they really fight. The bulls remain on their knees, lock horns, and ram each other briefly. Serious injury is rare. The intruding bull often walks away, grazing as he goes.

Young males and bulls without territories form bachelor herds. Bachelors are often forced to live on the fringes of the wildebeest group. There, among the tall grasses, enemies such as lions often lurk. If a herd of bachelors wanders into a bull's territory, the bull quickly chases the group out.

Groups of females and young roam in nursery herds. They may wander from one bull's territory to another. When a bull sees the cows approaching, he

Wildebeest

◁ *Thousands of western white-bearded wildebeests graze on a preserve in Kenya. Even in the dry season, the area has enough water to support many animals.*

calls out with loud, deep grunts. If he fails to lure them with his calls, he may chase them and try to keep them in his territory.

About eight and a half months after mating, a female bears a single calf. The calf, able to stand shakily within minutes of its birth, can walk and run soon afterward. In a few days, it is fast enough and strong enough to keep up with the herd.

Most wildebeest calves are born during a three-week period. The calves are not strong enough to outrun such enemies as spotted hyenas, lions, cheetahs, leopards, and wild dogs. But the presence of many calves helps protect the young during their first few days. Their enemies may have trouble singling out one calf to prey on.

Find out about some relatives of wildebeests— gazelles, gerenuks, and impalas—in their own entries. Read about other antelopes on page 52.

WILDEBEEST

HEIGHT: 45-55 in (114-140 cm) at the shoulder

WEIGHT: 350-550 lb (159-249 kg)

HABITAT AND RANGE: grassy plains and open woodlands in southern, central, and eastern Africa

FOOD: mainly grasses

LIFE SPAN: as long as 21 years in captivity

REPRODUCTION: 1 young after a pregnancy of about 8½ months

ORDER: artiodactyls

Broomlike tufts of hair stand straight up on the neck and face of a black wildebeest. This animal's short, stiff mane, handlebar horns, and light-colored tail set it apart from its closest relative, the blue wildebeest. Once hunted nearly to extinction, black wildebeests now live protected on preserves and private farms.

Black wildebeest: 47 in (119 cm) tall at the shoulder

575

Wolf

HEAD THROWN BACK, a wolf points its nose toward the sky and begins to howl. The call soars to a high note, then slides down in smooth, rippling tones. Wolves may howl at any time of the day or night.

Wolves keep in touch by howling. A rising and falling "lonesome howl" may mean that an animal has become separated from the pack, or group. A howling pack may be warning other packs to stay away from its hunting grounds. Wolves also howl to call the pack together after a hunt is over. It often seems that wolves howl simply for the pleasure of being together. When one wolf starts to howl, other members of the pack join in.

The wolf is the largest member of the dog family. It looks much like a German Shepherd dog. It has thick, shaggy fur and a bushy tail. With its long legs, it can run great distances. And a wolf's powerful jaws can seize prey and hold it tightly.

Wolves can have coats of different colors. The gray wolf usually has a coat that is a mixture of white, black, gray, and brown hairs. Sometimes the animal may have black fur. Other gray wolves may have reddish coats. Gray wolves that live on the tundra, the treeless plains of the Far North, have thicker, longer fur that may be almost white. These wolves are called tundra wolves.

Another kind of wolf, the red wolf, has shorter fur than the gray wolf. Some red wolves do have reddish coats, but others vary in color from light tan to gray or black.

Wolves once roamed almost all of the lands that are north of the Equator. These animals were at home everywhere, except in tropical regions and in deserts. They lived in the forests and on prairies, grasslands, and tundra.

Today gray wolves—often called timber wolves—have been hunted almost to extinction in the United States, except in Alaska and Minnesota. A few packs have recently returned to Michigan, Wisconsin, and Montana. People have brought others back

◁ *Casting long shadows on the snow, gray wolves cross a frozen lake in Minnesota. The pack follows a trail made on earlier rounds of hunting deer and moose. In deep snow, wolves usually travel in single file. Each wolf can follow the trail more easily, because it does not have to break its own path through the drifts.*

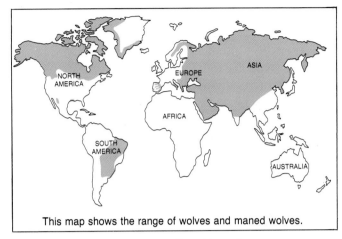

This map shows the range of wolves and maned wolves.

WOLF AND MANED WOLF 🐾 **2 of 3 species**

LENGTH OF HEAD AND BODY: 36-63 in (91-160 cm); tail, 13-20 in (33-51 cm)

WEIGHT: 40-175 lb (18-79 kg)

HABITAT AND RANGE: forests, tundra, swamps, and prairies in parts of North America, Europe, and Asia. Maned wolf: grasslands and swamps in South America

FOOD: large and small mammals, birds, fish, lizards, snakes, frogs, insects, and fruit

LIFE SPAN: 16 years in captivity

REPRODUCTION: 5 to 7 young after a pregnancy of about 2 months

ORDER: carnivores

Whining wolves wait as their pack leader eats. Wolves may go for days without making a kill. When they bring down large prey, they gorge themselves. A wolf may eat almost 20 pounds (9 kg) of meat in one meal.

Wolf

to Idaho and Wyoming. There are many in Canada, Alaska, and parts of Asia, but few in Europe. Red wolves of the southeastern U.S. were destroyed in the wild but saved in captivity and restored to North Carolina. Distant relatives called maned wolves live on grasslands and in swamps in South America.

Few animals have been feared so much, with so little reason, by people. Unless a wolf is sick, it will rarely attack a human. Yet, for centuries, people have hunted, poisoned, and trapped wolves.

The biggest threat to wolves is their changing habitat. As settlers move into the wilderness areas where wolves live, people may raise livestock there. Wolves sometimes attack the livestock. Then farmers and ranchers try to get rid of the wolves.

Wolves will eat almost anything—small mammals, birds, fish, lizards, snakes, and fruit. They usually depend on large prey, however—moose, elk, caribou, sheep, and deer—for their food.

Because their prey is often so much larger than they are, wolves must hunt together in packs. Tails wagging, the wolves crowd around the pack leader. They frisk about, touch noses, and lick the leader's mouth. A few whines and a long, low howl may signal the beginning of the hunt. The members of the pack all join in the call. Each animal howls on a different note. The excitement peaks in a wild chorus.

The wolves set out at a smooth, easy trot. Wolves can lope along for many miles, and they can run quickly for short distances. Usually wolves travel in

On a hilltop in a national park in Italy, a pack of gray wolves rests and stretches during a winter afternoon.

△ *Nose pointed skyward, a gray wolf fills the frosty air with a howl. A wolf can vary its call by sucking in its cheeks. It can also change the sound by curling and uncurling its tongue.*

Nose to nose, two gray wolves gently nuzzle each ▷ other. The wolf with the lighter fur is the female leader of a pack in Minnesota.

single file. In winter, they may travel great distances to find enough food.

Wolves try to attack any prey they find. Strong and healthy animals can often escape, and many chases end in failure. The victims caught are usually sick, injured, or very young or old animals.

Wolves hunt different animals in different ways. They may chase a caribou herd until they spot a weak animal and attack it. Mountain sheep may try to escape from wolves by running up steep, rocky cliffs. Wolves can surprise them by attacking from above. When musk-oxen are threatened, they form a line to protect themselves. Generally, the only way that wolves can bring down a musk-ox is to find an animal that has been left alone.

A moose is a wolf's largest and most dangerous prey. A moose can be ten times as large as a wolf. Charging and whirling, a moose kicks at attackers with its hind feet and slashes with its front feet. But if the wolves can make a moose run, the larger animal

cannot easily kick. Then the wolves can bring it down by attacking from behind.

A wolf pack often includes about six wolves. All the members are usually related. One male acts as the leader of the entire pack. One female leads the females and the young. In larger packs, she also leads less important males. Each wolf has a place in the pack. A leader shows its rank by holding its head up and holding its tail straight out. Less important wolves roll over, wriggle, or crouch before the leader. They

Wolf _____

lay back their ears and tuck their tails between their legs. Sometimes pack members bare their teeth, growl, or snap at one another. But these threats seldom turn into real attacks.

The two leaders keep the wolf pack together and lead the defense against such enemies as bears or wolves in other packs. The leaders decide when to hunt, and they choose the prey. They also settle fights over food or between cubs. The leader is usually the first wolf to feed after a kill. The male and female leaders are often the only members of the pack to mate and bear young.

Before the young are born in the spring, the male and the female prepare a den. Sometimes

Brightly colored salmon attract a gray wolf in ▷ Alaska. The water churns with fish swimming upstream to lay eggs. Wolves catch fish in shallow streams by snapping them up in their jaws. Despite the plentiful prey, this wolf needed several bites to land a meal. ▽ Red wolf follows a trail through the brush. The species is now in danger of extinction through loss of habitat and cross-breeding with coyotes.

Red wolf: 47 in (119 cm) long; tail, 15 in (38 cm)

wolves dig a new den. They may also enlarge a fox den or use a beaver lodge. A wolf den may be 15 feet (5 m) long and high enough for a wolf to stand in.

Usually from five to seven pups are born in a litter. A newborn wolf has short legs and a blunt nose. The offspring is covered with dark fur. When the pups are about two weeks old, their eyes open. At about three weeks of age, they crawl out of the den for the first time. Then they begin to eat solid food. The pups

may continue to nurse for another month, however.

The entire pack takes an interest in a new litter. All the adults help care for the pups, bringing food to them and sometimes baby-sitting when their parents are hunting. When a wolf returns from hunting, the pups rush up to it. They whine and wag their tails and lick the adult's face. The wolf then brings up some of the meat it has swallowed and brought back to the den in its stomach.

Soon the pups start exploring the world around their den. Rough-and-tumble play helps decide which young wolves will become leaders of the pups. One pup sneaks up and pounces on another. That sets off a wild chase. Pups attack each other in play. They practice hunting by attacking insects, birds, and rodents. These games help the pups learn hunting skills they will need later on.

During the summer, pups stay in several resting

spots while the adults hunt. By fall, the young wolves may be able to join the pack as it travels. They help to run down prey, but they usually let the older wolves make the kill.

When winter arrives, the young are nearly grown. But they will not be expert hunters until they are almost two years old. Then some young wolves will stay with the pack. Others will leave to find mates and to start new packs.

◁ *Maned wolf gallops through tall grass in South America. A black mane stands up on its neck, and black hairs cover its muzzle and legs. Maned wolves hunt small mammals and birds.*

Maned wolf: 42 in (107 cm) long; tail, 15 in (38 cm)

Wolverine

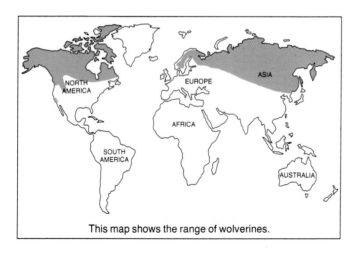

This map shows the range of wolverines.

WOLVERINE 🐾 I of I species

LENGTH OF HEAD AND BODY: **26-34 in (66-86 cm); tail, 7-10 in (18-25 cm)**

WEIGHT: **24-40 lb (11-18 kg)**

HABITAT AND RANGE: **forests and tundra in northern North America, Europe, and Asia**

FOOD: **remains of dead animals, large hoofed animals, small mammals, birds, eggs, fruit, and plants**

LIFE SPAN: **as long as 16 years in captivity**

REPRODUCTION: **I to 4 young after a pregnancy of about 9 months**

ORDER: **carnivores**

AN AIR OF MYSTERY has long surrounded the wolverine. People rarely see this furry, bearlike animal with the short, bushy tail. But it is legendary for its fierceness, its great strength, and its huge appetite. The wolverine lives only in wilderness areas—forests and treeless plains—in parts of northern North America, Europe, and Asia.

Despite its appearance and the sound of its name, the wolverine is not related to the bear or to the wolf. One of the largest members of the weasel family, the wolverine may weigh 40 pounds (18 kg). It measures 3 feet (91 cm) long, including its tail.

In summer, the wolverine eats a wide variety of food—berries, plants, eggs, rodents, and rabbits. In winter, the wolverine feeds mainly on dead animals it finds, such as caribou, elk, and deer. With its keen sense of smell, the wolverine can find food buried under snow. It may also dig some rodents out of the burrows where they hibernate (HYE-bur-nate), or sleep, all winter. The wolverine may kill more prey than it can eat at one time. It stores the meat and returns to it later to feed.

Occasionally, a wolverine may attack a caribou that is weak or bogged down by snow. With its furry paws, the wolverine can move quickly across snow, when travel is difficult for larger animals.

As it looks for food, the wolverine lopes slowly

△ On a midsummer afternoon, a wolverine hunts for rodents along a ridge. The animal, a large member of the weasel family, is legendary for its great strength and fierceness.

△ Blanketed by heavy, dark fur, a male wolverine in Alaska pauses in the snow.

throughout a wide range. It often travels as far as 15 miles (24 km) in a day. The wolverine marks its range with a strong-smelling substance that is produced by glands in its body. The scent marks may mean, "I am hunting here." The animal also marks trees with scratches and bites.

A male shares his range with two or three females. In late winter or early spring, about six months after mating, the female makes a den under the snow or in a hidden place. There she gives birth to a litter of one to four young. They are fully grown in about six months, and by the following winter they go off on their own.

Trappers in North America once hunted wolverines for their fur, which was used to line parkas. By the early 1900s, the animals had almost disappeared. Since the 1960s, wolverines have been protected by law in several states.

583

Wombat

Hairy-nosed wombat: 36 in (91 cm) long; tail, 2 in (5 cm)

Hairy-nosed wombat waddles among clumps of grass in its feeding grounds. The plump marsupial's front teeth have sharp edges that can easily cut tough grasses, roots, and bark.

ROLY-POLY AS A BEAR CUB, a stocky wombat basks in the early morning sunlight. Then this marsupial (mar-SOO-pea-ul), or pouched mammal, gets up and waddles into its nearby burrow. It curls up there and sleeps most of the day. At night, the wombat heads for its feeding grounds, where it searches for roots, grasses, and bark to eat.

Wombats live in forests and on grasslands in parts of Australia and its nearby islands. There are two kinds of wombats. The coarse-haired wombat, which weighs as much as 80 pounds (36 kg), has rough brown or black fur. The smaller hairy-nosed wombat has a silky, gray-and-brown coat.

Like badgers, wombats dig large burrows with their short, powerful legs and sharp claws. They line their dens with pieces of bark.

When alarmed, the shy wombat runs into its burrow. But if a dingo, a kind of wild dog, tries to follow it

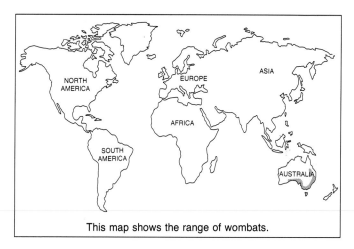

This map shows the range of wombats.

inside, the wombat kicks the attacker with its strong hind legs.

A female wombat gives birth to one tiny offspring between April and June of each year. The young wombat crawls into the rear-opening pouch on its mother's belly and continues to grow and develop there. As the mother walks about, her offspring can sometimes be seen peeking out between her hind legs.

At about five months of age, the young wombat begins to leave the pouch for short periods. It returns frequently to nurse or to seek shelter. By December, it is able to take care of itself.

WOMBAT 🐾 **2 of 3 species**

LENGTH OF HEAD AND BODY: 28-47 in (71-119 cm); tail, as long as 2 in (5 cm)

WEIGHT: 32-80 lb (15-36 kg)

HABITAT AND RANGE: forests, grasslands, and dry regions in parts of Australia and nearby islands

FOOD: grasses, roots, and bark

LIFE SPAN: about 25 years in captivity

REPRODUCTION: 1 young after a pregnancy of about 1 month

ORDER: marsupials

Deep burrows on a dry plain in Australia provide homes for a colony of hairy-nosed wombats.

Woodchuck

The woodchuck is a kind of marmot. Find out about marmots on page 352.

Yak

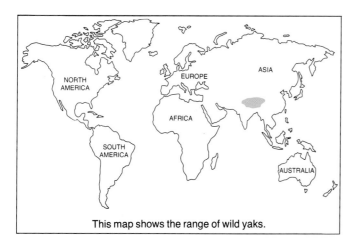

This map shows the range of wild yaks.

THE WINDSWEPT HIGHLANDS OF TIBET provide a home for the wild yak of central Asia. Few other large mammals live at such heights. The massive yak roams cold, treeless plateaus and the mountain ranges nearby. It can climb as high as 20,000 feet (6,096 m) above sea level.

The yak has a low-slung body, and it often keeps its broad head close to the ground. Males have long, curving horns that may measure 3 feet (91 cm) from tip to tip. When fully grown, male wild yaks may reach 6 feet (183 cm) at the shoulder and weigh as much as 1,800 pounds (816 kg). Females are much smaller and have shorter, thinner horns.

Surefooted relative of the cow, the sturdy yak is suited to the harsh lands where it lives. During the winter, a soft, dense undercoat grows beneath coarse, longer hairs and helps protect the animal from the cold. In spring, yaks shed their woolly undercoats. Often, as the wool falls out, chunks of it get caught in the long fringes that hang from the yaks' shoulders, sides, and legs.

Yaks graze on grasses and herbs. They also browse, nibbling the leaves of small shrubs. Like cows, they do not chew their food thoroughly before swallowing. After eating, they bring up wads of partly digested food, called cuds. The animals chew the cuds further, then swallow and digest them.

Female yaks and their young travel in herds that

▽ *Sturdy and surefooted, shaggy domestic yaks travel a narrow trail in Nepal. They climb near Mount Everest, the world's highest mountain.*

Casting shadows across the snow, yaks and porters approach a mountain pass in Pakistan.

may number hundreds of animals. In such large groups, they can protect themselves from wolves. Yaks have a keen sense of smell. If members of the herd pick up a scent of danger, they may rush together. They face the enemy with heads lowered and defend themselves with their horns.

Older males usually stay with the females only during the mating season, in the fall. During the rest of the year, males roam alone or in small groups.

About nine months after mating, a female bears one calf. It remains with her for at least a year.

During the hottest part of the summer, yaks leave lower pastures, where they spend the winter. They head for cool mountain heights, where snow remains on the ground all year. Yaks are skilled at feeding in the snow. They brush it aside with their muzzles or use their hooves to uncover patches of grass. When water is scarce, they may eat the snow.

Centuries ago, people of Asia began to domesticate, or tame, the yak. Domestic yaks are much smaller than wild yaks. Their black or brown coats may have patches of white or red. Domestic yaks make sturdy pack animals. They supply their owners with milk, meat, hair, and hides for leather. Their waste is burned for fuel.

YAK 🐾 I of I species

HEIGHT: 37 in-6 ft (94-183 cm) at the shoulder

WEIGHT: 400-2,200 lb (181-1,000 kg)

HABITAT AND RANGE: mountainous regions of central Asia; domestic yaks are found throughout a wider area of central and southern Asia

FOOD: grasses, herbs, leaves, shoots, and twigs

LIFE SPAN: about 25 years in captivity

REPRODUCTION: I young after a pregnancy of about 9 months

ORDER: artiodactyls

Z

Zebra

(ZEE-bruh)

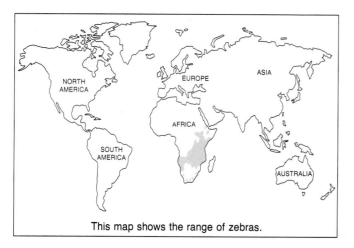

This map shows the range of zebras.

NO TWO ZEBRAS have stripes that are exactly alike. Each set of stripes is a little different from the next, just as one person's fingerprints are always different from another's. Even the patterns on opposite sides of a zebra's body do not match exactly.

No one knows why zebras have stripes. They may help hide the horselike animals in tall grass or in shimmering sunlight. When a group of zebras runs, it may be hard for an enemy to pick out a single animal. The different patterns may also help zebras tell each other apart. Scientists think the stripes may help protect the animals against some biting flies. These insects can only make out large patches of black or white. They probably do not see the zebras' narrow stripes, so they rarely bother the animals.

People have always been fascinated by the zebra's stripes. Two thousand years ago, Romans exhibited captured zebras in parades in Rome. Their name for the zebra meant "tiger horse."

Three kinds of zebras live in Africa. The most numerous are the plains zebras, sometimes called Burchell's zebras, which are found in open, grassy areas. Mountain zebras spend their time on rocky hillsides. They have become rare. Grevy's (GRAY-veez) zebras are larger than the other kinds. These animals live on

Tail waving, a plains zebra in eastern Africa leaps into the water as it crosses a stream.

588

Plains zebra: 51 in (130 cm) tall at the shoulder

Zebra

△ Nipping and nuzzling, young plains zebras play at fighting. Zebras often groom each other. They sometimes rest their heads across each other's backs.

▽ Although no two zebras' stripes match exactly, each kind of zebra has a similar pattern. Short stripes run crosswise over the rump of a mountain zebra. Narrow, black stripes, spaced close together, mark a Grevy's zebra. A plains zebra has broader stripes. Fainter bands sometimes alternate with the darker stripes.

Mountain zebra

Grevy's zebra

Plains zebra

△ *Flying hooves send up clouds of dust as plains zebras move across a dry grassland in Africa. Antelopes called springboks travel with them. If alarmed, zebras bunch together for protection.*

the dry plains and on hillsides, and are also rare.

Plains and mountain zebras—no bigger than ponies—roam in family groups. A male, called a stallion, stays with several females, called mares, and their young. Even when families graze in herds of as many as 10,000 animals, each family stays together. If family members become separated, they call to one another with barking cries.

Each stallion protects the females and young in his family. Ears pricked forward, he listens carefully. If enemies approach, such as lions, hyenas, and wild dogs, the mares bunch together and hurry away with their offspring. The stallion follows, fighting off the attacker with bites and kicks.

A stallion always stays alert for rival stallions. If two rivals meet, they may sniff, touch noses, then leap apart. If one tries to steal a mare from the other to start a family of his own, the two may kick, bite, and wrestle neck to neck.

At night, plains zebras remain on flat, grassy plains where they can see in every direction. At least

---

ZEBRA 🐾 **2 of 3 species**

HEIGHT: **41-59 in (104-150 cm) at the shoulder**

WEIGHT: **440-990 lb (200-450 kg)**

HABITAT AND RANGE: **mountains and open, grassy plains in eastern, central, and southern Africa**

FOOD: **grasses**

LIFE SPAN: **about 40 years in captivity**

REPRODUCTION: **usually 1 young after a pregnancy of 11½ to 13 months**

ORDER: **perissodactyls**

△ *Plains zebras and antelopes called gemsboks gather at a water hole in Namibia. One zebra kneels to lick salt from the ground. Zebras often share water holes with other animals.*

▽ *Plains zebra mare rolls in the dust to rid herself of insects. Her days-old offspring stands close by. Young zebras can run and play just an hour after birth.*

one adult stays awake, on guard. Just after sunrise, the zebras move off in single file to graze on tall grasses. They stop to drink at water holes that dot the plains. Elephants, wildebeests, gazelles, buffaloes, and giraffes may feed and drink nearby. With so many eyes, ears, and noses alert for danger, all of the animals at a water hole are safer from the predators who may be watching silently.

Grevy's zebras live in different kinds of groups than other zebras. Although they may come together to graze, they do not always stay together. Some individuals even travel on their own.

During certain months of the year, little rain falls in parts of Africa. Then the herds of zebras wander widely looking for food. Pawing the ground, mountain zebras may dig for water. When there is plenty of grass to eat, zebras usually remain in one place. Most young are born then. A newborn zebra's stripes are brown and white. Its mane is still wispy. When it is an hour old, the baby can frisk and run. For the first few days, its mother keeps other members of the group away until the foal recognizes her.

592

Zebra

Narrow stripes of Grevy's zebras blend ▷ *with tall grass in the noonday sun. These zebras have long, hairy ears, and they bray like donkeys. Though other kinds of zebras live in the same family group all year round, Grevy's zebras move freely from group to group.*

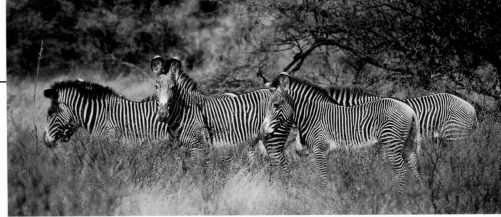

Grevy's zebra: 59 in (150 cm) tall at the shoulder

Zebu   The zebu is a kind of cow. Read about cows on page 158.

Zorilla

(zuh-RILL-uh)

In a rare daytime appearance, a zorilla in Africa hunts for insects or rodents. The zorilla roots for prey with its snout or digs for food with its long claws.

ZORILLA

LENGTH OF HEAD AND BODY: 13-15 in (33-38 cm); tail, 8-12 in (20-30 cm)

WEIGHT: 2-3 lb (1 kg)

HABITAT AND RANGE: brushy plains and grasslands in parts of Africa

FOOD: insects, small mammals, reptiles, birds, and frogs

LIFE SPAN: 13 years in captivity

REPRODUCTION: 2 or 3 young after a pregnancy of 5 weeks

ORDER: carnivores

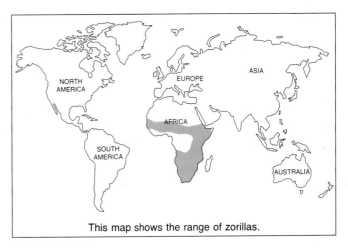

This map shows the range of zorillas.

WITH A THICK, BLACK COAT marked by white stripes, the zorilla of Africa resembles its relative the skunk. Like the skunk, the zorilla has scent glands under its bushy tail. When alarmed, the animal raises the hair on its body and tail, making itself look bigger. If that action doesn't frighten its attacker away, the zorilla screams, lifts its tail, and sprays a strong-smelling fluid at its enemy.

At night, the zorilla trots across open grasslands and brushy plains on its short legs. It searches for insects, small mammals, snakes, and birds to eat. During the day, the zorilla rests in a rock shelter or in a shallow burrow.

A female gives birth in the burrow or in another well-hidden place. Usually two or three young are born after a pregnancy of five weeks.

593

Glossary

The **Book of Mammals** may contain words that are new to you. Their meanings are explained below. Knowing what these words mean may help you to better understand the **Book of Mammals** and other books about animals.

adapt—to become suited to one's surroundings. Animals can adapt to changes in the environment over many generations.

aestivate—to spend the hot months in a sleeplike state. While aestivating, an animal breathes more slowly and has a lower body temperature and slower heart rate than while active.

amphibians—cold-blooded vertebrates, such as frogs, toads, and salamanders. Amphibians spend part of their lives in the water and part on land.

ancestor—a forerunner; a progenitor of an existing species or group.

antlers—a pair of solid bony forms on the heads of most species of male deer. Antlers sprout, continue to grow, and fall off every year. Female caribou also grow antlers.

bachelor herd—a group formed by young male animals and males without territories. Bachelor herds are common among many kinds of hoofed mammals.

baleen—plates of hard, flexible material, with fringed inner edges, that grow from the upper jaws of some whales. Baleen plates serve as strainers. They allow water to pass through a whale's mouth, but they trap small animals for food.

behavior—anything that an organism does involving action and response to stimulation.

blubber—the fat of whales and other large marine mammals.

◁ *Bold and majestic, a tiger, largest of the cats, stares from a forest in India.*

brachiate—to swing with the arms in a hand-over-hand movement from one hold—often a branch or a vine—to another.

breed—to mate and produce young. Also, a breed is a group of domestic animals of one species in which certain characteristics, such as size, color, and type of hair, have been gradually developed and maintained by humans.

bristle—a short, stiff, coarse hair or filament.

browse—to feed on the leaves, twigs, and young shoots of shrubs and trees.

brush—a growth of small trees or shrubs.

burrow—a hole in the ground often dug by an animal and used as a place to live, to hide, and to bear young.

bush—an area covered with low shrubby plants.

camouflage—a disguise, such as body coloring, that helps an animal blend in with its surroundings.

captivity—the state of being confined, as when an animal is kept in a zoo or an animal park.

carnivore—a flesh-eating mammal.

climate—a region having specified atmospheric conditions.

coat—the external growth on an animal.

courtship—the process of performing actions to attract a mate.

cud—a wad of partly chewed and digested food brought up to the mouth from the stomach of certain hoofed mammals. The cud is chewed again, swallowed, and then further digested.

den—a hollow space that an animal uses as a place to live, to hide, and to bear young.

descendant—an animal coming from, or proceeding from, an ancestor.

desert—a dry, generally treeless region that usually receives less than 10 inches (25 cm) of precipitation a year. A desert may be hot or cold.

displays—actions that serve as signals to other animals. Animals may use displays to attract mates. Displays may also help to ward off enemies and to show how important or strong an animal is to the other animals in its group.

domestic animals—animals, such as dogs, cats, cattle, or sheep, that have been tamed by humans.

echolocation—a system by which an animal sends out beeps or pulses of high-pitched sounds and listens for the echoes that bounce back when the sounds hit an object. Bats, porpoises, solenodons, whales, and some shrews use echolocation to find their way, to avoid obstacles, and to detect prey.

endangered—reduced in numbers to the point of near extinction.

environment—surroundings, including air, land, water, and living things.

extinct—no longer in existence.

feral animal—an animal, now living in the wild, that was once domestic or had ancestors that were once domestic.

flank—the fleshy part of the side of the body between the ribs and hip.

flipper—a broad, flat limb used for swimming. Seals, porpoises, and whales have flippers.

flukes—tail fins or the flattened parts of a whale's tail.

food chain—a sequence of plants and animals that provide food for members of a community. Plants make their own food and are eaten by plant-eating animals. These animals are consumed by meat-eating animals. For example, grass may be eaten by a mouse. The mouse may be eaten by a weasel. The weasel may be eaten by a hawk.

forest—an area with thickly growing trees and underbrush.

freeze—to become very still.

fur—the hairy coat of a mammal.

grassland—an area covered with grasses and herbs.

graze—to feed on grasses and herbs.

groom—to clean the skin and hair by removing dirt and insects. For many animals, grooming one another is important in maintaining the social relations of their group.

grub—a soft, thick, wormlike larva of an insect.

guard hairs—long, coarse hairs that cover and protect an animal's soft, thick underfur.

habitat—the terrain in which an animal lives naturally, such as a desert, a forest, a grassland, or a swamp.

herbivore—a plant-eating animal.

herd—a group of wild or domestic animals of one or more kinds that feed and travel together.

A river otter stands alert on the banks of a stream in Colorado.

hibernate—to spend the cold months in a sleeplike state. While hibernating, an animal breathes more slowly and has a lower body temperature and slower heart rate than while active.

hide—the skin of an animal.

home range—the entire area where an animal lives.

hoof—a hard fingernail-like covering on the lower part of the foot of certain mammals, such as horses and deer.

horn—a hard growth made of a hairlike material that forms around bony cores on the heads of many hoofed mammals. Horns are permanent. Unlike antlers, they do not fall off and grow back every year.

hunt—to traverse in search of prey.

incubation period—the time during which an animal uses the warmth of its body to hatch eggs. Female echidnas and platypuses are the only mammals that lay eggs.

invertebrates—animals without backbones, such as jellyfishes, worms, snails, spiders, and insects.

krill—small, shrimplike animals that are found most abundantly in cold waters. Krill are the main food of baleen whales.

larvae—wormlike forms that hatch from the eggs of many kinds of insects.

life span—the average or recorded length of time that an animal lives in the wild or in captivity.

litter—the offspring born at one time to an animal that usually gives birth to more than one young.

lope—an easy, natural gait.

mammal—a warm-blooded vertebrate that feeds its young with milk from special glands in the mother animal's body. All mammals except monotremes give birth to living young. All mammals have some hair on their bodies.

mammalogist—a scientist who studies mammals.

mane—long and heavy hair growing about the neck of some mammals.

marsh—an area of usually wet land covered with plants, such as grasses, cattails, and rushes.

mate—either member of a breeding pair of animals.

mating season—the time of year when males and females of the same species breed.

migration—the seasonal movement of animals from one place to another.

molt—to shed hair at certain times of the year.

muzzle—the projecting jaws and nose of an animal.

nurse—to feed young with milk from special glands in the mother's body.

nursery herd—a group formed by female animals and their young. Nursery herds are common among many kinds of hoofed mammals.

offspring—the young of an animal.

order—a scientific classification that groups together animals that share certain characteristics. An order is divided into families, genera, and species.

pasture—land used for grazing.

plain—a large area of treeless land that is either flat or rolling.

plateau—a large, flat, elevated area of land. A plateau is higher than surrounding land on at least one side.

poacher—a person who hunts illegally.

polar regions—the areas around the earth's geographic poles.

prairie—a large area of flat or rolling land with tall, coarse grasses and few trees.

predator—an animal that hunts, kills, and then feeds on other animals. Wild cats, for example, are predators of rodents.

pregnancy—the condition of having unborn young inside of the body.

prehensile tail—a tail that can be used for grasping. Some kinds of monkeys have prehensile tails that can hold on to tree branches and support their weight. Binturongs, kinkajous, tree pangolins, and most opossums also have prehensile tails.

preserve—a natural area that is set aside for the protection of animals.

prey—an animal that is hunted for food.

prowl—to move about as if in search of prey.

quill—a hollow, sharp spine.

rain forest—a tropical area having a heavy annual amount of rainfall. Rain forests have broad-leaved evergreen trees.

range—the region throughout which an organism naturally lives.

reproduction—the process by which animals produce offspring like themselves.

reptiles—air-breathing, cold-blooded vertebrates—such as snakes, turtles, and lizards—that are usually covered with scales or bony plates.

rival—an animal striving for competitive advantage.

roam—to range or wander over.

root—to dig in the ground with the snout.

savanna—a grassland in tropical regions that contains scattered trees or bushes.

scale—a small, flattened, rigid plate forming part of an external body.

scavenger—an animal that feeds on the remains of dead animals that it finds.

scent glands—glands in the bodies of some animals that produce a substance that is often strong smelling.

scent marks or **scent posts**—marks made by an animal rubbing its scent glands against an object. Scent marks or scent posts may also be made by spraying urine. Animals often use marks to announce their presence and to help find mates.

scrubland—an area that is covered with shrubs or stunted trees.

snout—a long, projecting nose.

species—a group of animals of the same kind that can mate and produce young like themselves.

sprint—to run with a burst of speed for a short distance.

swamp—an area of wet land that is covered with trees and shrubs.

terrain—the physical appearance of an area of land.

territory—an area that an animal, or a group of animals, lives in and defends from other animals of the same species.

thicket—a dense growth of shrubbery or small trees.

tundra—a relatively flat, treeless plain found in the world's arctic and subarctic areas. Cold desert is another term for tundra.

tusks—the large teeth of an animal that usually stick out when its mouth is closed. Elephants, walruses, wild boars, and male musk deer have tusks.

underbrush—bushes, small trees, or shrubs that are found growing among the tall trees of a forest.

undercoat—a growth of short hair or fur partially concealed by the longer guard hairs of a mammal.

urine—fluid waste material secreted by the kidneys.

velvet—the soft vascular skin that covers and nourishes the growing antlers of deer.

vertebrates—animals with backbones, such as mammals, birds, fishes, amphibians, and reptiles.

wallow—to roll about in dust or mud.

water hole—a pool where animals gather to drink.

wild—living in a state of nature and not ordinarily tame or domesticated.

wingspan—the distance from one wing tip to the other, when both wings are extended.

woodland—a grassland with small trees and shrubs.

The Orders of Mammals

Every mammal belongs to one of 19 scientific orders. The chart below lists the orders and presents some characteristics that distinguish their members. The chart also groups all the animal entries in the *Book of Mammals* by order.

Monotremes (MON-uh-treemz)	A monotreme lays eggs. Each egg hatches into a young animal that laps milk from pores on its mother's belly: *echidna, platypus*
Marsupials (mar-SOO-pea-ulz)	Marsupials usually have pouches. These animals give birth to tiny, underdeveloped young: *bandicoot, cuscus, kangaroo, koala, marsupial mouse, numbat, opossum, phalanger, quokka, sugar glider, Tasmanian devil, wallaby, wombat*
Insectivores (in-SEK-tuh-vorz)	*Insectivore* means "insect eater." Most insectivores have long, narrow snouts and sharp claws that are well suited for digging for food, usually insects: *gymnure, hedgehog, mole, shrew, solenodon, tenrec*
Dermopterans (der-MOP-tuh-runs)	A dermopteran glides from tree to tree. It does this by stretching well-developed folds of skin that extend from the sides of its neck to all four feet and that enclose its tail: *flying lemur*
Chiropterans (kye-ROP-tuh-runs)	A chiropteran is a winged mammal, the only kind of mammal that actually flies: *bat*
Primates (PRY-mates)	Primates have the ability to grasp with their fingers. They have hard nails on some of their fingers. Their eyes are often specialized for depth perception. Some have highly developed brains: *aye-aye, bush baby, chimpanzee, gibbon, gorilla, lemur, loris, monkey, orangutan, potto, tarsier*
Xenarthrans (zen-ARTH-runs)	Xenarthrans have very small teeth, usually in the back of the jaw, or, in some cases, no teeth at all: *anteater, armadillo, sloth*
Pholidotes (FOLL-ih-dotes)	Large, horny scales cover the long, tapering body of a pholidote: *pangolin*
Lagomorphs (LAG-uh-morfs)	Most lagomorphs have hind legs that are suited for leaping. Like a rodent, a lagomorph has chisel-like front teeth that grow throughout its life. But it has two pairs of front teeth in its upper jaw: *hare, pika, rabbit*
Rodents (ROE-dents)	A rodent has chisel-like front teeth, one pair in the upper jaw and one pair in the lower jaw, that grow throughout the animal's life: *agouti, beaver, capybara, chinchilla, chipmunk, coypu, dormouse, gerbil, guinea pig, hamster, hutia, jerboa, kangaroo rat, lemming, mara, marmot, mole rat, mouse, muskrat, paca, pocket gopher, porcupine, prairie dog, rat, squirrel, tuco-tuco, vizcacha, vole*
Cetaceans (see-TAY-shunz)	A cetacean spends its entire life in the water. It breathes air through a blowhole in the top of its head and feeds on fish, squid, or plankton: *porpoise, whale*
Carnivores (CAR-nuh-vorz)	Most carnivores are meat eaters, but many also eat plants. They usually have sharp teeth that are well suited for cutting and tearing flesh. Some have specialized claws to help seize prey: *aardwolf, badger, bear, binturong, bobcat, cat, cheetah, civet, coati, coyote, dingo, dog, ferret, fossa, fox, genet, grison, hyena, jackal, jaguar, kinkajou, leopard, linsang, lion, lynx, marten, mink, mongoose, otter, panda, polecat, raccoon, raccoon dog, ratel, ringtail, skunk, suricate, tiger, weasel, wolf, wolverine, zorilla*
Pinnipeds (PIN-ih-pedz)	*Pinniped* means "fin-footed," and a pinniped has four long flippers. These meat eaters spend much of their lives in water, but they come ashore to give birth: *seal and sea lion, walrus*
Tubulidentates (too-byu-luh-DEN-tates)	The aardvark, because of unique tubelike teeth in the back of its jaw, was put alone in this order: *aardvark*
Proboscideans (PROE-buh-SID-ee-unz)	A proboscidean has a long, flexible trunk and hooflike nails: *elephant*
Hyracoids (HIGH-ruh-koidz)	A hyracoid has hooflike nails on its toes. Its upper front teeth are a little like tusks: *hyrax*
Sirenians (sigh-REE-nee-unz)	A sirenian lives in shallow coastal waters and rivers where it feeds on water plants. It has paddlelike forelimbs and a flattened tail: *dugong, manatee*
Perissodactyls (puh-RISS-uh-DAK-tulz)	A perissodactyl is a hoofed animal with an odd number of toes on each foot: *ass, horse, rhinoceros, tapir, zebra*
Artiodactyls (art-ee-oh-DAK-tulz)	An artiodactyl is a hoofed animal with an even number of toes on each foot: *antelope, babirusa, bison, buffalo, camel, caribou, chamois, cow, deer, elk, gazelle, gerenuk, giraffe, goat, hippopotamus, hog, ibex, impala, llama, moose, musk-ox, okapi, peccary, pronghorn, serow, sheep, tahr, wildebeest, yak*

Index

(**Bold type** refers to illustrated text; regular type refers to text.)

A

ANTEATER

Aardvark (Orycteropus afer) **44-45**
Aardwolf (Proteles cristatus) **46-47**
African civet (Civettictis civetta) 154, **155**
African clawless otter (Aonyx capensis) **417**
African climbing mouse (Dendromus mesomelas) 393-394, **396**
African elephant (Loxodonta africana) **2-3, 21, 34-35, 190-195**; speed 30
African hedgehog (Atelerix albiventris) **257**
Agoutis (Dasyprocta spp.) **25, 47**
Alaskan brown bear (Ursus arctos) **6, 84,** 85, **86-87**
Alpaca (Lama pacos) 337, **338, 339,** 341
Alpine ibex (Capra ibex) **26, 286, 287, 288,** 289, 290
Alpine marmot (Marmota marmota) 26, **355**
American black bear (Ursus americanus) **88, 89,** 90
American marten (Martes americana) **357, 358,** 359-360
American mink (Mustela vison) **361**
Ankole (Bos taurus) **161**
Anteaters **48-51**
Antelope jackrabbit (Lepus alleni) **254**
Antelopes **4, 20-21, 33, 42-43, 52-61**
Apes see Chimpanzee; Gibbons; Gorilla; Orangutan
Arabian camel (Camelus dromedarius) **114-115, 116, 117**; foot **14**
Arabian oryx (Oryx leucoryx) **42-43**
Arctic fox (Alopex lagopus) 206, 208, **210, 211**
Arctic ground squirrel (Spermophilus parryii) **519**
Arctic hare (Lepus arcticus) **255**
Argali (Ovis ammon) 504, 507
Armadillos **24, 62-65**
Asian elephant (Elephas maximus) 193, **196, 197**
Asiatic black bear (Ursus thibetanus) **92,** 93
Asses **66-68**
Australian hopping mouse (Notomys fuscus) 12, **396**
Australian sea lion (Neophoca cinerea) **497**
Australian water rat (Hydromys chrysogaster) 477, **478,** 479
Aye-aye (Daubentonia madagascariensis) **69**

B

BEAR

Babirusa (Babyrousa babyrussa) **70-71**
Bactrian camel (Camelus bactrianus) 115-116, **117**
Badgers **18, 72-75**
Bahamian hutia (Geocapromys ingrahami) **277**
Baird's beaked whale (Berardius bairdii) 23, **568**
Baird's tapir (Tapirus bairdii) 531, 533
Banded linsang (Prionodon linsang) **328**
Banded mongoose (Mungos mungo) **368-369**
Bandicoots **76**
Bank vole (Clethrionomys glareolus) **546**
Banteng (Bos banteng) 160,**161**
Barbary macaque (Macaca sylvana) **380,** 383
Barred bandicoot (Perameles gunni) **76**
Bat-eared fox (Otocyon megalotis) **20, 209,** 210, 211
Bats **15, 29, 77-83**
Bears 6, **18, 84-93**
Beavers **35, 94-98**
Beech marten (Martes foina) **27,** 357, **359,** 360

Belding ground squirrel (Spermophilus beldingi) **520**
Beluga (Delphinapterus leucas) **22,448, 452**
Bent-winged bat (Miniopterus schreibersi) **83**
Bharal (Pseudois nayaur) **238-239**
Bicolor white-toothed shrew (Crocidura leucodon) **510**
Binturong (Arctictis binturong) **99**
Bison (Bison bison) **100-103**
Black-and-white colobus (Colobus guereza) **382**
Black-and-white tassel-ear marmoset (Callithrix humeralifer) **377**
Black buck (Antilope cervicapra) 53, **58**
Black flying fox (Pteropus alecto) **83**
Black-footed ferret (Mustela nigripes) **202-203,** 457-458
Black-footed tree rat (Mesembriomys gouldii) **477**
Black lemur (Lemur macaco) **320,** 322
Black-mantle tamarin (Saguinus nigricollis) **377**
Black-naped hare (Lepus nigricollis) **254**
Black rat (Rattus rattus) 478, 479, 480
Black rhinoceros (Diceros bicornis) 13, **482-483, 485**
Black-tailed deer (Odocoileus hemionus) **33**
Black-tailed jackrabbit (Lepus californicus) **18, 255;** speed 31
Black-tailed prairie dog (Cynomys ludovicianus) **36, 454-457;** foot **14**
Black wildebeest (Connochaetes gnou) 571, 572, **575**
Blossom bat (Syconycteris australis) **82**
Blue hare (Lepus timidus) **26, 252-253**
Blue whale (Balaenoptera musculus) 23, 562, **568**
Blue wildebeest (Connochaetes taurinus) 571, 572, **573**
Bobcat (Lynx rufus) **104-105**
Bohor reedbuck (Redunca redunca) **59**
Bongo (Tragelaphus eurycerus) 56, **58**
Botta's pocket gopher (Thomomys bottae) **440**
Bottlenose dolphin (Tursiops truncatus) **446, 448, 568**
Bowhead whale (Balaena mysticetus) **22**
Brazilian tapir (Tapirus terrestris) **25, 530, 531, 532**
Brocket deer (Mazama americana) **24,** 173
Brown hyena (Hyaena brunnea) **282**
Brown lemur (Lemur fulvus) **321**
Brown rat (Rattus norvegicus) **477,**479, 480
Brush-tailed possum (Trichosurus vulpecula) 15, **430**
Buffalo, American see Bison
Buffaloes **106-111**
Burchell's zebra (Equus burchelli) **20** see also Plains zebra
Bush babies (Galago spp.) **112-113**
Bush dog (Speothos venaticus) **179,** 180
Bush hyraxes (Heterohyrax spp.) 283, **284-285**
Bushpig (Potamochoerus porcus) 266, **268**

C

CAT

Cacomistle (Jentinkia sumichrasti) 488
Camels **114-117**
Canada lynx (Lynx canadensis) **344**
Cape buffalo (Syncerus caffer)
Cape ground squirrel (Xerus inauris) **522**
Cape hare (Lepus capensis) **254**
Cape hunting dog (Lycaon pictus) **21, 180-181, 296**
Cape pangolin (Manis temmincki) **15, 28, 426**
Capybara (Hydrochoerus hydrochaeris) **24, 118-119**
Caracal (Caracal caracal) 128, 130, 133, **135**
Caribou (Rangifer tarandus) **16, 41, 120-125**

Cats **126-137;** domestic breeds (Felis catus) 128, **136-137**
Cavies **248,** 249
Chacma baboon (Papio ursinus) **371**
Chamois (Rupicapra rupicapra) **26, 138-139**
Cheetah (Acinonyx jubatus) **21, 29, 34, 140-145;** speed 31
Chilla (Dusicyon griseus) **208**
Chimpanzee (Pan troglodytes) **146-151;** foot **14**
Chinchilla (Chinchilla laniger) **151**
Chinese pangolin (Manis pentadactyla) **426**
Chipmunks **152-153**
Civets **154-155**
Coati (Nasua narica) **156-157**
Collared lemming (Dicrostonyx groenlandicus) **317**
Collared peccary (Tayassu tajacu) **428, 429**
Collared pika (Ochotona princeps) **437**
Common dolphin (Delphinus delphis) **30**
Common dormouse (Muscardinus avellanarius) **184**
Common genet (Genetta genetta) **217**
Common grison (Galictis vittata) **246**
Common paca (Agouti paca) **420**
Common shrew (Sorex araneus) **510**
Cotton-top tamarin (Saguinus oedipus) **377**
Cows **158-161;** domestic breeds (Bos taurus) **158-159,** 160, **161**
Coyote (Canis latrans) **162-165,** 457
Coypu (Myocastor coypus) **166-167**
Crabeater seal (Lobodon carcinophagus) **490,** 492
Crested porcupine (Hystrix cristata) **444, 445**
Cuscuses **168-169**

D

DEER

Dall's porpoise (Phocoenoides dalli) **23**
Dall's sheep (Ovis dalli) **502, 504, 505**
Deer **24, 27, 170-177**
Deer mouse (Peromyscus maniculatus) **396**
Defassa waterbuck (Kobus ellipsiprymnus) **54**
Desert cavy (Microcavia australis) **248,** 249
Desert cottontail (Sylvilagus audubonii) **466,** 468
Desert golden mole (Eremitalpa granti) **364**
Desert jerboa (Jaculus orientalis) **303**
Desert kangaroo rat (Dipodomys deserti) **309**
Desert wood rat (Neotoma lepida) **479**
Desman (Desmana moschata) **363**
Dhole (Cuon alpinus) **179,** 180
Dingo (Canis dingo) **178**
Dogs **21, 178-183;** domestic breeds (Canis familiaris) 181, **182-183**
Domestic ferret (Mustela furo) **203**
Dorcas gazelle (Gazella dorcas) **215**
Dormice **184-185**
Dugong (Dugong dugon) **186-187**
Dusky dolphin (Lagenorhynchus obscurus) **450**
Dusky titi (Callicebus moloch) **374**
Dwarf lemur (Cheirogaleus major) **320,** 322
Dwarf mongoose (Helogale parvula) **20, 367, 369**

E

ELEPHANT

Eastern chipmunk (Tamias striatus) **152, 153**

Echidnas **188-189**
Eland (Taurotragus oryx) 53, 55, 56, **58,** 60
Elephants **2-3, 21, 190-197**
Elk (Cervus canadensis) **198-201**
Emperor tamarin (Saguinus imperator) **25, 376**
Eurasian lynx (Lynx lynx) **27, 345**
Eurasian red squirrel (Sciurus vulgaris) **522, 523**
European badger (Meles meles) 72, **74-75**
European brown bear (Ursus arctos) **93**
European hare (Lepus europaeus) **254**
European harvest mouse (Micromys minutus) **394-395**
European hedgehog (Erinaceus europaeus) **256**
European mole (Talpa europaea) **362, 363**
European polecat (Mustela putorius) **203**
European rabbit (Oryctolagus cuniculus) 466, 468, **469;** young **468-469**
European wild boar (Sus scrofa) **27, 264,** 266

F

FOX

Fallow deer (Dama dama) **172,** 173
Fanaloka (Fossa fossa) 154
Fat dormouse (Glis glis) 184, **185**
Feather-tailed glider (Acrobates pygmaeus) **431**
Fennec (Fennecus zerda) 206, **208,** 210
Ferret badger (Melogale moschata) **75**
Ferrets **202-203**
Fin whale (Balaenoptera physalus) **568**
Fisher (Martes pennanti) 357, **359**
Fishing bat (Noctilio leporinus) **29, 78;** hunting **80-81,** 82
Fishing cat (Prionailurus viverrinus) 130, **132-133**
Fluffy glider (Petaurus australis) **432**
Flying lemurs **204**
Forest buffalo (Syncerus caffer) 108-109
Fossa (Cryptoprocta ferox) **205**
Fox squirrel (Sciurus niger) **522**
Foxes **20, 206-211**
Frog-eating bat (Trachops cirrhosus) **40, 78**

G

GIRAFFE

Ganges susu (Platanista gangetica) **448,** 450
Garden dormouse (Eliomys quercinus) **185**
Gaur (Bos gaurus) **160,** 161
Gazelles **21, 144, 212-216**
Gemsbok (Oryx gazella) **54-55,** 60, **592**
Genets **216-217**
Gerbils **218-219**
Gerenuk (Litocranius walleri) **220-221**
Giant anteater (Myrmecophaga tridactyla) **48, 49, 50-51**
Giant armadillo (Priodontes giganteus) **24, 64, 65;** foot **14**
Giant forest hog (Hylochoerus meinertzhageni) 264, 265, 266
Giant otter (Pteronura brasiliensis) 417, **418-419**
Giant panda (Ailuropoda melanoleuca) **421-424**
Gibbons **222-225**
Giraffe (Giraffa camelopardalis) **20, 226-231;** speed 31
Goats **232-239;** domestic breeds (Capra hircus) **237**
Golden hamster (Mesocricetus auratus) **250**
Golden jackal (Canis aureus) **296,** 299

601

Photographers' Credits

FRONT COVER © Tim Davis/Tony Stone Images. **BACK COVER** © Reinhard Kunkel. **(1)** Keith Gunnar. **(2-3)** Thomas Nebbia. **(3)** PITCH/P. Montoya. **(4)** Kenneth W. Fink/ARDEA LONDON. **(6-7)** Steven C. Kaufman. **(10-11)** Robert Caputo. **(12)** *left,* Loren McIntyre; *top right,* Karl Weidmann; *bottom right,* Hans & Judy Beste. **(13)** R. S. Virdee/Grant Heilman Photography. **(14)** Jeff Foott. **(15)** *top,* Merlin D. Tuttle; *bottom left,* Bannister/NHPA; *bottom right,* Hans & Judy Beste. **(16)** *top,* Stanley Breeden; *bottom,* Stephen J. Krasemann/DRK Photo. **(18)** *top,* David Hiser; *bottom left,* Larry R. Ditto; *bottom right,* Robert P. Carr. **(19)** ANIMALS ANIMALS/Stouffer Productions. **(28)** *top,* Hans & Judy Beste; *bottom,* Joan Root. **(29)** *top,* © Reinhard Kunkel; *bottom,* Merlin D. Tuttle-J. Scott Altenbach. **(30)** Tupper Ansel Blake. **(31)** Wolfgang Bayer. **(32)** © Jean-Paul Ferrero. **(33)** *top,* Fred Bruemmer; *bottom left,* Tom & Pat Leeson; *bottom right,* © Peter Johnson. **(34)** George W. Frame. **(34-35)** Sven-Olof Lindblad. **(35)** *bottom left,* Wolfgang Bayer; *right,* Stanley Breeden. **(36)** *top,* Thomas D. Mangelsen; *bottom left,* Helen Rhode; *bottom right,* John M. Burnley. **(37)** Rolf O. Peterson. **(38)** *left,* Keith Gunnar; *right,* Jeff Foott. **(39)** *top,* James K. Morgan; *bottom left,* Greg Beaumont; *bottom right,* Jen & Des Bartlett. **(40)** Merlin D. Tuttle. **(41)** *top right,* Rollie Ostermick; *bottom left,* Bates Littlehales/N.G.S. Photographer; *bottom right,* Christopher Springmann. **(42-43)** George D. Lepp. **(43)** *top,* Wolfgang Bayer; *bottom,* George D. Lepp. **(44-45)** Alan Root. **(46)** Alan Root. **(47)** PITCH/Francois Gohier. **(48)** Francois Gohier. **(49)** Loren McIntyre.

(50) Wolfgang Bayer. **(50-51)** Francisco Erize/BRUCE COLEMAN INC. **(51)** *left,* George B. Schaller; *right,* Jen & Des Bartlett. **(52-53)** Clem Haagner. **(54-55)** *top,* © Peter Johnson; *center,* PITCH/Jean-Claude Carton. **(54)** *left,* © Frederic/Jacana/The Image Bank; *right,* Clem Haagner/BRUCE COLEMAN INC. **(55)** *top,* © 1974 Gail Rubin; *bottom,* © Reinhard Kunkel. **(56)** *top and center,* © Peter Johnson; *bottom,* Kenneth W. Fink/ARDEA LONDON. **(57)** Peter Davey/BRUCE COLEMAN LTD. **(58)** *left,* Kenneth W. Fink/BRUCE COLEMAN INC.; *right,* Belinda Wright. **(58-59)** © 1979 Patricia D. Moehlman. **(59)** *top,* PITCH/P. Montoya; *bottom left and right,* Gerald Cubitt. **(60-61)** George Holton/OCELOT INC. **(62)** Laurance B. Aiuppy © 1980. **(63)** *top and bottom,* Laurance B. Aiuppy © 1980; *center,* Larry R. Ditto/BRUCE COLEMAN INC. **(64)** *top,* Francois Gohier; *bottom,* George B. Schaller. **(65)** *top,* N. Smythe/National Audubon Society Collection/PR; *bottom,* Tracy S. Carter. **(66)** © 1980 Patricia D. Moehlman. **(67)** David Cavagnaro. **(68)** Stanley Breeden; *inset,* © Gail Rubin. **(69)** Anthony & Elizabeth Bomford/ARDEA LONDON. **(70-71)** Tom McHugh/National Audubon Society Collection/PR. **(72)** *left,* Charles G. Summers, Jr./BRUCE COLEMAN INC.; *right,* ANIMALS ANIMALS/Ernest Wilkinson. **(73)** Robert P. Carr/BRUCE COLEMAN INC. **(74-75)** PITCH/D. Heuclin. **(75)** *top,* M.P.L. Fogden/BRUCE COLEMAN INC.; *bottom,* C.B. & D.W. Frith/BRUCE COLEMAN INC. **(76)** *left,* Douglas Baglin/NHPA; *right,* Stanley Breeden. **(77)** Merlin D. Tuttle. **(78-79)** Merlin D. Tuttle. **(78)** *top and center,* Merlin D. Tuttle. **(79)** *top and bottom right,* Merlin D. Tuttle; *bottom left,* Hans & Judy Beste. **(81)** J.A.L. Cooke/Oxford Scientific Films. **(82)** *top,* PITCH/Billes; *center left,* Adrian Warren/ARDEA LONDON; *center right,* Hans & Judy Beste; *bottom,* Merlin D. Tuttle. **(83)** *top,* Stanley Breeden; *far left,* Rene-Pierre Bille; *left,* Kenneth W. Fink/BRUCE COLEMAN INC.; *right,* M.P.L. Fogden/BRUCE COLEMAN INC.; *far right,* PITCH/Jean-Paul Ferrero. **(84-85)** Martin W. Grosnick. **(85)** Stephen J. Krasemann/DRK Photo. **(86)** Patrick E. Powell. **(86-87)** Jeff Foott; *inset,* Steven C. Kaufman. **(88)** *top,* Sonja Bullaty-Angelo Lomeo/courtesy Time-Life Books; *bottom,* Douglas H. Chadwick. **(89)** *left,* Jen & Des Bartlett; *right,* Lynn L. Rogers. **(90)** *top,* George W. Calef; *bottom,* Mickey Sexton/AlaskaPhoto. **(91)** © Canada Wide. **(92)** *left,* Jean-Paul Ferrero; *right,* Tom McHugh/National Audubon Society Collection/PR. **(93)** *left,* PITCH/Binois; *top and bottom right,* Bernard Peyton. **(94)** Jen & Des Bartlett. **(95)** *top,* Wolfgang Bayer/BRUCE COLEMAN INC.; *bottom,* Jen & Des Bartlett. **(96)** *left,* Wolfgang Bayer; *right,* Jen & Des Bartlett. **(97)** Wolfgang Bayer. **(98)** *top,* Leonard Lee Rue III; *bottom,* Rollie Ostermick. **(99)** Tom McHugh/National Audubon Society Collection/PR.

A young chimpanzee in Tanzania, a country in Africa, balances between two vines.

(100-101) Laurance B. Aiuppy © 1980. **(101)** John M. Burnley. **(102)** Erwin & Peggy Bauer. **(103)** *top left,* Jeff Foott; *top right,* Jim Brandenburg; *bottom,* Francisco Erize/BRUCE COLEMAN INC. **(104)** Charles G. Summers, Jr. **(105)** *top,* Leonard Lee Rue III; *center,* Gary R. Zahm; *bottom,* L. West. **(106-107)** PITCH/P. Montoya. **(108)** *top,* PITCH/G. Vienne-F. Bel; *bottom,* George W. Frame. **(109)** Dieter & Mary Plage/BRUCE COLEMAN LTD. **(110)** *top,* Jim Brandenburg; *bottom,* Loren McIntyre. **(111)** *top,* Jean-Paul Ferrero; *bottom,* Bob Abrams/BRUCE COLEMAN INC. **(112)** *top,* Bob Campbell; *bottom,* Gary Milburn/TOM STACK & ASSOCIATES. **(113)** Lee Lyon/BRUCE COLEMAN LTD. **(114-115)** Victor Englebert. **(116)** Gerald Cubitt. **(117)** *top,* Victor Englebert; *bottom,* Leonard Lee Rue III. **(118)** George B. Schaller. **(119)** *top,* Loren McIntyre; *bottom,* Sven-Olof Lindblad. **(120)** George W. Calef. **(121)** Helen Rhode. **(122)** Martin W. Grosnick. **(122-123)** Helen Rhode. **(124-125)** Rollie Ostermick. **(125)** *top,* Steven C. Wilson/ENTHEOS; *bottom,* Farrell Grehan. **(126-127)** Wolfgang Bayer. **(128-129)** Maurice Hornocker. **(129)** *top,* Maurice Hornocker; *bottom,* Charles G. Summers, Jr. **(130)** *top,* Livan & Rogers/BRUCE COLEMAN INC.; *bottom,* A. A. Geertseman. **(131)** *top,* Karl Weidmann; *bottom left,* © Jean-Paul Ferrero; *bottom right,* Francisco Erize. **(132)** *left,* Belinda Wright; *right,* Stanley Breeden. **(133)** *top left and bottom right,* Stanley Breeden; *top right,* Belinda Wright. **(134)** George B. Schaller. **(135)** *left,* Bob Campbell; *right,* Tadaaki Imaizumi/ORION PRESS. **(136)** *top,* Jane Burton/BRUCE COLEMAN INC.; *bottom left,* © Stephen Green-Armytage 1981; *bottom right,* Hans Reinhard/BRUCE COLEMAN LTD. **(137)** © Stephen Green-Armytage 1981. **(139)** © Jean-Paul Ferrero. **(140-141)** © Reinhard Kunkel. **(141)** Robert Caputo. **(142-143)** Robert Caputo. **(143)** *top,* Norman Myers/BRUCE COLEMAN INC.; *bottom,* George W. Frame. **(144)** *top,* Robert Caputo; *center,* Robin Pellew; *bottom,* Clem Haagner. **(145)** Bob Campbell. **(146)** Derek Bryceson. **(147)** *top,* Derek Bryceson; *bottom,* Jane Goodall. **(148)** *top,* Hugo Van Lawick; *bottom,* Jane Goodall. **(149)** Derek Bryceson; *inset,* Jane Goodall.

(150) *top and bottom left,* Jane Goodall; *top right,* Hugo Van Lawick. **(151)** Russ Kinne, National Audubon Society Collection/PR. **(152)** L. West. **(153)** *top,* Wayne Lankinen/BRUCE COLEMAN LTD; *bottom,* Leonard Lee Rue III/BRUCE COLEMAN LTD. **(154)** Anthony and Elizabeth Bomford/ARDEA LONDON. **(155)** *top,* Rod Williams/BRUCE COLEMAN LTD; *bottom,* BRUCE COLEMAN INC. **(156)** *top,* Jeff Foott; *bottom,* Francois Gohier. **(157)** *left,* Stephen J. Krasemann/DRK Photo; *right,* Jen & Des Bartlett. **(158)** Jim Brandenburg/BRUCE COLEMAN INC. **(159)** *top,* Jonathan T. Wright/BRUCE COLEMAN INC.; *bottom left,* Harste/BRUCE COLEMAN INC.; *bottom right,* J. B. Blossom/NHPA. **(160)** Stanley Breeden. **(161)** *top,* Loren McIntyre; *bottom left,* S. C. Bisserot; *bottom right,* Tom McHugh/National Audubon Society Collection/PR. **(162)** Gary M. Banowetz. **(163)** *left,* Glenn D. Chambers; *right,* Jane M. Pascall. **(164)** Jon Farrar. **(164-165)** Charles G. Summers, Jr. **(165)** David Hiser. **(166-167)** Bildarchio Paysan Stuttgart. **(167)** PITCH/J. C. Bacle. **(168).** © Jean-Paul Ferrero. **(169)** *top,* Jack Fields/National Audubon Society Collection/PR; *bottom,* Belinda Wright. **(170-171)** Thase Daniel. **(171)** William J. Weber. **(172)** *top,* Francisco Erize; *left,* George H. Harrison; *right,* Jean-Paul Ferrero. **(173)** *left,* George Holton/OCELOT INC.; *center,* Stanley Breeden; *right,* George H. Harrison. **(174)** Charles G. Summers, Jr. **(174-175)** Belinda Wright. **(175)** *top,* Francois Gohier/National Audubon Society Collection/PR; *bottom,* Andrew Laurie. **(176)** PITCH/Francois Gohier. **(177)** Tetsuo Gyoda/ORION PRESS. **(178)** Jen & Des Bartlett. **(179)** *left,* Stanley Breeden; *right,* Pauline R. McCann/BRUCE COLEMAN INC. **(180-181)** © Reinhard Kunkel. **(181)** *top,* © Reinhard Kunkel; *bottom,* Patricia D. Moehlman. **(182)** *top left,* Richard W. Brown; *top right,* Hans Reinhard/BRUCE COLEMAN INC.; *bottom left,* © Stephen Green-Armytage 1981; *bottom right,* James L. Stanfield/N.G.S. Photographer. **(183)** *top,* © Stephen Green-Armytage 1981; *bottom,* Momatiuk/Eastcott/Woodfin Camp Inc. **(184)** Kim Taylor/BRUCE COLEMAN INC. **(185)** *top,* PITCH/J. L. Blanchet; *bottom,* Rene-Pierre Bille. **(186-187)** Ben Cropp. **(188)** *top,* Brian J. Coates/BRUCE COLEMAN LTD; *bottom,* Jen & Des Bartlett. **(189)** *top,* PITCH/Jean-Paul Ferrero; *bottom,* Jen & Des Bartlett. **(190)** © Peter Johnson. **(190-191)** George W. Frame. **(192)** *top,* © Patricia D. Moehlman; *bottom,* © Reinhard Kunkel. **(193)** M. P. Kahl. **(194)** © Reinhard Kunkel. **(194-195)** Bob Campbell. **(195)** *top,* © Peter Johnson; *bottom,* F. J. Weyerhaeuser. **(196)** Stanley Breeden. **(197)** Dieter & Mary Plage/BRUCE COLEMAN LTD. **(198-199)** Steven C. Wilson/ENTHEOS.

(200) Steven Fuller. **(201)** *top,* Gary R. Zahm; *bottom,* Charles G. Summers, Jr. **(202-203)** *sequence,* B. J. Rose. **(203)** ANIMALS ANIMALS/Michael & Barbara Reed. **(204)** Peter Ward/BRUCE COLEMAN INC. **(205)** Zoological Society of San Diego. **(206-207)** Farrell Grehan. **(207)** *top,* Wolfgang Bayer; *bottom,* Lynn L. Rogers. **(208)** *top,* Glenn D. Chambers; *bottom left,* Jen & Des Bartlett; *bottom right,* ANIMALS ANIMALS/John C. Stevenson. **(209)** *left,* P. Morris/ARDEA LONDON; *top right,* © Reinhard Kunkel; *bottom right,* Steve Maslowski. **(210-211)** Robert A. Garrott; *inset,* Douglas H. Chadwick. **(212)** © 1978 Patricia D. Moehlman. **(212-213)** M. P. Kahl. **(214)** Gerald Cubitt. **(215)** *top,* PITCH/P. Montoya; *bottom,* PITCH/F. Charmoy. **(217)** George Holton National Audubon Society Collection/PR. **(218)** Edward S. Ross. **(219)** *top,* Carol Hughes/BRUCE COLEMAN LTD; *bottom,* Moira & Rod Borland/BRUCE COLEMAN INC. **(220)** PITCH/P. Montoya. **(221)** Peter Davey/BRUCE COLEMAN LTD. **(222)** Tom McHugh/National Audubon Society Collection/PR. **(223)** Teleki-Baldwin. **(224-225)** Tom McHugh/National Audubon Society Collection/PR. **(226-227)** © Peter Ward/BRUCE COLEMAN LTD. **(228)** Ian Beames/ARDEA LONDON. **(229)** *top,* Stewart Cassidy; *bottom,* © 1978 Patricia D. Moehlman. **(230)** *top,* M. P. Kahl/National Audubon Society Collection/PR; *bottom,* Clem Haagner/BRUCE COLEMAN INC. **(231)** Gerald Cubitt. **(232)** Douglas H. Chadwick. **(233)** Tom & Pat Leeson. **(234)** Keith Gunnar; *inset,* Karen B. Reeves. **(234-235)** Tom & Pat Leeson. **(236)** Douglas H. Chadwick. **(237)** *left,* Kenneth W. Fink/BRUCE COLEMAN INC.; *right,* © Robert L. Dunne/BRUCE COLEMAN INC. **(238-239)** George B. Schaller. **(239)** *top,* George B. Schaller; *center,* Kenneth W. Fink/ARDEA LONDON; *bottom,* Javier Andrada. **(240)** Craig R. Sholley. **(241)** *top,* Dian Fossey; *bottom,* David P. Watts. **(242-243)** David P. Watts; *inset,* Craig R. Sholley. **(244)** *top,* David P. Watts; *bottom,* Craig R. Sholley. **(245)** Craig R. Sholley. **(246)** *top,* PITCH/Francois Gohier; *bottom,* Tony Morrison. **(247)** Jean-Paul Ferrero/ARDEA LONDON. **(248)** Jen & Des Bartlett. **(249)** S. C. Bisserot.

(250) Jane Burton/BRUCE COLEMAN LTD. **(251)** Thomas D. Mangelsen. **(252-253)** Rene-Pierre Bille. **(253)** *left,* Rollie Ostermick; *center,* Stephen J. Krasemann/DRK Photo; *right,* Franz J. Camenzind. **(254)** *top left,* Clem Haagner; *top right,* Joanna Van Gruisen/ARDEA LONDON; *center,* M.P.L. Fogden; *bottom left,* Derek Middleton/BRUCE COLEMAN LTD; *bottom right,* PITCH/Cordier. **(255)** *top,* David R. Gray; *bottom,* Larry R. Ditto. **(256)** *top,* Hans Reinhard/BRUCE COLEMAN LTD; *bottom,* S. C. Bisserot/BRUCE COLEMAN LTD. **(257)** *top left and right,* Peter Ward/BRUCE COLEMAN INC.; *bottom left,* PITCH/J. Delacour. **(258)** Gerald Cubitt. **(259)** © Peter Johnson. **(260)** © Peter Johnson. **(260-261)** Hervy/Jacana/The Image Bank. **(262-263)** ARDEA LONDON. **(262)** Alan Root. **(263)** Philip Coffey. **(264)** PITCH/Billes. **(265)** Ivan Polunin/NHPA. **(266-267)** T. W. Ransom. **(266)** *top,* Gerald Cubitt; *bottom,* Bildarchio Paysan Stuttgart. **(267)** Gerald Cubitt. **(268)** *top,* Webbphotos/Ted McDonough; *bottom,* Frank W. Lane. **(268-269)** Victor Englebert. **(270-271)** © Jonathan T. Wright/BRUCE COLEMAN INC. **(272-273)** © Stephen Green-Armytage 1981. **(274)** *left,* H. W. Silvester/RAPHO; *right,* James L. Stanfield/N.G.S. Photographer. **(274-275)** © Elisabeth Weiland/National Audubon Society Collection/PR. **(275)** George B. Schaller. **(276)** *top,* Sally Anne Thompson/Animal Photography Ltd.; *bottom,* Thase Daniel. **(277)** Tom McHugh/National Audubon Society Collection/PR. **(278-279)** *top,* Carol Hughes/BRUCE COLEMAN LTD; *bottom,* George W. Frame. **(279)** *top,* Robert Caputo; *bottom,* David Bygott. **(280)** M. P. Kahl. **(280-281)** David Bygott. **(282)** *top,* Clem

Haagner; *bottom,* Philip Coffey. (**283**) Hendrik N. Hoeck. (**284-285**) Peter Davey/BRUCE COLEMAN LTD. (**284**) *bottom left,* © Gail Rubin; *bottom right,* Bob Campbell. (**285**) © Gail Rubin. (**287**) © Jean-Paul Ferrero. (**288**) *top,* © Jean-Paul Ferrero; *bottom,* Rene-Pierre Bille. (**289**) © 1977 Gail Rubin. (**290-291**) © 1977 Gail Rubin. (**292**) M. P. Kahl. (**293**) Clem Haagner/BRUCE COLEMAN INC. (**294**) M. P. Kahl. (**294-295**) © Reinhard Kunkel. (**295**) Wolfgang Bayer. (**296**) © 1978 Patricia D. Moehlman. (**297**) © Reinhard Kunkel. (**298-299**) © 1978 Patricia D. Moehlman.

(**300-301**) Loren McIntyre. (**302**) Loren McIntyre. (**303**) Mark Rosenthal-Kimberly Lile. (**304-305**) Jen & Des Bartlett. (**306**) *top,* Tom & Pam Gardner; *bottom,* Jen & Des Bartlett. (**306-307**) Jen & Des Bartlett. (**307**) Jen & Des Bartlett. (**308**) *top,* Hans & Judy Beste; *bottom,* PITCH/Jean-Paul Ferrero. (**309**) © Bob & Clara Calhoun/BRUCE COLEMAN INC. (**310**) *top,* M.P.L. Fogden; *bottom,* James H. Carmichael, Jr./BRUCE COLEMAN INC. (**311**) Loren McIntyre. (**312**) Jen & Des Bartlett. (**313**) © Jean-Paul Ferrero. (**314-315**) Jen & Des Bartlett. (**316**) Alvin E. Staffan. (**317**) *top left,* Varin-Visage/Jacana/The Image Bank; *bottom left,* ANIMALS ANIMALS/Mark Chappell; *right,* Bob & Clara Calhoun/BRUCE COLEMAN INC. (**318**) *top,* Norman Myers/BRUCE COLEMAN LTD; *bottom,* Chris Zuber/BRUCE COLEMAN LTD. (**319**) Russ Kinne/National Audubon Society Collection/PR. (**320**) *top,* George Holton/National Audubon Society Collection/PR; *bottom,* Anthony and Elizabeth Bomford/ARDEA LONDON. (**321**) *top,* W. T. Miller/BRUCE COLEMAN INC.; *bottom left,* Gerald Cubitt; *bottom right,* Tom McHugh/National Audubon Society Collection/PR. (**322**) Russ Kinne/National Audubon Society Collection/PR. (**323**) Dieter & Mary Plage/BRUCE COLEMAN LTD. (**324-325**) Thomas Nebbia. (**326**) Dieter & Mary Plage/BRUCE COLEMAN LTD. (**326-327**) Stanley Breeden. (**327**) *top,* © Reinhard Kunkel; *bottom,* Stanley Breeden. (**328**) Tom McHugh/National Audubon Society Collection/PR. (**329**) Patricia D. Moehlman. (**330**) © Peter Johnson. (**331**) Robert Caputo. (**332**) *top,* M. P. Kahl; *bottom left,* PITCH/Carton; *bottom right,* Bob Campbell. (**333**) © Peter Johnson. (**334-335**) *top,* George B. Schaller/BRUCE COLEMAN INC.; *bottom,* David Bygott. (**335**) *top,* George B. Schaller/BRUCE COLEMAN INC.; *bottom,* Belinda Wright. (**336-337**) Loren McIntyre. (**338**) Loren McIntyre. (**339**) *top,* Francisco Erize; *bottom,* Tony Morrison. (**340**) *top,* Loren McIntyre; *bottom,* Francisco Erize. (**340-341**) Francois Gohier. (**342**) Belinda Wright. (**343**) *left,* Ivan Polunin/NHPA; *right,* Stanley Breeden. (**344**) Tom Walker. (**345**) PITCH/Cordier. (**346-347**) Fred Bavendam. (**348**) Fred Bavendam. (**349**) *left,* Fred Bavendam; *top and bottom right,* Jeff Foott.

(**350-351**) Jen & Des Bartlett. (**352**) Douglas H. Chadwick. (**353**) *left,* Helen Rhode; *right,* Douglas H. Chadwick. (**354**) *top,* Stephen J. Krasemann/DRK Photo; *bottom,* Rollie Ostermick. (**355**) *top,* Stephen J. Krasemann/DRK Photo; *bottom left,* James H. Carmichael, Jr.; *bottom right,* Rene-Pierre Bille. (**356**) *left,* Hans & Judy Beste; *right,* Stanley Breeden. (**357**) Leonard Lee Rue III. (**358**) Greg Beaumont. (**359**) *top,* Jim Brandenburg; *bottom,* Hans Reinhard/BRUCE COLEMAN LTD. (**360**) Goichi Wada/ORION PRESS. (**361**) Leonard Lee Rue III. (**362**) *top,* Pilloud/Jacana/The Image Bank; *bottom,* Varin/Jacana/The Image Bank. (**363**) D. H. Thompson/Oxford Scientific Films. (**364**) *top left,* Edward S. Ross; *top right,* Lynn L. Rogers; *bottom,* Christopher Springmann. (**365**) *top,* Peter Davey/BRUCE COLEMAN LTD; *bottom left and right,* Jen & Des Bartlett. (**366**) *left,* Candice Bayer/BRUCE COLEMAN INC; *right,* Belinda Wright. (**367**) *top,* Clem Haagner; *bottom,* Alan Root. (**368-369**) Jonathan Rood. (**369**) *top,* Anthony & Elizabeth Bomford/ARDEA LONDON; *bottom,* Gerald Cubitt. (**370**) Akira Uchiyama/National Audubon Society Collection/PR. (**371**) *top,* Francisco Erize; *bottom,* Gert Behrens/ARDEA LONDON. (**372-373**) PITCH/Guy Dhuit. (**373**) *left,* Wolfgang Bayer; *right,* Karl Weidmann. (**374**) *top,* PITCH/Cresto; bottom, Tony Morrison. (**374-375**) Karl Weidmann. (**375**) *left,* Tony Morrison; *right,* Nicole Duplaix. (**376**) *left,* Wolfgang Bayer; *right,* G. Ziesler/PETER ARNOLD INC. (**376-377**) Loren McIntyre. (**377**) *left,* Edward S. Ross; *center,* © Jean-Paul Ferrero; *right,* J. Mason/ARDEA LONDON. (**378**) Loren McIntyre. (**379**) *top,* Adrian Warren/ARDEA LONDON; *bottom,* Francisco Erize. (**380**) Tom McHugh/National Audubon Society Collection/PR. (**380-381**) Jane Teas. (**381**) *left,* Stanley Breeden; *right,* Tom McHugh/National Audubon Society Collection/PR. (**382**) *top left,* © Jean-Paul Ferrero; *top right,* Kenneth W. Fink/BRUCE COLEMAN INC; *bottom,* Bob Campbell. (**383**) Edward S. Ross. (**384**) *left,* M.P. Kahl/BRUCE COLEMAN INC. (**384-385**) T. W. Ransom. (**385**) *top,* T. W. Ransom; *bottom,* Bruce Coleman/BRUCE COLEMAN INC. (**386-387**) Helen Rhode. (**388-389**) Stephen J. Krasemann/DRK Photo. (**390**) *top,* Stephen J. Krasemann/DRK Photo; *bottom,* Tom Walker. (**391**) Franz J. Camenzind. (**392**) M.P.L. Fogden. (**393**) *top left,* William J. Weber; *bottom left,* PITCH/D. Heuclin; *right,* P. A. Hinchliffe/BRUCE COLEMAN INC. (**394-395**) G. I. Bernard/Oxford Scientific Films. (**396**) *top left,* Peter Ward/BRUCE COLEMAN INC; *top right,* © Robert P. Carr; *bottom left and right,* Hans & Judy Beste. (**397**) John R. Lewis/TOM STACK & ASSOCIATES. (**398-399**) Francisco Erize. (**399**) *top,* Jen & Des Bartlett; *bottom,* Stephen J. Krasemann/DRK Photo.

(**400**) Harry Engels/BRUCE COLEMAN INC. (**401**) *top,* Jen & Des Bartlett; *bottom,* Gary R. Zahm. (**403**) Hans & Judy Beste. (**404**) George Holton/OCELOT INC. (**405**) L. West. (**406**) *top,* Len Rue Jr.; *bottom,* Jack Dermid. (**407**) Jen & Des Bartlett. (**408**) *top,* Kim E. Steiner; *bottom,* Tony Morrison. (**409**) Tom McHugh/National Audubon Society Collection/PR. (**410-411**) Rod Brindamour. (**412**) Rod Brindamour. (**412-413**) Mike Price/BRUCE COLEMAN LTD. (**414-415**) Michael S. Quinton. (**416**) *top,* Jeff Foott/BRUCE COLEMAN INC.; *bottom left and right,* Jeff Foott. (**417**) *top and center,* M. & R. Borland/BRUCE COLEMAN INC.; *bottom,* G. D. Plage/BRUCE COLEMAN INC. (**418**) *top,* Loren McIntyre; *bottom,* Wolfgang Bayer/BRUCE COLEMAN INC. (**418-419**) Jacques Jangoux/PETER ARNOLD INC. (**420**) Karl Weidmann. (**421**) © Jean-Paul Ferrero. (**422-423**) PITCH/Jean-Paul Ferrero. (**424**) Stan Wayman/National Audubon Society Collection/PR. (**425**) Nicole Duplaix. (**426**) *top,* M.P.L. Fogden/BRUCE COLEMAN INC; *bottom,* Joan Root. (**427**) © Jean-Paul Ferrero. (**428**) *top,* Tom McHugh/National Audubon Society Collection/PR; *bottom,* Larry R. Ditto/BRUCE COLEMAN INC. (**429**) Jen & Des Bartlett. (**430**) *left,* Stanley Breeden; *right,* Jen & Des Bartlett. (**431**) Hans & Judy Beste. (**432**) Stanley Breeden; *inset,* Ralph & Daphne Keller. (**433**) *left and bottom right,* Stanley Breeden; *top right,* Ralph & Daphne Keller. (**434**) *top,* Ralph & Daphne Keller; *bottom,* S. R. Morris/Oxford Scientific Films. (**435**) Stanley Breeden. (**436**) Jeff Foott. (**437**) *top,* Michael S. Quinton; *bottom left,* Helen Rhode; *bottom right,* Charles G. Summers, Jr. (**438-439**) Robin Smith/Photographic Library of Australia PTY LTD. (**440**) *top,* C. Allan Morgan; *bottom,* Jim Brandenburg. (**441**) TIERBILDER OKAPIA, Frankfurt/Main. (**442**) Jen & Des Bartlett. (**443**) *top,* Martin W. Grosnick; *bottom,* Rollie Ostermick. (**444**) Joan Root. (**445**) *top,* Tony Morrison; *bottom,* David Bygott. (**446-447**) David Doubilet. (**448-449**) Ken Balcomb. (**449**) Francisco Erize.

(**450-451**) Jen & Des Bartlett. (**451**) Lewis Trusty. (**452**) *top,* Fred Bruemmer; *bottom,* Russ Kinne/National Audubon Society Collection/PR. (**453**) Eugene Maliniak. (**454-455**) Jim Brandenburg. (**455**) William J. Weber. (**456-457**) Greg Beaumont. (**458**) Charles G. Summers, Jr./TOM STACK & ASSOCIATES. (**458-459**) Jim Brandenburg. (**459**) *left,* Wendell Metzen; *right,* Charles G. Summers, Jr. (**460**) George H. Harrison. (**461**) Gary R. Zahm. (**462**) *top,* Jim Brandenburg; *bottom,* Larry R. Ditto. (**463**) Nicholas deVore III/BRUCE COLEMAN INC. (**464-465**) Hans & Judy Beste. (**466**) Stephen J. Krasemann/DRK Photo. (**467**) Thomas D. Mangelsen. (**468**) G. I. Bernard/Oxford Scientific Films. (**469**) *top,* G. I. Bernard/Oxford Scientific Films; *bottom,* Jane Burton/BRUCE COLEMAN LTD. (**470**) *left,* Hans Reinhard/BRUCE COLEMAN LTD; *right,* Jeff Foott. (**471**) Leonard Lee Rue III. (**472**) Wolfgang Obst. (**473**) Karl H. Maslowski. (**474**) *top,* Leonard Lee Rue III; *bottom,* Jen & Des Bartlett. (**475**) *left,* Perry Shankle; *right,* William J. Weber. (**476**) Shin Yoshino/ORION PRESS. (**477**) *left,* Jane Burton/BRUCE COLEMAN LTD; *right,* Stanley Breeden. (**478**) *top,* Clem Haagner/ARDEA LONDON; *bottom,* Graham Pizzey. (**479**) *top,* M.P.L. Fogden; *bottom,* M. K. & I. M. Morcombe. (**480**) Jen & Des Bartlett. (**481**) Clem Haagner/ARDEA LONDON. (**482-483**) © Reinhard Kunkel. (**484**) Thomas & Gitte Nebbia. (**485**) *top,* © Reinhard Kunkel; *bottom,* Gerald Cubitt. (**486**) Gerald Cubitt. (**486-487**) Andrew Laurie. (**488**) Leonard Lee Rue III. (**489**) Jen & Des Bartlett. (**490-491**) Jen & Des Bartlett. (**492**) *top,* Fred Bruemmer; *bottom,* Jeff Foott/BRUCE COLEMAN INC. (**493**) Flip Nicklin. (**494**) G. Carleton Ray. (**494-495**) Marion Morrison. (**495**) *top,* Jen & Des Bartlett; *bottom,* Erwin & Peggy Bauer. (**496**) © Peter Johnson. (**497**) *top,* Jen & Des Bartlett; *bottom,* David Doubilet. (**498-499**) © Masayuki Egawa/Nature Production (PPS)/PR.

(**500-501**) Larry R. Ditto. (**502**) *left,* Charles G. Summers, Jr.; *right,* Michael S. Quinton. (**503**) *top right,* Jeff Foott; *bottom left and right,* Michael S. Quinton. (**504**) *top,* Martin W. Grosnick; *bottom,* Rollie Ostermick. (**505**) *left,* Martin W. Grosnick; *top right,* Helen Rhode; *bottom right,* Stephen J. Krasemann/DRK Photo. (**506**) *top,* Richard W. Brown; *bottom left,* Rene-Pierre Bille; *bottom right,* © Hans Reinhard/BRUCE COLEMAN INC. (**507**) George B. Schaller. (**508**) *top,* Galen B. Rathbun; *bottom,* Robert P. Carr. (**509**) ANIMALS ANIMALS/Stouffer Productions. (**510**) Stephen Dalton/NHPA. (**511**) Lynn L. Rogers. (**512**) *top,* Francois Gohier; *bottom,* C. Allan Morgan. (**513**) © Robert P. Carr. (**514**) *top,* Loren McIntyre; *bottom,* Wolfgang Bayer. (**515**) Wolfgang Bayer. (**516**) *left,* Tony Morrison; *right,* Francisco Erize. (**517**) N. Smythe/National Audubon Society Collection/PR. (**518**) Jen & Des Bartlett. (**519**) *top,* Martin W. Grosnick; *bottom,* Helen Rhode. (**520**) *top,* M.P.L. Fogden; *bottom left,* Joseph G. Hall; *bottom center,* William J. Weber; *bottom right,* George D. Lepp. (**521**) ANIMALS ANIMALS/Stouffer Productions. (**522**) *left,* Gerald Cubitt; *top right,* Lynn L. Rogers; *bottom right,* Jon Farrar. (**523**) © Hans Reinhard/BRUCE COLEMAN INC. (**524**) *top,* E. Hanumantha Rao; *bottom,* M. K. & I. M. Morcombe. (**525**) Stanley Breeden. (**526-527**) Clem Haagner. (**528**) Dieter & Mary Plage/BRUCE COLEMAN LTD. (**529**) George B. Schaller. (**530-531**) Francois Gohier. (**532**) *top left,* Francisco Erize; *top right and bottom,* Loren McIntyre. (**533**) Tony Beamish/ARDEA LONDON. (**534-535**) M.P.L. Fogden. (**536**) Erwin & Peggy Bauer. (**537**) *left,* Howard Uible/National Audubon Society Collection/PR; *top and bottom right,* Russ Kinne/National Audubon Society Collection/PR. (**538-539**) © Jean-Paul Ferrero. (**540**) Rajesh Bedi. (**540-541**) Jean-Paul Ferrero. (**541**) *top,* Belinda Wright; *bottom,* George Holton/OCELOT INC. (**542**) Tom McHugh/National Audubon Society Collection/PR. (**543**) Jen & Des Bartlett. (**545**) *top,* Gunter Ziesler/PETER ARNOLD INC; *bottom,* Francois Gohier. (**546**) *top,* © Hans Reinhard/BRUCE COLEMAN LTD; *bottom,* Stephen Dalton/NHPA. (**547**) *top,* John Shaw; *bottom,* G. I. Bernard/Oxford Scientific Films. (**548**) Jen & Des Bartlett. (**548-549**) M. K. & I. M. Morcombe.

(**550**) *left,* Ralph & Daphne Keller; *right,* M. K. & I. M. Morcombe. (**551**) Hans & Judy Beste. (**552**) Tom Walker. (**553**) *top,* Stephen J. Krasemann/DRK Photo; *bottom,* Fred Bruemmer. (**554-555**) Leonard Lee Rue III. (**555**) *top,* G. Carleton Ray; *bottom,* Tom Walker. (**556-557**) G. Carleton Ray; *inset,* Geoff Carroll. (**558**) William R. Curtsinger. (**558**) Jon Farrar. (**559**) Thomas D. Mangelsen. (**560**) *top,* Rollie Ostermick; *bottom,* Rene-Pierre Bille. (**561**) Bill Ruth. (**562**) *top,* James Hudnall; *bottom,* Chuck Nicklin. (**563**) Chuck Nicklin. (**564-565**) *sequence,* Sylvia A. Earle. (**565**) *bottom,* Flip Nicklin. (**566**) Franz J. Camenzind. (**567**) Howard Hall. (**569**) Ron & Valerie Taylor. (**570**) David Lavallee. (**571**) © Reinhard Kunkel. (**572**) *top,* © Reinhard Kunkel; *bottom,* © George W. Frame. (**573**) © Peter Johnson. (**574-575**) Robert Caputo. (**575**) © Leonard Lee Rue III. (**576**) David Hiser. (**577**) Jim Brandenburg. (**578**) Giorgio Boscagli/UNION PRESS. (**579**) *top,* Udo Hirsch/BRUCE COLEMAN LTD; *bottom,* Jim Brandenburg. (**580**) ANIMALS ANIMALS/Stouffer Productions. (**580-581**) Rollie Ostermick. (**582**) Francisco Erize. (**583**) *top,* Rollie Ostermick; *bottom,* William W. Bacon III/AlaskaPhoto. (**584**) Francisco Erize. (**585**) David Goulston-/BRUCE COLEMAN LTD. (**586**) Dieter & Mary Plage/BRUCE COLEMAN LTD. (**587**) George B. Schaller. (**588-589**) © Reinhard Kunkel. (**590**) Carol Hughes. (**590-591**) Gerald Cubitt. (**592**) *top,* © Peter Johnson; *bottom,* Carol Hughes. (**593**) *top,* Leonard Lee Rue III; *bottom,* D. T. Rowe-Rowe. (**594**) © Jean-Paul Ferrero. (**597**) ANIMALS ANIMALS/Stouffer Productions. (**604**) Irven de Vore/Anthro-Photo. (**607**) Fred Bruemmer.

Acknowledgments

The National Geographic Society is grateful to the individuals and organizations listed here for their generous cooperation and assistance during the preparation of the *Book of Mammals:* David Horr Agee, J. Scott Altenbach, American Museum of Natural History, American Rabbit Breeders Association, Inc., Paul K. Anderson, Sydney Anderson, Renate Angermann, Kenneth B. Armitage, Rollin H. Baker, Julie Ball, Marion Ball, Carl Brandon, Anton B. Bubenik, John A. Byers, Carnegie Museum of Natural History, James W. Carpenter, Tracy S. Carter, Joseph A. Chapman, Tim W. Clark, Garrett C. Clough, Malcolm Coe, C. G. Coetzee, Richard W. Coles, Larry R. Collins, Ian McTaggart Cowan, Dorcas D. Crary, A. W. Crompton, Anne Dagg, Robert J. Davey, Joseph A. Davis, Jerome E. DeBruin, James G. Doherty, James M. Dolan, Jr., Iain Douglas-Hamilton, Duke University Center for the Study of Primate Biology and History, Nicole Duplaix, Harold J. Egoscue, John F. Eisenberg, Elephant Interest Group/Department of Biological Sciences/Wayne State University, Margaret Ellis, Robert K. Enders, Albert W. Erickson, Purcell Erquhart, Richard D. Estes, M. Brock Fenton, Fish and Wildlife Service of the U. S. Department of the Interior, Florida State Museum, Dian Fossey, Bristol Foster, Richard R. Fox, Hans Frädrich, George W. Frame, Lory Frame, William L. Franklin, Biruté M. F. Galdikas, Alfred L. Gardner, Valerius Geist, Hugh H. Genoways, Patricia Goodnight, Edwin E. Goodwin, David R. Gray, Mervyn Griffiths, Barbara Grigg, Heinz Heck, Steven R. Hill, Hendrik N. Hoeck, Judith Hopper, Maurice G. Hornocker, Nicholas Hotton III, Sandra L. Husar, Mary Alice Jackson, Jennifer U. M. Jarvis, A. J. T. Johnsingh, Wiletta V. Jones, Charles J. Jonkel, Beatrice Judge, Lloyd Keith, Karl W. Kenyon, Charles A. Kiddy, John Kirsch, Devra Kleiman, Hans Klingel, Karl Koopman, Donald L. Kramer, Karl R. Kranz, Andrew Laurie, Sam Lewis, Boo Liat Lim, Raymond Linder, Muriel C. Logan, Charles A. Long, Nicholas J. Long, William Lopez-Forment, Dale F. Lott, Yael Lubin, Richard E. McCabe, Audrey McConnell, Michael E. McManus, Mark MacNamara, Phyllis R. Marcuccio, Joe T. Marshall, James G. Mead, L. David Mech, J.A.J. Meester, Derek A. Melton, Arlene Michelirer, Russell A. Mittermeier, Patricia D. Moehlman, Peter L. Munroe, James Murtaugh, Norman Myers, National Museums of Canada, National Zoological Park/Smithsonian Institution, A. E. Newsome, New York Zoological Society, Kenneth S. Norris, Alvin Novick, Ronald M. Nowak, Margaret A. O'Connell, Bart W. O'Gara, Robert T. Orr, Ed Peifer, Jr., Michael Pelton, R. L. Peterson, Ivo Poglayen-Neuwall, Roger A. Powell, George Rabb, Mary Rabb, Urs H. Rahm, Adele S. Rammelmeyer, Galen B. Rathbun, G. Carleton Ray, Elizabeth H. Rinker, Miles Roberts, Jonathan Rood, David T. Rowe-Rowe, Daniel I. Rubenstein, James K. Russell, Hope Ryden, Oliver A. Ryder, George B. Schaller, Victor B. Scheffer, Jan Schwartz, John Seidensticker, Geoffrey B. Sharman, James H. Shaw, Paul W. Sherman, Jeheskel (Hezy) Shoshani, A.R.E. Sinclair, R.H.N. Smithers, the Smithsonian Institution, Smithsonian Tropical Research Institute, Lyle K. Sowls, R. E. Stebbings, Eleanor E. Storrs, Michael D. Stuart, Fiona Sunquist, Mel Sunquist, Lee M. Talbot, Ian Tattersall, John J. Teal, Geza Teleki, Clair E. Terrill, Richard W. Thorington, Jr., Merlin D. Tuttle, University of Maryland's Appalachian Environmental Laboratory, U. S. Department of Agriculture/Beltsville Agricultural Research Center, Richard G. Van Gelder, Franklyn Van Houten, C. G. van Zyll de Jong, Charles Walcott, John S. Ward, Janet Warner, Everett J. Warwick, Washington University Tyson Research Center, Christen M. Wemmer, Ralph M. Wetzel, Robert J. Whelan, Judith White, Wildlife Management Institute, David P. Willoughby, Henk Wolda, Charles A. Woods, the World Armadillo Breeding and Racing Association, World Wildlife Fund, William A. Xanten, Hoi Sen Yong.

On an ice floe in Canada's Gulf of St. Lawrence, a female harp seal stretches out in the late-winter sun with her white-coated, week-old pup. The pup will nurse for less than two weeks. It will gain weight rapidly and soon weigh about 100 pounds (45 kg). By spring, the pup will be able to care for itself.

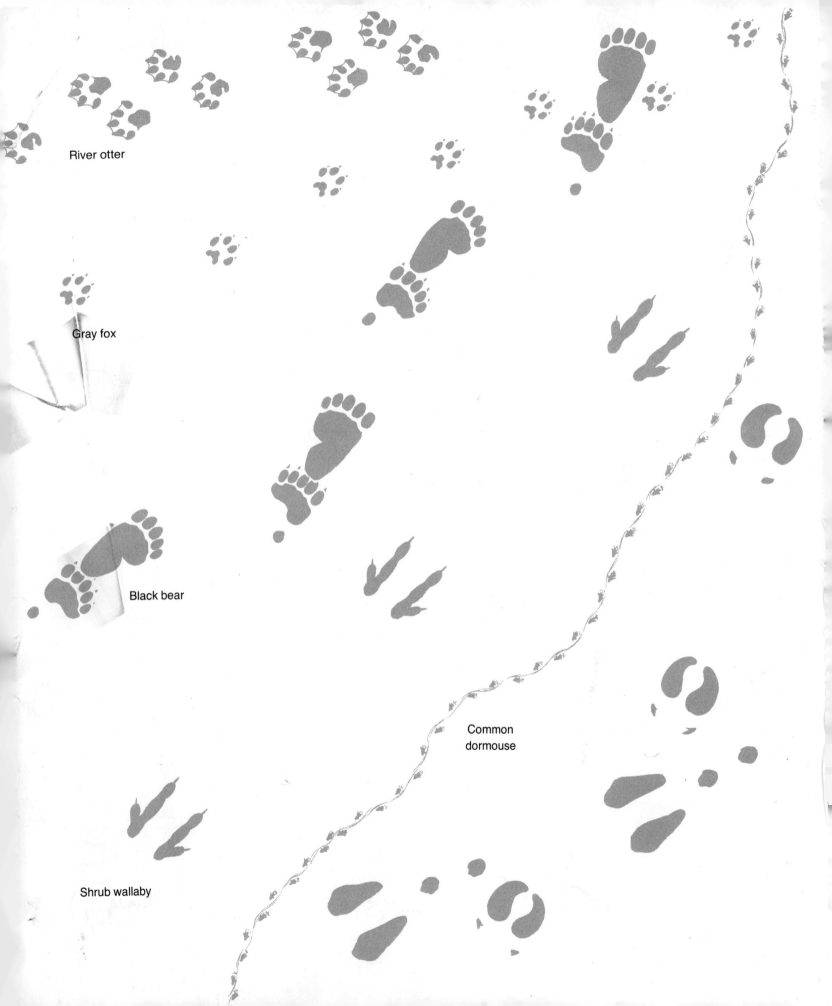

River otter

Gray fox

Black bear

Shrub wallaby

Common
dormouse